THE AUDACITY OF SPIRIT

Published 2008 by
Veritas Publications
7/8 Lower Abbey Street
Dublin 1
Ireland
Email publications@veritas.ie
Website www.veritas.ie

ISBN 978 1 84730 054 6

Lines from Denise Levertov's 'Annunciation' (p. 96) are taken from *Selected Poems* and appear courtesy of New Directions Books, 2002; lines from Denise Levertov's 'Poetics of Faith' (p. 123) and 'On the Parables of the Mustard Seed' (p. 128) are taken from *The Stream and the Sapphire* and appear courtesy of New Directions Books, 1997.

Cover design by Paula Ryan
Printed in the Republic of Ireland by ColourBooks Ltd

*Veritas books are printed on paper made from the wood pulp of managed forests. For every tree felled, at least one tree is planted, thereby renewing natural resources.*

Jack Finnegan

# The Audacity of Spirit

The Meaning and Shaping
of Spirituality Today

Veritas ✳

# Acknowledgements

I am grateful to many individuals, friends and colleagues, for their support, guidance and encouragement. It is all deeply appreciated. My primary reader was Dr Chris O'Donnell who peer-reviewed the text for me and made many valuable suggestions, which I gratefully took on board. Rita Canavan, friend, wise woman in the ways of Spirit, and patient listener made an inestimable contribution to the shaping of the book. Dr Una Agnew advised and encouraged me in many ways, and my conversations on Rahner and Trinity with Dr Declan Marmion were rewarding. Emer Ryan's editorial support was much appreciated. Thanks, too, to Dr Bernadette Flanagan and Dr Michael O'Sullivan for their constant support, and thanks, too, to Donna Doherty and Ruth Kennedy of Veritas who made this publication possible. I am particularly grateful to my students who teach me new things and open new questions for me; and the many people at home and abroad who trusted me with their spiritual stories. They have inspired me more than they can ever know.

> *Light of Light to you,*
> *the sight of the Trinity to you,*
> *and audacity of Spirit to follow the way.*

31 January 2008

# Contents

# The Audacity of Spirit

Wild seeds of audacious spirit carried by the winds of Spirit:
such is the image underlying my thoughts as I set out
on this spiritual journey, this attempt to keep pace
with the audacity, the shaping audacity of spirit today.

Soul, spirit: words that hint at the depths and heights
of human life, of transcendence, of the sacred;
of encounters far beyond the banality and materialism
consuming every day.

Poetic words crafting a guiding imagination;
now analogical, now dialectical,
now contemplative, but always dynamic,
always in process, pushing words speculatively
far beyond their common boundaries, their prisoning bars.

Crafted words poeming the unsayable,
yet connecting height and depth,
beauty and truth, goodness and the best in us.

Spirit, soul: words that hint at glory and wonder
and the struggle with suffering and sorrow and strife;
rasping words to wrestle with,
wrestle Jacob-like with an angel at a Jabbok ford.

Words that catch us on the hip and leave a memory,
a wound from which the waters of life
and soul-song murmur and flow;
a remembering that points beyond,
towards a divine destiny; a wound
that generates longing, intention,
desires that refuse partial satisfactions
and constantly seek beyond the states of
mind we impose escapingly on our lives.

Spiritual, spirituality: shifting, soft, fuzzy, oftentimes murky words hiding their true meaning from easy view; mercurial words ready to take new shapes; words that leave us searching behind images, and metaphors and stories, and songs and poems, even beyond our densest abstractions and thickest descriptions and clusters of knowledge, because we intuit, glimpse, hear on the winds of mind an echo of something profoundly simple, profoundly healing: traces of a More Than that is innately and caringly, mysteriously transformative and always Otherwise.

Spiritual, spirituality: these are words that stimulate life and growth and change: metanoia words evoking reflective moments of lifting up and going deep; soaring and plumbing words; inviting words that beckon us beyond our addictions and captivities; aporia words that stop us in our tracks; revitalising words that remind us of our humanness and humaneness, of our freedom and the iron cage of conditioning and habit, of serenity and a nastiness that grows like a cancer in our midst; words that wonder if the whole truth can ever be spoken, and if not, why not?

Spiritual, spirituality: words that bring a softening of glance and heart, open to a murmuring deep within that wants to soar and fly and swoop on eagle's wings, dance on the mountains, rejoice with feet rhythming good news, embrace the cosmos. These are words that flirt with us, call us forth, seduce our resistances, soften the hard places, balm the painful aching places of emptiness and discord and grief-stricken absence, the fragmented places of social isolation and loneliness, of social injustice and the dismissive abuses of power.

Spiritual, spirituality, soul, spirit: words that open chinks, give glimpses of worth, let in a shining, scattering darkness, and a musical murmuring evoking a deeper listening, a more attentive awareness: an awakening from our consensual slumber, our politically correct secular slumber, an awakening to a new consciousness, to an enlightenment and an illumination melting barriers, overcoming divisions and separations, false boundaries too strongly and erroneously held for forgotten reasons, born in times long forgotten but holding us in thrall. Spiritual, spirituality, soul, spirit: words that offer unity and oneness, that cleanse and purify, that soften and lighten and give a lilt of laughter at early foolishness, better humour bringing together things once perceived as separate.

Wild seeds of spirit carried on a Wind, a divine Breathing, breathing life, breaking the foolish patterns of the past that have no oil and give no light, spirit-less practices of a dead past deadening the present – how many years of dead devotions that triggered no change, still trapped in the clawing power of primordial experience that found no true container?

How many years of dead words killing the music of the soul, clipping the wings of spirit, deadening, spirit-less habits unruffled by Spirit-Wind-Breathing-Life; dead words encrusting soul with weights and burdens and scalding yokes that refuse review, that cringe from critique, angrily defensive of a dead, deadening past: deceptive illusions of life? False havens of flight from existence?

Spiritual, spirituality, soul, spirit: words that challenge the past in the present, words to paint new possibilities of lives leaning into a future pulsing with promise. Words gifting graciously; energising words: soaring, sifting, stimulating words; words sensing selfish centres of inaction, apathy: dull sleep-like apathy shuttering the eyes of soul, corrosive corrupting apathy, stumbling zombie-like from ego-built, illusory, self-defeating walls of angry-fearful boredom blocking the contemplative gaze that penetrates our many veils of ego-illusion and ego-inflation, the grandiose false world of perceptions and assumptions we believe to be real, the prison of our own misremembered imaginal making.

Soul, spirit: relational words, words reaching out to otherness, I–Thou words embracing difference and the utterly different; words of compassion defeating obsession, words of care and concern; words of response, responsiveness, responsibility; words evoking ethical stances, challenging us to stand lightly on the earth our home, our origin, standing morally and critically in our systems; words favouring technologies that care for the earth and recognise the rape of the earth for what it is: rape, crime, rapacious greed gone mad, ecologically, socially, destructively mad, symptoms of an economic pathology stealing the future from our children; symptoms of a spiritual pathology, a diminished life all too many of us have forgotten how to name – words once gone, how can we truly say what needs to be said?

Symptoms, too, of a loss of political will in the face of power elites and their short-term interests, their greed, their bone-grinding grimacing greed. Spirit, soul: words that demand radical and active involvement in history and politics; that demand engagement and activism; that demand a socially and ecologically engaged mysticism. Words that seek change, seek a re-enchanting of the world. A disenchanted world, our secular inheritance, our violently shadowed inheritance, is easy to pillage and exploit, easy to rape and destroy because its magic and its beauty have been stolen by a materialistic deterministic ideology that is blind to anything it deems unreasonable, with a deeming that dances to a damning death it thinks is a better, more rational life.

What else is planetary warming if not a harbinger of things to come? What else is the destruction of rainforests to grow soya beans to feed chickens to be sold cheaply in Western multiples? What else if not the results of economic and political hubris and greed with which we have all colluded and connived, we of the West with our voracious appetites, our vauntingly flauntingly conspicuous consumption, our consumerism that commodifies everything under the sun and is ready to sell it – or him or her or them – at the right price?

At what price for soul and spirit? Those who live from soul and spirit ponder these precipice questions, stand at the edges, stand in the border-lands and glimpse the consequences of mass collusion, conniving with diminishment and depletion because they have come to understand, reflectively understand, how modernity and its parent the Enlightenment have shaped perceptions of life and world in the West today and in so doing has shaped – misshaped? – our attitudes to the things of human soul and spirit: their reality, their needs, and their unique personal and social modes of expression.

What happens to a society that represses its spirit and its spirituality, marginalises its religious impulse, ignores its soul, lives a purely materialistic, thoroughly secular existence? The signs are all around us: addictions, violence, narcissistic disorders, suicide, crime, child abuse of horrific proportions done by those with supposed faith and those with none, and all the other descriptors of ethical and moral decadence of a culture in decline. It is in such times that spirituality tends to rise phoenix-like from the ashes of disenchantment. As societies go into ethico-moral and cultural decline the spiritual search re-emerges, not because spirituality is a symptom of socio-cultural deterioration but because it represents an active reaction against it. These are the times in which we now live. Will we grasp the chance?

Spirituality grows as more and more people search for more meaningful, more responsible forms of life in a confused and spiritually bankrupt world. Then why are we surprised today to discover growing evidence of wild seeds of spirit scattered by Spirit Wind, of the creative touch of Divine Breathing everywhere? Why are we surprised by the audacity of spirit? Questions are being asked, people are embracing spiritual quests, a revolution of spirit is underway, the re-enchantment of spirit has begun. Will the world be the same again?

*The Meaning and Shaping of Contemporary Spirituality*

This book is an exploration of contemporary spirituality. It is alert to the fact that spirituality is about many things. It is about the sublime and the deep, and the inward and the outward turn. It is about oneself and others, about the world and everything in it and the quality of the webs of relationship we spin and knit. Spirituality is about life and how we live it. It is about culture and society and how we shape them. It is about stillness and great efforts, about solitude and the insight it brings; it is about knowing and acting on the quality of that knowing. Spirituality is the space where we work with the creative potentials of human similarity and difference, or struggle with the enemy-making forces that betray the potentials for harmony and peace with all that is. It is about social justice; it is about equality and a world to save. Spirituality generates ecological awareness and response as the earth is rediscovered as the Holy One's good gift. It is a space of healing and purification, a place of enlightenment and a call to wholeness.

Spirituality is the place where we meet primordial reality and wrestle with the forces of primordial experience that date back to the very origins of our human lives. It is a space for self-knowledge and self-transcendence and the processes they set in train. It is the space where we encounter the forces of shadow and repression and interpret or misinterpret them, contain them safely as we respond to the upward call of the divine and the awe-inspiring wonder of God, or give way to the darker powers of disorder and destruction. Spirituality is a space where lovers meet and in the meeting God is found. It is holy ground and sacred space, a place where pilgrims meet as journeys pause, a space where rituals flourish and worship prospers. It is a space for prayer, meditation and the wise contemplative gaze. It is the meeting place of harmony, community, integrity, generosity, love, faith and hope, motivation and intentionality, and the turning of the mind away from sole concern with the self.

Spirituality is the meeting place of worldviews and calls to action, the place where compassion is the principle of discernment and ethical living its proof. Spirituality is a place of participation, a place for sorrow and a place for joyous celebration. It is a place for quiet self-reflection on the deep questions of life, a place where ultimate reality is befriended. Spirituality is a place of confrontation, a place of enigma and paradox. It is a centre point, the dynamic pivot where opposites meet and create potentials for change: the lost and the found, the bright and the dark, the hard and the soft, the inclusive and the exclusive, the vain and the humble, the reasonable and the unreasonable, the conscious and the unconscious, the intellectual and the affective, the masculine and the feminine, the general and the specific, as well as good and evil. Such forces meet in dynamic flows. Our responsibility is to so choose that they flow towards the compassionate and the humane, towards the discovery and expression of true humanity. Spirituality, after all, is a place for transformed lives to emerge like butterflies and blossoms in early summer.

Spirituality is a journey, a quest, a path, a way. It is a journey of discovery, a quest for meaning, a path to a fuller life, a way of love and embraced destiny; dancing with the Holy One, new songs of devotion and awe rising from the depths of soul. Spirituality is a deep valley of contentment, a high mountain where holiness challenges and the divine expansiveness is dangerously encountered. It is a space where the forces of coercion and connivance, of collusion and diminishment are confronted, where God is chanced upon along the way and often missed, so light is the divine touch in the midst of human preoccupations and their hypnotic, conditioned effects. Spirituality is the way of liberation from their automatic control, the way into a more coherently aware existence. It is the capacity to see through the decadence of an individual life and turn again in life-beckoning directions. Spirituality is a place of dignity, a place of resilience and freedom where power is recognised as the ambivalent force it really is, and its corrupting influences duly noted as spirit flows into action as false interpretations of the world are duly conceded and repented.

Spirituality is the place where the whole of a person's religious experience, beliefs, relationships and action, is put to the test; the place where resistances to transformation are acknowledged and overcome. It is the place where the world is re-sacralised and re-enchanted, where a radiating beauty breaks through and a brighter concord brightens the world, our home again, our ethos, our abode. According to Gregory of Nyssa, spirituality is about freedom, the freedom that flows from the soul as the image of God, and spiritual progress is the process of growth into the freedom of the children of God (Romans 8:21). This is a growing freedom from three forms of slavery grounded in different forms of ignorance: psychological slavery to illusion and deformed imagination, social slavery to the forces of tyranny, violence and mainstream opinion, and religious slavery to anti-gospel forces, stances and beliefs.

℄ *Audacity of spirit*

In writing this book I have continually returned to a cluster of six image metaphors. The first is the *audacity of spirit* for which the book is named and which acts as the book's principal organising centre. The active presence of audacity of spirit is clearly implicit in the increasingly revolutionary stance against the disenchantment and desacralisation that typifies the globalising, late modern consumer world in which we live today, a stance that has emerged as a key theme in the contemporary development of Western spirituality. Audacity points to courage, to revisioning, to hope. That is what is happening in the West today. People are reawakening to the force of spiritual courage, they are challenging the forces of secularisation and working for a re-sacralised and a re-enchanted world. They are challenging the forces of injustice and demanding a better world. They see what is happening to the planet and seek a deeper value. They see through the illusions of materialism and say: enough! We are not buying empty lives! Minds are being renewed. Deeper visions are reawakening because people today are rediscovering an ancient lesson: when the vision disappears the people perish (Proverbs 29:18), and they are seeking afresh a vision fit for fuller lives, they are seeking afresh the way of transformation.

The audacity of spirit is certainly about ethical integrity, but audacity of spirit is also about divine action. How audacious of God's Spirit to move again in the West, to awaken hope in many hearts, to sow seeds of deeper meaning and a softer, humbler, more compassionate world with room enough for all. Under the influence of divine audacity more and more people are asserting their essential worth in a consumer world that would reduce them to nothing more than units of production, mere consumers in a media-driven world of discontent and exploitation. In Martin Luther King's famous saying, we are all somebody; and the Divine Spirit is audaciously inspiring us to audaciously redeem that fact. Audacity names the way to respect, respect for difference in a world where different people seek differently with integrity for liberating truth in the context of interspiritual and interfaith dialogue. In a secularised world the demand for public space for spiritual conversation itself requires audacity. This book keeps returning to the image of audacity of spirit because it is a sign of the times. Three other image metaphors keep audacity of spirit company throughout the book: *rhythm, dance* and *song*. These three images are used to evoke the expressive dynamism of symbolic life, to stir up a sense of the cyclic nature of life on this planet and the dynamics of eternal return and rebirth that are always with us as we seek fuller, more meaningful, more ethically responsive, more historically and politically responsible lives.

## ℂ Rhythm

Rhythm reminds us of times and seasons, of the beat of life, the flow of breath, the warmth of love, the turn of the tide, the course of time, the turning of seasons, the change of weather, the interplays of rest and work, of joy and sorrow, and the spiralling progress of lives towards ultimacy. In his last book Gerald May explores this rhythm in a wonderful reflection on time. He reminds his readers that nature knows nothing of time but everything about presence, presence to cycles and successions, sounds and silences, coolings and warmings, stillings and movings, light and darkness, birthings and dyings, courting and nesting, rhythms and seasons.[1] Rhythms confront us with absolute reality, with utter presence, with the way things are, and contemplation is the capacity to be fully there, fully in tune with Presence and the way things truly are.

Rhythm connects us to the seasons of the heart, and the longings of the spirit, the interplay of prayer and work, of stillness and action, of effort and tranquillity, of need and fulfilment, of listening and remembering, of religious awe and worship, and the rhythms of ritual and celebration. It reminds us of the interflow of times of prayer and meditation, of reflection and retreat, of pilgrimage and the spiritual quest. A secularised world not only risks losing contact with the rhythms of life, of nature, of spirit and a caring ethic, it also risks losing contact with the world itself and soon sees nothing wrong with destroying its own dwelling place. The price is immense because it is the land, nature, that teaches us the rhythms of life and teaches us to lift our eyes to the mountains, the abode of the sacred. Then there is the audacity of confronting deadening habits and the forces of illusion and isolation: rhythm continually reminds us that we are part of something greater than ourselves. Spirituality, too, has its rhythms, its sonorities and movements, its respirations and pauses that mirror the power of breath and wind; rhythms that mirror spirit and the processes of soul.

Attention to rhythm reveals a dynamic space full of imagination and creativity, full of tone and the promise of splendour crying holy! to the awe-struck beat of the human heart. Attention to rhythm empowers us to move within the currents of sound and energy and event that are all around us: a laughing child, the dawn chorus, the wind in leaves, the gurgling of streams, the crash of waves, the whistling wind, silent mist, drifting snow, and the gently drifting rain of a soft day in Ireland. Rhythm is part of who we are: rising with the sun, lying down with the moon, preparing and eating our food, caring and learning, and responding to the deep solar and lunar, the deep biological, cultural and spiritual rhythms of our deepest human nature. And attention to those rhythms draws us into contemplative harmony with the pulse of divine life. In the African religious tradition, for example, there are certain drumbeats and rhythms that speak only of God, beats and rhythms that serve as divine text and sacred message, rhythms that are religious narratives, a kind of gospel. Spirituality is what draws us to the rhythms that speak of God, and these rhythms in turn shape the flow of spiritual longing and make it audacious, ready to sing and dance, sometimes slow, sometimes fast, but never inert, for these are living rhythms made by God, rhythms that free us from the prisons of time.

Rhythm names the dynamic flow of spirit opening to Spirit and learning to fly on the winds of grace. What is required is the imaginative intensity to engage with grace, an intensity that itself beats to rhythms of new life, a humbler, richer, fuller life lived to the subtle rhythms of Spirit. What is required is attention to the harmonies of incarnation that empower audacity of spirit, the audacity to share the gifts of the Spirit with the world. The tragedy is that so many of us have thrown these rhythms away and then wonder why we suffer. What have these rhythms to do with life in the fast lane, with the fragmented rhythms of urban existences, those places where broad horizons disappear, deafening rhythms that have no sensitivity to a still small voice and the rhythms of prophetic vision (1 Kings 19:12)? The rhythms of spirit and Spirit are different and spirituality learns to sing and dance to their loving beat: they teach us to sense the movements of God moving in lives, moving in the world and all that is. After all, rhythm is life, and spiritual life responds to a spiritual tempo, a tempo of creation, a crescendo of creative experience.

### ❡ Dance

Dance is another window onto rhythm. To dance is to pray rhythmic form into being. To dance is to create patterns, weaving them together in three-dimensional space. Dance is response to primordial experience, transforming thought and feeling into living movement that makes them visible in the world. Dance allows something of the divine to shine in the world, revealing the divine that permeates life and inner being. A living spirituality is a living dance, an expressive response to the rhythms of being. Spirituality is embodied response, response making active the deep, primordial resonance of being as spirit transforms the dance, taking it beyond art, making it gifted contemplation. Was it not St Ambrose of Milan who linked the dance of spirit with an ecstasy of faith spilling out into the whole ring of creation, in a dance that lifts spirit up to the stars, mirroring the dance of heaven? Our spirits dance in the winds of Spirit and in the dancing find the way beyond self and so enter the audacious paths of transcendence where two worlds meet, one human and the other divine, and dance something new into being, something beyond ego.

The dance of spirit allows body to become attuned to spiritual values and rhythms, to spiritual movement and practice, to enter the flow of ritual. Dance connects us to the energy of life and spirit and finds ways to give delightfully disciplined expression to the beauty of embodied spirit. Dance draws body into the praise of God, rejoicing in a flow of worship that spills over into space and movement, expressing unity with all that is in ways not known to the logical mind, giving deeper expression to deeper, liberating meaning. On the dancing feet of contemplation we fly to God, we walk softly in sacred spaces, full of wonderment and awe. Such dance flows from intelligence; it has its own reasons, and voices its own imagination in an embrace of transforming communion, a communion beyond words but not beyond expressing. Like contemplation and its deep sense of the sacredness of life, dance represents more than an event. It represents a way that finds its deepest inspirations in its paradoxical hiddenness in God and makes the hidden plain in a flurry of expressive possibility that melts borders imprisoning the audacity of spirit. Dance reminds us that spirituality is a festival, a celebration of life, an unself-conscious attention to the dynamisms of spirit delightfully transforming the world.

❦ *Song*
Song expresses the reality of soul. Soul is the song's deep message because the music of soul has the power to bring soul and spirit, mind, heart and body together in a deeper, more attuned unity. Song is soul finding its unique voice. Soul-song is intimately linked to spirit-dance. It is also an image metaphor for attunement to the rhythms of human and divine life through a melody that finds harmony with the creating word of God and seeks jubilant expression. In the Celtic tradition it was taught that every soul has a unique song, a unique spark of the divine, and that the task of spirituality was to engage in an attentive vigil until that unique song was first heard, then recognised and sung, freeing this song-spark to set the world on fire with Divine Presence. This is a deep song easily drowned out by the noises of a busy world, easily lost in the midst of its cares and woes. The invitation to recognise this song is there in the constant invitation in the Hebrew Psalms to sing a new song, to let new music soar. Contemplatives attending to soul attend to the song of soul and give it life in the world, rescuing life from the shallow and the banal that surround us on every side, giving it new tone and depth. In a sense, soul-song already reaches beyond mortality. It has an almost angelic tone, a lilt of pure praise of God that is founded in transcendence.

Greek has a specific word for spiritual song from which the English *ode* descends, with its poetic implications for inspiration and imaginative expression. Soul-song enters the world of the most sublime ode and lets glorious jubilation soar into the divine Presence in a ritual of eternal return. St Paul sees spiritual song as a gift of the Spirit, an evocative gift drawing people into the rhythms of melody, singing and making music in grateful hearts to God (Ephesians 5:19-20). Soul-song arises from a still place where the divine is alive, where spirit, carried on the voice of the heart, seeks melodic windows to the world. Such song belongs wholly to the singer, a unique expression of a unique and irreplaceably irrepressible soul. The spirituality of the singer fills the song; the spirituality of the dancer fills the dance, and the rhythmic melodies of soul discovering spirit find unity in a spiritual flower fragrantly blossoming in the world and touching it with beauty. In this sense the images of song and dance bespeak soul rising above the constraints of history and human contingency in a soaring flight of spirit that knows no bounds till it comes to rest in its Beloved's arms like a dove in the cleft of a rock (Song of Songs 2:14).

In its unique melody soul-song is always full of life, full of the essence of life and the promise of life to the full. It subverts the deadness of shallow worlds built for consumption. Full of deep motive and meaning soul-song engages and expresses all of being in all its aspects. It engages and expresses the essence of ensouled being-in-the-world even when being is hidden under the layers of experience that overlie and encrust it. It is a mystical song that lilts of meaning beyond meaning and in its beauty gives voice to the inexpressible, gives melodic definition to the indefinable. The imagery of rhythm, dance and song reminds us that real change is measured by a creative shift that allows soul to sing and spirit to dance a deeper spiritual awareness into life: for melody is the universal language transcending all difference, a path to union and communion. Soul music means there is breath-wind to lift spirit and let it sail the ways of the world, dancing its way beyond self into the iridescent traces of God. Song invites soul; dance expresses spirit; rhythm names the spiral flow of life. Spirituality needs all three if it is to flourish and be audacious in the world today.

These three image metaphors have movement in common, movement and breath: movement from lower to higher consciousness, for example, and movement made possible by healing transformation. Rhythm, dance and song represent movement that is choreographed and disciplined through training and commitment. They also name movement that is gloriously spontaneous, full of energy and creativity. Rhythm, dance and song evoke changing states of being, mood shifts, flows of feeling, processes of awakening, of budding and arousal, as well as movements that return to centres: to still spaces and quiet dells of spiritual renewal and restoration. Rhythm, dance and song evoke possibilities and potentials for discovery. They bespeak disruption, the breaking of automatic reactions, but they also bespeak deeply aware sensitivity.

Rhythm, dance and song hint at the dynamic nature of spiritual encounter and the nature of its processes because soul gives song its power, spirit gives dance its energy: the wind set a-blowing when the divine and the human meet; and so they bespeak resilience, that sine-qua-non of the spiritual journey, and of life that chooses to go on living. Rhythm, dance and song challenge us to set ego and self-referred concerns in context. They rhythm the shrinking of the inflated ego in the presence of what is not-ego; not just the id in the Freudian sense, that most primitive, passionate, and irrational pleasure-seeking psychic force, but all that is Other, and in the Other celebrate freedom and the wonder of being free. Rhythm, dance and song utter God to a forgetful world: we are incomplete without soul and spirit, incomplete without their audacity, without their rhythms, without their song and dance. We need their vibrant utterance. We need their power to change the world.

### ℭ Dangerous memory

Two other thematic refrains complete the set of image metaphors that recur throughout this book. One is from a man, the other from a woman. The times in which we live demand recurring insistence on Johann Baptist Metz's iconic theme of *dangerous memory*. A spirituality for the twenty-first century cannot afford to forget the horrors that went before it, must not forget the victims of violence and oppression, must not forget how easy it is for whole peoples to turn away in fear and collude with tyranny, must not forget a profoundly ethical political and social commitment. A truly audacious spirituality will not allow itself the false luxury of such forgetting, even in order to 'move on': putting horror behind us has to mean making sure it does not happen again. This is a profoundly Christian stance, one that grows out of a conviction of the social significance of the cross and the social demand of the victim of tyranny and injustice. The authentic starting point for an audacious spirituality is found when what it means to be fully human is firmly and consciously grounded in history and society, both of which demonstrate the endangered and fragmented nature of present human being-in-the-world.

We are people who construct history; and we also construct its fragmentation. Only a false spirituality will cover over and ignore social and historical fragmentation and its dangerous implications for justice and the peace of the world. That is why we need audacity of spirit, soul-song and spirit-dance: the audacious capacity to wrestle with the unethical power agendas and structures that damage the world and exploit its people. What is at work in the choice of Metz's recurring theme is a hermeneutics of danger, an interpretive sense that people and the structures they build can be politically, socially and personally dangerous and endangered: impacted by the irrationality of evil and the corruptions of power. The theological implication is that final meaning, so dear to contemporary definitions of spirituality, is deferred, obstructed, deviated, depleted, postponed by the struggle with the unpredictability of life and the unforeseen contingencies of existence.

The struggle with existence under the emblem of dangerous memory brings us face to face with the reality of the spiritual life. It raises two options for us. We can embrace spirituality as a mode of flight from alienation and despair, or we can face the challenge of existence. Taking a cue from Søren Kierkegaard, it is possible to define authentic spirituality as *a creative and transformative containment and expression of primordial human experience, something that is uniquely personal to every one of us.*[2] According to Ann and Barry Ulanov, primordial experience names the original strata of human life.[3] The central elements of human life are met in primordial experience, elements of great power capable of shaking lives and bringing ordinary preoccupations to a standstill: wonderful and ecstatic, or terrible and destructive, dating back to separation from the unity and harmony of the womb. Primordial experience makes consciousness flesh. Primordial experience shapes the narrative structure and typical behavioural patterns of individual and group lives precisely because it has to do with the undercurrents of human existence and the darker sides of human behaviour. Its presence is felt in all our disturbing experiences of gap, break, lack, and the void. The impacts of primordial experience are encountered everywhere: in history, community, relationships, revelation, vocation, work and the spiritual practices and commitments that deal not only with the forces of psychological repression and the shadow side of life, but also with their ethical and spiritual consequences.

In Kierkegaard's terms, what is required is a movement from a generic or fuzzy kind of spirituality to a spirituality that has the clarity of conscious choice, one that recognises not only the mutual challenges and implications of psychological and spiritual growth, but the necessity of dangerous memory if spirituality is to be more than self-gratifying wish-fulfilment: a dance of clear awareness is of the essence. A spirituality that clearly acknowledges the mutuality of psychological and spiritual development learns how to move away from chaotic imbalances towards unity, union and communion. A spirituality that clearly acknowledges dangerous memory learns how to stand with the victims of tyranny and social inequality. Primordial experience is present in personal struggles for meaning, identity and individuality; it is also present in the struggle for justice in the face of primal anxiety. Primordial experience lies behind every act of individual and social self-interpretation. It lies behind the quality of every human engagement with existence, the lens through which concrete existence and relationships are interpreted and misinterpreted. Primordial experience is there in every counselling, psychotherapeutic, or spiritual accompaniment encounter. It makes its presence felt in every personal, social and occupational relationship. Primordial experience is the backdrop to the dark night and other painful, self-revealing experiences known to authentic spirituality, the kind that are always encountered somewhere along the way.

For Kierkegaard a twin movement is entailed in coming to terms with primordial experience: a movement from existence and self to religion and God, and a movement back from God to existence and the self. This self-God-self rhythm may at first glance appear contradictory or even potentially neurotic, but the task of authentic spirituality is to transcend the God-self contradiction and build a process of formative and transformative integration. In that integrating dance the graced encounter with God begets a more creative and ethically conscious encounter with both self and reality. This is more likely to take place when the social and political significance of dangerous memory is grasped. In Christian spirituality the dynamic movement back from God to self and existence must take place in the shadow of the cross, in the light of dangerous memory and the power of primordial experience in mobs gone mad. If that level of awareness does not arise, spirituality is revealed as an escapist haven from reality, a kind of panacea, a neurotic form of self-referred solace and comfort. Such spirituality deserves to be critiqued because it serves as a false, a distorting container for primordial experience.

Neither authentic religion nor authentic spirituality, precisely because they remain consciously and responsibly open to the interweaving dance of human life and the interpreting/misinterpreting forces of primordial experience, can serve as a disengaged or uninvolved haven from the impacts of the neurotic absurdity that typifies so many lives. Authentic spirituality is not flight from the absurd. It subsumes a return to existence after the manner of Abraham (Genesis 22:1-19). Note how the existence-God-existence rhythm is yet again revealed. The same is true in the story of Tabor (Mark 9:2-8). Spirituality, when it is grounded in dangerous memory, always remains in touch with reality, does not flee from the contemporary triad of absurdity-alienation-despair, or the exploitation-manipulation-evasion triad that reveals their presence. Authentic spirituality permits these interweaving triads to be dealt with at a deeper, more wholistic level. This makes it possible to contend with existence in a way that reveals spirituality as a creative, conscious dance with the challenges of human existence, guided by an attitude of mind characterised by a thoughtful, reflective consideration of numinous knowledge.[4] Authentic spirituality does this by providing a context of tradition and belief, of spiritual wisdom and knowledge that allows the immediacy of awesomely divine and powerfully primordial religious experience to be authentically contained and observed.[5]

The positive role of spirituality is to encourage and protect the immediacy of such experience, not block or distort it. Authentic spirituality allows soul to sing and spirit to soar audaciously and creatively in the world as it is. That audacity also shows that an individual or group's concrete, biographical situation is the basic context for authentic spirituality, and the human basis for understanding it. Authentic spirituality teaches people how to live closer to the primordial, subterranean levels of their lives without being flooded by psychosis. In the light of dangerous memory, spirituality also teaches them how to live without needing to repress the presence of darker forces, without engaging in substitutive satisfactions like addictions, and without needing to deny the powerful influence such forces have on human action and the human search for emancipatory meaning because there are healthy ways to manage and transcend these forces.[6] Authentic spirituality, by embracing emancipatory meaning, also safeguards individuality and the individual person against the mass-consumerism of the times and its hidden exploitations. This is another space where dangerous memory reveals its spiritual and religious importance.

In theological terms, truly liberating meaning is fundamentally eschatological, descriptive of a sacred time. It pertains to an objective future that cannot be defined by any one political ideology or vision, or be subsumed by its demands. Christian spirituality understands that ultimate emancipatory meaning is in the hands of God who wills to be found and in the finding allows ultimate meaning to be glimpsed and fleetingly touched. Ultimate meaning is made possible by God's descent into a dangerous and endangered world, a descent that invites personal and social cooperation and the expressive convictions of an audacious spirit. A spirituality that is not informed by dangerous memory, then, lacks a sense of the real; it is out of touch with history and God's paradoxically victorious self-revelation. Dangerous memory reminds us that any search for meaning that ignores or forgets the fact that life, and today all of planetary existence, is endangered, becomes an illusion, a comforting abstraction that is out of touch with the real world and of no authentically transformative or liberational use.[7] Such is the path of delusion and neurotic existence. Spirituality seeks more, seeks a life that transcends delusion and its escapist fantasies.

€ *Vive Jésus/let Jesus live*
That is why the other returning refrain in the book is borrowed from St Jane de Chantal (1572–1641). Her life can be summed up in the spiritual maxim, *vive Jésus*, which she shared with her soul friend St Francis de Sales (1567–1622) and inscribed on all her letters. I have translated it programmatically as *let Jesus live* rather than the more literal *live Jesus*. At first glance the phrase looks like a pious inscription of the kind that was once popular on letters and envelopes, but that impression would be

deceptive. *Vive Jésus* is a summary of the everyday mysticism Jane de Chantal lived so audaciously and the gentle, kindly yet disciplined methodless method she offered to others: gentle, yes, and kindly compassionate, but clear, conscious, disciplined. *Let Jesus live* is a mysticism and a demanding process of Christian living, a spirituality of the ordinary that is alive and well and necessary today, soaked as it is in the imagery of a gentle Christ offering rest for a weary soul and a sweet yoke for exuberant spirits (Matthew 11:28-30). *Let Jesus live* is a maxim, a motto, a spiritual statement, an aspiration, a celebration, a practice, a program, a liberatingly disciplined process, a presence, an experience, a graced reality, a quality of awareness, a mode of commitment, a living rhythm, a call to metanoia, a call to stillness, a rule of life, the gracious hinge around which a whole life pivots, spirit dances and soul sings. It is the summary of a spiritual path, the expression of a spiritual vision, a process of surrender, the naming of a transformed life, and the naming of a graced engagement with love that dances up from the deep heart's core of Christian spirituality and unassumingly sings it to the world.

*Let Jesus live* puts Jesus and the way he teaches firmly at the centre of the spiritual life. It contemplatively awaits his gracious pleasure in watchful awareness and in gentle surrender to an immeasurable stillness that sings of the sacred within and in that singing evokes a dance of compassionate service and passionate solidarity. *Vive Jésus* means we desire nothing more than what God desires for us in grace, and therein lies a profound challenge for contemporary people living in discontented consumer societies. In that Christ-shaped space endlessly desiring, busy, noisy self-referred lives are transformed by a paradoxically quiet sense of fruitful uselessness, a kind of empty-handed-active-passivity, a quiet resting, a gentle patience, a graciously contented simplicity and yet an audacious activity that lets Jesus live and dance and sing in the world. The phrase *let Jesus live* sings with the melody of a key Pauline text: I no longer live because Jesus lives in me (Galatians 2:20). But this is a song that develops organically within the social realities and responsibilities of real human lives dealing with the impacts of primordial experience. This is a song that lets Jesus shine through real human faces, and be heard in the compassionate tone of real human voices. *Vive Jésus/let Jesus live* bespeaks a transformed centre, a transformed mind, a transformed heart, the very places where Jesus seeks to live in transforming grace.

Jane wrote *Vive Jésus* at the head of every letter she wrote and quoted it frequently in all her writings. It summarises a deeply personal way of life, a committed way, a way of ego-transcending transformation. *Vive Jésus* also appears in Francis de Sales' two best-known works, in the dedicatory prayer to his *Introduction to the Devout Life* and in Book XII, chapter 13 of his *Treatise on the Love of God*, as well as in many of his letters and other writings. *Vive Jésus/let Jesus live*, lies at the very centre of Salesian spirituality and orients its every value and practice. To let Jesus live is to embrace the divine and be changed, utterly changed, because it means confronting the relational and dialogic shape and texture of daily life itself, allowing it to be touched by God's expansiveness. In Jane's vision there is no place for an isolated contemplation and therein lies the challenge for a fragmented society that favours isolated identities adrift in a sea of lonely individualism. Letting Jesus live calls for an innately social understanding of spirituality, one marked by mutual regard and a genuine affection that transcends self-referred boundaries. And if there is suffering in letting Jesus live it is the suffering of love, of rebuffed kindliness and the understanding patience it demands, love bearing fruit in Spirit peace, striking back with the heart of love.[8]

### ( Poetics of spirit

The book is organised in twelve chapters that trace the complex contours of contemporary spirituality before attempting to identify the basic characteristics of a spirituality for the twenty-first century. The methodology is that of a poetics of spirit, an approach that favours imaginative and speculative reflection on the theory and practice of contemporary spirituality and their dynamic interactions.[9] Poetics recognises that the truth of a spirituality cannot be separated from the action that brings it to life in the world. To know something is to develop a relationship with what is known, a relationship that gives expression to who we are becoming: to reflect on spirituality is to enact spirituality. The consequences of spiritual knowing are ongoing because spirituality is dialogical, a process, a struggle, a negotiation, something ethical, something meant to be fruitful in transformed lives, a place where the ancient distinction between skill and moral judgment dances its dance.

The Greek words for this ancient distinction are *poiesis* and *praxis*, words used to name different understandings of action that trace their origins back to Aristotle. In the Greek tradition praxis, rational reflection, is seen to be superior to poiesis, a productive skill; while poiesis builds a world, praxis fulfils rational intentions. Can there be a synthesis? Perhaps there can if we place praxis within poiesis, elevating the one without diminishing the other. Certainly, when we reflect on God as creator we encounter a hint of this synthesis in action where both poiesis and praxis come together on account of something good. Spirituality values the link poiesis suggests to a creating God, but it also values transformative intention. In this view, if praxis is intentional life then poiesis names the art of building a home for life, life humming with productive power.

There is a problem with this suggestion. Spirituality challenges us to move beyond imitative replay to something real, something that is not centred on humanity, something not centred in a kind of postmodern tinkering with fragments. A robust spirituality, able to express the audacity of spirit and let Jesus live in dangerous memory, envisages something more than a bit-player in a game of cyber networks. What is required is a different, a more radical understanding of creative imagination, of what is involved in the making of a true abode for life that transcends the limits of ego-based consciousness and the misinterpretations of primordial experience. What is demanded is an ethical-poetic-contemplative imagination capable of embracing a vision beyond the self. Not even self-making can be centred on the self in the absence of the Other.

The building of a spirituality sings a story that reveals more than the need for skill and technique, more than tools for an audacious spirit. The story of spirituality also sings of a capacity for deep contemplative reflection that is of its very nature performative, transformative and self-implicating. The poetics of spirit used here is not simply about aesthetics and the subjectivity of beauty as is so often the case with poetics today. The ancient meaning uses the word poetics performatively: not a surprise since its origins lie in Aristotle's study of Greek theatre and tragic drama. Poetics aims at decision but decision requires the discernment and recognition of purpose. It is in this sense that the word poetics is used in this book. It affirms the unity of knowing and acting, of truth and action in the drama of human existence. A poetics of spirit brings praxis and poiesis together: praxis, a process of reflexive action, offers poiesis, a process of creative crafting, a sense of ultimate purpose, a goal to be discerned, accepted, chosen and implemented. It is not enough for a spirituality to be well-designed; it must also have a well-defined purpose that simultaneously orients it and is revealed in action. A poetics of spirit is performative. It recognises that spirituality actively orients a choice and creates a space where authentic personhood is crafted through an interweaving process of formative techniques, transformative intentions, and ethical action in the service of a transcendent goal.[10] On the way it recognises that to become truly human means searching for and choosing the uniquely true self.[11]

Chapter one sets the scene by exploring the rise of global spirituality. These are transitional times, and transitional times bring new challenges to those seeking to live genuinely spiritual lives. Today, that challenge has taken on both ecumenical and interfaith dimensions as spiritual ideas and practices from all over the world become available as a result of the communications and information revolutions. This chapter also looks at the European enigma. Europe has become an officially secular desert in a world of burgeoning religion and exploding spirituality. It seems that no one has told the powers that be in Europe that the Enlightenment and its myth of scientific and rational progress is just that, a myth. Europe is a place where secular materialist philosophy has been in the ascendancy for over a hundred years, a period of horror and destruction on an industrial scale unimaginable to earlier generations. It seems that Europe still has to learn that secularism does not save us from our dark side. Something else, a different, more human ethic and awareness is required, an awareness that a renewal of emancipatory spirituality can support and encourage. The question is, however, whether Europe is paying attention.

Chapter two moves on to examine the cultural and contextual forces that shape contemporary spirituality. It addresses the forces that contour contemporary mentalities and the challenges and disenchantments they enact once the decision to live by human reason alone is made. This is a decision that is exacerbated by the ethical banality of consumer culture and its fuelling of endless discontents and desires. Attention then turns to the rhythms of re-enchantment and re-sacralisation that the present revolution in contemporary spirituality suggests is already underway in the West. The postmodern milieu seems particularly favourable to this surprisingly audacious turn, but it also favours a non-creedal, non-institutional, deregulated approach to things spiritual. This represents a real challenge for institutional expressions of spirituality. Nevertheless, growing evidence points in the direction of a new audacity of spirit: the challenge is to notice and read the signs of the times. Chapter two also seeks to identify the principal shaping forces at work in contemporary spirituality: ecological concerns, the suspicion of institutional expressions of religiosity and spirituality, consumerism and its discontents, ethics, and the impacts of media-driven superficiality. Then the late-modern turn to the self is explored. The importance of this turn for spiritualities described in terms of the search for the true self is noted.

Chapter three starts with a deceptively simple question: what is spirituality actually about? It is in the process of answering that question that the poetic method shaping the book comes to the fore. The method has already been encountered in the prologue and in the first part of this introduction. It is called a *poetics of spirit*. Poetics is a speculative attempt to explore the choices and intentions that underpin the making processes at work in the production of contemporary spirituality. The chapter begins with ten descriptive reflections on contemporary spirituality. It then attempts to explore the many layers of spiritual experience and what influences these layers today: religion, meaning, alienation, and caricature. The poetic spirit is a creating spirit, a bearer of possible worlds. It views spirituality as an inner work of making that finds audacious public expression through engaged and transformed lives. The chapter concludes by reflecting on the advantages and disadvantages of the poetic approach before describing spirituality as a way of uncovering and becoming aware of the hidden music of being-in-the-word as it comes to a mysterious crescendo: the truth of spirituality is in its living.

The poetic method has a variety of advantages in spirituality and five of these are explored: a poetics bespeaks exploration and expression, it bespeaks a polyphony of possibilities, it also points to a process of transformative interpretation, recognises the forces of context, and finally reveals a space where many potentials dance and sing together to rhythm new horizons of meaning into being. Chapter four is in direct continuity with the poetics of spirit introduced in Chapter three. Chapter four explores the universal use of metaphor in spirituality and suggests that metaphor, as the language of spirit, must be recognised as the principal instrument of a poetics of spirit. Metaphor is used in spirituality as a way to engage creatively and critically with the forces that shape spirituality and contour contemporary expressions of soul and spirit. As well as investigating the creative and evocative power of metaphor, this chapter looks at how metaphor works and then considers the presence and use of metaphor in faith-based spiritualities. The identity of revealed faith in spirituality as *event-process-relation* is then explored. A reflection on metaphor in spirituality that does not inquire into the influential role of masculine and feminine metaphors would be incomplete at best and at worst would suggest that spirituality is gender blind. Jazz is introduced as a metaphor for the revolution underway in contemporary spirituality. Can spirituality let Jesus live to different, individualised, or even spontaneously improvised rhythms?

Chapter five goes further into the meaning of the word spirituality, particularly in terms of life-style choices. Two elements shape the approach taken: J. B. Metz's dynamic concept of dangerous memory and Jane de Chantal's call to let Jesus live, aspects of which we have already explored. Do such images impact consciously ethical life-style choices today? The question has to do with the forces that shape us as responsive and responsible human beings intentionally dancing towards a sacred future, embracing its rhythms and singing its songs. The core question posed in this chapter is: what is spirituality today? The search for an answer navigates through a series of thematic descriptions of the wild profusion and complexity of contemporary Western spirituality as it swirls its coats of many colours in the global winds of spirit. Themes of awareness and unawareness are raised, themes of the desert and silence as places of temptation and wildness but of angelic presence, too (Mark 1:12-13); places of discovery and shifting identity. Related themes of self-implicating activity, of creative expression, of depth and transcendence are also discussed. Attention is then given to the soft, nomadic edges of contemporary spirituality and its passionate landscapes. In this chapter thirty-four brief descriptions of contemporary spirituality are offered. These help us to understand the imprecision typical of definitions used in the contemporary spiritual revolution and the forces that shape it. The present fuzziness is examined before the chapter concludes with a review of the defining themes of spirituality that help us to understand the moulding of a life that allows soul to sing and spirit to dance an audacious remaking of a dry world into a place of springs (Psalm 107:35).

The forces that impact the meaning and shaping of contemporary spirituality shape Chapters six, seven and eight. Soul and spirit are the pivotal focal points in these chapters. Chapter six returns to the genealogy of the word spirituality, and explores its origins in order to retrieve the dynamism and rhythm of its foundational meaning. The Hebrew *ruach* and the Greek *pneuma* are unfolded in order to reveal the creative, life-giving force behind spirit and spirituality. This is done against the backdrop of a suggestive listing of twenty-one contemporary uses of the word and twenty-two typical expressions of contemporary spirituality. A brief history of English usage follows before emerging manifestations and questions are explored. The problem of religious and spiritual amnesia, loss of memory, in the new spirituality is then addressed. Then the link between memory, imagination and the spiritual landscape is more fully explored against the horizon of the influential image of holy ground as Ellen Ross unfolds it. Attention then turns to the shaping impact of the Enlightenment and Romanticism, the important influence of Paul Tillich and Thomas Luckmann, and the diverging and often esoteric processes that presently typify the new spirituality.

Chapter seven continues in a similar vein, this time concentrating on the question of soul. Again, the genealogy of the word is the starting point for reflection, beginning with the Greek and Hebrew origins of the word before turning to reflect on the meaning of soul in the Western Christian tradition. The soul-body unity is then considered, a unity that dances before God in the world, a unity that is wonderfully and divinely made to be fully alive in love, lovingly alive to the divine gift of life to the full (John 10:10). The chapter concludes with a poetics of soul that identifies life, love and creativity as the great descriptors of soul, soul understood as the precondition for complete and healthy existence in the world, soul as the ground of a vital and vibrant spiritual anthropology. Chapter eight continues the reflection on spirit. This reflection unfolds in conversation with Simone Weil, David Hay and Michael Gelven. Attention then turns to the relationship between the Divine Spirit and the human spirit. Images of fragrance, invitation, inspiration, love, beauty and freedom focus on the vibrant challenge to transcend self-interest and self-defensiveness that personifies images of audacious spirit soaring on the winds of the world. Life is the song of spirit and the fruit of the Spirit grows graciously in the singing. So does holiness, the expansiveness of God in human lives. Prayer emerges at this point as the space made by soul and spirit, the space where soul and spirit meet, the space where soul and spirit move the focus of living away from self-obsession towards God.

Chapter nine turns at last to the vexed question of definition. It offers a field guide to the proliferation of definitions that arise around spirituality in a world of clamouring and contesting voices. The fragmenting forces of postmodern culture are only too easy to see in the wild proliferation of definitions that are at work here. It is as if a mustard seed of definition was set free and then spread wildfire through the world, competing for space in mind-body-spirit festivals of many different kinds. The nature, task and characteristics of definitions is unfolded, and issues of meaning and value, of assumption and presupposition, of symbolic and social interaction are engaged with before a process of mapping spirituality is attempted. In order to give a flavour of the competing voices, forty-eight different kinds of definition encountered in spirituality are identified in a brief descriptive summary. The question of meaning in spirituality is then explored before an attempt to summarise the forest of forms, definitional contours, and thematic categories that typify contemporary spirituality is undertaken. The chapter concludes with a reflection on the Christian spiritual vision.

Chapter ten turns to the shape of contemporary spirituality as an interweaving set of practices, literacies and discourses. This approach permits us to explore a number of important themes in contemporary spirituality. The pathos or pain involved in the struggle towards authenticity, and the challenges involved in searching for a humbler vision of being are raised. Particular attention is paid to the spiritual challenges posed by the routines and anomalies of everyday embodied lives and their shaping impact on the practices ordinary people use in the construction of contemporary spiritualities. De Certeau's 'spiritual bricolage' and Wuthnow's 'patchwork religiosity' are offered as typical examples. Toolkit spiritualities with their individual sets of symbols, rituals, prayer-practices and stories ready for every spiritual eventuality are another.

Practice is viewed here as a carrier of intentional meaning and purpose: their living expression. Living practice is the space where living words, meanings, ideas, images and intentions are made flesh in the world: twenty-two fields of spiritual practice are summarised by way of typical example. Then the interactive issues of literacy and discourse are explored as they come together in the world of practice. Literacy is important to a developing spirituality because language serves social and developmental as well as communicative purposes. Without appropriate levels of literacy sacred texts become closed books, spiritual development suffers through lack of appropriate language, and the communication of spirituality runs the risk of falling to the level of the lowest common denominator, if it is not ignored completely. Teachers of spirituality will recognise the problems inherent in poor levels of spiritual or religious literacy. The challenge to practitioners and students of spirituality alike is to understand how living practice brings developing literacy and deepening discourse together in the service of life.

Chapter eleven is an attempt to dream into the future by describing the hoped-for basic contours of a post-postmodern spirituality. The inspiration is Christian and Western, and the dream takes place in conversation with the cultural impacts of postmodern deconstruction. Two foundational pillars for an emergent post-postmodern spirituality are addressed: the apophatic turn to stillness and non-discursive meditation in a noisy world, and the turn to passionately ethical social solidarity in a world of fragmented, isolating and uncaring individualism. Wordless and imageless apophatic stillness interacting with passionately ethical social solidarity have the power to shape a new spiritual ethos. They are also capable of creating a spiritual abode for a spiritually alert people as they confront a desacralised world and seek to enchant it afresh. The chapter explores the techniques of meditation associated with apophatic spirituality in some depth. It attends in particular to the contemporary growth of depression, that ancient sickness of the human soul, before exploring its ancient spiritual antidote: the spiritual serenity and clarity that is the true fruit of sustained meditative and contemplative practice. Attention is also given to the qualities of the discursive and non-discursive mind. The chapter also examines the need for a passionately befriending solidarity if, in Bonhoeffer's terms, the dreamed-of spirituality is to have any real social significance: the goal, after all, is to imagine a spirituality capable of dancing a new world into being.

Chapter twelve offers a series of reflections on a variety of theological themes important to Christian spirituality today. These reflections recognise the challenges posed to spirituality by the seductions and abuses of power that are so clearly evident today, and the dangers inherent in elitist understandings of spirituality. The first reflection focuses on Bonhoeffer's challenge to Christians to live completely in the world, and in the contemporary West that means a world that blindly commodifies the dance of the human spirit and reduces it to a disposable product in a disposable world. The commodification of the spirit is a spiritual challenge for theology and a theological challenge for spirituality at a time when both must write new songs about the dire needs of a planet in crisis. What is unfolded here is a reflection on the contemporary relation between theology and spirituality that prepares the way for a reflection on God-as-Trinity. Such a reflection is necessary precisely because Trinity represents the foundational grammar of all Christian experience. Trinity orients Christian spirituality and simultaneously anchors it as a love-impelled, dancing journey of perpetual return to its Loving Source.

Attention then turns to Thomas Merton's identification of the creative imagination as the place where contemplative experience is constantly remoulded in a landscape alive with the rhythms of radical love. Such is the landscape that supports the discovery of the true, the contemplative self, a self wise in the graced ways of letting Jesus live and dancing with God-as-Trinity. Spirituality dances wisely or it is lost. Other themes addressed in this chapter include the crisis of transformation facing us in the contemporary West. The challenge of weakness, pain and suffering is identified as the dark medium of encounter with God. There is an eschatological bias to this view of Christian spirituality, a bias in favour of a paradoxical presence that makes it impossible for us to ignore our dark side and its potentially toxic impacts. There then follows a reflection on Bernard Lonergan's understanding of metanoia and conversion and its implications for a spirituality firmly grounded in a radically unconditional encounter with the gift of divine love. Rahner's non-elitist vision of Christian spirituality is then visited before a final reflection on life in grace brings the chapter to a close. Grace is pivotal because Christian spirituality is about the graced emergence of an identity-in-Christ that resists evil and loves God because Perfect Love drives out fear (1 John 4: 18).

NOTES

1. Gerald G. May, *The Wisdom of Wilderness: Experiencing the Healing Power of Nature.* Foreword by Parker J. Palmer (New York: HarperSanFrancisco, 2006) 69–90.

2. See Avi Sagi, *Kierkegaard, Religion and Existence: The Voyage of the Self.* Translated from the Hebrew by Batya Stein (Amsterdam, Atlanta, GA: Rodopi, 2000) 25–44.

3. Ann and Barry Ulanov, *Religion and the Unconscious* (Philadelphia: The Westminster Press, 1975) 13–24.

4. John W. Welch, *Spiritual Pilgrims: Carl Jung and Teresa of Avila* (New York/Mahwah, NJ: Paulist Press, 1982) 79.

5. Ann and Barry Ulanov, *Religion and the Unconscious* op. cit. 36.

6. ibid. 25–45.

7. See James Matthew Ashley, *Interruptions: Mysticism, Politics, and Theology in the Work of Johann Baptist Metz* (Notre Dame, IN: University of Notre Dame Press, 2002).

8. See Wendy M. Wright and Joseph F. Power, eds, *Francis de Sales, Jane de Chantal: Letters of Spiritual Direction.* Translated by Péronne Marie Thiebert with a Preface by Henri J.M. Nouwen (New York/Mahwah, NJ: Paulist Press, 1988); Wendy M. Wright, *Heart Speaks to Heart: The Salesian Tradition* (Maryknoll, NY: Orbis Books, 2004).

9. See Edward K. Kaplan, *Holiness in Words: Abraham Joshua Heschel's Poetics of Piety* (Albany, NY: State University of New York Press, 1996).

10. See Richard Kearney, *The Wake of Imagination: Towards a Postmodern Culture*

(London and New York: Routledge, 1988, reprinted 2001); Terence
Ball, *Reappraising Political Theory: Revisionist Studies in the History of Political
Thought* (Oxford: Clarendon Press, 1995) 221; Karsten Friis Johansen, *A
History of Ancient Philosophy: From the Beginnings to Augustine*. Translated by
Henrik Rosenmeier (London and New York: Routledge, 1998) 392; Ray
S. Anderson, *Spiritual Caregiving as Secular Sacrament: A Practical Theology for
Professional Caregivers*. Foreword by John Swinton (London and
Philadelphia: Jessica Kingsley Publishers, 2003)17–20.

11. See Adrian van Kaam, *On Being Yourself: Reflections on Spirituality and Originality*
(Denville, NJ: Dimension Books, 1972) 9–24.

## CHAPTER 1

*The Emergence of Global Spirituality*

*If spirituality is about a quality of presence,*
*an inner and an outer presence, something divine,*
*then spiritual living is about making sure*
*there is a clear path to the door.*
*Spirituality is also about directions in contexts.*
*Like religion it waxes or wanes in time and place.*

## INTRODUCTION

One of the words that helps us map spirituality today is the word *contemplation*. It is a powerfully evocative word that reveals rich facets of human experience and potential. It triggers thoughts and feelings; it initiates insights and intuitions about things and captures them in precious revelatory moments. Contemplation is a gifted capacity for openness and breadth of vision, a graced capacity for unbounded presence schooled in the synergies and arts of listening and reflecting. Contemplation sings with a sense of all-embracing awareness, dances in a vast space full of the rhythms of the divine, and spins out into the world of action ready to discover and embrace the deep essence of human being and existence. Contemplation unfolds an all-embracing vision, an enlightened and spiralling awareness visioning depth beyond illusion. It learns how to find the extraordinary in the ordinary, the pearls hidden in fields easily passed by in the consumer rush and its media-spin-made discontents. Contemplation is a state of fluid awareness that sees through to the inner nature of reality and makes new modes of knowing possible.

Contemplation always reveals an operative and orienting attitude of heart and soul, a spirit rising in creative freedom, a seeking for a true abode in the teeming vastness of the cosmos. Contemplation opens up the potential self, rescues it from the chains of the past and the driven ego; it enables the potential self to come newly alive into the world. Above all contemplation is about a quality of sharing presence creatively unfolding in an ever-expanding now, that not only builds a clear path to the awesome doors of life, perception, understanding and welcome, but also walks in sacred paths and knits newness with their ancient challenges; and today those challenges are many and vitally demanding. Contemplation is a mode of encounter, a point of convergence, an abode of freedom-in-the-presence-of-the-Other. Contemplation sits companionably with mystery and gazes deeply into the seminal questions of the times, fluidly penetrating their opaque and unpredictable surfaces. Contemplation makes room for questions and there are many such questions confronting any serious review of contemporary spirituality today.

What sort of world is shaping contemporary spirituality? What contextual forces are at work in people's lives as they enter into personal and communal conversations about religion and spirituality today? What sort of cultural or philosophical ethos is challenging spirituality as this new century unfolds? Does spirituality have a deep innovative élan or liberating power that can be successfully harnessed for the good of all? Does spirituality have a constructive role to play in a world of rapidly changing values and problems, and if so, what kind of spirituality? Are we really being challenged to develop a new global consciousness along with the global spirituality that will give it operative expression? Is a new spirituality of action and convergence of the kind suggested more than forty years ago by Teilhard de Chardin what is needed? Is it inevitable that this emerging global spirituality be a dialogical blend of the best elements of Eastern and Western mystical paths? Who will decide what those elements are? What of the potential and real distortions of spirituality?

What of the African and Latin American experiences of spirituality and mysticism? What, then, of traditional and aboriginal ways of spirituality and mysticism? Was Kathleen Fischer correct in 1988 when she described global spirituality as another name for inclusive spirituality?[1] Is a common global spirituality either possible or desirable? And if a unitary global spirituality were to emerge how might it avoid the dangers of totalising power on the one hand and a frozen universalism on the other? How might spirituality develop if the emergence of a global economy and ideologically driven one-world visions are discovered to be primary motivating forces behind a totalising drive for a global religiosity, a global spirituality? If such were the case what is the prospect of a global non-religious, secular or civil spirituality surfacing and sweeping all other religious and sacred forms away, regardless of how subtle the methods used? What might the role of spiritual and religious leadership be in all of these matters?

These are many-sided questions and they will be answered in a multiplicity of ways, depending on the points of view of those who respond or react to the profound changes such questions imply are already underway in spirituality, especially in the West. Nor is answering such questions made any easier by the tendency today for many people to define spirituality in inner, subjective, personal and experiential terms in opposition to outer, objective, organisational or institutional terms.[2] Are spirituality and the sacred only to be discovered within, or do they also sparkle between and among people in their living environments?[3] If spirituality is only discovered within, if it is defined as a purely private affair of little public consequence as modernity insists, how is a globally influential spirituality ever to arise in the first place? What is the probability that such efforts would remain uncontested? In contemporary Europe, for example, how might such a global spirituality be organised and by whom, given that the public voice of mainstream religion is effectively marginalised and excluded by political and media interests regardless of the fact that religion is on the rise in the rest of the world?

A number of things, however, are clear. Critical answers to the questions raised above, and many others like them, require genuine respect for the heritage, insight and wisdom of differing mystical, religious, and spiritual traditions. Radical difference is part of what these traditions have to bring to frank, constructive and critically reflective dialogue in favour of a more globally conscious, more globally humane world. Contemporary spirituality shows every sign of evolving at a deep human level, responding in a variety of ways to the changing motivations, interests, rhythms and challenges of the times in which we now live and the global nature of the challenges we now face. Contemporary spirituality is also challenged to respond creatively and wisely to the global explosion of pluralistic, urban socio-economic and socio-cultural settings and their socio-political and socio-religious problems. People are beginning to break free of the slough of spiritual lassitude; a new confidence is arising at grassroots levels.[4] Transitional space has become the bearer of promises of spiritual well-being in complex and conflicted times and places.

It is also clear that Christian spirituality is itself in transition as it engages with and is confronted by both transnational challenges and the realities of global crisis and change. Spiritualities that were content to be local are now challenged to address global issues, not least of human and ecological justice. Within spirituality these challenges underline the need for respectful interspiritual dialogue that recognises the need for shared communal responses to the world's problems. Nonetheless, the emergence of a single global spirituality seems improbable. The concept of *global spiritualities* that build networks and communities of consensus and creative response to global concerns makes more sense, not least because of the wide range of affinities, differences and sensibilities already at work in contemporary religiosity and spirituality.

The challenge is to recognise and encourage the creative and emancipatory resources of spirit and appreciate them analytically so that ancient suspicions may be laid to rest and common action for the benefit of the world and everything in it undertaken.[5] While diversity will continue to be characteristic of this new movement, we are also challenged to rediscover in love the religious and cultural roots of a sanely optimistic and creative spiritual humanism that cares for the whole world: sanely optimistic lest we forget the despairs and terrors of our shared history. What is urgent, however, is the emergence of an operative consensus among religions and spiritual traditions about the state of the world and the mobilising of forces and resources to respond creatively to the emancipatory and ecological needs that face everyone in the world today. Therein lies a profound historical responsibility with broad political consequences. There is another aspect to this turn. If the globalising of spirituality means anything, it means that a purely individualistic and self-referred understanding of the spirit or the spiritual life has little to offer in the face of pressing global needs.

## Spirituality and Transitional Times

These factors are reminiscent of other transitional and liminal or threshold-crossing moments in the annals of spirituality, moments of civilisational and religious conflict, or moments when socio-cultural and socio-political chaos presented new challenges for the discovery of spiritual meaning and modes of presence.[6] Two examples come immediately to mind. The formative years of the Christian tradition were themselves times of great political, economic, cultural and intellectual upheaval. Socio-political and socio-economic upheavals also form the backdrop to St Benedict's (480–540) prophetic spiritual stance during another time of great political, social and religious disruption in the aftermath of the fall of Rome in 410. Benedict's vision became a beacon of hope in a dark time of great change and turmoil in Europe, a time that had begun before he was born and continued until the eleventh century. It offered continental Europe a dynamic way of allowing all of human life, beset by the challenges, dangers and disruptions of transitional times, to be caringly shaped by the liberating message of Jesus Christ.[7] But then, Christian spirituality has always been about entering into what God is doing in the world.

The history of the Christian tradition has much to teach us as we seek to respond creatively to the spiritual needs of the twenty-first century. For example, Christian spirituality has faced transnational challenges since St Paul and others began their journeys to the teeming urban centres of the Roman Empire. Soon, Christian communities grew up in Rome and Constantinople, Antioch and Alexandria and the many other cities like Corinth that welcomed the Christian message of the triumph of love over fear, of hope over despair. Spirituality has always evolved in response to new social, cultural and philosophical challenges. It constantly rediscovers itself as the world changes. Today we are witnessing a new grassroots awakening as technological, cultural, economic, and social globalisation gathers momentum and offers new channels for the development of a new religiosity and new ways of being spiritual in the world. Such pivotal moments in the history of Christian spirituality point us unmistakebly in the direction of the wellsprings of biblical spirituality and the depths of the Christian mystical tradition.

The idea of a global spirituality responding creatively to the potentials of transitional spaces and times and their new hints of the sacred is not something new in the Christian context. Christian spirituality has encountered and responded creatively to the Spirit dancing to the revealing drumbeats of transition and the opportunities of liminal space many times over in its 2,000-year history, not least in its emergence as a global reality in its own right.[8] What all transformational times and spaces have in common is their non-normality. They are in-between spaces coloured by potentially dangerous and unpredictable forces. They signal times of uncertainty, ambiguity, fragmentation and confusion. But they are also times of potential blessing, moments of profound spiritual intensification. The task of spirituality is to support this turn, to offer it a critical methodology, to show it new approaches to inner and outer harmony and learn to sort unconscious distractions from genuine insight.

Both transitional and liminal spaces and times are full of opportunities for transformative learning and deep metanoia, especially when the knowledge that is innate to the contemplative eye, to the discerning spirit is brought to the fore. Transitional and liminal times and spaces open windows onto the awesomeness of unrecognised sacred space; and they reveal the human spirit's drive to uncover the hidden potentials of creative expression even in moments of deep chaos as it seeks to dance a new dance with Spirit, its anchoring source of life and creative nourishment. The contemplative eye sees beyond the uncertainties and confusions to hidden dimensions and depths and seeks to bring them into clear view, especially when they represent repressed and marginalised potentials and possibilities unwanted and unappreciated by a social or cultural mainstream in decline. In the echoes and rhythms of Spirit song they have the power to reveal pathways across mysterious boundaries and scary edges to something different, something new: they give glimpses of new life and new spaces for new life. Transitional times and spaces challenge those who recognise themselves in them to risk finding their way to a changed future. As old ways are challenged new understandings and new connections become possible.

As times of crisis, transitions are also characterised by deep disruptions, and as times of uncertainty they confront us with multiple possibilities. In transitional spaces change occurs spontaneously to the extent that people are prepared to relinquish something in order to gain something:

to relinquish something outworn to gain something new and creative. As far as spirituality is concerned, transitions have to do with the unfolding of unrecognised identity, of connecting to the as-yet not-me, and in the connecting unfold new self and communal potentials. Transitional spaces are portals to possible futures. Transitional times allow agents and agencies of change to create new possibilities and new spaces for reflection that favour personal transformation and change. The same is true of organisations and their operative structures. What they have in common is the invitation to embrace with astonished delight the dynamic Spirit-borne rhythms of transformation.

In spirituality transitional spaces and transitional times are understood to be places where Spirit Wind blows through the crags of uncertainty and confusion, driving fear away in the embrace of divine love: they hold the bright promise of liberation. Today we need the spiritual courage to journey through dangerous transitional spaces and find new ways to construct a better world. We dare not abandon globalisation processes to self-referred power elites if we seek a fairer, more just, more compassionate world. People who are committed to the ways of spirit need to cross the boundaries of prejudice and learn to work together for the sake of God's good creation. If such people do not risk transition then space risks becoming enclosed, risks becoming a cosy cocoon, a space and a time that opens up to nothing and goes nowhere. This is not the mystic way.

What is at stake is the practicality of spirituality in the messy dynamics of real lives, and today that practicality raises practical issues of global connectedness, ecumenical conversation and interfaith dialogue. Unfortunately, for some people the idea that spiritual ecumenism is part and parcel of the Catholic tradition is a new and daunting concept. At their best such conversations take place in a trusting and open fashion; a committed praxis of dialogue and cooperation represents the wise way forward.[9] It is all too easy to forget that a spirituality that is not ready to share its spiritual treasures, that builds no welcoming path to its door is rightly suspect. Genuine spirituality is expansive. It resists being locked away and hidden in the dark. Genuine spirituality is a fruitful seed seeking watered soil and light in which to grow and blossom and send its intense yet subtle perfume into the air of the world.

The truth is that the human spirit is a bright and precious jewel that needs to let its bright facets shine in the world, swirling and dancing with the bright colours of brothers and sisters seeking the transcendent good. The truth is that spirituality lies at the heart of all genuine, all congruently active ecumenical and interfaith dialogue.[10] Spirituality lies at the heart of efforts to go beyond the barriers and structures of prejudice wherever they appear in the world. In order to do that spiritual ecumenism and interfaith dialogue need to be recognised as indispensable elements in contemporary spirituality. They are creatively conducive to the kind of critical reflection that favours depth, not least through the demands of self-implicating service and witness.[11] In Heribert Muhlen's terms a spirituality of imperturbability, untouched by clear proposals for concrete praxis, will be of little use to the world in the years ahead.[12] Spirituality faces a global challenge of great complexity and importance and there is no point in us arriving breathless and late.[13]

## GLOBAL SPIRITUALITY

During much of the twentieth century, efforts were made to identify the core themes of a potential world religion and an accompanying global spirituality that would help to build world peace. There is a recognition here that the coming together of religious as well as political practices and modalities of thought are crucial to any such global project, and the same may be said about the plight of the planet. The work of religion scholars like Mircea Eliade, Joseph Campbell, Huston Smith, Wilfred Cantwell Smith, and Ninian Smart looked optimistically in that direction. More recent scholarship has been less sanguine, but even then scholars like Peter Berger, Martin Riesebrodt, Mark Jurgensmeyer, and Roland Robertson have identified religion as a valuable, imaginative and ethical resource for the emerging global society. Hans Küng's work on a global ethic is an important case in point.[14] What many scholars in the world of comparative religion seem to be concerned about is the need for an inclusive paradigm of tolerance and understanding as the spiritual and ethical dimensions of a rapidly globalising world make new demands on the religious imagination and the flexibility of transnational religious and spiritual traditions.[15]

Spiritualities change in a globalising world as they respond to and engage with the new rhythms of life, rhythms impacted for better or worse by changes in lifestyles, culture and society, economics and technology, travel, migration, and political change. What globalisation makes necessary is openness to respectful and honest dialogue, a new and critically considerate conversation between religions and spiritual traditions about their similarities and their differences, about the educational value of mutual interaction, and joint actions in favour of a better, more just, more peaceful, more equitable global system. Why should all of these matters be entrusted to the hands of politicians and their civil functionaries? If this is what is meant by global spirituality, well and good: it represents a challenge to religious and spiritual groups and bodies to assume historical and political responsibility for the world in new ways in changing times.

However, there is another vision at large, one that favours the eclectic blending of the ideas and practices that emerge from comparative studies and from world level conversations between the global religions that favours the emergence of one new global religious and/or spiritual ideology. This agenda raises two important questions. Whose interests and sensibilities would be served by such a development? Would its imposition lead to the subtle persecution or marginalisation of those who do not agree? There are already some hints of the latter danger at work in liberal European democracies where genuine religious sensitivities and voices are ignored in the name of equality and minority rights: and therein lies an intriguing conundrum. In the name of one minority a new minority is brought into being. In ameliorating one injustice another is committed through the tyranny of the new politically correct majority. A spirituality concerned for justice reflects critically on such situations and seeks a more humane praxis.

Not surprisingly, then, global religions also show signs of consolidation in response, at least in part, to such tendencies, as incompatibilities of vision and thought become clearer, and deeply valued differences and sensibilities are more analytically understood and respected and thus inform shared praxis. Common themes and affinities are not difficult to identify: civility, compassion, respect for human rights, liberty, love, democracy, ethical values, equality, tolerance for difference, non-violent stances against tyranny and the soullessness of modern systems and structures, stances that counter the global tendencies to totalise power, stances that raise crucial environmental and ecological concerns, and stances that counter the forces of alienation and despair in the world. There is no reason, beyond sectional political interest, why transnational religions should not come together and develop strategies for dealing with such crucial issues. After all, their adherents make up the vast majority of the global population. Interfaith dialogue on major world concerns is essential today. It represents the work of a global sense of spiritual responsibility for the state of the peoples of the world and the state of the planet.

The differences between the world religions and their spiritual and mystical traditions are also easy to identify. The most obvious have to do with visions of ultimate reality and their concomitant understandings of human nature and human destiny. Other differences help us distinguish between religions of grace and salvation such as Christianity on the one hand and religions of consciousness such as Buddhism on the other. Then we need to respect the difference between theist and non-theist religions, and this increasingly includes adherents of secular humanism. All of these differences are significant and are part and parcel of the religions and philosophies that hold them dear. Experiences of affinity and difference need to be equally valued, especially if mutual respect is to be a guiding principle in the emergence of global religious and spiritual dialogue. The image of the möbius strip, a one-sided figure of eight, comes to mind as a rich metaphor for the interconnectedness of all these things. Both affinities and differences are crucial to the exercise of critical reflexivity, not least about the nature of spirituality as a human and a religious characteristic of profound significance to the contemporary world.

Critical reflection shows that behind the word *spirituality* lurks an indeterminate array of differing and often contesting concepts. The severing of the word spirituality from its religious and Christian origins complicates the search for a contemporary definition. Everyone wants a piece of the word and in the process its originating meaning is obscured, where it is not lost. Some of these usages are easy to understand while others are easily misunderstood; some are based on polarisations, splits and dichotomies, while others struggle to maintain a sense of the personal-communal-planetary whole: the religion-spirituality split is a typical example; some take on a subversive quality while others become subtly insidious: violent fundamentalisms are obvious examples.

In spirituality we encounter belief, cultural and symbolic systems, and all of them need to be understood in their webs of significance, in their interconnected and interconnecting stories, all with their local flavours and all with their global implications for dialogue and the challenges of mutual understanding.[16] In the postmodern culture in which we now live many forms of spirituality seek to blossom and send their seeds blowing on the winds of change. Christian spirituality in its many expressions encounters many different expressions of new spirituality. Eclectic, evan-escent, unfocused, vaguely religious, fragmented, fleeting, dilettante spiritualities rub shoulders with spiritualities that seem to lack any organising centre. Spiritualities that seem to lack any reference to the human person or human suffering encounter spiritualities that make no reference to the divine.

Conservative world resisting and world denying spiritualities squabble with liberal spiritualities, new ageisms and 'occultures' that colonialise and repackage Oriental practices for Western audiences. Some spirit-ualities seem difficult to distinguish from magic. Others seem to be not much more than collections of useful practices and rituals borrowed by psychology for therapeutic purposes. And others still embody closed forms of classic fideism that reject as utterly false everything outside their particular faith visions. A growing majority of new spiritualities seem to represent emotional reactions to the soulless rationalism of modernity and its one-sided love affair with productive economic efficiency and material progress. This potentially maze-like choice of possibilities suggests that in a pluralist world spiritual consensus may prove lamentably elusive.

We are everywhere confronted by the ambiguities and possibilities of the spiritual revolution and the spiritual reawakening that is presently sweeping the world. But the roots of this ambiguity are ancient. They take us back to the shaping differences between the Greek and the Hebrew imaginations and their impacts on Christian understanding. When we imagine the Divine Spirit, when we imagine God as spirit, what do we glimpse? If we enter the Greek imagination then spirit points us towards the immaterial. If we enter the Hebrew imagination then spirit is a desert whirlwind, a storm, an irresistible power. If we are to imagine spirituality afresh for a postmodern world, which kind of imagination will guide us? What kind of wisdom emerging from what kind of imagination will direct us? These are pivotal questions that confront all who wonder about the meaning and orientation of spirituality today, especially if they are concerned to understand the uniqueness of Christian spirituality.

The term spirituality (*spiritualitas* in Latin) has a long history of Christian usage but its more popular application takes us back only as far as the Renaissance. Its expansion begins in earnest only recently, largely in reaction to the unfolding challenges of late modernity. Between the Renaissance and the popular eruption of the word in the late twentieth century, spirituality was effectively excluded from modern discourse, derided as a form of neurotic alienation. With the postmodern turn this ideological exclusion has come to a rapid end. We are now witnessing an explosion of interest in and a burgeoning of forms of spirituality of great diversity: frequently secular, often contradictory; frequently recreational, often severed from any kind of religious belief; frequently nostalgic for a lost past, often seeking the comforting illusion of a pure, unstructured expression of spirit freed from the shadowed baggage of human and religious history and collective responsibility for it.

The new spiritualities are growing in parallel with other cultural, social and economic changes. They tend to favour the empirical and the pragmatic – the scientific study of links between spirituality and health is a typical example. The new spiritualities are frequently interested in the technical side of spiritual practices and their economic potentials. They are often interested in the technologies of the self and human potential; and, given the postmodern turn to the individual as an autonomous source of spiritual authority and truth, they are fascinated with the esoteric and the gnostic. Abetted by the turn to the emotional and the sentimental that characterised modern romanticism and its rejection of the cold intellectualism of Enlightenment philosophy, the new spiritualities represent a distinct change in spiritual practice and discourse away from any critical interest in the objective relevance and credibility of specific spiritual life styles: a visit to the internet will make this point clear. Instead, the new spiritualities reveal an often uncritical, self-referential, syncretic tendency that has the power to throw the innovative influence of spirituality into question.

Not surprisingly, then, key words like *spirit, spiritual life, spirituality* evade precise definition because of the breadth of contesting meanings attributed to them today. These meanings tend to be grounded in a rainbowed and many-coloured understanding of the human person on the one hand, and equally divergent understandings of the world and religion on the other, especially those that reveal the forces of disenchantment of the world and of institutional religion.[17] The result is a radical process of change unfolding against the background of what Gordon Mathews has described as a global cultural supermarket where the roots of human identity become increasingly matters of consumer choice, and where the influence of cultures or religions of origin declines.[18] The available evidence suggests that large-scale changes of spiritual allegiance are underway. This process is clearly visible in rapidly changing societies like Ireland as they embrace economic success. Similar movements have been identified in Latin America and Africa, though not necessarily in the same direction.

Globally, there is unlikely to be any aspect of local life, economics, politics, religion or spirituality that has not felt the impact of global capitalism and its alliance with the shaping forces of secular modernity, not least the growth way of life on which the market economy depends.[19] The growth way of life characteristic of consumer societies impacts strongly on attitudes towards traditional religion and spirituality. The most obvious example comes from the advertising industry whose core task is to generate a volatile mix of desires and discontents: and the advertisers do their job well. Happiness is whatever product is positioned to assuage the latest discontents. Consumer society as a whole is complicit in the industrial-level production of consumer discontents precisely by encouraging us to define our aspirations in terms of the new and the different. In growth-oriented societies expectations are constantly being raised, and happiness becomes a postponed illusion of material contentment. Happiness has become a postmodern simulacrum, an empty sign, an ephemeral thing, a ghost.

In the global spiritual supermarket personal satisfaction has become the key meaning horizon. But it is a horizon in flux, always receding as we approach it, always beyond reach. And so our standards keep shifting and changing as we are lured down the meandering track of never-ending consumption intended to cure a commercially engineered discontent. Even in spirituality we risk becoming naïve pawns in a game of consumer manipulation, living an illusion of freedom and choice that cloaks but does not hide the forces of mass conformism and mass domestication. Have we all unknowingly exchanged one pervasive cultural tyranny for another? Growth societies have the capacity to undermine authentic personal well-being by down-playing the importance of such core foundations of an authentically happy life as genuine love, real friendship, caringly supportive community, and commitment to something beyond the self. The market economy, by constantly fuelling new desires and discontents, impairs these very qualities, demanding their sacrifice as the price of economic success with its ever changing definitions of what is currently important to personal happiness.[20] Something similar happens in the construction of contemporary spiritualities. It is not difficult to see that exploitive cultural and social discontents favour the novel and the different in spirituality as readily as in any other aspect of life, and the frequent trading-in of old models for new as new fashions and styles become de rigueur.

We are witnessing today the emergence of a new, often vague or abstract globalised vision of spirituality as, for example, Christian, Jewish, Buddhist, Hindu, Taoist, Confucian, and Islamic concepts and practices encounter and are merged with capitalist, cosmological, eco-logical, environmental, economic, feminist, Marxist or pacifist concerns and practices, all delightfully interwoven with the ideas of quantum science to create exciting new spiritual blends for tired spiritual palates. The roots of much of this trend may be traced back to the orientalising influence of the Theosophical Society and the first Parliament of Religions held in Chicago in 1893. As a result of the processes of bricolage that underlie this globalising process, the blending of whatever personally appealing spiritual concepts and practices are to hand, a very different understanding of spirit, spiritual life, and spirituality has come to the fore, in a process that has gathered particular momentum in the past forty years.[21]

In the new spirituality influences arising from the worlds of religious pluralism, then, vie with influences arising from a variety of secularised philosophical, humanist and ideological concerns that are themselves increasingly challenged by the parallel globalisation of countervailing spiritual and religious trends.[22] In line with a global upsurge in religion there is also evidence of the growing influence of alternative spirit-ualities.[23] After all, we live in a shrinking world where information on all kinds of spiritual concepts and practices are available at the click of a computer mouse. Spirituality is no longer confined within the parameters of a single religious tradition, a specific geographical area or even a hemisphere: spirituality shows clear signs of becoming a global enterprise grounded in global thinking, and appealing to a global community. Are we witnessing the birth of a global spirituality for global citizens, a spirituality that favours inclusiveness and collaboration across religious, political and cultural divides? While the evidence suggests something of the kind, it also intimates how unlikely the emergence of a worldwide federated, syncretic religion or spirituality actually is. The considerable differences between religions and spiritual traditions suggest that such a turn remains historically improbable.

At the same time, the academic study of global spirituality has emerged as a new discipline.[24] We are increasingly confronted by what Ewart Cousins described in 1985 as a collective spiritual journey in which the convergence of different mystical and spiritual paths is taking place at global levels.[25] In Cousins' view this global spirituality is at once characterised by the blending of religious and mystical traditions with deep ecological concerns: the riches of the mystical traditions are being harnessed to respond to profound material and planetary challenges and environmental concerns.[26] It represents a new ecumenical and interfaith challenge, an essentially communitarian challenge with implications for world peace. A not dissimilar idea was already present in Erich Fromm's humanistic psychology. In a book published in 1966 Fromm suggests that the emergence of a global religiosity or spirituality is a necessary evolutionary step in the history of religion, an idea grounded in his love of the Old Testament.[27] Teilhard de Chardin also contributed to Christian moves towards a more cosmologically alert understanding of spirituality and its global implications.[28] The contemporary move towards a global spirituality is influenced in no small part by the parallel development in world economics of a global developmental process. For example, in the contemporary context, spirituality is attracting global interest in ways that Douglas Hicks has found to be consistent with shifts in the global economy from heavy to light industry, and the parallel development of the services and entertainment industries.[29] Spirituality does not evolve in a socio-cultural or economic vacuum. It remains profoundly contextual, impacted by contextual shifts and changes whether local or global.

One of the implications of the global shift is the growing range of contested meanings attributed to the word *spirituality*. Spirituality began life as a Christian term signifying the practice of the Christian life, a communal walking in the Divine Spirit that gives a preferential attention to the intimately loving, relational and sacred dimensions of existence. It is now just as likely to denote a life progressively oriented towards individually chosen and designated higher purposes, frequently serving self-referred psychological or gnostic understandings of self-transcendence. In the new global spirituality such a purpose may be naturalistic, materialistic or atheistic, and have no discernible connection to recognisably religious purposes, traditions, practices or concerns. In fact the terms *spirit, spiritual life, spirituality* are also employed in modern philosophical and secular conversations about the nature and meaning of human existence without any reference to a transcendent or divine dimension. In many such contexts *spiritual life* tends to name a lifestyle informed by aesthetic, moral, or philanthropic principles having to do with the secular pursuit of human happiness. Similarly *spirituality* is used to refer to the interweaving of the values and processes that emerge from such secularised conversations, while *spirit* is used to identify an organising culture without regard to divine or transcendent referents.

More to the point, a range of relevant, interactive distinctions are frequently overlooked or obscured in the new spirituality: reason and passion, intelligence and feeling, the subjective and the objective, the sensible and the intentional, the aesthetic and the ethical. This has not been helped by the modern assumption that humankind is the sole maker of its own destiny, a global population adrift on a shaky raft in a vast ocean of possibility. An operative sense of the unity of things is largely absent; and so love is severed from intelligence, reason from passion, and mind from heart. Many want to explain life, not live it; many want to dominate the world, not care for it. Many have lost any kind of connection to prophetic wisdom. Many have lost any sense of contemplative relationship with all that is. Many, sadly, have lost the intelligence of the heart. Many have no felt need of God. Many have no sense that the secular city devours its citizens and makes them slaves to processes and structures that inexorably devour the sacred. Many have no sense that Christ is forever new. Many follow the path of refusal. Once the spiritual value of the person before God is lost, people are reduced to things, pawns to play games with, and disposable units of production.

Viewed from a theological perspective much secular writing on spirituality tends to be reductive and naturalistic. Recent secular writing on spirituality usually responds creatively to the challenges and opportunities offered by postmodern thought, but in ways that often fail to evoke a vision of the whole, or lead to a loss of the central focus on human interiority as both a relational and social reality. It is generally written in a humanistic key with often helpful developmental overtones, but there is also an embarrassment about the use of religious language, an embarrassment that leads to the de facto marginalising of the divine and a subsequent theological impoverishment. The elements of eclecticism, as well as the fragmented and isolated individualism that characterise the postmodern milieu tend to dominate the overall vision. On the other hand, the eclectic nature of secular spirituality should come as no surprise. Multiculturalism as a global discourse seems to be the heir to Enlightenment humanism: as older identities and relations fail, the consumer search for new integrative ideals becomes very appealing.[30] Such is the challenge facing spirituality today: nothing less than the core values in human and Christian spirituality are at stake. The net result is that Christian spirituality is challenged to rethink and re-imagine its own reality. Do we discerningly and audaciously embrace the newness of Spirit or cling to the apparent securities of a superseded past?

## Measuring the Spirit: The European Enigma

Measuring the spirit is like measuring the wind. Spirit keeps moving and chants many different melodies. Some of them are like gently whispering breezes, difficult to detect. Spirituality is also about directions in contexts. Like religion its songs wax or wane in tune with the rhythms of time and place. Some of them reach hurricane force and unleash destructive potentials. According to JP Larsson, who was writing against the background of religious violence, we live in a world with more than 9,000 distinct religions with adherents in more than 200 countries worldwide.[31] Statistics show that most of the world is religious and many otherwise historical, political or economic conflicts reveal religious components. It is also true that not always wise media or other public representations have complicated religious antagonisms and misunderstandings to serve non-religious ideological ends. In the fields of religion and spirituality, claims are often made about states of affairs, for example the practices or operational beliefs in a spiritual tradition, that mask their claimants' personal attitudes and conflicting beliefs.

Not surprisingly, then, attitudes to religion and spirituality surface in an array of viewpoints that range from the simplistic to the profound. The sharp positions evident in the recent 'Clash of Civilisations' debates and the arguments about Turkey's potential membership in the EU are indicative of such conflicts. Some otherwise intelligent people think that religion is the root of all evil, some uphold it as the solution to all the world's problems, and still others think that it and its iconic figures should be parodied, sidelined, marginalised or indeed ignored except when they usefully serve as colourful or shocking expletives. Influenced by the agendas of modernity some consistently act to remove religion completely from the public arena and make it a purely private matter, a question of taste and good intentions. Some have tried to impose state-sponsored atheism. Others have created state Churches. Many view everything in life through a religious lens: family, society, politics and the state.

Religion and its spiritual traditions have always played a role close to the heart of human civilisation. Today religion is in a state of resurgence almost everywhere except Europe and a few other countries where institutional practice continues in decline even as interest in spirituality paradoxically achieves unheard-of heights. In Europe a secular philosophy has been in the ascendancy for many decades with roots going back to the nineteenth century. Born of the Enlightenment myth, it claims that a secular world can deliver lasting human peace and contentment. France constitutionally embraced this position in 1905 and its influence has been felt everywhere in Western and Central Europe. At the beginning of the twentieth century the classic European power relationship between Church and State was effectively severed. What came next were the world-engulfing wars of the twentieth century. After Hiroshima and the Holocaust confidence that secularist ideology and politics could successfully deliver world peace has, like faith and religion, been seriously damaged. And so the drama evolves.

We have learnt the hard way that if religious power structures could lead to wars and violence, and the new forms of religious violence are contemporary markers of this potential, secular politics is just as lethal and destructive in its power ambitions. No single power structure has a monopoly on humanity's violently imaginative depravity and its destructive inventiveness. The enlightened world of secular ideology has shown the self-same capacity to unleash the dark demons of human ingenuity and depravity once (and sometimes still) attributed to religion alone. The task of dangerous memory is to remind people who look to religious and spiritual inspiration in their lives of the dark potentials that lurk below seemingly pleasant and comforting surfaces. Europe is as it is for a complexity of reasons beyond our scope here. However, the complexity of Church-State power relationships has a long history in this part of the world with its roots in times when popes made kings, when powerful prince-bishops and abbots exercised political and economic power, and cardinals served as chief ministers and chancellors. Such has never been the case in the USA, but in Europe the dance for influence in people's lives between politics and religion obscures a long and complex history.

We are living through a new movement in that dance today. Just as power allegiance moved first from Church to State and then gave us communisms and fascisms, and they proved disastrous, now Europe is giving its allegiance to global consumerism and the happy-ever-after instant utopia its media gurus and adherents promise. Even birth rates have collapsed in this brave new self-indulgent Europe, down to somewhere between 1.2 to 1.45 per couple on average, well below the 2.1 needed to maintain present population levels. Interestingly, Americans are more likely than native Europeans to read these shifts and turns in Europe through a religious lens. That is, until the question of Turkish membership in the EU and the growth of Islam in Western and Central Europe – through immigration and higher birth rates – enter the debate and show Islam to be the fastest-growing religion in Europe.[32] Then many who personally give little personal importance to religion have little difficulty evoking Europe's classic Christian heritage and identity and pay lip-service to a belief-system they operatively reject.

Up to quite recently European populations tended to be homogeneous with a common ethnic and religious identity. This is no longer the case, and so religion is once again part of the volatile mix in European political debate, clear evidence of a pluralist turn grounded in large movements of immigration that have brought new ethnic and cultural understandings and customs to Europe and new religious forms and practices. In fact, it is worth asking a pivotal question. Are the changes in European religiosity really the result of the impact of secularist ideology? Or are they better understood as the consequence of an increasingly pervasive interactive and competitive pluralism?[33] The latter certainly seems to be at least partly the case here in Ireland if my own research in contemporary Irish spirituality and the growing bricolage, or patchwork,[34] or personalised, or non-traditional tendency that characterises it is anything to go by in a world of globalising religion.[35]

I am certainly persuaded by Grace Davie's argument that Europe, in particular Western and Central Europe – and I would include Australia – is the exceptional case in the study of world religion.[36] Her case becomes very clear when Europe is contrasted to the very different scenes in the USA, Latin America, as well as in modernising Africa, the Near East and large parts of Asia where secularisation theory is hard-pressed to explain what is happening. Supply-side theorists suggest that the religious problem in Europe may have much more to do with the presence of highly regulated and constrained religious markets that block healthy competition, rather than the onward march of modernity or the persuasiveness of secularist ideology. Established or National or dominant mainstream Churches are typical examples of what such theorists have in mind. The perceived failure of Churches to respond to rapidly changing social and spiritual needs must also be taken into consideration.

Newly emerging evidence suggests that people respond positively when Churches and Church-related movements actively and effectively compete for their attention. In the US, this seems to be what lies behind the phenomenon of religious switching. If clergy fail or felt needs are not met, people do not simply abandon Church as seems to be the dominant response in Europe. They tend to go to another congregation; they shop around.[37] Competition also helps to explain the rapid changes in religious allegiance taking place in Latin America. In effect, the reality in Europe is far more complex than secularisation theorists have traditionally recognised. On the other hand, there is no doubting the existence of a secularist intelligentsia in conflict with the religious world in Europe, the USA and elsewhere, but that is not the same as secularism and its claim to explain or single-handedly prophesy the global demise of religion. One is an ideology seeking power, the other a theory seeking proof; and the distinction is hugely important.

In any event, pluralist and interreligious conversation is now a fact in most Western countries, helped by immigration and the information explosion. This is particularly true as we experience the religious economy or supply-side move towards choice and intentional or voluntary religious belonging and the breakdown of religious monopolies especially in countries with state Churches. There are complex implications here for religious institutions, especially those that hold seriously to a doctrine of religious freedom. But in Europe, institutions, including mainstream religious institutions, are suspect while personal experience and individual choice are favoured, explaining Grace Davie's powerful image of believing without belonging.[38] Add rigidly conservative and relativising liberal tendencies to the mix and gain a sense of how complex the world of European religion actually is. Then reflect on the implications of all of this for contemporary spirituality in a world of postmodern supply-side consumer choice. Applied to spirituality, supply-side theory clarifies the socio-economic backdrop to the growing demand for personal spiritual experience in the West, and there is no doubting its implications for religion. The *World Values Survey* clearly indicates that even in the most secularised countries a growing percentage of people spend time reflecting on the meaning and purpose of life.[39]

Propositional reflection suggests that attention to a broad range of religious and spiritual factors is both relevant and necessary. These include the critical analysis that helps people discern whether what they believe to be true is actually false or dangerous; the analysis of the specific implications of age and gender cohorts and other demographic factors.[40] It is also important to recall that the Renaissance helped to trigger a process that not only supported the privatising of religion and its exclusion from politics, but prepared the way for the split between religion and the spiritual search we now observe, particularly in Europe. Evidence also points to a loss of religious and spiritual literacy and language as links with family-based or school-based religious traditions are weakened or severed, especially in younger age cohorts. As the influence of established religion declined, many began to believe that a secularist libertarian vision had successfully taken its place as the principal source of a cohesive public vision and what it means to be human.

In the face of present sociological evidence it seems that the secular vision itself is also in crisis. The split between the private and the public domains of life that we can trace back to the Reformation and the Renaissance still continues to exert influence on how religion and spirituality are perceived in Europe. The former public but considered suspect, the latter private but considered experientially or subjectively trustworthy. The challenge facing institutional religion in much of Western Europe is the iron-cage imagery that institutional religious structures still seem to convey to many people today. If mainstream religious traditions represent rafts in the ocean of life, then the statistical evidence shows that many have decided to dive off and swim on their own, either because they have decided to jump for personal reasons or because in some way they have been pushed off by institutional dynamics or repulsed by revelations of abuse.

Awareness, literacy and liberation are interlinked in this worldview, and, in the presence of awareness and literacy, liberation will be sought from religious and spiritual traditions that lack congruent inner and outer vitality or whose agents are found spiritually or ethically wanting. Today we live more in a religious and spiritual economy than in a yesteryear religious or spiritual monoculture. The change will shape personal and collective understanding, affectivity and intentional action in many different and surprising ways. In Europe generally the religious market is still highly regulated but the spiritual market is unregulated and free. This sets the scene for the audacity of spirit and its capacity to fly in unexpectedly new ways in a religious world that ignores the vital presence of spirit at its peril.

## RELIGION AND SPIRITUALITY: FINDING THEIR MEASURE

Quantitative studies in the field of religion offer some indication of the state of the spiritual quest in Europe, particularly in the absence of Europe-wide qualitative reviews. Statistical information on European religiosity is available through national census offices,[41] as well as through such sources as ISSP[42] and EVS[43] and a variety of research councils, polling organisations, and academic institutes. Combined figures show that Ireland, Malta, Poland and Romania tend to have very high figures for ascribed religious identification. Figures tend to be lower elsewhere in Europe. Overall European statistics represent a public decline in the importance people give to institutional Christianity. What is certain is that classic Christendom and its sacred canopy are dead and that Christianity as a religion and as a family of spiritual traditions has to fend for itself in increasingly consumer-driven pluralist and competitive societies.[44]

Lynda Barley's work is a good source of information on UK religious statistics. Her studies clearly demonstrate significant growth in spiritual awareness.[45] Research by David Hay and Kate Hunt who studied the spirituality of people who have no formal connection with Churchly religion is particularly relevant to this debate.[46] Hay's research indicates that some 75 per cent of the UK population report spiritual experience, an increase of some 60 per cent over thirteen years, a period when Church attendance plummeted in Britain.[47] In his keynote address to the *British and Irish Association for Mission Studies* at Selly Oak, Birmingham in September 2000, Hay highlighted a number of significant issues arising from his own research. Most contemporary spirituality is grounded in highly individual stories and in most cases belongs to the quest mode. He also noted the generic nature of the depictions of God that tend to arise, with Christian echoes audible mainly in the older cohorts. He noted a reluctance to be explicit in talking about God where the problem of suffering remains a major shaping influence.

Hay's work also shows that while monotheism is still dominant, it comes in a highly watered-down form reminiscent of the household gods of a much earlier period in human history. References to Jesus came from people with a childhood background in Christianity but they too were also quite vague. For the majority of respondents spiritual experience pointed to 'something there', a kind of transcendent providence, something mysterious that eluded description and refused conventional religious language. He also noted that people in the younger cohort who had no religious background tended to construct their own theologies. This highlights the lack of a common language for contemporary spiritual experience, which for Hay explains the lack of impact new forms of spirituality have at political and legislative levels.[48] There is no longer a shared domain of spiritual literacy; its place has been taken by an array of fragmenting practices, literacies and discourses. The loss of a shared spiritual literacy remains a problem for all researchers and demands an exquisite capacity for respectful listening. Hay confirms the view that rapidly increasing numbers of people recognise spiritual experience as part of their lives while the institutions traditionally associated with the spiritual life are in a process of severe decline.[49]

French figures for 1999–2000 suggest that 40 per cent of the population acknowledge some degree of Church attendance. Germany shows similar tendencies of decline. When European figures indicating belief in God are given priority the situation shifts dramatically. Figures relative to belief in God across Europe tend to be high, though once again equivocal forces are at work. Figures relating to confidence in the institutional Churches show a downward trend, and cross-EU figures indicate a growing detachment from institutionalised religion. However, anecdotal evidence from the Netherlands seems to suggest that the decline in religious practice there has bottomed out and Church attendance has begun to rise. At the same time, European figures relating to informal religion remain high even though it is difficult to evaluate the significance or the-meaning-of-life influence such informal practices may have. These trends raise interesting questions for students of spirituality. The implications for relational consciousness are, to say the least, intriguing.

The variations in these indicators make it difficult to assess what is really happening in the European religious context. What is clear is that religiousness remains a more powerful force than social scientists expected, not only in Europe but on a worldwide level, where estimates of 85% religious belonging of some kind have been suggested. It is also interesting to consider the seeming failure of intensive official attempts to eradicate religion in such places as the Soviet Union, China, Albania and Cuba during the second half of the twentieth century. Figures for professed as distinct from virtual atheism also seem to be in worldwide decline.

As it stands, Christianity, Islam, Hinduism and Buddhism represent the religions of the majority of people on the planet, and all are present in Europe, part of the emerging religious and spiritual market place. Religion and spirituality share the shaping of human identity with a broad range of correlative factors, principally race, education, ethnicity, social status, class and gender, as well as age, sexual orientation and politics. While each of these factors operates autonomously, they are experienced simultaneously. This is one of the reasons why looking at statistics on religion in isolation from other shaping factors is potentially misleading. Each of these factors has the capacity to introduce distinctive variables into the overall social picture. Neither the religious nor the emerging spiritual reality in Europe is as simple as it seems.

## A Concluding Thought

Let me conclude with this interesting example from Introvigne and Stark. Competition even within Roman Catholicism in Italy has spurred a substantial religious revival: Church attendance has risen, and there has been a remarkable resurgence of Christian beliefs.[50] Deregulation, competition, and consumer pluralism: these are the keys to understanding the spiritual revolution, especially in Europe. As Introvigne and Stark have noted, most of the world is more religious now than it was thirty years ago.[51] Secularisation theory was developed to explain decline. It does not seem to be in a position to explain spiritual resurgence. Religious economy or supply-side theory seems to have a capacity to do both. It can help us to understand why when religious participation is low in Europe, belief remains quite high. Interest in spirituality is rising exponentially in a free pluralist market where neither state support nor state regulation apply; hence the emergence of patchwork spiritualities with new modes of practice and transmission, and new spaces and resources.

## Themes and Questions for Further Reflection

1. Identify the challenges facing spirituality in a multicultural, globalising world.
2. Identify the implications of the European enigma for religiously-anchored spiritualities.
3. What are the demands made by a dynamic and transformative spirituality in transitional times?
4. The challenge of finding a coherent way to the doors of spirit and its

creativity: how do you personally enter the mystery and embrace its unfolding; can you identify the diversity of religious, spiritual and transpersonal beliefs encountered in contemporary Western spirituality?

FURTHER READING

Peter L. Berger, *The Desecularization of the World: Resurgent Religion and World Politics* (Grand Rapids, MN: Eerdmans Publishing, 1999).

NOTES:

1. Kathleen Fischer, *Women at the Well: Feminist Perspectives on Spiritual Direction* (New York/Mahwah: Paulist Press, 1988) 44.

2. See for example Don Swenson, *Society, Spirituality, and the Sacred: A Social Scientific Introduction* (Ontario: Broadview Press, 1999) 101–111.

3. ibid. 387.

4. See for example, Robert K. C. Forman, *Grassroots Spirituality: What It Is, Why It Is Here, Where It Is Going* with a contribution by Kathryn Davison, PhD (Exeter & Charlottesville: Imprint Academic, 2004) 45–74.

5. See Joel Beversluis, ed., *Sourcebook of the World's Religions: An Interfaith Guide to Religion and Spirituality*, third edition (Novato, CA: New World Library, 2000).

6. See for example John Anderson, *Religious Liberty in Transitional Societies: The Politics of Religion* (Cambridge: Cambridge University Press, 2003).

7. See for example Esther de Waal, *Seeking God: The Way of St Benedict* (Norwich: Canterbury Press, 1999). See also Aquinata Böckmann, O.S.B., *Perspectives on the Rule of St Benedict: Expanding Our Hearts in Christ* (Collegeville: Liturgical Press, 2005).

8. See Richard J. Woods, *Christian Spirituality: God's Presence through the Ages*, New Expanded Edition (Maryknoll, NY: Orbis, 2006); Philip Sheldrake, *A Brief History of Spirituality* (Malden & Oxford: Blackwell Publishing, 2007).

9. See Edward Idris Cardinal Cassidy, *Ecumenism and Interreligious Dialogue: Unitas Redintegratio, Nostra Aetate* (New York/Mahwah, NJ: Paulist Press, 2005) 110 & 130.

10. See Arie R. Brouwer, *Ecumenical Testimony* (Grand Rapids, MN: Eerdmans Publishing, 1991) 195.

11. See Walter Kasper, *A Handbook of Spiritual Ecumenism* (Hyde Park, NY: New City Press, 2007).

12. See Wolfgang Vondey, *Heribert Mühlen: His Theology and Praxis. A New Profile of the Church*, with an Epilogue by Heribert Mühlen (Lanham & Oxford: University Press of America, 2004) 10.

13. See Enda McDonagh, *Gift and Call: Towards a Christian Theology of Morality* (Dublin: Gill & Macmillan, 1975) 156.

14. Hans Küng, *A Global Ethics for Global Politics and Economics* (Oxford: Oxford University Press, 1998).

15. See Mark Jurgensmeyer, 'Thinking Globally about Religion' in Mark Jurgensmeyer, ed., *Global Religions: An Introduction* (Oxford and New York: Oxford University Press, 2003) 3–13 at 9–13. All of the essays in this collection make important contributions to thought on global religion. The implications for spirituality are not difficult to draw. See also Richard H. Roberts, *Religion, Theology, and the Human Sciences* (Cambridge: Cambridge University Press, 2002).

16. See Clifford Geertz, *The Interpretation of Cultures* (New York: Basic Books, 1973) 5; see also his *Local Knowledge: Further Essays in Interpretative Anthropology* (New York: Basic Books, 1983) 182.

17. See, for example, Robert C. Fuller, *Spiritual, but Not Religious: Understanding Unchurched America* (Oxford & New York: Oxford University Press, 2001).

18. Gordon Mathews, *Global Culture/Individual Identity: Searching for Home in the Cultural Supermarket* (London: Routledge, 2000) i.

19. See Wimal Dissanayake and Rob Wilson, eds, *Global/Local: Cultural Production and the Transnational Imaginary* (Durham, NC: Duke University Press, 1996) 37–38.

20. See Paul Wachtel, 'Overconsumption' in David V. J. Bell, Leesa Fawcett, Roger Keil, Peter Penz, eds, *Political Ecology: Global and Local* (London: Routledge, 1998) 272–291 at 266–267.

21. For a discussion of global spirituality see Steven L. Chase, *Doors of Understanding: Conversations in Global Spirituality in Honor of Ewart Cousins* (Quincy, IL: Quincy University Franciscan Press, 1997). See also Robert Muller, *New Genesis: Shaping a Global Spirituality* (Anacortes, WA: World Happiness and Cooperation, 1991), the first edition of this book was published by Double Day in 1982; Ninian Smart, *The World's Religions: Old Traditions and Modern Transformations* (Cambridge: Cambridge University Press, 1989).

22. See Richard Falk, 'Secularism, Globalization, and the Role of the State: A Plea for Renewal' in Barbara Sundberg Baudot, *Candles in the Dark: A New Spirit for a Plural World* (Seattle: University of Washington Press, 2002) 47–66 at 50.

23. See Christopher Partridge, 'Alternative Spiritualities, New Religions, and the Re-enchantment of the West' in James R. Lewis, ed., *The Oxford Handbook of New Religious Movements* (Oxford: Oxford University Press, 2004) 39-67. See also Bettina Grey, James Morrison, Michael Tobias, eds, *A Parliament of Souls: In Search of Global Spirituality: Interviews with 28 Spiritual Leaders from Around the World* (San Francisco: Bay Books, 1995).

24. See Bernard McGinn & John Meyendorf, 'Introduction to the Series' in Bernard McGinn & John Meyendorf, with Jean Leclercq, *Christian*

*Spirituality: Origins to the Twelfth Century.* Volume 16 of *World Spirituality: An Encyclopedic History of the Religious Quest* (New York: Crossroad, 1985) xiii.

25. Ewart H. Cousins, *Global Spirituality: Towards the Meeting of Spiritual Paths* (Madras: Radhakrishnan Institute for Advanced Study in Philosophy, University of Madras, 1985) 3.

26. See for example, Daniel Ross Chandler, *Towards Universal Religion: Voices of American and Indian Spirituality* (Westport, CT: Greenwood Press, 1996) 215. See also Joel Springs, *How Educational Ideologies Are Shaping Global Society: Intergovernmental Organizations, NGOs and the Decline of the Nation State* (Mahwah, NJ: Lawrence Earlbaum Associates, 2004) 105–106, 119, 124, 180. For a discussion of this new form of spirituality and its expression among Catholic religious women see in particular Sarah McFarland Taylor, *Green Sisters: An Ecological Spirituality* (Harvard: Harvard University Press, 2007). See also Roger S. Gottlieb, *A Greener Faith: Religious Environmentalism and Our Planet's Future* (New York & Oxford: Oxford University Press, 2006); Thomas Berry, *The Dream of the Earth* (San Francisco: Sierra Club Books, 2006).

27. Erich Fromm, *You Shall Be as Gods: A Radical Reinterpretation of the Old Testament and Its Tradition* (New York: Holt, Rhinehart and Winston, 1966). See also Pat Duffy Hutcheon, *Leaving the Cage: Evolutionary Naturalism in Social-Scientific Thought* (Waterloo: Wilfrid Laurier University Press, 1996) 353.

28. See for example, Margaret McGurn, *Global Spirituality: Planetary Consciousness in the Thought of Teilhard de Chardin and Robert Muller with a Proposal for a World Bimillennium Celebration of Life* (Ardsley-on-Hudson, NY: World Happiness and Cooperation, 1984); Ursula King, *The Spirit of One Earth: Reflections on Teilhard de Chardin and Global Spirituality* (New York: Paragon, 1989).

29. Douglas A. Hicks, *Religion and the Workplace: Pluralism, Spirituality, Leadership* (Cambridge: Cambridge University Press, 2003) 38.

30. See Inés Dussel, 'What Can Multiculturalism Tell Us About Difference? The Reception of Multicultural Discourses in France and Argentina' in Carl A. Grant & Joy L. Lei, eds, *Global Constructions of Multicultural Education: Theories and Realities* (Mahwah, NJ: Lawrence Erlbaum Associates, 2001) 93–114 at 94.

31. J. P. Larsson, *Understanding Religious Violence: Thinking Outside the Box on Terrorism.* (Aldershot: Ashgate Publishing, 2004) 1. For an in-depth study of global religious violence see Mark Jurgensmeyer, *Terror in the Mind of God: The Global Rise of Religious Violence.* Third edition, revised and updated. (Berkeley, Los Angeles, London: University of California Press, 2003).

32. For a discussion of the clash of civilisations thesis see Pippa Norris and Ronald Inglehart, 'Islam and the West: Testing the "Clash of

Civilizations" Thesis' published by the John F. Kennedy School of Government at Harvard University (accessed 27/01/2008): http://ksghome.harvard.edu/~pnorris/Acrobat/Clash%20of%20 Civilization.pdf

33. On religious pluralism see Peter Berger's *Religion in a Globalizing World* http://pewforum.org/events/index.php?EventID=136 (accessed 27/01/2008).

34. The term was coined by Robert Wuthnow. See Robert Wuthnow, *After Heaven: Spirituality in America Since the 1950s* (Berkeley, Los Angeles, London: University of California Press, 1998) 2.

35. See, for example, Linda Woodhead et al., eds, *Religions in the Modern World: Traditions and Transformations* (London & New York: Routledge, 2002). See also Krzysztof Michalski, ed. *Religion in the New Europe.* (Budapest & New York: Central European University Press, 2006).

36. Grace Davie, *Europe: The Exceptional Case. Parameters of Faith in the Modern World* (London: Darton, Longman & Todd, 2002).

37. See Massimo Introvigne and Rodney Stark. 'Religious Competition and Revival in Italy: Exploring European Exceptionalism' in *Interdisciplinary Journal of Research on Religion*, Vol. 1 (2005) 1, Article 5, pp.1–20. http://www.religjournal.com/ (accessed 27/01/2008).

38. Grace Davie, *Religion in Britain Since 1945: Believing Without Belonging.* (Oxford: Blackwell, 1994).

39. See the review of the WVS from the University of Michigan News Service at http://www.umich.edu/news/index.html?Releases/2004/ Sep04/r092104 (accessed 27/01/2008).

40. See Richard Cobb-Stevens, 'The Beginnings of Phenomenology: Husserl and his Predecessors' in Richard Kearney, ed. *Twentieth-Century Continental Philosophy.* (London: Routledge, 1994) 5–37. See also Simon Blackburn, *Essays in Quasi-Realism* (Oxford: Oxford University Press, 1993).

41. http://www.cso.ie/; http://www.statistics.gov.uk/CCI/SearchRes.asp? term=religion (accessed 27/01/2008).

42. See http://www.gesis.org/en/data_service/issp/data/ 1998_Religion_II.htm (accessed 27/01/2008).

43. http://www.gesis.org/en/data_service/topics/50-CD-ROM/index.htm (accessed 27/01/2008).

44. For the statistical evidence cited in this chapter see the following list of accessible websites with reliable and extensive information on world religions (all accessed 27/01/2008). The most recent information is available from the Baylor and Barna sites. http://www.baylor.edu/content/services/document.php/33304.pdf http://www.adherents.com/ http://pewforum.org/ http://www.barna.org/

http://www.thearda.com/Archive/browse.asp
http://www.gc.cuny.edu/faculty/research_briefs/aris/aris_index.htm
http://www.pluralism.org/index.php
http://are.as.wvu.edu/
http://www.worldvaluessurvey.com/
http://www.bikupan.se/wvs/value.html
http://www.innovativeresearch.ca/Canadian%20Values%20
Study_Factum%20280905.pdf
http://www.democ.uci.edu/resources/archive.php
http://www.nanzan-u.ac.jp/SHUBUNKEN/publications/
Bulletin_and_Shoho/pdf/23-Kisala.pdf
http://www.religionstatistics.net/statofrel1.htm
http://www.statistics.gov.uk/cci/nugget_print.asp?ID=958
http://www.census.gov/prod/www/religion.htm

45. Lynda Barley, *Christian Roots, Contemporary Spirituality* (London: Church House Publishing, 2006).

46. David Hay & Kate Hunt, *Understanding the Spirituality of People Who Don't Go to Church* (final Report of the Adult Spirituality Project, Nottingham University, 2000).

47. David Hay, 'The Spirituality of Adults in Britain – Recent Research' in *Scottish Journal of Healthcare Chaplaincy* 5 (2002) 1, 4–9; see http://www.sach.org.uk/journal/0501p04_hay.pdf (accessed 27/01/2008) for a pdf version of this article.

48. David Hay, 'The Spirituality of the Un-Churched' (BIAMS Conference, Selly Oak, Birmingham, 2000) http://www.martynmission.cam.ac.uk/BIAMSHay.htm (accessed 27/01/2008).

49. David Hay, 'The Spirituality of Adults in Britain – Recent Research' op. cit. 4.

50. Massimo Introvigne and Rodney Stark. 'Religious Competition and Revival in Italy: Exploring European Exceptionalism' in *Interdisciplinary Journal of Research on Religion*, op. cit. 4.

51. Ibid. 16.

## CHAPTER 2

*Cultural and Contextual Forces*

> *We think we can even invent ourselves at random*
> *by assembling convenient and pleasing but transient*
> *identities out of the bits and pieces we find around us.*
> *We pick up fragments to shore against our ruin.*
> ROBERT SOKOLOWSKI

## UNFOLDING THE CONTEXT

Spirituality is a universal human characteristic and phenomenon that is culturally and historically situated. It is influenced by the social, linguistic, historical, religious, economic, ecological and political realities of its human locations. Spirituality confronts us with and reacts to all the forces that impact existential reality. It impacts on every aspect of life: inner and outer, personal and communal. Spirituality emerges in geographical landscapes: deserts, mountains, valleys, villages, cities, in holy places and holy spaces, in the wilderness, and in hidden places of the human heart and soul, mind and memory, imagination and creativity, joy and sorrow, well-being and woe.

Spirituality is like the wind and the rain, like the air and the mists of morning. It is ubiquitous and fluid, flowing, moving, changing with the changes of life itself, sometimes simple, sometimes subtle, sometimes strong and courageous, sometimes weak and tenuous, barely holding the boundaries of sense and meaning. And it can seemingly disappear. Above all it responds to the times in which we live, is mapped by them and traces paths through them. Unnoticed, it frames and organises them, shaping their concepts, illuminating their images. Spirituality helps us to rethink life itself, helps us to deal creatively and imaginatively with our times.

We live in remarkable times. In the West it seems that we are standing in transitional space between two worlds: the late modern and the postmodern worlds. Certainly, change is all around us. In more ways than one, a new map of the world is in the making.[1] This new map is changing how we view every aspect of human life. These are times of economic, cultural, political and social change; times of globalisation, of rampant consumerism, of unbridled free trade and worker exploitation, of human trafficking and mass migration, and a widening range of real and potential ecological threats and disasters: even our water is at risk. We live our lives in the bloody shadow of the world-engulfing wars of the twentieth century and their ideological and political offspring. A pivotal epoch such as this deeply impacts the shaping and meaning of spirituality and its modes of response or reaction.

We live in remarkable times. We carry the memory of the madness that gave us ethnic cleansing on a horrifying scale: the Holocaust, Cambodia, Rwanda, the Balkans and more recently Darfur. Echoes of colonialism and the influences of neo-colonial attitudes still resonate. New economic and political imperialisms are on the rise. Various parts of Africa are in serious ecological and economic difficulty. The Middle East is unsettled. Political and religious fundamentalisms have become commonplace. People rage against the limits of the human condition. Human migration is happening on an unimaginable scale. A new generation of terrorist movements has emerged. Human rights abuses are regularly reported by concerned organisations attempting to uphold an international ethic. Reports of institutional and state corruption of various kinds arise on an almost daily basis. Integrity is challenged.

We live in remarkable times. Social disorder and physical and sexual violence are on the rise. We see pain and disorder on our streets. We meet drugs and drug-related criminality and violence in our neighbourhoods. Poverty, sometimes in new forms, continues to afflict peoples everywhere. Scientists insistently tell us that our own unbridled economic actions have put the planet itself at risk. Global warming is a reality; the ice sheets are melting; waterways are polluted; species loss is predicted on a massive scale. The rainforests are being destroyed; aboriginal peoples are being displaced and disowned. Energy resources are approaching critical tipping time. Nuclear weapons are being developed; advances in weapons technology are being vigorously and clamorously pursued. These are the historical, political, societal, economic and ecological symptoms, the contextual particularities that embody the challenges facing anyone who wishes to embrace – or indeed study – contemporary spirituality.

The times are also changing how increasing numbers of people are reviewing and responding to questions of meaning, how they are engaging and re-engaging with humankind's spiritual propensities and desires. Modernity's triumphalist convictions about the demise of religion and the disappearance of humankind's spiritual creativity, its convictions about the disenchantment of the world, the desacralising and secularising of life in the West, are being challenged on all sides. There is convincing sociological evidence of the re-enchantment of the world and the re-sacralisation of life. Seemingly on the cusp of victory the secularist agenda has begun to pall. With regard to religion, spirituality's more organised sibling, secularisation theory – modernity's dominant social paradigm – is under attack. This, too, has major implications for spirituality.

As sociologist Peter Berger explains it, the dominant assumption that we live in a secularised world has proved false.[2] Religion and spirituality have not gone away. Interest in mysticism has not gone away. The world as a whole is as religious as ever it was and more, even if Europe remains an exception. New forms and new expressions of spirituality are evolving in the face of organised and vociferous efforts to maintain the political dominance of secularism. Spiritual re-enchantment is taking place despite the clear evidence of religious disenchantment in Europe, and clear indications of social and cultural change. The audacity of spirit is being revealed in abundant ways.

## THE CHALLENGE OF MODERNITY

The challenge faced in this chapter is to reveal the forces behind these changes, forces identified by the terms *modernity, late-modernity* and *postmodernity*, as they impact on and alter the contours and contexts of contemporary spirituality. The challenges and disenchantments of modernity are ubiquitous, consequences of the convergence of social and intellectual forces that have fashioned western society since the seventeenth century.[3] It names a turbulent, world-changing period in European history shaped by the Enlightenment and definitively impacted on by the French and Industrial Revolutions, giving rise to a world dominated by the turn to autonomous human reason. Modernity names a rationalist and historical ideology seeking something good: the liberation of the human subject. The problem is that it sought to do this by making religion its enemy and working for the spiritual disenchantment of the world. Faith is separated from reason.[4] Grounded in a decision to live by human reason alone, rational science became the only basis for human certainty. Modernist approaches to things religious and spiritual disdained what could not be scientifically explained to the satisfaction of a secularist rationale.

As a result, reason was set in sharp contrast and opposition to religion.[5] In the process, religion is separated from revelation. In the name of freedom and progress, rationalist dogma replaced religious dogma. The result is that European society and culture have been de-traditionalised and moved in new anti-religious, secular directions. There is a hidden power game in all of this: what cannot be explained is difficult to control and that made religion suspect to those seeking intellectual and political domination. What could not be controlled had to be marginalised in other ways, at the least by being dismissed, disparaged and parodied as mediaeval or superstitious nonsense. The same images and terms are still in use today in certain media and ideologically-driven representations of global religiosity.

Unfortunately, the twentieth-century aptitude for domination and control gave the world the twin evils of Nazi Fascism and Stalinist Communism and their offshoots. It also gave us capitalism and consumerism. How free is freedom? Even then science and humanistic reason were represented as the Apollonian pillars on which the twentieth century was ostensibly built. History suggests a much more complex picture, and so does sociological research. The long disruptive shadow of Apollo's mad twin Dionysus was simultaneously at work as it always is, erupting from the dark, subterranean recesses of the human mind. While Apollo constructs the illusions of well-established life, Dionysus breaks through their veils and confronts us with raw reality. Where Apollo represents the dynamics of stability in human affairs, Dionysus represents the dynamic – the daimonic? – unpredictability of wild and ecstatic emotivity.[6] In effect, modernity is a myth, a myth of unending progress made possible by rationalist science, or scientism, in which the turn to Apollonian reason is presented as the only sure path to cure individual and social ills. The Greeks knew different.

The modernist myth has been met increasingly since the 1980s with a strong hermeneutics of suspicion and has itself become the subject of consistent critical deconstruction by philosophers and theologians and by others in the human sciences. For example, Nicholas Lash has astutely reminded us that the word *religion* as we have received it in recent usage is itself a theoretical invention of the seventeenth and eighteenth centuries, itself a child of the Enlightenment.[7] The earlier notion of religion as a pervasive mood or condition of reverence, enchantment and connectedness was displaced in favour of a boundaried, strongly privatised locality of experience subject to free choice. According to Lash, the roots of this limited, limiting and boundaried model are lodged in the so-called Wars of Religion when nation states moved to exercise control and sovereignty by inventing what we now think of as religion and exploiting it as a means of social control.

Where religion was not nationalised it was privatised. This raises an interesting possibility. It is entirely likely that the decline of institutional religion in Europe today is actually the collapse of this narrow Enlightenment theory of religion and the return of an older, more culturally pervasive, more mystical condition of reverence for all that is – something Ernst Troeltsch had already noted during the period between the two world wars of the twentieth century.[8] It appears today as if Troeltsch foresaw the present reality and that Lash has identified a concept of religion that has reached its sell-by date.

What is apparently collapsing is itself an Enlightenment invention. Religion, especially in its spiritual and mystical manifestations, is demanding its freedom through a renewed audacity of spirit urging soul to break free of the conformity-enforcing Procrustean bed the Enlightenment cleverly designed to domesticate religion and serve political ends. This gives rise to new questions. How is a freed religion, a religion reconnected to reverence for all that is, to speak to the voices of contemporary ethico-economic and political power whose purposes still require the marginalising of religion, its very subservience to economic and political hegemonies? How are we to recuperate an effective concern for human life and the planet we all share in all its situated detail? So much of value has been lost, not least an audacious spirit of non-exploitive, mature reverence.

In this process science became the defining tenet, the controlling idiom, the prevailing dogma, and religion was shown the red card. In embracing these beliefs modernity not only turned away from religion, rejecting it and its many spiritual expressions as products of a presumed darkness grounded in a purportedly erroneous grasp of reality. It also saw religion and its spiritual expressions as foolishness, perhaps a comforting illusion or an escapist panacea, but most assuredly a block to the accomplishment of modernity's socio-political and economic goals. In modernity's worldview, beliefs and values are legitimate only to the extent that they are sanctioned by rationalist science in accordance with Enlightenment thought, their roots nourished by Cartesian philosophy and Newtonian physics. Such are the foundations of the myth by which Europe still seeks to live and order lives.

Interestingly from an Irish perspective, the *Oxford English Dictionary* dates the term *modernism* to a letter written by Jonathan Swift in 1737. The implication is that modernism is itself a situated reality that can be located historically, culturally and geographically, a phenomenon of a particular time still making universal claims, a phenomenon that does not readily recognise its own generalised shadow or its own grim historical consequences. Reflect for a moment on the nature and implications of individualism and consumerism as they are experienced today. Reflect for a moment on the myth of disinterested scientific inquiry and then consider its ties to industrial control and the rationalisations of massive profit. Reflect on what has been lost to society and to culture as a result of the twentieth-century's dark side. Reflect on the implications for the well-being of the human spirit, when soul is perforce forged in suffering caused by nothing other than the power ambitions of privileged elites.

Please don't get me wrong. I am not attacking either reason or science here or the good that they can do and have obviously done. That would be foolhardy in the extreme. What I am concerned about is the strong naturalistic, materialistic and reductionistic ideology that is taken for granted within modernity, and uncritically – or perhaps cynically – presented as a fact. What I am concerned about is the domination of 'physicalism' and the exclusion of the spiritual from public life and administration. In fact, modernity is a secularist belief system set against other, usually religious belief systems in a search for social dominance and control. If it had a space for religion, it was only for an utterly rational religion of nature or a religion indistinguishable from humanistic ethics, or a theology grounded in Enlightenment thought and in service to the Enlightenment agenda. That is why revelation and faith are first privatised, then marginalised. They represent a rejected centre of influence. There is a fundamental philosophical question to be answered here. There is also a question of honesty, integrity and equality.

Modernity claims that we have no other certain source of knowledge beyond reason and its scientific twin. This is an amazing assumption; it asserts that no other reality could possibly exist beyond the sensory physical reality that science can measure. The result is relativism, subjectivism and fragmentation on a large scale and a consequent loss or relativisation of meaning in almost every aspect of life, human or otherwise. Little wonder that modernity is in crisis. Reflect even for a moment on the far from neutral impacts of globalisation, its monist agendas and manipulative, profit-driven dynamics. Reflect on the reduction of persons to consumers, and literally everything else in the world to objects of consumption, provided that the price is right. Reflect on the exploitation of individual desire functioning in such a world and how that exploitation works. Reflect on the socio-cultural impacts of savage individualism, subjectivism and capitalism. Reflect on the information revolution, the dominance of techno-economics and their implications for the creative expression of soul and spirit. Reflect on the flattening of the world that they imply.

It is not difficult to see that such forces have clear implications for religion and spirituality. Spirituality had four options: accept modernity and work within its world view, ignore it, react to it, or develop a new path. Indications of all four strategies are discernible in a range of responses that find expression in fundamentalist and traditionalist movements, in a variety of liberal approaches, and in others that adopted various strategies of critical dialogue. In the aftermath of the Enlightenment the forms of spirituality that emerged are themselves intriguing. In the period up to 1900, representative forms of spirituality within Christianity alone include Quietism, Pietism, Wesleyan, Puritan and Shaker spiritualities, the Oxford Movement, and Evangelical and Pentecostal spiritualities. The twentieth century brings about a radical change. The ecumenical movement begins. Interfaith dialogue opens. A renewed interest in charismatic, mystical and contemplative spirituality comes to birth. A turn to prophetic-political-liberational spirituality begins to surface. Emancipatory, ecological and cosmic spiritualities come to the fore.

Many of these changes converge around influential writers and teachers.[9] The list includes such names as Thomas Merton, Evelyn Underhill, Dorothy Day, Simone Weil, Dietrich Bonhoeffer, Pierre Teilhard de Chardin, Brother Roger Schutz, Sandra Schneiders, Dorothee Sölle, Oscar Romero, Mother Teresa, Gustavo Guttierez and many others including figures like Mahatma Gandhi and Pope John XXIII. Pilgrimage became popular again. People set out on spiritual quests and wisdom sojourns; they went on retreat. Interfaith dialogue continued to expand. In the second half of the century, the religious phenomenon of believing without belonging noticeably grew.[10] Political, liberational, and feminist spiritualities came to the fore. So too did Theosophical, New Age, New-Pagan and varieties of esoteric and eclectic spirituality.

Such are the contextual forces and forms of spirituality encountered in the twentieth century, a century that a newly emergent spirituality shared with Darwinian evolutionary thought, Marxism, Quantum thinking, Capitalism and Psychoanalysis as the shapers of a new century. Simply by creating new contexts all of these forces called for new responses. The twentieth century also demonstrates that in times of dramatic change some forms of religion and spirituality tend to continue to embody traditional religious and spiritual modes and images; not simply as forms of resistance to change but more particularly as potentials for future religious and spiritual renewal, providing checks and balances, preserving alternatives, keeping older potentials in reserve.[11] Today's spirituality is a child of the interaction between secularising and re-emerging religious-spiritual forces as they reshape contemporary culture, especially now that modern societies are consensually structured by market economies and liberal democratic politics.

At the same time, modernity has reached an impasse and is in the process of being critically discredited. People are making their own informed choices. It is against this background that people today are seeking such pivotal elements as meaning and value, freedom, abundance, and social justice.[12] For a time it appeared that secular humanism's triumph in the West was assured. There is no doubting religious disenchantment in the West, a result of the convergence of cultural and intellectual forces that have been shaping Western society for many years. But as we have seen, the statistics of religious decline in Europe are crosscut by impressive indicators of spiritual resurgence. As we approach the end of the first decade of the new millennium, we still live in cultures that are secular in theory but are rapidly becoming pluralist in practice. Pluralism seems set to become a pivotal shaping element in the spirit of the new century.

Modernity is credited with these changes, aided by various elites in a variety of walks of life, from academia to journalism to politics, who continue to serve fundamentally secularist goals. In Europe, a mass media that serves a strident secularism fights to keep religion out of the Public Square except when scandals or ethical controversies dear to libertarian constituencies arise. Faith has been forced to seek refuge at the margins of society and has been transformed into a matter of private preference and individual choice, refused a place in the public forum.[13] On the other hand, Christianity did originate in a Near Eastern wilderness in politically fraught times. There are complex forces at work in the West to be sure, but the obvious result is easy enough to see: a majority of people in the West no longer seem to view the world through predominantly religious lenses.

### Re-enchantment and Re-sacralisation

And yet there is another story at work. While it is evident that institutional Christianity has been wounded, sometimes by its own unaided efforts as recent scandals lay bare, new forms of spiritual life are blossoming in the West. The deep longings of the human spirit for a more connected, more meaningful existence have taken on new urgency. They have begun to seek new expressions. An unexpected consequence of this change is that secularisation theory itself is increasingly criticised by one-time supporters in sociology precisely because it did not predict this spiritual revolution.[14] The fact is that, while the statistical evidence pointing to the ascent of secularism and the decline of mainstream institutional religious practice in the West is readily available, it does not tell the whole story. The forces at work are too complex for easy statistical analysis.

Phenomena like religion, spirituality and mysticism are notoriously difficult to define and not surprisingly they insistently evade the reductive tendencies of much contemporary thought. In the process, they become largely invisible to ideologically driven secularist and physicalist assumptions. The available evidence shows that humanity's basic religious impulse, the quest for a meaning that somehow transcends the natural limits of human existence, is far from extinguished and is in a resurgent state.[15] According to Professor Christopher Partridge, spiritualities are emerging today that represent a new spiritual awakening that utilises thought forms, ideas and practices that are already familiar to the majority of contemporary Westerners.[16]

Ideas and forms, practices and expressions of spirituality that have not been traditionally associated with institutional or popular religion in the West are also growing in all kinds of unexpected places. In all of this it is important to recall that the term *spirituality* is prone to an array of different meanings grounded in very different personal stories and the languages and literacies available to their tellers in the particularities of their various locations and circumstances. Contemporary spirituality confronts scholars and practitioners alike with a spectrum of oblique descriptions defying singular definition, but there is no denying that we are witnessing the emergence of new forms of spirituality, harbingers if not of a spiritual revolution, then of a new spiritual springtime.

Interest in things spiritual is growing by the day, pointing away from disenchantment and secularisation in the direction of the re-sacralisation and re-enchantment of life in the West. It seems that as older expressions of religiosity and spirituality fall into decline new or renewed forms are taking their place. It appears that people's spiritual desires are adapting to changed circumstances and evolving new ways of expressing soul and spirit, developing new strategies of action with their own operational logics and modes of transmission, and making use of new means of communication and learning. Imagine texting or blogging as spiritual practices alive with transformative potential. As these forces of spiritual re-sacralisation and re-enchantment grow, modes and forms of spirituality concealed by the mainstream consensus have also begun to break free from the dominant forms of Western spiritual culture.

Michel de Certeau explored these phenomena, which are after all practices of everyday life, more than twenty years ago.[17] In de Certeau's terms, the new spirituality uses functional combinations to produce new expressions by making use of resources that are readily available and then begins to construct and do new things with them, a process usually referred to as bricolage. In this sense the new spirituality is difficult to pin down. It is socially dispersed yet insinuates itself everywhere by using the spiritual products of the dominant order even in the act of changing them. In fact, how spirituality is taught or spread tells us very little about those who use it, especially when those users are not themselves its primary makers. In this sense the new spirituality may be described in de Certeau's terms as secondary productions that are nonetheless personally and socially meaningful and significant.

There is the rub. Such new forms and structures may disappointingly represent forms domesticated by contemporary needs: individualistic, fragmented, pantheistic, serving egocentric needs that risk leaving spirit and soul still alienated and lost. What is new does not necessarily represent a radical or groundbreaking departure. Present evidence points to a kaleidoscope of often-conflicting forms. Still, the sacred persists in the West, often in forms not easily recognised by the Christian family of spiritual traditions. These new expressions of spirit and the spiritual are often subjective, inner-focused, or nature-based, and practitioners tend to use a self-conscious terminology that is not necessarily linked to the spiritual literacies of the great world religions.

Yet these new expressions may also represent responses to the challenge to live life to the full and engage in the kind of personal and social transformation intended to benefit humankind and the whole of creation. In a word, Western society desperately needs the spiritual re-enchantment that appears to be underway. But there is another challenge in all of this, the challenge to embrace, develop and grow a socially engaged spirituality, a spirituality open to human and planetary solidarity. To echo a phrase from Laurence Binyon's 1942 poem *The Burning of the Leaves*, 'now is the time for stripping the spirit bare' and giving it space to blossom afresh, blossom audaciously in the world.[18]

Yet that begs another question: what spirit, and what shapes will it take if we strip it bare? And yet it is clearly more than time to free spirit from the encrusting dross that has repressed it, from the social and cultural forces that have publicly marginalised it in the name of triumphalist secularist dogma. It is time for ears to be opened afresh to the call to engage with authentic transformation, for tongues to be loosened to speak in favour of a new, renewed vision of life, and for eyes to be opened to a new way of seeing all of reality: and our responsibilities to it and for it, particularly with regard to the forces of domination and oppression. What is taking shape is a spiritual condition in which new convergences of belief and behaviour seek transforming embodiment.[19]

### THE POSTMODERN MILIEU

Postmodern spirituality begins with the twentieth-century shift to consumption as the organising principle in contemporary economic, cultural and religious life. The impact on spirituality begins to emerge as conformity encounters the strengthening desire for self-expression. Targeted and specialised marketeering soon moved from the economic to the spiritual sphere. The emphasis in the media on image, difference, fashion, spectacle and branding has unerringly migrated to the spiritual sphere and spirituality has begun to travel along the new trade routes as religion did in the past. New mediated rituals are emerging: the techno-pagan Burning Man festival in Black Rock City, Nevada, and the Day of the Dead celebrations that are growing in Latin America are typical examples; and the spread of Christian Bookstores is indicative of the parallel commodification of Christianity. Spiritual practices are being repackaged, reshaped and transported into new cultural markets, some-times to the interests of particular political and economic agendas. In the postmodern milieu these reshaped and repackaged spiritual products also respond to the social and cultural forces that are shaping and reshaping individual and communal identities.[20]

Interestingly, postmodern people tend to be far more open to the supernatural and to spirituality than their modernist predecessors. The result is an incredible diversity of spiritualities, even within Christianity, especially where the emphasis on the individual has led to a discernible diminishing of communal concerns. Within postmodern contexts Christian spirituality is challenged to discover a new way of expressing holiness, a new way of embracing the expansiveness of God in the new spiritual marketplace and along its new, often virtual, trade routes.[21] The spirituality widespread in the postmodern milieu tends to be quite pragmatic and subjective. There are two challenges here. The first, of particularly Christian interest has to do with the complex, consumer-driven interaction of the human spirit, the spirit of the age, and the Divine Spirit in the new spiritual marketplace. It also has to do with the diversity of spiritual expression and style that characterise such complexity as people search for a vibrant sense of the divine, often in non-traditional ways.[22]

The second challenge has to do with the contested role of critical reason within the postmodern milieu and in the diverse spiritualities being shaped by postmodern forces. If the Enlightenment was about the public use of reason – it was also called the Age of Reason – the postmodern runs the risk of becoming the opposite, a romantic marketplace where reason is increasingly absent. Is the new spirituality to be accountable to critical and discerning reason? Is it acceptable that the new spirituality remains a surface celebration of the ephemeral and the momentary? Is it acceptable that the new spirituality remains of little ethical or social consequence? Is individualism to be central and community excluded from the new spiritual prospectus? The implications for humanity are immense, not least in terms of the death of the subject in a swirl of fragmenting identities: though it is also important to consider what the word *subject* means in this context.[23] What happens when, on the shifting sands of postmodernity, a vanishing self becomes the site of encounter with a vanishing God?[24]

The core question is: does the *postmodern turn* name an imploding of modernity, its turning in on itself as it were, or the emergence of new forms of experience, thought, and social organisation? And the corollary: what are the implications for contemporary spirituality? Whatever the answer to the core question – and it will probably contain elements of both possibilities – recent decades have witnessed a series of critical intellectual, cultural, religious and social challenges to the convictions of modernity that carry momentous implications for newly emerging spiritualities. The postmodern involves a radical critique of what people today see as the faulty, constraining, even dangerous assumptions of the modern worldview, a worldview held accountable for the state of spiritual bankruptcy that characterises much of the Western world, and Western Europe in particular. It is in this sense that postmodernity, or late modernity, is probably best described as a *mood* or *condition* of history, whose impact is particularly evident in the areas of knowledge and belief. The problem is the extent to which new spiritualities will resist socially, politically and ethically the significant experiences of subjugated, marginalised and repeatedly terrifying otherness and difference that are endemic in the postmodern world.[25]

There are three conditions for knowledge in modernity: a foundational grand narrative as the criterion of legitimacy; the development of strategies to legitimise some forms of knowledge and exclude others; and a desire for knowledge-based criteria for moral legitimacy. Late modern or postmodern thought contests all three of them. In this sense the postmodern turn names a loss of faith in knowledge and/or belief based on grand narratives and their exclusive character. It sees them as mere narratives, stories alongside other stories, texts alongside other texts. The implications for ethics understood as right action based on universal principles, and for spirituality understood in terms of universal meaning and sense-making, are evident. In effect, the late modern and the post-modern represent a suspicion, a contesting stance, a mood of incredulity towards modernist philosophies and their impacts on society, culture, ethics, identity, science, psychology, theology, religion and spirituality.

The late modern – and the postmodern – represent a fragmenting move from common values to individualised cultures and beliefs. They favour individual and small group forms of spirituality and spiritual belonging. These are often superficial, derived from commodified media images where traditional links to meaning are rendered tenuous at best. The question is the extent to which media influence is cultural rather than directly religious or spiritual, given that both religion and spirituality are culturally located. In either case the implications for institutional religion in a consumer culture are obvious.[26] The main advantage of the postmodern is a far from neutral undermining of the conformist pressures associated with modernity. It also represents a kind of spiritual nostalgia, a longing for an expressive spirituality freed from the need to conform to the demands of the systemworld and its so-called scientific standards and the ways in which life is rationalised and dominated by routine and bureaucracy.

The postmodern paradoxically favours the lifeworld, the natural, expressive, communicative, and organic sphere of human existence, the place where people seek to live life to the full, seek meaning and value in life, and honour the things of the spirit.[27] In so doing it makes a subject-based spirituality possible, one that respects the unique and irreplaceable dignity of the human person before God. This is not simply a return to a pre-modern spirituality. It is the attempt to discover a spiritual dimension to contemporary life in the wake of the collapse of modernity. In general it is non-dogmatic in its beliefs, often tending, as de Certeau revealed, towards bricolage and the idiosyncratic. Community is not excluded, but it is re-imagined. Concern is with self-identity and the narrative that gives it shape.

If Paul Ricoeur is correct, identity is culturally mediated through symbols, texts, narratives, language and the range of culturally situated bearers of meaning and meaning resources, the very forces that shape contemporary spiritualities: spirituality and human identity are linked experiential structures. Identity grows out of the complex interactions between symbols, texts, narratives and language and the self-evaluations they activate as we seek to make sense of our lives; so, too, does spirituality. In the process, disparate and contingent elements are woven together in dynamic and changing ways.[28] In postmodern contexts the spirituality that tends to emerge from this weaving process is frequently non-creedal and theologically vague, revealing a religious or spiritual literacy gap, a loss of connection or continuity with spiritual discourse. Again, late-modern and postmodern spirituality tends to be transmitted and communicated in non-traditional, non-institutional ways, often through fairs, spontaneous groups, night courses, and small ads in health-food shops or complementary health clinics.

Spiritual practices tend to be rooted in individual logics that soften and blur the boundaries of fixed forms and traditions, and imaginative invention also plays a role. All of this shows a connection to the prevailing cacophony of postmodern culture and its individualistic trends. The result is that faith is whatever a person makes it to be in terms of potentially transient subjective meaning, even if it is not unique. The question arises: should we be optimistic or pessimistic in response to this situation? The answer depends on the role that religion plays in the evolving cultural matrix. If religion serves as an alternative centre to politics in the search for identity, if it becomes a source of alternative interest and insight, an optimistic answer is in the making. If not, a more pessimistic view will prevail. In either case, however, religion and spirituality remain players in the cultural arena.[29]

The postmodern is also characterised by a stance of incredulity towards any sense of universal reason and universal or objective truth. It also contests any sense of a universal history, or any kind of unifying theory. Postmodern reason is always situated, relative to the prevailing narrative in a society or institution. In the postmodern world even language is seen not as neutral but as a changeable social construct. The postmodern emphasises discontinuity, difference, otherness, plurality, fragmentation, and complexity, and it sees power and ideological issues behind every universal knowledge, history or truth claim. This is the narrative shaping emergent spiritualities. Identity is constructed in the telling of stories, and stories change. So does spirituality because there is always more than one way to tell a story. Anyone who is experienced in spiritual accompaniment will recognise the reality of this claim.

Just as importantly, the postmodern also represents a revolution of consciousness. Consciousness is seen as a task, not a given, precisely because we live in embodied situations subject to material, social, cultural and linguistic conditions and contingencies. The postmodern mood influences not only how we think about the world, it influences how we experience it and how we talk about our experiences. It influences how we construct meaning and how we construct our understandings of embodiment. A simple example will suffice. Think of our contemporary way of being when space/time has been flattened out by instant communication and commerce, consumerism and commodification. Reason is removed from its pedestal and situated in the messiness of a human context flooded by information and sound bytes. Who am I then? What does embodiment mean then?

We become flattened selves sitting in front of flat screens seeking flattened enlightenments. One result is a nomadic existence in a world without certainties seeking an end to the boredom of a flattened world. The postmodern nomad is uprooted from fixed place and time, has no fixed location but improvises an ungrounded existence while playing with improvised identities minimally organised, now one thing, now another.[30] The same thing happens to flattened spiritualities. But this is also a world that allows the return of the messianic, of prophetic and mystical religion and spiritualities that invoke justice and the gift, and risk to seek in faith beyond the Void, the Nada. It names the return of the repressed and the embrace of the other. In such contexts our obligations towards the other cannot be calculated. At the very least it is about letting the other be while respecting particularity and difference. The return of the repressed also allows theology and spirituality to claim their places as discourse in the postmodern milieu. This runs directly counter to the modernist agenda and its materialistic monopoly.

Late-modern and postmodern spirituality suggest that it is time to break down this monopoly, to reject its power to exclude, to reflect outside its borders, to embrace dangerously what is other to modernity. The turn to religion and spirituality, to a theological mode of reflection, is part of this project, a sign of a new move beyond the gaps and dead ends of modernity. Beyond them lies the gift, the offer of a new beginning, something mystics know, a new song: or at least its opening chords and rhythms. Religion once again becomes possible because presence is once again beckoning. A radical change is possible. A different undersong begins to echo as spirit arises in the shaping of new personal and new cultural identities. This is also the naming of a changed spirituality, of a spiritual condition in which belief and practice come together in differently embodied shape. It names the possibility of a spirituality grounded in lived testimony, a prophetically wise spirituality rooted in engaged and performed narrative. The recovery of religion and spirituality in all their diversity are sanctioned: such is the phenomenon arising in the contemporary Western spiritual milieu.

Postmodern spirituality resists closure in favour of continuing transformation. It points us to the Spirit's creative presence in the messy and often muddy and murky contingencies of human life and history. It helps us to recuperate icon and identify, reject and transcend idols and their illusions of the sacred. Postmodern spirituality favours the full flourishing of Spirit-shaped human life in all its diversity. It supports a spirituality of life in this world, open to the questioning of the other and the different. Christian spirituality rediscovers itself as living before the face of Jesus Christ, the Other who had been reduced to an expletive but who still embodies suffering and offers hope in a community of persons, none of whom are perfect but nevertheless seek something beyond themselves.

Postmodern spirituality engages with life-shaping practices. It facilitates the rediscovery of sacrament and the recovery of intense bodily participation in prayer and worship. It faces the impact of capitalism as it serves to reveal inadequate spiritual practices and insights found wanting in the face of the disorientations, inequalities and suffering caused by polarising and exploitive change. It requires practices that respect the particularities of age, gender, culture, language, race, class, and all the other ways legitimate difference and authentic individuality is made manifest. It supports practices that affirm the beauty of each human face before God, and the diversity of spiritualities that such an affirmation implies. The postmodern creates new space for liturgy, prayer and worship. New approaches to scripture, lectio divina, meditation, conversation, community-building and fellowship are made possible. The postmodern brings to the surface new calls to ethical action and engaged mysticism; and it makes it possible to orient life to the reign of God while immersed in the contingencies of history and the unpredictabilities of human life. It also demands the courage to embrace the gift.

On the other hand, this is a world that is potentially highly solipsistic and narcissistic: self-referred and self-absorbed. It is a world made of fragments; and in a world of fragments we encounter fragmented identities following fragmented desires that rob us of coherent or congruent identities. In psychoanalytic terms we live in an age when the pleasure principle is in the ascendancy. We encounter playfulness but sell it short for entertainment and the promiscuities of style, fashion, and spiritual pastiche that lack any external validation, refuse any external challenge to their self-referred universe. It does not disclose the path to joyful worship. We slide on surfaces and engage in surface learning lacking depth, dancing with a desperation that fears transformation, satisfied to mimic freedom in fragmented, fluctuating environments where strobe lights flash and fruit machines beckon. We risk becoming bearers of virtual transformations in virtual spaces, carriers of illusory spirit and empty soul: but, then, who decides what is virtual? In flattened, fragmented, fluctuating worlds, knowledge tends to be tentative, many-sided, and not always rational, especially when the boundaries between fact and fiction dissolve.

At the same time, the postmodern mood represents a number of important shifts: from rigidly pre-determined to openness to the new and unexpected; from reductionism to holism; from an impersonal clockwork world to a participatory universe; from transcendence to immanence; from materialism to spirituality; and from a physical to a relational and communicative reality. New frontiers emerge, prior oppressions fall away, and new self-creating activities and integrities grounded in relational motivations become possible. In this new world we are called to be team-players and participators, collaborators and co-facilitators, co-creators and co-authors of brave new stories in a land where meaning lies in the dialogue between people, and relational models of life prevail. The emerging spiritualities challenge us to be creative, open to new meaning, open to new possibilities and new, world- and life-enhancing projects with other people.

REFLECTION: FIVE SHAPING FORCES

Late modernity and the postmodern offer much fertile terrain for religious and spiritual reflection. Clearly, the mood they represent can be helpful to the search for spiritual meaning. But the condition they represent is not neutral and needs to be handled with care and attention because dangers lurk within. It is important to remember that late modernity and the postmodern face us with a complex phenomenon grounded in the convictions and the doubts, the strengths and weaknesses, of the contemporary West. The convergence of these convictions and doubts raises serious questions about personal and social meaning and value, identity and destiny: themes that speak to the heart of spirituality and religion. Questions arising from the doubts and uncertainties raised by late modernity and the postmodern lead in turn to the search for alternatives to the prevailing mainstream consensus and its secularised disenchantments. Practitioners and seekers alike need to be alert to these problems. A number of contributing forces have been identified over the past twenty-five years, five of which we shall discuss here.[31]

The first has to do with the more savage and ecologically disastrous aspects of global capitalism and consumerism and their planetary impacts. Much of the contemporary spiritual quest is grounded in a counter-cultural imagination and ethical choice in the face of what has been accepted as clear evidence of socio-cultural decadence and distortion. A second element concerns the nature and state of late-modern institutions, including mainstream religious institutions. Institutional failures and betrayals with their consequent losses of trust are identified in ways that make more personal, more subjective solutions to spiritual and religious concerns more attractive, seemingly more trustworthy. When institutions betray trust, the turn to self and to the sole authority of personal experience becomes predictable.

Not surprisingly, then, the emerging counter-cultural imagination tends now to find the classical institutional forms of life and activity inadequate, irrelevant or, indeed, oppressive. Under such circumstances institutions and bureaucracies are easily depicted as traps, as chicken-coops reinforced by rigidly and legalistically applied regulations of contested kinds. Against this background the spiritual task is easily redefined as the discovery of personal, subjective freedom from apparently rigid or legalistic forces and their perceived frustrations and hindrances. Spirituality quickly becomes the search for personal identity, internalised autonomy, and subjective authenticity to the exclusion of more communal expressions. On the other hand, in disenchanted worlds new forms of spirituality are predictably and seriously concerned with the discovery and the nature of a sacred sense of self, the discovery of a self space where spirit is allowed to dance to new rhythms and find new songs to sing.

A third, clearly related factor highlights the struggle with the all-pervasive forces of materialistic consumption and the perceived failure of materialism to satisfy higher, non-material, transcendental personal and social needs. A fourth related issue lies in the identification of the corrosive impact of late modernity and the postmodern on contemporary personal and social life, especially in terms of private and public morality as well as professional and business ethics. In short, both well-being and well-doing are made problematic in contexts where a sense of the sacredness of the person has been lost. Traditions and institutions have been undermined to the extent that many people have not only been de-traditioned, de-institutionalised or un-churched, they have also been rendered religiously and spiritually illiterate, robbed of the ability to sing of soul and dance through spirit vistas. These are times of social saturation. Too much is happening too fast for most people, and so individuals look to themselves to re-work things to their own seeming advantage. The human mind seeks to build new structures of personal and social stability and renew older ones to serve newer purposes; and in the process non-conventional forms of religion and spirituality arise. Interest in mysticisms of many, often esoteric, kinds expands. But if spiritual literacy is lost, such explorations run a twin risk: the dangers of spiritual masochism, and the spiritual exploitation and manipulation of others.

The last factor to be identified as significant to the changing face of spirituality and religion in the West today is the banality and super-ficiality of consumer culture. This is a powerful factor impacting on approaches to religion and spirituality in the contemporary world, particularly in counter-cultural incarnations. It is important to note that consumer cultures tend to undercut the doctrinal content of religious beliefs, to seek practices emptied of their originating discourses. Consumer interest focuses on the power of spiritual practices to deliver immediate satisfactions, not on their doctrinal underpinnings or modes of expression. This makes the consumption of practices more likely than commitment to a doctrinal base. Quite simply, consumer ideology changes the world in which spiritual and religious beliefs, teachings, theologies, symbols, rituals, sacred texts and practices are encountered. They are reshaped for other more immediate and individual purposes.

Consumer ideology changes the way in which people tend to relate to and understand religious and spiritual beliefs, rituals, practices, and traditions. Not surprisingly, they are all reclassified as products and commodities. They are taken for granted, seen as no more than means to satisfy individual needs or ends without much thought or concern for their religious or cultural origins. Little or no thought is given to the ethics of social appropriation that such usage involves, itself a form of plagiarism in a milieu that is heedless of where spiritual products come from, or the impact of the consumer mentality on religious and spiritual congruence and integrity. It is important to understand that in the consumer world *function* replaces *meaning*. Use and the satisfaction of individual desire predominate. As Vincent Miller notes, the problem is not about getting things right, or being open to different voices, but in how the contents of a tradition are engaged and used.[32] Late modernity favours those aspects of a religious or spiritual tradition that have broad consumer appeal. Personally demanding doctrinal requirements are simply ignored and set aside.

We live in an entertainer's and a merchandiser's world and religious and spiritual products find shelf space in the shopping mall, or on the stalls at the local Mind-Body-Spirit Festival, or are exploited by the advertising industry. In much the same way, sacred narratives must take their place alongside other texts, other forms of story or myth. In a consumer universe, branding and uniformity in the service of a new yet politically correct conformism replace contrast, difference and uniqueness. In a world of media-based cultural intermediaries, in a world of desire and discontent where instant satisfaction rules, in a world where the pulpit has been factually as well as figuratively removed, celebrity replaces moral greatness and in its hurdy-gurdy ebb and flow the influence of integrity is effectively obscured. A world built on desire and its lacks makes the task of distinguishing and discerning between desires well nigh impossible. And yet; and yet more people are reading more spiritual and mystical texts than ever before; and it is important to remember that it is the power of beliefs and doctrines that energises counter-cultural communities and brings them into being.

## THE TURN TO THE SELF

The convictions and certainties of late modernity support a radical self-referred turn in contemporary spirituality. Late modernity also supports the active construction of a de-traditioned self, while the privatisation of religion and spirituality remain culturally influential themes. However, the late-modern self is neither situated nor defined within a social context; it is set against it, constructed in contrast to it. We run the risk of developing isolated selves fearful of difference and otherness, fearful of change. Am I myself or am I someone else's construction? Am I no more than a figure in someone else's dream-world? The postmodern self has many faces, many voices, has a part in many dramas. The conundrum is that, while it dreams of self-sufficiency, it has to work itself out in practice.[33]

The late-modern self is an individualistic self, an actor in a drama of utilitarian individualism: I value myself alone; I empower and look after myself alone. The goal is no longer the common good but the unalloyed satisfaction of individual desires, interests and wants. Reflect on the growth of addictions of every kind. Reflect on the fact that neither social nor planetary solidarity are really on individualism's agenda. More than anything else, late modernity supports the quest to discover and express the truest and deepest aspects of the individual self. That is not of itself a dangerous thing. In fact the uncovering of the true self is an appropriate spiritual goal. The problem is otherwise. In the search for the self, the outside world as carrier of ethical and spiritual value and meaning all too easily disappears. In a world which has been stripped of cultural and religious tradition the search for the true self can be easily led astray.

As we consider the spiritual quest for the true self we need to reconsider the spiritual loss modernity entails. The guiding presumption is that what is left after cultural and religious de-traditioning and de-institutionalising is good, namely the individual self as the sole carrier of human depth, value and potential. For the person guided by late-modern ideology religion as an organised, community-based phenomenon is either suspect or bad in principle, while spirituality as an individualistic, subjective, self-constructed privatised reality is good. Unfortunately these understandings of the self are also at the heart of and orient much late-modern therapeutic practice. It should be no surprise, then, that their influence has also been felt in late-modern approaches to spiritual guidance and teaching.

These organising images of the self are also found in education, in self-help movements, in the turn to complementary health practices, mind cures, positive thinking, prosperity movements, and in key aspects of enterprise culture. They lie at the heart of contemporary esoteric visions of the new spirituality. The reinventions for Western audiences of karma and reincarnation clearly show this self-referred turn. It seems to proclaim that the individual is fully in control, fully self-referred in every aspect of individual life, past, present and future. Self-referred understandings of the human person are widespread in educated populations. Developing and expressing one's authentic potential, one's unique identity, empowering oneself: these are central motivating themes. We meet them everywhere. In consequence, spiritualities that affirm the reality and ethical demands of the outside world, the shaping demands of social otherness and difference, of social and ecological engagement and solidarity, of self-sacrifice, of traditionally sanctioned and regulated communal practice, become increasingly unacceptable.

Why? Quite simply because of the internalisation of authority and truth that is typical of late-modern visions of the self. The interiorising and personalising of authority has significant implications for organised and structured religious and spiritual organisations and movements. Spiritualities in the New Age style have been typically representative of this dynamic. They favoured and supported late-modern forms of individually internalised authority and truth that gave rise to fluid forms of self-referred belonging and belief. Similar forces are at work in mainstream religious and spiritual organisations and traditions. Changes in Christian practice have made the re-sacralised self feel completely at home. Self-authority has transformed religious and spiritual discipline into a matter of personal choice: personal consumption on personal terms in response to personal desires grounded in personal authority.

The nature of religious and spiritual obedience is changed; the role of external authority structures is questioned; figures in authority and leadership are given a suggestive or orientative or consultative rather than a decisive role in what are considered to be matters of essentially individual choice. In its most radical form late-modern and postmodern obedience is to the self, not to anyone else on earth or in heaven. The demands of commitment are not always binding. Politically correct consensus rather than prophetic response to situations of suffering and injustice is the dominant domesticating force. At a time when spiritual experiences are multiplying, the Pelagian, the Esoteric, the Gnostic and the Theosophical have returned with a vengeance and don't even know their ancient names. Is it any wonder that people rage against the limits of the human condition and seek a secure pre-existent self?

It is not so in the Western contemplative and mystical tradition. There the true self is not confused with some primordial pre-existent self, hidden under layers of perceived psychological, social or religious oppression, waiting to be uncovered and activated with the help of some psycho-meditative technology. The mystic and the contemplative embrace a true self that is radically other than the late-modern self-sufficient, autonomous self. The true self of the mystic is giftingly born of creative encounter with God, midwived in Spirit action, delivered into responsive being in the waters from the side of Christ. It has no real existence apart from God and God's awakening call and gift, but is responsively born of the transforming contemplative encounter with God and awakened by grace. It is drawn into being out of the alienation of the ordinary self and frees it into utter receptivity and union. The discovery of the true self is the discovery of a relationship with God, gifted by God.

This is the true spiritual self: a self called into being by a graced receptivity and relationality rooted and watered in love. The true self comes to birth in mutuality, in the gift of the Divine Other. True personal identity rises out of this gifted mutuality, this gifting Trinitarian presence. The true self is graciously and lovingly uttered into being by a God who, in Trinity, utters an act of loving otherness and draws the human other into a transforming relation where neither becomes a mere adjunct of the other. The true self is a consequence of the ordinary contingent self encountering something utterly, incomprehensibly, infinitely and open-endedly beyond it. We come to know ourselves truly to the extent that we come to know ourselves as utterly known, utterly lovingly known by God-as-Trinity.

This is a truly self-revealing love that gifts us with a uniquely and infinitely loved identity, gifts us to flourish as uniquely irreplaceable persons, sets the potential self free. The true True Self is the Self of God: we are true selves to the extent that we know ourselves as *imago dei*, image of God, remade by God's sovereign action: this is what surprises the mystic and astounds the contemplative as alienation falls away and walls of isolation crumble. This is the Christian understanding: the true self, the contemplative self, the spiritually potential self is an unimaginable gift. Such is the mystical invitation. Our task is to respond willingly to the rhythms of its revealing and awakening. This is the fullness of life, the fullness of a personhood freed from the limits of human subjectivity.[34] How do you stop such a spring from flowing into and transforming the world? But that is another question for another time.

THEMES AND QUESTIONS FOR FURTHER REFLECTION

1. How aware are you of the relevance of culture and processes of sociocultural change in shaping contemporary spirituality; the ways spiritual sensitivities influence understanding of socio-cultural concerns, for example, issues of social justice?
2. Identify the late-modern or postmodern milieu: how influential are they as an influential cultural and spiritual phenomenon?
3. What is involved in developing a spiritual identity in a postmodern milieu?
4. Identify the implications of the turn to the self and the stress on individualism in contemporary spirituality.

FURTHER READING

David Hay, *Why Spirituality is Difficult for Westerners* (Exeter & Charlottesville, VA: Societas Imprint Academic, 2007).

NOTES:

1. Andrei Codrescu, *The Disappearance of the Outside: A Manifesto for Escape* (St Paul, MN: Ruminator Books, 2001) 57.

2. Peter L. Berger, 'The Desecularization of the World: A Global Overview' in Peter L. Berger, ed., *The Desecularization of the World: Resurgent Religion and World Politics* (Grand Rapids, MN: Eerdmans, 1999) 2.

3. What follows has been influenced by a number of authors. See Stephen Toulmin, *Cosmopolis: The Hidden Agenda of Modernity.* (Chicago: Chicago University Press, 1990); Frank Boyle, *Swift as Nemesis: Modernity and its Satirist.* (Stanford: Stanford University Press, 2000); Larry Riggs, *Moliere and Modernity: Absent Mothers and Masculine Births.* (Charlottesville, VA: Rockwood Press, 2005); Luc Anckaert, Danny Cassimon, Hendrik Opdebeeck, eds, *Building Towers: Perspectives on Globalisation.* (Leuven: Peeters Publishers, 2002); Bryan S. Turner, ed., *The Blackwell Companion to Social Theory.* Second edition. (Oxford: Blackwell Publishing, 2000); Barbara Sundberg Baudot, ed., Foreword by Vaclav Havel, *Candles in the Dark: A New Spirit for a Plural World.* (Seattle and London: University of Washington Press, 2003).

4. See Philip Sheldrake, *A Brief History of Spirituality* (Oxford: Blackwell Publishing, 2007) 139–140 and 172–173.

5. See John D. Caputo and Michael J. Scanlon, eds, *God, the Gift, and Postmodernism* (Bloomington and Indianapolis: Indiana University Press, 1999).

6. See Allan Megill, *Prophets of Extremity: Nietzsche, Heidegger, Foucault, Derrida* (Berkeley/Los Angeles/London: University of California Press, 1987) 38–46. See also John W. De Gruchy, *Christianity, Art and Transformation: Theological Aesthetics in the Struggle for Justice* (Cambridge: Cambridge University Press, 2001) 13–16.

7. Nicholas Lash, 'The Church in the State We're In' in L. Gregory Jones and James J. Buckley, eds *Spirituality and Social Embodiment.* (Oxford: Blackwell Publishers, 1997) 121–137.

8. Ernst Troeltsch, *The Social Teaching of the Christian Churches,* two volumes, translated by Olive Wyon, with a Foreword by James Luther Adams (Louisville, KY: Westminster/John Knox Press, 1992). The text was originally published in 1931. See in particular vol. I, 381 & vol. II, 993–994.

9. Philip Sheldrake, *A Brief History of Spirituality* op. cit. 139–204.

10. See Grace Davie, *Religion in Britain since 1945: Believing Without Belonging* (Oxford: Blackwell, 1994).

11. See David Martin, *On Secularization: Towards a Revised General Theory* (Aldershot: Ashgate, 2005) 144.

12. See George Weigel, 'Roman Catholicism in the Age of John Paul II' in Peter L. Berger, ed., *The Desecularization of the World: Resurgent Religion and World Politics* op. cit. 19–35 at 23.

13. See Kevin J. Vanhoozer, 'Theology and the Condition of Postmodernity' in K.J. Vanhoozer, ed., *The Cambridge Companion to Postmodern Theology* (Cambridge: Cambridge University Press, 2003) 16.

14. See for example, David Martin, *On Secularization: Towards a Revised General Theory* op. cit., and Peter L. Berger, ed., *The Desecularization of the World: Resurgent Religion and World Politics* op. cit.

15. P. Berger, 'The Desecularization of the World: A Global Overview' in *The Desecularization of the World: Resurgent Religion and World Politics* op. cit. 3.

16. Christopher Partridge, 'Alternative Spiritualities, Occulture, and the Re-Enchantment of the West' in *The Bible in Transmission,* Summer 2005, 2. The text is available online at http://www.biblesociety.org.uk/exploratory/articles/partridge05.pdf (accessed 27/01/2008). See also his *The Re-Enchantment of the West,* 2 volumes (London: T & T Clarke, 2004).

17. Michel de Certeau, *The Practice of Everyday Life* (Berkeley: University of California Press, 1984).

18. See http://www.poemhunter.com/p/m/poem.asp?poet=7249&poem=198561 (accessed 27/01/2008) for the full text of the poem.

19. See Kevin J. Vanhoozer, 'Theology and the Condition of Postmodernity' op. cit. 23.

20. For an in-depth examination of these forces see Lynn Schofield Clark, ed., *Religion, Media, and the Marketplace* (New Brunswick, NJ and London: Rutgers University Press, 2007). See also Richard Cimino and Don Lattin, *Shopping for Faith: American Religion in the New Millennium* (San Francisco: Jossey-Bass, 2002).

21. See for example Ann W. Astell, ed., *Divine Representations: Postmodernism and Spirituality* (Mahwah, NJ/New York: Paulist Press, 1994).

22. See Marie L. Baird, *On the Side of the Angels: Ethics and Post-Holocaust Spirituality*

(Leuven-Paris-Dudley, MA: Peeters Publishers, 2002) 20–29.

23. See James Matthew Ashley, *Interruptions: Mysticism, Politics, and Theology in the Work of Johann Baptist Metz* (Notre Dame, IN: University of Notre Dame Press, 2002) 112 and 197–198.

24. Mark A. McIntosh, *Mystical Theology: The Integrity of Spirituality and Theology* (Oxford: Blackwell Publishing, 2005) 216–219.

25. See David Tracy, *On Naming the Present: God, Hermeneutics, and Church* (Maryknoll, NY: Orbis Books, 1994) 4.

26. See Stewart M. Hoover, *Religion in the Media Age* (Abingdon and New York: Routledge, 2006).

27. See Jürgen Habermas, *The Theory of Communicative Action. Volume Two: Lifeworld and System: A Critique of Functionalist Reason* (Boston, MA: Beacon Press, 1985).

28. See Paul Ricoeur, *From Text to Action*. Translated by Kathleen Blarney and John B. Thompson (Evanston: Northwestern University Press, 1991) 15, and *Oneself as Another*. Translated by Kathleen Blarney. (Chicago: University of Chicago Press, 1992) 141–145 and 165–168.

29. Stewart M. Hoover, *Religion in the Media Age* op. cit. 269–271.

30. See David Morley, *Home Territories: Media, Mobility, and Identity* (London and New York: Routledge, 2000); see also Mark Hansen, *Embodying Technesis: Technology Beyond Writing* (Ann Arbor, MN: The University of Michigan Press, 2000).

31. For a review of the identification of these forces see for example, Eileen Barker, ed., *Of Gods and Men: New Religious Movements in the West* (Macon: Mercer Press, 1983); Peter L. Berger, Brigitte Berger & Hansfried Kellner, *The Homeless Mind* (Harmondsworth: Penguin Books, 1974); Kenneth Gergen, *The Saturated Self: Dilemmas of Identity in Contemporary Life* (New York: Basic Books, 1991); Paul Heelas, *The New Age Movement: The Celebration of the Self and the Sacralization of Modernity* (Oxford: Blackwell Publishers, 1996, reprinted 1999); Vincent J. Miller, *Consuming Religion: Christian Faith and Practice in a Consumer Culture* (New York: Continuum, 2004); Jacob Needleman, *The New Religions* (New York: Crossroads, 1984); Philip Sampson, Vinay Samuel and Chris Sugden, eds, *Faith and Modernity* (Oxford: Regnum Books, 1994); Roy Wallis, *The Elementary Forms of the New Religious Life* (London: Routledge & Kegan Paul, 1984).

32. Vincent J. Miller, *Consuming Religion: Christian Faith and Practice in a Consumer Culture* op. cit. 5.

33. Mark A. McIntosh, *Mystical Theology: The Integrity of Spirituality and Theology* op. cit. 213-216.

34. See ibid. 219-239.

## CHAPTER 3

## Towards a Poetics of Spirituality

> *Poets teach us that words have the power*
> *to take root weed-like in the no-place of*
> *the desert and its shifting sands.*
>
> DAVID JASPER

### INTRODUCTION

What is spirituality about? This is a question that we have already begun to explore and will delve into more and more fully as this book unfolds, but for now the answer is that spirituality concerns what we do with the experience of being and becoming. At its best, spirituality reveals a self-forgetting attunement to a socially engaged self-transcending life. This is a life that implicates newer levels of cognitive, affective and operative congruence. At its most painful, spirituality is the search to fill a primal absence, the result of childhood loss or wounding. At its best, spirituality is an ascending path to a richer, more meaningful, healthier mode of being and living, one that engages with an honest and liberating discovery of the self-before-God. At its most aching, spirituality is a dark descent into the spaces of pain and loss, an addict's struggle to reconnect with a primal sense of lost goodness: the way forgotten under a dark blanket of unseeing.

Spirituality is a way of being authentically and lovingly human in the whole web of meaning, creativity, freedom, responsibility, sociality and relationality that mark human life on the planet today. As a process, spirituality engages with the rhythms of an often repressed centre of orientation and creativity that lies beyond the human ego. This centre allows dynamic expression to our inner depths, to the expansive, progressive and probing qualities of the human spirit, capacities that translate as creative and imaginative thought-and-action-in-the-world. Spirit is an axis that is alive, uniquely personal, purposeful, and courageous. Spirit is a centre of depth that makes new modes of experience possible: provided the human spirit is acknowledged and set free as the organising nucleus of a mature spirituality. Spirit engages with the paradox of a humanity that is always unique, always shared but not always responsibly owned.

Spirituality has to do with how we experience life and how we respond to life by actively engaging with the shaping forces of experience and its spiritually formative potential. Such engagement reveals spirituality as a life-transforming dance where the rhythms of self-transcendence and the songs of ultimate value weave new dynamics for fuller living. As we enter the dance and sing the songs we discover that spirituality is both a formative process and a life project that embrace the interweaving dynamics of human individuation and integration and their social consequences. As soon as we actively and self-implicatingly begin to confront the deeper questions of human life in the world today, especially when we learn to respond to them from a space of non-exploitive, respectful stillness and receptivity, we have begun to create a space for the sacred, to see beyond illusion, to find a new light for living. We have begun to craft a spirituality. That crafting work is a poetics of spirit, and metaphor is its creative building block.

More simply the question 'What is spirituality?' provides a spirit-based answer to the question, 'What does it mean to become fully human, fully alive?' In this chapter we will explore in some detail what this statement might mean. Before doing that, however, it is important also to note that spirituality grows in response to the challenges and invitations that emerge in the contexts of real life. Spirituality is always descriptive of the spirit-based and faith-based experiences lived by real people in real situations and in real locations, especially when they are revealed as moments in a spiritually formative and transformative process. This means that no two of us experience spirituality in precisely the same way because our life contexts and histories differ in so many distinctive ways.

The focus of this chapter is on a deepening reflection on the nature of spirituality today. The presentation is divided into several parts. What they all have in common is the desire to enter more fully into the undersong of spirituality today. We engage first with ten brief descriptions of the primary dimensions of human experience that are engaged when a person sets out on the path to a vibrant, transformative spirituality. Take each of the descriptions that follow as an invitation to critical self-reflection on the assumptions that guide your present understanding of spirituality and its formative elements. Then engage critically with the fuller reflections that follow.

## TEN DESCRIPTIVE REFLECTIONS

1. When we have begun to grapple with the question of what it is to be an authentic and effective human being; when we become aware of and grapple reflectively with the bright and the dark sides of our human experience, we have begun to craft a spirituality. As soon as

we have begun to question our own destructive and chaos-causing potentials; as soon as we begin to grapple with our own attractions and repulsions, with the shifting emphases that configure our identity, we have begun to craft a spirituality. When we begin to recognise and favour kindness and compassion, tenderness and care, appreciation and love; when we begin to favour active concern in our approaches to the other and the world, we have begun to craft a spirituality.[1] When we do such things we enter the world of poetics: imaginative and creative art in the service of spirit.

2. More specifically, as soon as we begin to reflect critically on the nature and demands of humane living, to develop a vision of human life to the full, to reflect on the nature and quality of being and existence in the world today, we have begun to construct a spirituality. As soon as we begin to question our self-concept; as soon as we choose to embrace growth and transformation, metanoia and conversion of life; as soon as we begin to attempt a decentred way of life, to embrace some form of responsible temperance and harmony, we have begun to construct a spirituality. As soon as we begin to walk lightly on the earth and through people's lives, we have begun to construct a spirituality. As soon as we focus on reflective action or praxis, and on ways of living more creatively; as soon as we begin to search for a more fruitful way beyond the obstacles that block the flourishing of virtue and the fullness of life, we have begun to step into the making of a spirituality.[2] Poetics names that mode of making in the service of spirit.

3. Spirituality also has to do with a commitment to awareness: without it nothing vital to the development of a spiritual lifestyle can really happen. Along with a commitment to awareness, spirituality also has to do with recognising ethical responsibility for meaningful change. Without such a sense of responsibility nothing much is going to change for the better. Responsive and responsible awareness lies at the heart of a life-changing spirituality. As soon as we begin to commit ourselves to conscious living, to awareness of what is happening inwardly and outwardly; as soon as we begin to attend with honesty and integrity to our streams of thinking and imagining, to the quality of our modes of knowing and experiencing, our ways of feeling and reacting, to the songs we sing and the dances we dance, we have begun to construct a spirituality and walk the poet's imaginatively crafting way in the service of spirit.

4. When we begin to reflect on the turbulence of our streams of thought and image, and attend with critical self-awareness to our sensory and

embodied experiences, we have begun to craft a spirituality. When we begin to reflect on unilaterally egoistical and self-centred, self-referred – or solipsist – and narcissistic forms of living and their inevitable personal and social diminishments, we have begun to walk a spiritual path. When we begin to seek a more enlightened understanding of all of the flows and streams that characterise our awareness, but more especially as we begin to meditate seriously and pray for the enlightenment of our minds, searching for the reasons of hope before God (Ephesians 1:18), we have begun to understand the core reflective and meditative practices that shape the crafting of a spirituality and the action it leads to in the world. Spirituality is about life in the real world. It serves spirit as a poet does through reflective and performative action, singing creatively in the world.

5. As soon as we begin to acknowledge consciously focused moral and aesthetic responses to life; as soon as we begin to search with commitment for a deeply reflective and responsible consideration of other forms of life and the natural world, we have begun to construct a spirituality. When we attempt to fill the creative and meditative spaces left vacant when science and technology have satisfied our material needs, we have begun to step into the realm of spirituality.[3] As soon as we begin to shake off the collusive consensual sleep that does not want disturbance, or change, or social responsibility; as soon as we begin to turn away from unconscious living and to responsibly recognise in ourselves the forces of social and religious marginalisation, the refusal to encounter otherness and difference whatever their form, we have begun to construct a spirituality and walk the way of the poet, that bearer of possible new worlds in the service of spirit.

6. We begin to construct a spirituality when we attempt to open the eyes of mind and heart, soul and spirit and gaze differently on the world; when we commit ourselves to taking more responsibility for life in all its worthwhile forms and expressions; when we begin to switch off habitual cruise controls and automatic pilots and the limiting and diminishing presuppositions, assumptions, habits of mind and expectations they reveal, we have begun to construct a spirituality. As soon as we begin to confront how literally absent-minded (out of mind) and blithely unaware we are of our own inner processes and their impacts, we have begun to construct a spirituality. We have found the way to a new, a poetic imagining, a new way of serving spirit.

7. Spirituality is about questions of heart and love, soul and spirit, mind and action, freedom and the limits of freedom, commitment and

integrity, insight, intuition and awareness. This means that as soon as we begin to come to terms with the challenges of congruent living where a harmony of inward and outward forces is demanded by honesty and integrity; as soon as we begin to wonder about the true nature of soul-making and spirit-living, of soul-song and spirit-dance, of divine rhythms and dangerous memory; as soon as we begin to ask questions about the universality of suffering, especially the suffering that accompanies the journey to self-knowledge and decentred living, as soon as we begin to wonder how to let Jesus live in the worlds we inhabit, we have begun to craft a spirituality. As soon as we begin to respond to suffering; as soon as we begin to grapple creatively with the disorienting dilemmas and crises that arise in real lives; as soon as we begin to engage, however hesitantly, with questions of ultimacy and death, we have begun to step into the realm of spirituality, hearing its creative challenges chanted on the winds of Spirit.

8. As soon as we begin to notice that religion is a realm of reverence and worship, that it is far more than a set of propositions; as soon as we begin to recognise that religion is a world in which awe and understanding, creativity and knowledge, reverence and the feeling of deep participation in ultimate reality and moral commitment are all of a piece; as soon as we begin to understand that such qualities are easily distorted, that they are easily cut off from each other and compartmentalised, we have begun to construct a spirituality really open to worship and wonder.[4] When we begin to hope for justice, fairness and hospitality in our local worlds, we have begun to construct a spirituality. As soon as we long for an honest world, open to utter Otherness, open even to the seemingly impossible, we have begun to understand the need for a politically and historically enlightened spirituality in a high-speed, high-tech, free-market, multi-media world of consumerised need and greed.[5] We have begun to discover the need to sing new songs and dance new dances to more disconcerting rhythms if spirit is to be served.

9. Spirituality is also about the sacred and the transcendent, the connection between believing and being. As soon as we begin to consider questions of self-transcendence, integration and transformation; as soon as we begin to engage in life orienting and supporting spiritual practices; as soon as we begin to develop spiritual literacies through reflective reading, conversation, study, pilgrimage, prayer or meditation, we have begun to craft a spirituality. As soon as we begin to reflect on and examine our mode of total functioning in the world and open our lives to transcendence and transformation, we have set our

feet on a spiritual journey, a journey into new spaces demanding new imagination, new ways to serve spirit.

10. Christian spirituality challenges us to consider maturely the question of God as the horizon of ultimate value in human life and experience.[6] As soon as we begin to wonder about God as creative and expansive presence, as soon as we begin to recognise Jesus as teacher-healer-and-saviour, as soon as we begin to ponder the Spirit as life-giver-and-empowerer, as soon as we reflect on the questions of difference in equality that a Triune God suggests, as soon as we begin to wonder about holiness as the gracious gift of the Holy One, as soon as we begin to consider their implications for a liberating way of life, we have begun to construct a Christian spirituality. As soon as we begin to seek the essence of human creativity as divinely gifted; as soon as we begin to seek to live with creative congruence and continuity, as soon as we discover that metaphor can evoke the God side of human experience, we have begun to walk a spiritual path, we have discovered the way of the contemplative poet who seeks to change the world by serving spirit, setting its creative rhythms to work in the world.

## THE MANY LAYERS OF SPIRITUAL EXPERIENCE

Spirituality may be depicted as a cluster of knowledges and practices that motivate and orient spiritual action in the world. Spirituality is the unifying field that brings together a wide array of concepts, ideas, beliefs, practices, literacies, narratives, texts, discourses, rituals, skills, techniques and understandings. In the best of all possible worlds, spirituality also includes an awareness of the destructive impact of human power relations with their inequalities and abuses; but often that awareness is sadly absent. Sometimes spirituality includes mainstream religious beliefs, sometimes not; sometimes it includes mainstream understandings of God, sometimes not. For believers, God, however hidden or absent and imageless, however present and iconically beautiful, is an essential partner in the spiritual journey, especially when God is experienced as the giver-and-gifter of personhood in the fullest and most creative senses of the word, the giver-and-gifter of all that is. In such contexts, theology becomes a significant conversation partner that helps us work through the private and public spiritual implications of our consciously and responsively held belief systems. Psychology is the conversation partner that helps us recognise our stages of development and maturity as we face the inner world of the self and the outer worlds of history and politics. Spirituality always raises questions of integrity and a harmonious or congruent life; and we wrestle with those questions in a world of metaphor.

### ℂ Religious and institutional influences

Contemporary spirituality has many forms and displays many expressions. These derive from the great world religions and their spiritual traditions as well as from non-religious or secular-humanist philosophical traditions.[7] What religious and non-religious forms of spirituality reveal is a concern for ways of life marked by integrity, creativity, ethical social engagement, love and justice. All authentic spiritualities today share a concern for the quality of human life and for the quality of planetary health, and are concerned about the socio-economic and political systems that impact so profoundly on human and planetary life. A spirituality that does not grapple with these issues and their implications for the well-being of all life on the planet is living a self-referred illusion. There is a problem here. None of the elements of life or the religious, social, cultural, economic or political structures that express them are encountered in neat and convenient ways. They are encountered in the messiness of existence itself and the self-interests that drive them. Issues around the quality of life, of planetary well-being, of economics and politics so often confront us with our inability to fully distinguish or separate spirituality from the socio-cultural contexts of life where it is challenged and lived.

The consequences of systemic and institutional life are also of founding concern to contemporary spiritualities, certainly to the extent that they are genuinely immersed in reality. Systems and institutions have actual impacts on life and the planet. Many of these are good and beneficial, but the ways in which they operate often include negative consequences. These are often the consequences of uncaring routine and bureaucratisation with their rationalisations: oppression, tyranny, injustice, deprivation, poverty, needless suffering and death, violence, addictions, pollutions, ecological disasters, species destruction, climate change – a list that grows by the day. Once spirituality is understood as an integral life project the challenge of such damaging forces becomes clear. They dare emerging spiritualities to engage progressively in building a better world, not just a comforting inner existence. Emerging spiritualities are challenged to redress such ills and to choose and empower life-giving and life-enhancing solutions when confronted by them. Spirituality has to do with depth. It uncovers the deep inner core of the human person where ultimate reality is experienced, and by implication the complex socio-political, socio-economic, and socio-environmental outcomes that flow from that experience: inward experiences have outward repercussions.

When the socio-cultural mainstream defines life in purely material and economic terms, when it is governed by a metaphor of unconditional personal happiness and greed, the results are systemically predictable:

- crime,
- corruption,
- wealth inequalities and imbalances,
- social dysfunction and violence,
- social and ecological disaster,
- corrupt abuses of personal and institutional power and position,
- and the self-aggrandising power-plays of hidden, secretive and self-interested power elites.

Spirituality is always contextual; it is always located in real lives and situated in real places. Spirituality finds its situated and located authenticity today to the extent that it is actively concerned with and confronts the working assumptions that govern the world and the power relationships they serve. Spirituality needs a vision. Whether we like it or not, spirituality has a responsibility to the future. In theological terms, spirituality has an eschatological character, a creative hope-filled openness to the future. It is meant to have a prophetic vision, to understand what needs to be done if things are to change. It is meant to have the active hope that people and society will change as the appropriate actions are taken, because hunger, injustice, and oppression are problems now; and our personal problem is the extent of our unaware collusions with them. We need engaged mystics attuned to the rhythms of soul and spirit in this world of ours.

❲ *The themes of meaning, suffering and alienation*
Spirituality also names clusters of value, virtue and meaning. It draws attention to aesthetic and moral value, to life and creational meaning. Spirituality draws attention to virtue as a naming of true human selfhood focused on qualitative styles of living. It draws attention to nature and the cosmos and the forces of nature and the cosmos, and how we interact with them. Spirituality draws attention to justice and the ways of justice, to the nature and uses or abuses of freedom. It also draws attention to the human situation and its situated predicaments: ecological and human devastation, the uncaring exploitation of human, social and natural resources. At its most incisive, spirituality is about human and creational purpose and destiny. It struggles to understand why we are here at all and it struggles with our grandiose self-centred illusions and the kind of world we are actually building today. In the end, spirituality is challenged to respond to humanity's deepest pain and torment, and to the groan of creation seeking its own creative completion as the cosmos seeks Christ. This cry is innately linked to and situated within the deafening dance of socio-economic and socio-political forces, ideologies and the power relations, rivalries and practices that underlie them.

All the great spiritual traditions have confronted and been confronted by the question of suffering. The same must be true even of partial or fragmented or patchwork contemporary spiritualities. Suffering is a space of convergence for all spiritualities even if they develop very different discourses on suffering that evoke very different practical responses and interventions. To do otherwise would be to gut the link between authentic spirituality and human creativity. After all, creativity is a defining human capacity. We are not meant to be slaves, colluders conniving with our own exploitation and the perversions of creativity that accompany it. Spiritually aware people know, recognise and act on these understandings of responsive and responsible creativity regardless of the fact that we live in a globalised consumer society – or would it be more accurate today to say that we exist in a globalised consumer economy?

In this sense, spirituality names the struggle against alienation of every kind. It names the search for freedom. Spirituality names the refusal to be trapped in an inverting world where alienation and fragmentation are daily confused with freedom. The spiritual stands against such inversions and the invisible cage that locks them into a purely material, purely economic view of humanity and the world. Authentic spirituality learns how to stand against economic determinism and the unilateral application of techno-economic ethics in human affairs. It knows that there is more to life. When imposed suffering, enslavements, addictions, collusions, and connivances become obstructions on the path of life, wisdom, portrayed as Lady Sophia (Proverbs 8), comes to our aid. We learn that these impositions and connivances are dead-ends not goals, blocks not portals. Lady Wisdom teaches us how to recognise them for what they are: the dead ends, illusions, and traps Dame Folly scatters in our way (Proverbs 9). Once recognised, such experiences become our teachers. They remind us that the goal of human freedom and creativity requires the direction of wisdom, but we have to be wisely awake and aware to discern it.

Teilhard de Chardin told us more than forty years ago that without hope-giving vision humankind is lost, lost here and now in pain and alienation precisely because there is no vision to motivate the necessary sacrifice, no vision to liberate the present as it faces the future.[8] Vibrant spirituality informs us that there is no need to wait. Reflective spiritual praxis has the wisdom and ability to let the vision grow and now is the time to do it. Spirituality is on the ascendancy, especially in the secular Western democracies. Elsewhere in the world religion is resurgent. There is a message here of some kind, a statement about the choices many people are making about life as it emerges from the horrors of the twentieth century. People seem to be saying that we need faith, ideals and values to guide our personal and social lives, to guide us onto paths of valid personal, social and ecological integration. People seem to be saying that it is time to re-engage with self-transcending motivations, the motivations that move spirituality and shape its wisdom-building literacies and transformative practices.

## ❦ *The dangers of spiritual rigidity and caricature*

It is also the time to be alert to the psychological and ethical dangers confronting spirituality in new rigidities, extremisms and self-oriented fanaticisms, as well as the dangers posed by a broad and often wilful ignoring of systemic, bureaucratic and institutional forms of oppression and the utter disregard they generate for people. This is especially so when people are perceived as vulnerable, or different, or powerless, particularly in situations where visions of rampant consumption have blinded people to the social meanings of redemption and the deep roots of genuine happiness. We need the audacity of spirit to confront these forces. In the best sense of the word, spirituality surfaces vital themes of human creativity, action, and practice as transcendence is discovered in the everyday challenges of ordinary life:

- in moments of love and concern,
- in moments of supportive solidarity,
- in moments of struggle against victimisation and unjust treatment,
- in moments of encounter with goodness, beauty and truth.

All of these are real. They are all tangible. They all echo to the challenge to be real, to be more than we believe we can be. They all challenge us to let Jesus live, to listen to soul-song and to let spirit dance again to the rhythms of deep, imaginative creativity, to become crafters of deeper visions.

Dislodged or severed from its self-implicating moral nature spirituality is revealed as a caricature, a parody, a puppet on a fraying string, a narcissist's comforting placebo. In such a guise spirituality is like the deluded Emperor's new clothes: visible only to the politically correct and the sycophantic, the servants of illusion, a lip-serving illusion lacking substance, a latter-day chant of cant and humbug. On the other hand, authentic spirituality is able to maintain a capacity for creative coherence and the well-grounded moral indignation it makes possible. Those who embrace authentic spirituality struggle to generate a better world even if it is only in their own small, local situations. Authentic spirituality must favour spirit. It must reject a world colluding with world-destroying forces. The challenge is to permit spirituality to emerge as a force for wise change in all the many creative ways and meanings the idea of change and change-based practices intimate. Authentic spirituality is in favour of healing, of peace, of reconciliation, of transformation. Transforming spirituality stands against systematic exploitation of every kind and the murderous intent that often shadows it.

Spirituality seeks nothing less than life to the full, life beyond the new imperialisms, colonialisms and racisms that litter our paths with their distorting distinctions. Real spirituality seeks a counter-cultural stance, something giftingly possible to an audacious spirit standing for the ways of liberating wisdom in a world of dismantled, deregulated fragments. Spirituality teaches us that alienation is not a natural law. It is always in the end the product of choice, the product of how life is organised, oriented and expressed, the result of anti-spiritual structures and dynamics. The present ecological crisis is emblematic of the new alienation. By allowing ourselves to be detached from our embeddedness in the natural world, we have all colluded with the present state of affairs and are still very reluctant to face its personal and social consequences. Issues around energy supply and energy use make that very plain. It seems that we want to leave the solution of such vexing issues to future generations as our soured, spoiled heritage. The result is that species survival is already at risk. If we continue to be spiritually alienated from the natural world, the more the disaster will threaten. In the end, real spirituality is about real lives and the world-impacting consequences of real choices. We have to listen to the song of soul; we have to rediscover the dance of spirit if we are to save the world.

## Towards a Poetics of Spirituality
( *The poetic spirit: bearer of possible worlds*
With origins dating back more than two millennia to the Greek philosophers, poetics has been closely identified with the world of literary criticism. Poetics sits in the centre of a triad of related words: *poet*, *poetics* (from the Greek *poiesis*), and *poetry*. The poetics is the inner-work-of-making that finds public expression in a poem. Spirituality is an inner work of the creating spirit that also finds audacious public expression in the creative rhythms of a transformed life: a living poem, a work in progress. Is it any wonder, then, to discover that mystics are often poets and singers and dancers, men and women attuned to the depths of human purpose and destiny? Think for a moment about Thomas Merton's poetry and Hildegard von Bingen's songs. Is it any wonder, then, that poets are often mystics? Think of Patrick Kavanagh, or Evelyn Underhill, or Francis Thompson, or Raïssa Maritain, or Helder Camara, or Emily Dickinson, or Gerard Manley Hopkins, or Denise Levertov. To live spirituality, to enter into its deepest potentials and engage in a making is to become a poet, a singer, a dancer, a weaver, a builder, a constructor, a creator: a crafter of unprecedented melodies that open portals to possible worlds.[9]

The poetic spirit reveals itself in the conventional and in the unconventional encounters with beauty, with what is good and true, the things that point to more, tracing a beckoning path beyond. It is there in the bright intensity of a gaze. It is there in a child's cry. It is there where the sharp panes of a face soften with a quizzical smile or a fleeting wink. The poetic spirit is there in the wheeling of birds and the splish-splash leaping of hungry fish, hoovering hovering may-fly and drifting spider. It is there in the drone of a bumble bee in summer, that weighty carrier of pollen-brushed promise of new life, and it plays peek-a-boo in the crackle of frosty grass underfoot of a winter's morning. It is there in the blushing buds that herald spring's child-like innocence. It is there in bronzed leaves dancing as bright reds rustle to the mature songs of trees on hills in autumn winds. The poetic spirit is there in a lover's look and the turn of a head. It is there in the noticed unpredictability of things and their playful wildness.

A poetics of spirit is fitting because it names a creative process of recollected composition, the making skill that moulds and orients a poet's and a mystic's ability to reveal the inner shape and meaning of things in a way that transcends modernity's fascination with bland branded sameness, the sameness of a deadening consensus. The poet, in the same way as the spiritual seeker, is also challenged by the realities of difference and indeterminacy that characterise the postmodern predicament we now face. The poet like the mystic pushes against the imprisoning boundaries of defensive certainties and their frozen, fettered visions. They push against every kind of totalising tendency and self-absorbing spirit. They seek the spaces of clearness and compassion that transcend the small-minded visions of those who have forgotten the question of life. As the Greeks of long ago understood it, poetics is both an active making and a creative enterprise that asserts the constructive visioning power of human imagination to express human longing and human transcending, and explore the deep questions of human ultimacy.

The ancient Celts believed that true poets carried within them the power not only to make new worlds but to unmake old ones. It was enough for the true poet to declaim the new for it to come into being and for people to live it. This is the power of spirit and spirituality when the audacity of creating spirit is set free to dance and fly in the world. Our forebears understood that poetics takes us beyond the conceptual; that it crosses into real lifeworlds where the challenges of life in all its rag-and-bone messiness and potential madness, its boiling wildnesses and foolish-nesses, are to be met. This is an accurate name for the making that comes to light in true spirituality. The poetic spirit makes things visible to us in ways that confront us with the whole gamut of human moods and emotions, with their highs and lows, their waxings and wanings, their heavenly and their underworld habitats full of sometimes bright, sometimes dark and often unrecognised stirrings of desire. This is also an accurate describing of the challenges and frustrations of spirituality: the encounter with the real and the unrecognised, the movements of openness and the movements of resistance. There is much for contemporary spirituality to engage with in these ancient intuitions.

What makes a poetics of spirit particularly attractive as an approach to the study of spirituality, then, is not just its discursive capacity but its capacity to make discourse sing and find its own particular rhythms and music. It gives spiritual practice and discourse a symbolic charge that hints at hidden meanings and a rich harvest of possibility awaiting active expression. We should not be surprised to discover, then, that spiritual, mystical and poetic texts are treasure gardens of creative combinations of meaning coming together in indeterminate arrays of rich and spirited metaphor. They have the potential to open portals to an equally indeterminate array of creative possibilities and lively enactments. They embody critical questioning and crucial imagining. They dance in worlds of embodiment and character portrayal that reveal ever-deepening paths to soul and soul truth. This is yet another reason why spirituality today successfully eludes concise technical definition. Poets do not simply define poetry, they write it and sing it, and try to live by it. So do saints and mystics. Here is another metaphor: spirituality is symphonic. If that is so, where are the limits to its possible personal and social trajectories?

### ℂ The nature of a poetics of spirit

Poetics is an act of seeing widely with clear eyes and a discerningly creative mind.[10] That poetics is a way of seeing the world and a way of wrestling with reality is the basis of its role in the study and practice of spirituality, itself a way of seeing the world and wrestling with reality. A creative poetics of spirit challenges any spirituality seeking contemporary authenticity to grapple with the absences, isolations, lonelinesses and oppressions that afflict so many people in the present-day world. As a way of seeing and wrestling with reality poetics also challenges us to take notice of the inarticulate; to pay heed to the silenced victims of voice stealers, to grapple with the marginal, the superficial, the fragmented, the disenchanted, dismantled, dissatisfied and ignored aspects of real lives; and to imagine what might lie hidden within such experiences. A poetics of spirit is tasked to imagine beyond the places of spiritual complacency and the crafting of safe spiritual comfort zones; though it will appreciate why such zones are crafted. That is why a poetics of spirit challenges us to embrace the visible with what it renders invisible, and the indeterminate arrays of bright/dark opposites that depict human lives and human selves in a contingent universe. The poetic criterion is to notice the world clearly as it is; to notice the traces of meaning, detect the auras of pathos, figure out the places of deception and corruption, and spot the hints of transcendent energy hidden in the hearts of things.[11]

The term 'poetics of spirit' is not used here in a Hegelian key. It refers instead to a process of continuing spiritual discovery and developmental unfolding throughout the human life cycle. It is a creative process: there is no ladder to the Absolute to discard.[12] Here, poetics of spirit describes a critically reflective spiritual practice that imaginatively and creatively crafts language and life in the continuing service of spirit. A poetics of spirit is itself an enactment of spirit, itself an engaged spiritual practice. It is a way of viewing the world from the perspective of spirit and its dynamic presence in the world. Properly understood, a poetics of spirit engages with the perceptual fields in which spiritualities flourish or decay. An engaged poetics of spirit seeks to evoke a felt-sense that leads to a self-implicating understanding of spiritual consciousness and its diverse enactments. By its very nature an engaged poetics of spirit challenges spiritual pilgrims to actively care for spirit and its manifold expressive and practical concerns in and for the world.

The test of any poetics is the notice paid to the surfaces that hide and obscure potential promises of depth: the dying body, the ritual gesture quickly made, and the lifted head (Psalm 3:3c). Such a poetics invites us not only to see what is, but to sense or intuit what is becoming; what is attempting to emerge from stasis and hiding, what is not able to say itself in the world: intricate patterns of iridescent wings not yet ready to risk the winds of freedom, unlike Mary in Denise Levertov's poem Annunciation:[13]

> Bravest of all humans,
> consent illumined her.
> The room filled with its light,
> the lily glowed in it,
> and the iridescent wings.

Poetics responds creatively to moments of earth-shattering consent. It understands that the human spirit dancing with Divine Spirit is the generative force in spirituality. Poetics also recognises the incompleteness of things, the unreadiness and the unwillingness of people to break free of unquestioned assumptions and risk the wings of Spirit. A spiritually attuned poetics explores the edge places where More Than beckons and giftingly calls; and the in-between spaces where fear fearfully whispers.

A genuine poetics will always respond to the rhythms of human desire: the interplays of a Moses baulking four times (Exodus 3 & 4) and a Mary responding at once (Luke 1:26-38). Such are the spaces where the creative urge trembles till at last eros and agape embrace each other and lift life into a new space, crafting new channels for the ways of Holy Spirit in the world. Poetics is well placed to wrestle with the fire of heaven and the God of light: that aspect of spirituality which images a walking in transforming, testing fire (1 Peter 1:7; 1 Corinthians 3:12-15). These new channels are also good places to recall the niggling links between poetics and politics, of flights into Egypt to escape infanticide (Matthew 2:13-15) and Gethsemane betrayals after the alleluias have been silenced (Mark 14:32-50). In a spirituality that is defined in terms of practice and performance poetics and politics inextricably intersect. Poetics as a way of seeing the world and politics as a way of organising and controlling social life confront us with the power gradients and inequalities that touch and wound lives.

The tangles of poetics and politics must be attended to if a socially passionate spirituality is to reshape the world to the rhythms of integrity: a recurring theme in the vision of spirituality that informs this text. The tangles of poetics and politics must be attended to if the whole world is to fall under the gaze of a passionate spirituality. This is why a poetics of spirit should hold a primary place in the study and practice of spirituality. Such a poetics is ethically challenged to see reality as it is, to embrace the contemplative vision that pierces veils of unexamined assumptions and illusions, and so engage with real-life spaces teeming with undecided presences and ambiguous caricatures hinting of promise. The task is to reach out however tentatively to the things ignored and the things repudiated in those spaces to discover what beauty, or truth, or traces of the holy might be hidden there. Such is the creative responsibility of every committed spiritual pilgrim. Spirituality is all too easily betrayed by the arrogances and intolerances that flow from the complacencies of self-crafted, self-serving perceptions of uniqueness. The integrity of a poetics of spirit rests on the ethically creative refusal to turn a blind eye to anything. That is the strength of a poetics of spirit, and its ground for humility and respect.

A poetics of spirit shares qualities with the poetics of testimony that is familiar to students of recent theology.[14] This is an approach to theology that breaks the silence that so often meets survivor accounts, victim stories, memoirs of marginalised people: the biblical cry of the poor and oppressed (Proverbs 21:13). A poetics of spirit calls for self-implicating action, an engaging with the jarring, disruptive, discordant notes such stories strike for comfortable, self-referred spiritualities. Like a poetics of testimony, a poetics of spirit provides a way of seeing and moving beyond the constraining threshold of rational discourse. It offers a way of reimagining, reshaping, refiguring and re-exploring spirituality; of reimagining its transformative role and responsibility in the world. To the extent they are self-implicating, personal and communal spiritualities uncover the potential to become paths of jarring, counter-cultural testimony.

Creative redescription of reality lies at the heart of the human spirit's meaning-making capacities. These capacities take on theological significance when they are opened in turn to the transforming grace of the Holy Spirit.[15]

Like a poetics of testimony, a poetics of spirit becomes a path to living testimony. It does this by changing the spiritual imagination of practitioners and their practices. In the grace of the Spirit, a changed spiritual imagination leads to changed socio-cultural expressions and impacts. By this means a poetics of spirit not only allows us to respect the aesthetic and mimetic or modelling aspects of spiritual practice by reimagining spiritual experience and its expression in the world, it also exposes the self-revealing nature of spirituality. A poetics of spirit unfolds how the dance of spirituality is understood and choreographed within the multifaceted modern-day quest for spiritual nurturance, expression and meaning. In so doing poetics is revealed as a space within which speech itself is a spiritual act with transformative force. And so a poetics of spirit must be willing to wrestle honestly with the polyphony of practices, voices and stories that characterise contemporary spirituality; to dance with a potent mix of intersecting religious, political, gendered, literary, ecological and cultural orientations, and the governing myths, metaphors, and narrative worlds they each imply.

Two foundational realities represent the point of convergence for the thematics introduced to this point, and what will follow. The first refers to the role ambience, awareness, consciousness, commitment, creativity, freedom, wisdom, value, action and engagement play in human spirituality. The second refers to the counter-role played by human weakness; its penchant for self-serving and defensive choices and the long, tragic, exploitive and oppressive shadows they cast. On the one hand, spirituality enacts the search for a fulfilled, meaningful, happy, and worthwhile existence. On the other, it is confronted by a more fraught, more disturbing, more Othello-like reality. Both have to do in the end with how we handle vulnerability, how we handle ambience and context, how we handle the forces of attraction and repulsion that shape and mould our ability to value life, and the attachments that serve or block it. The converging impact of creative awareness and self-serving weakness is felt in a wide variety of different ways, and poetics of spirit, an inventive mode of metaphorical speculation about spirituality, offers a creative approach to exploring their endless interplay.

The difference between poetics and technical language lies in the use of metaphor. Through the lens of metaphor a poetics of spirit enables a progressive, critical investigation of the worlds of spirit and their many manifestations. Such investigation engages with spirituality in its numerous forms, practices, expressions, literacies, discourses and narratives.

It remains alert to the acts of contextual communication, interpretation and definition through which soul-song and the dance of spirit reach out to touch the world. A poetics of spirit enables spiritual pilgrims to dance responsively to metaphor's rhythms and give fresh voice to the songs of soul. By its very nature a poetics of spirit is endlessly responsive. It responds to both the spontaneous and the ritually constructed aspects of spirituality; it responds to the artistry and creativity of spirituality and its idiosyncratic, commonplace expressions. An engaged poetics of spirit responds to place, to the desert and to the lush places, to chapels and caves, to holy wells, and lakes and seas. It responds equally to particularity and universality, to the individual and the collective, to the one and the many.

The spaces for a poetics of spirit are limited only by a lack of creative imagination grounded in attentive, embodied awareness. A poetics of spirit responds to times of socio-political upheaval, poverty and distress, and to times of peace, prosperity and social wellbeing. An engaged poetics of spirit responds to delusion and clarity, ignorance and wisdom, greed and loving kindness, anger and compassion, hatred and forgiveness, revenge and reconciliation. Only the songs and dances change. A poetics of spirit is at home in the interweaving processes of creativity and receptivity. It is at home in processes that run clear like crystal streams, and those that are muddied, turgid and opaque. A poetics of spirit dances with processes of association and dissociation, with processes of circulation and closure, of rapport and disagreement, of presence and absence. A poetics of spirit affirms that the human spirit is active, dancing with the Holy Spirit in the sometimes-arduous worlds of social relations, the worlds where subject and object swirl and whirl together, now in a dance of creative unfolding, now in the rhythms of emancipation and the singing of free people: self-serving, conniving weakness overcome in a flow of transforming awareness.

The core themes of spirit, psyche and soul arise against this double horizon of creative awareness and self-serving weakness. Soul, as the ground of spirit and psyche, is not only the living, beating axis of spirituality it is also a prime focus for a poetics of spirit. But such a poetics is in some guise at the mercy of what is happening to the concept of soul today, and the clusters of disparate and discordant meanings that constellate around it. In the contemporary West, soul has suffered the loss of a wise and richly informed spiritual literacy, and many of us have only blurred, childhood-based notions of what soul might mean. There are many lost subtleties of meaning to be rediscovered as we attempt to construct vibrant and creative spiritualities for today. We have to learn afresh that soul names the animating essence of life; that soul is the depth within where the life-giving portal of divine presence awaits fresh discovery.

Soul also facilitates our deepest, most reflective, most potentially transformative and integrative perspectives on life and God, and all that is. And then we have to take into consideration the impacts of psychology and philosophy on understandings of soul, especially those grounded in the Enlightenment agenda and its turn to rationalist, reductive and naturalist forms of science.

Because of its grounding in soul and spirit, spirituality resists and evades attempts at tight technical definition. It is best served by an approach grounded in poetics. Poetics, in the form of poetics of spirit, also names a particular approach to writing about spirituality, writing that is less about critical argument and the logic of concepts and more about experience, feeling, narrative, imagination and representation. It names a metaphoric and imaginative approach to spirituality intended to focus responsive, transformative and generative attention. A poetics of spirit does this by describing contemporary issues and connections in spirituality and speculating on them in ways that are critically grounded in experience. But even then poetics is not simply about description. More to the point, a poetics of spirit names a form of critical relational and illustrative reflection intended to focus attention on spiritual meanings, definitions, approaches, practices, literacies and discourses as these arise within spiritual contexts. Poetics does this by making the structuring and orienting presences in spiritual contexts decipherable through the imaginative use of metaphor.

A poetics of spirit starts with situated realities but stretches responsively and generatively beyond them, becoming a spiritual practice and discourse in the process. A poetics is a praxis in which responsive understandings interacting with ethical action play a critical role. In a poetics, focus turns to people's living and embodied practices, the new worlds of spirit these practices reveal, and the responses they evoke. A poetics of spirit helps us to ask serious questions about the ways spiritual practices connect to the whole of life. Poetics does this by shaping an orienting experience-based metaphor that allows a creative unfolding of spiritual themes, issues, and questions. It also unfolds how they actually organise and orient different forms of human experience. We have already met the metaphor that is central to this chapter: it is there in the words *way, path* and *journey*. It is also present in words like *seeking* and *questing* and *sojourning*, and it is there in related references to *life, change* and *authenticity*. A poetics of spirit is provisional, nomadic, a work in progress. It represents a snapshot of a moment in an unfolding story. A poetics of spirit is desperately needed in the worlds of religion and spirituality as late modern and postmodern consumer visions of life and motivations for living bite and dismantle our received ways of understanding what is real.

Poetics is especially appropriate to times of change and crisis because poetics allows us to grapple resourcefully and hopefully with an uncertain future. It is particularly suitable to spaces where experiences dynamically swirl and merge and twirl again and disappear into the welter of movement that walking along the way entails. Poetics is about the dance of reality and illusion and discerning the difference between them. A poetics of spirit shifts between themes, attending to contemporary evolutions, to traditional discourses, to popular movements and pieties and their characteristic practices. It traces fragments of life as they reveal the traces of soul and spirit, the hints and seeds of divine presence, recognising husks empty of life, pointers only to the illusions that never nourish soul or spirit. To engage in a poetics of spirit is already to engage with a foundational spiritual practice. To look reflectively, to engage as a participant observer in a field where all of life intermingles and reveals tangles of spirit, is already to become a practitioner of spirituality if only because the poetics becomes a mirror in which facets of self and self-transcending choice are glimpsed.

At the end, poetics is about incidence and expression, about the dancing in and out of things, about serendipity and the patchwork bricolage that makes use of whatever is to hand, about the muddled, superficial quality of much of life and so of much of spiritual life. It is also about incisive moments and unexpected insights, and the utterly ordinary muddiness and messiness and drama of things and what makes them unique to a moment or a person, or a group, or a practice, or a discourse. Poetics helps us to deal with the spontaneity and unexpectedness of things, the things that keep us alert and the quieter things we more easily miss in our often distracted lives. Ultimately, a poetics of spirit is about pertinence and making sense in spiritual lives and contexts; but it is also about impertinence and parody and the capacity to laugh at the deceptively heroic and the mulishly arrogant theatricalities of the human drama. A poetics of spirit embraces the position of the wise-holy-fool and so comes to a different, more creative awareness.

## Five Advantages

A method grounded in poetics offers at least five advantages to the exploration of spirituality. First, it permits us to identify and develop two basic vectors of contemporary spirituality: exploration and expression. Like all good poems, all good spiritualities share these two qualities. They explore life and relationships; they explore their meanings. Then they express value and commitment and loving compassion in the realities of every day. A poetics, like spirituality, is also suggestive, evocative, motivational and reflexive rather than technical and scientific. It favours the exploration and expression of such foundational themes as life and death, prayer and meditation, heart and soul, spirit and psyche.[16] As well as being expressive in both private and public behaviours a poetics of spirit also honours the cognitive and affective dimension of human life in ways that challenge attention and demand imaginative engagements and behaviours.

Secondly, if a poetics is a symphony, a polyphony of themes and images, constructions and possibilities, then a spirituality is a living polyphony of understandings, practices, engagements and orientations. It is a symphonic testimonial to soul and spirit and psyche alive and active in the world, attempting to make a difference, finding expression in the poetry of a vibrantly transformative life project. A poetics of spirit is rich in conceptual metaphor and imaginative analogy. Conceptual metaphor and imaginative analogy are both at home with symbolic language and the various modes of meaning mapping open to the human mind as it seeks liberating truth. The truth of spirituality, like the truth of poetry and music and art, is participative. Like meaning, spiritual process is presented in ways that are always unfinished, a dance in process. There is always more to be accomplished, more to be imaginatively said.

Like art, spirituality manifests meaning by simultaneously revealing and veiling it. They both hint at what our ancestors called thin places, places where the divine is glimpsed through a diaphanous veil that hides even as it gloriously and mysteriously reveals. Like art, spirituality invites self-implicating, living response. What this means is that participating in it, living its beauty, expressing its goodness, orienting life by it, reveals the truth of spirituality. This is true also of spiritual theology. Both are invitations to a way of life, ways of reflecting deeply on life before God and the awesome expansiveness of God in lives that are faithfully open.[17] However, while spirituality, theology, and poetics share common interests, a spiritual poetics is not the same as a systematic theology. The two can be readily told apart, even in the complementary nature of their relationship; the clue is in the descriptive word, *systematic*. That said the intimate relationship between an approach to spirituality informed by a poetics of spirit and practical theology is more obviously apparent. There, too, the clue is in the descriptive word, *practical*.

By claiming, however implicitly, that the truth of spirituality is revealed by living it we encounter two pivotal questions. How conceivable are patterns of spiritual life? How intelligible are they? The answer is sought by looking critically at questions of coherence and concord focused on the interplay of three significant processes:

- · understandings of reality,
- · the quality of loving kindness or compassion towards all that is,
- · the demands of justice.

But we need to be careful not to turn references to these three processes into another systemsworld rationalisation, a set of rigid rules. Rather than defining what spirituality manifests they are intended to help in recovering and responding to what is made visible in spiritual styles, practices and engagements. Reality, loving-kindness and justice are themselves situated and located in lifeworlds. They are not abstractions. They are human experiences subject to human distortions and power plays. In effect, they are to be used with critical awareness and applied discerningly.[18]

The third advantage of a poetics of spirit concerns the uncovering of the interpretive grammar or meaning matrix that lies behind the structuring and orienting of a specific form of spirituality. This has to do with the ways in which such structural elements operate. A spiritual grammar is fundamental to the recognition of shaping forces. Elements in such a grammar include:

- goals, perceptions, and justifications;
- issues around authority and power;
- questions to do with identity, relationships, and commitments;
- modes of spiritual transmission and formation;
- stages of human, spiritual and faith development;
- questions to do with openness and rigidity;
- issues related to sites of truth and sources of legitimation;
- the typical forms of emotional energy or affect, thought, and action;
- understandings of ego and self, especially of the wounded ego and the potential self;
- understandings of the other and respect for the other;
- the health or otherwise of understandings of love and self-giving;
- understandings of struggle and suffering;
- questions of ultimacy and the sacred.

In faith-based spiritualities central theological and creedal issues become significant elements in this grammar of spirit. An accurate grammar of spirit helps us to understand the forces and processes that converge in the various features that give a specific spirituality its characteristic tone, validity and pattern of praxis.

Fourthly, a poetics is concerned to unfold the contexts and processes underlying the locations, endeavours and predicaments of everyday life that confront spirituality as a coherent form of social practice. This helps us to recognise that a spirituality open to social solidarity is also open to self interrupting concerns and the potential irritations of the other who makes demands or is disturbingly different. For example, does a spirituality help those who practise it to stand consistently against social oppressions? Do practitioners refuse to be spiritual voyeurs, self-indulgent watchers rather than concerned activists? Does a spirituality help practitioners to shoulder social responsibility? Does it help them to break free of self-absorbed lifestyles and their corrupting potentials? Spiritualities that are socially open and supportive in such ways refuse to forget those who suffer, refuse to close eyes to what is happening around them and the socio-political or socio-economic needs that are apparent. Authentic spiritualities refuse pretence. They seek authenticity and coherence. They remain socially receptive. Above all they remain alert to the forces of social and moral depletion and diminishment, to the forces of hate, to the anguished cry for freedom. Questions such as these have the potential to take us beneath the surface of the rich array of spiritualities that dot the contemporary landscape and discern their social value.

The fifth advantage of a poetics is its interdisciplinary openness, its capacity to weave a way through the borderlands and transitional spaces where different approaches, methodologies and disciplines sometimes uneasily, sometimes playfully and creatively meet. Poetics reminds us to allow spirituality to be an audacious space where many possibilities and potentials learn to dance something new into being. This is particularly evident in the way poetics allows critique and imagination to play together with the stuff of spirituality to support new understandings, new horizons of meaning. Good examples of such a space are to be found in interdisciplinary approaches to the study of forgiveness and reconciliation, foundational aspects in a personally and socially transformative spirituality. Other examples are found in the cross-disciplinary study of spirituality in the health and social services worlds, and the worlds of business and adult education. At the same time, an appropriately critical poetics alerts spirituality to the dangers of self-involved reflection. Genuine spirituality is always confronted by the other, the surprising, gifting Other in the quest for meaning and life.[19] In its openness to meaning and life poetics inevitably leads us to the places where metaphors sing.

### ℭ The role of analogy and identification

Analogy, that other powerful engine of discovery, is a way of thinking found everywhere in spirituality and spiritual texts. Its role is intricate, complex, powerful and foundational. Much the same can be said of mental images as well as metonymy – where an attribute of something stands for the thing itself (her heart was throbbing with love, is a typical example). The narrative reasoning characteristic of many spiritual texts that uses story form and shared imaginative worlds to explore the causes, connectedness and outcomes of experiences and events embodies the quality of analogy. Parables, fairy-tales and myths are typical examples, so are biographical accounts and hagiography. Most expressions of affect and emotional energy also make creative use of analogy: *he hedged his delight with expressions of self-doubt and resistance* is a typical example where the image of a hedge grounds the analogy with St Augustine's *ready, but not yet*; so is *an outpouring of Spirit* with its imaginative analogy to flowing water.

Analogy is a means of understanding a thing or a relationship by reference to another thing or relationship that is similar in some respects and different in others. It is based on the perception of partial likenesses. A typical example in theology is Augustine's famous analogy: *the soul is to the human body what the Holy Spirit is to the Body of Christ* (*Sermones* 267). The *analogy of spirit* is the pivotal example in spirituality. Through the analogy of spirit the human spirit is depicted as a centre of dynamic, self-present and probing creativity by analogy with the Holy Spirit. By matching and aligning the two, analogy makes understanding easier. Analogy is also a form of mapping that allows inferences to arise, reasons for change to be identified, and spiritually transformative identification to take place. In Christian spirituality, for example, identification with Christ plays an essential underpinning role in understanding the dynamics of spiritual processes, purposes and aspirations (1 Corinthians 2: 12-16), and the representative behaviour and integrity of Jesus remains fundamental to the Christian practice of identification.

Identification with persons and places unleashes psychospiritual power that impacts consciously and unconsciously on people. It influences how they feel, think and behave and in the process generates personal and communal identity. Processes of identification form the basis for life orientation in spirituality, especially the identification of relevant human or religious qualities. Processes of identification generate fidelity to a tradition with its practices and discourses. For example, identification processes influence the bonds of unity, solidarity and mutual support that typify twelve step spiritualities; they help us to see in ourselves what we see in others, and in the process they also help us not only to disidentify from destructive practices but to re-identify with healthier, more creative possibilities. Identification also helps us to grasp how forces of meaning integrate and come together through imaginative and valuing processes when we engage in reflection and thought, in narrative, discourse, writing and conversation. And given the power and influence of identification processes it should come as no surprise that they also form the base of brand success in consumer societies.

Like poetry and song, spirituality is indebted to metaphor, analogy and identification and their sibling tropes as it seeks to explore, understand, integrate and describe the domains, terrains, forms and expressions of spirit. In fact, we take the underlying mental dynamics of metaphor, analogy and identification so much for granted that we are rarely aware that we are using them. Along with the use of figurative language, all three lie at the heart of both poetry and spirituality. In effect, poetics helps us to understand that spirituality is a kind of living poem in search of completion, a kind of unfinished symphony, a work in progress.[20] Do not be surprised then to encounter intimations of metaphor and analogy, identification, integration, imagination and value everywhere in spirituality. Spirituality like love is an adventure of discovery, a precious object to be handled gently and reverently, relished like a fine dish prepared by the Master Chef.

### ℂ The problem of fixed definitions

Poetics and spirituality both serve to reveal, express, question, promote, invite and persuade; though it is worth recalling that poetics prefers to surmount purely conceptual systematisations and the globalising or fixed definitions so beloved of the modern mind. How are dimensions of experience that verge on the inexpressible to be finally categorised? How is the dynamically unfolding expression of the human spirit to be captured in tight and generic synthesis when the forces of uniqueness and difference that shape its individual, local, and gendered expressions are taken into account? How can fixed definitions be given to the search for and the attempt to give living expression to humankind's deepest existential anxieties? A vibrantly transformative spirituality must disentangle itself from such rigidities and limits. How can closed definitions be given to the unique creativity and thrust for freedom that reveals the human spirit? We need an imaginative approach today that respects the reality of spirit and its inherent need to express dynamic, self-present, probing creativity. We need an inventive approach to the repressed spirituality hidden in these anxieties and questions We need a generous and respectful standpoint (1 Peter 3: 15) that is not afraid to dialogue with the wild variety and profusion of spiritual forms dancing into deregulated postmodern freedom in a world desperately seeking re-enchantment, desperately in need of the dynamic audacity of spirit.

Both poetics and spirituality confront us with uncertainty, bewilderment, mystery, awe, depth, and insight. They also confront us with the shallow, the petty, the small-minded and the rigidly one-dimensional. Through creative play spirituality protests how things are and contends with present presuppositions, rigidities and compromises, just as spirit strains towards a different visioning and a self-altering, transforming desire. Properly understood, spirituality is complex, many-voiced, multi-local, multi-modal. It is socio-politically and socio-historically charged. This is why a poetics of spirit is so appealing: it offers a way of doing justice to a term that itself proves extremely difficult to restrain and constrain, such is the breadth of meaning and the range of linkages assigned to it in contemporary usage. We live in a transitional time when a disenchanting modernity is losing its arrogant swagger and smirk; its power to decide what everything means challenged by a flowering of new possibilities.

The aptitude for a generous, gentle and respectful response is what makes poetics so appealing as a mode of expressing and exploring the innovative nature and mission of spirituality today. This is especially so in postmodern contexts with their cacophonies of competing and contesting voices. A generous, gentle, contemplatively aware and respectful stance is particularly necessary in fragmented and provisional contexts heaving with power-laden, conflicted and conflicting encounters. It is also demanded in contexts where affect-laden monologues shout across each other like deaf political hacks, closed faces shouting to little purpose and less effect as they slither on surfaces that provide little access to the depth of spirit.

So many lives are lived out today in shadowed and shallow spaces that provide little support for constructive self-care or communal commitment, callous worlds of lost social concern and absent responsiveness. Such worlds challenge elitist spiritualities, deadening religiosities and reality-denying ghetto mentalities, and rightly call them to account. Spirituality is more than a chameleon's shadowy comfort zone. It is not a security bunker. Spirituality is both a life project and a form of discourse and practice that calls incessantly for healthy self-scrutiny and critical reflection on personal and collective governing assumptions and meaning systems, as well as their perceptual frameworks and accompanying habits of mind. How else is spirituality to dance or sing with the temporal, economic, socio-cultural and socio-religious challenges that constantly and relentlessly rhythm the human spirit into being, spurring it to make creative not destructive choices?

Spirituality bespeaks a making and an unmaking, a dying and a rising; it is a potentially transforming force seeking transcendence and justice, arguing for a world where all are respected; searching for spaces where suffering, poverty and devastation are defied with inventive honesty. Spirituality not only plays with metaphors and myths, it also plays with the images and intimations that flow from our shared cultural and religious heritage, heritages that invite us into the dance with paradox and mystery, that help us to intuit and unfold the creative rhythms of their deep essence. Attention to poetics helps us to remember that spirituality is a meditative, reflective process that allows imaginative thinking and rethinking about life to take place in resourceful languages that serve to bring together thought and feeling, values and ideals, integrity and justice, and common sense actions for the good of all that is.

## POETICS: ADVANTAGES AND DISADVANTAGES

Attention to poetics helps us to uncover a splendour that reveals the rhythms and timings and seasonal colours of the spiritual world, mapping its many forms, identities, expressions, ideals, and actions. Poetics allows spirituality to give voice to the lush diversity of the human spirit as it is embraced and experienced by practitioners, including teachers and writers, who recognise the need for rich descriptive imagery that goes beyond basic assumptions and seeks a broader and deeper understanding: *thick descriptions* as they are called in research contexts.[21] But to do this well a poetics of spirit must be capable of recognising and doing justice to two opposing pulls. The first is the capacity to wrestle with complex and largely indefinable realities. The second is to recognise the human tendency to idealise, rigidify, or idolise images and expressions, thus depriving them of their capacity to transform, rendering them barren of transformative empowerment. Both are essential to the critical development of accurate understandings and descriptions of spirituality.

Spirituality may be understood, then, as a dynamic of poetic activity, in Christian terms a divine-human *poiesis* – or making – that surfaces in the construction of soul and spirit, a portal to and a graced sharing in the radiant beauty of Christ who invites a transforming participation in the divine dance of Trinity. Spirituality as a creative activity persuades in the way poetry persuades, opening new vistas and visions as poetry does. A poetics of spirit convinces through its descriptive veracity, its power to envision the vibrant potential and painful predicament of the human soul recognised, sought, followed, embraced, celebrated, given honest, vital and living expression. To engage in spirituality is to engage in a creative process, to engage with creative and constructive imagination, to become a poet of the soul, a singer of spirit, a dancer in life. Spiritual engagement allows us to reflect the shape of soul, prayerfully and meditatively construct a soul-based life, give it living identity. To engage in spirituality allows soul-based life to take on metaphorical suggestiveness, to paint pictures of its hopefully finished form precisely because poetics suggests transitive power, a grammar of change, an openness to sculpt new forms and discern new expressions and levels of insight.

An approach grounded in a poetics of spirit allows us to embrace spirituality precisely as a mode of making: a making of a style of life; an uncovering of intention, a releasing of something beautiful and true and good. A poetics of spirit also helps us to understand when self-referred spirituality becomes something ensnared within the marbled mire of human disappointment. A spiritual poetics is constructive. It is an unfolding of motive and desire, of will and choice, of ideality and direction; and it reveals their presence in the living action of construction itself. A spiritual poetics allows intention to emerge, take shape, find more powerfully distilled form in the action of building a spiritual discipline, of evolving a spiritual practice, of recognising and moving towards a spiritual goal, of deepening a spiritual understanding, of walking a transformative path and sharing the journeying with others. It recognises that desire, implicit and explicit, gradually emerges and takes shape in the very act of walking the walk into the world of transcendence.

If poetics, including a poetics of spirit, harbours a danger it is that of eluding or insufficiently acknowledging the need for a transparently ethical praxis in the very act of spiritual making that poetics signifies. Poetics means making. It is not enough to think: thought and imagination must flow into action and become a living, vibrant song, a song that refuses to remain on paper and lifts hauntingly into the air, a song that sings itself into beguiling being. What we are concerned with here is authentic spirituality, not some flight from either history or politics in a search for new and novel forms of diversion and comfort in a dangerous world. The poetics of spirit we are concerned with here is prophetic, wise, politically astute, a poetics that contemplatively penetrates illusion, that recognises the heritage of diminishment flowing from the grotesque parodies of existence that so often masquerade as life and freedom in a consumer-shaped universe that has forgotten not only how to be self-dispossessed, but also how to be self-transcending. In reclaiming poetics, spirituality makes it possible to open new doors to a self-transcendent mode of being in the world, of being shapers of history, engaged voices in the public politics that shape the communities and societies in which we live.

Poetics reminds us that spirituality is not just a mode of cognition. It is eminently practical, a life craft. Spirituality is a mode of making and shaping that cannot be reduced to a form of experience that merely looks to self or only looks within. Like poetics, spirituality is about the interweaving dance of thought, word and deed; sowing seeds of spirit that are meant to bear social and political fruit in the work of justice and peace, the work of ecological responsibility. Spirituality is certainly about contemplation, about recognising the forces of human alienation, but it is also about the creative deeds and actions that bring contemplation to life and give it embodied social shape. By revealing spirituality as a creative act, poetics draws us into a space of concerned and concerted action. It confronts us with the reality of the world as it is: a wonderfully creative and celebratory place, but a place of suffering, of pain, of destructive abuses of power, and the search for dominating influence and control.

Spirituality is either real or it risks becoming a parody, a parroted mimicry, a moment of jerking puppetry, a versified sham. Spirituality not only has the potential to become a new space of meaning and value; it also has the capacity to break free of the limits set on the human spirit by the ideologies that diminish human liberty. It is not enough for spirituality to be privately sincere and well meaning as contemporary thought would have it. It is not enough to look to the inner spaces, as if spirituality were simply a private, privatised, privatising phenomenon. This husk of modernity must be utterly rejected. The external world is just as relevant, just as demanding, just as needy of the transforming impact of spiritual commitment as the inner world is. Spirituality must demand its place in the public forum and insist on being heard in favour of more humane, fairer, more compassionate lifeworlds and systemworlds. Every spiritual action, precisely as an act of crafting and making, is also an authorial process, a creative process of choosing, a simultaneity of embrace and surrender, of receptivity and transcendence. These dynamics are clearly revealed in the change-producing forces of self-implicating-disclosure and self-implicating-commitment, and in every moment of ethically creative choice. Spirituality is about constructing after all, not least because it has the power to unearth imaginative forces and free them to generate newness of life in the audacious presence of the gifting Spirit.

Understood from the perspective of a poetics of spirit, spirituality actively supports a constructive interweaving and creative converging of:

- facets,
- glimpses,
- metaphors,
- stories,
- intimations,
- margins,
- edges,
- brights and darks,
- possibilities and potentials,
- rituals and symbols,
- plantings and birthings,
- dyings and risings,
- tragedies and sufferings,

as well as practices and repertoires of healing and empowerment. Spirituality at its best always recognises the vast evocative power of such interweavings and convergings. It resists the temptation to reduce the complexities of life to sets of Euclidian geometric detail, or at least seeks so to do. Spirituality faces the challenge of intrusions and voices that disturb comfortable silences in order to invite creative engagement. It supports a joining of minds and imaginations. Spirituality walks a dialogical path, engaging in meaningful conversation with sisters and brothers on the way. It explores with eyes alert to a different light. Spirituality is respectful of different ways of viewing complex realities: such as spirituality itself.

❑ *The relevance of poetic making*

A poetics of spirit reminds us to remain flexible in the face of the demands – especially the demands of justice, congruence and integrity – surfaced by the particularities of context, with their continuities and discontinuities, their ever-changing contingencies of time and place. A poetics of spirit teaches spirituality how to reconstitute fragments of experience and identity into creatively and flexibly empowering wholes. A spiritual poetics teaches us how to dance and be still in sacred spaces. It teaches us how to sit patiently before walls of boredom and psychic resistance. A poetics of spirit comforts and then disturbs. It confronts practitioners and students alike with paradox. It has the potential to weave the inward, outward and upward dimensions of life into something new and true and beautiful.

Spiritual poetics brings playfulness to the surface. It invites us to play with aspects and features and qualities and parts in the manner of Gerard Manley Hopkins's Christ who plays in ten thousand places. A poetics of spirit leaves room for other playings; it alludes to other journeyings. Spiritual poetics insinuates other ways of dancing with the spirit into the hide and seek of ever-deepening paths to rediscovered relationships and unexpected connections. A poetics of spirit may not be the favoured domain of a rational philosopher or systematic theologian, but it is the familiar workspace of a seasoned spiritual practitioner, a crafter and celebrator of things that point beyond themselves, allowing their song to be heard and a future glimpsed. Quite simply a poetics of spirit has the capacity to open portals onto unexpected vistas where spiritual inscapes and outscapes meet in a dance of mutual renewal.

A spiritual poetics develops awareness of shimmering intimations and whispers that evade more rationalistic forms of expression. It more creatively echoes the particularities of cultural imagery and context as they inspire tender buddings of spiritual experience. More to the point, a poetics of spirit helps us to dance in the borderlands where text and discourse and action weave new tapestries of possibility and insight. It allows a livingness to emerge; one that sees in the iridescent beauty of a butterfly the Risen One radiant with the vast infinitude of the gifting gifts of life; or in an acorn the infinite creativity of God. In the imaginative world of spiritual poetics ways are found to allow metaphor and paradox to seek and find expression in nuanced language that warms the heart and paints the promise-filled rainbow colours of spirit. This is evident in the voices of the mystics and the prophets who tint intentionality and discovery into being by painting word pictures replete with all the evocatively mystical colours figurative language allows. They illuminate spirit dancing in rhythmic harmony with interior movements themselves in tune with divine inspirations. The voices of the mystics and the prophets celebrate soul singers jubilantly emancipated from self-referred agendas in an expressive exchange that bursts the languaged bounds of text and syntax.

The use of figurative language helps spiritual discourse to celebrate more fully and so to befriend the realities of transforming desire. The primary example of this in Western spiritual literature is found in the poetry of John of the Cross. It is also vividly present in the Psalms and the Song of Songs of the Hebrew Bible. Figurative deviation and dislocation allow spirituality to find a radical tone that refuses to be ignored even unto death. This tone is what is revealed in the life and death choices and stances of an Oscar Romero, an Etty Hillesum, or a Dietrich Bonhoeffer. Spiritual and moral integrity comes at a price. Confronted by mainstream culture and its marginalising tendencies spirituality must grapple with deviational expression: it must turn away from the mainstream course. At such junctures spirituality must seek beyond the conventional: it must search for a language of intensification, for a more finely tuned expression of the real, and the challenges and consequences concomitant with being real in the real world.

Figurative language has the creative ability to impel spirituality away from the merely conceptual towards felt ways that energise life; and it does this in the very act of making an *aha* impression on life. What a poetics of spirit seeks above all is an unencumbered expression of the humbling awesomeness of existence, its power and potential, and the original amazement still faintly echoing at the heart of things. There is something here of the child-like identity the gospels describe (Matthew 18:3). A poetics of spirit is concerned with transcending the mere external as the spiritual seeker struggles with the challenges and often unexpected responsibilities of personal identity and autonomy as they dance in and out and around to the deep rhythms of real life. In this sense, spirituality is an existential search concealed in a swirl of creative repetitions, returns and innovations that take us down deep to the level of being itself. The person on a spiritual path is a seeker, one whose knowing is not yet complete, whose journey is unfinished, and whose task is ever and always to allow the surprise of life to rise, singing into the gifting light.

In such spaces spirituality operates at the outer levels of situational reference and uses metaphorical descriptors to indicate proximities, themes, issues and realities that, like the Gospel Kingdom, are at hand, nearby, just there, just here. By being able to operate imaginatively in these edge spaces, spirituality opens up transcendences and shared knowledges that flirt with larger, less boundaried, more mysterious situations. It uses location, tense and aspect to suggest time and flow and related rhythms that in turn allow deeper engagement with the dynamics of trans-formative encounter and experience. Imagination allows a different kind of seeing, one that allows hidden, less well-limned things to emerge. A poetics of spirit allows us to see a yellow-flowered tree a-flutter with birds in a mustard-seed (Luke 13:18-19), the *imago dei* in the human soul promising infinite possibility; and it allows us read their practical implications. Above all a poetics of spirit denotes a way of looking at and depicting a reality that is now replete with breath-holding immanence, now star-bursting beyond with breath-taking assurance of transcendence aglow with a Spirit-filled hope for the future. And then it grounds itself in the care of a raped earth and a wounded neighbour.

Since Plato there has always been a reluctant acknowledgement that the true poets knew or indeed know the secret of coming face to face with being. Like poetry, spirituality is a dramatic, imaginative, sometimes socially naïve, sometimes sad and tragic, sometimes festive performance that embraces an expressive view of life and language, one that grapples with the figurative possibilities of alternative vocabularies and lexicons. Like poetry, spirituality too demands an honesty and integrity ready to penetrate deceit and self-deceit contemplatively, to see through illusion and the lie. Illusion, deceit, the lie: forces that lurk at the heart of spiritual activity and distort it with claims of personal omniscience or omnipotence, of spiritual privilege, or even the grandiosity of literal divinity when the play of metaphor is unrecognised. Spirituality, like poetry, has the capacity to break free from social convention and mainstream social dominance. It has the capacity to reveal the hidden and the contradictory, the chaotic and the unpredictable aspects of human existence.

## ℂ A concluding triad

There is also a second triad of words associated with the art of making that is relevant to spirituality as a crafting project: hermeneutics – from the Greek *hermeneusis*, the creative process of interpretive reading; psychogenesis – the birth processes and constructions of the self; and poetics. There is a far-reaching connection between poetics and interpretation. In fact, poetics like spirituality may be defined as the drama of constructive and imaginative interpretation of life and reality encountering the challenges of transcendence. The link between poetics and the formation of the contemporary self is just as significant. As modes of making, poetics and spirituality interweave so intimately with the maturing of personal and community identity that it is sometimes difficult to tell them apart. They are constructively imaginative projects with

profound impacts on personal and communal development. Transformative living – like poetic composition – is a holy making that takes
place in the sacred spaces where potential lives seek new birth in wisely
expressed forms. In Christian spirituality this form evolves along a
vocational path that reveals the intimate dance of divine invitation and
human response: it is the graced embrace of transforming Spirit.

Like poetry, spirituality too may be encapsulated in the written word
but its preferred medium is life itself: its page is the fullness of a
creatively self-implicating life. The spiritual life is its own artistic canvas,
and the best test of a spiritual life is in the artistry of it performance. It is
in the testing and probing of the web of life, through its interpretation
and through the development of a spiritual identity that spirituality
legitimises its public statements of human meaning and possibility, of
human purpose and divine destiny. In so doing spirituality interprets life
and the nature and goals, the paths and responsibilities of well-founded
human existence. But what is creative interpretation when it is applied
to spirituality? Is some form of conceptual explanation or descriptive eluci-
dation sufficient? Or is spirituality an endeavour pointing in a direction,
the lived opening-up of an orientation, an active embracing of existence
in all its unpredictability? Obviously, the complete answer incorporates
all three possibilities, but a vibrant spirituality always gives primacy to
congruent, mindful, responsive engagement in the actualities of personal
and communal existence.

Spirituality is a way of uncovering the hidden dimensions of being-in-
the-world, tracing the hidden music of something that is simultaneously
hidden and made visible in the self-implicating acts that build human
identity. Its very concealment demands exploration, interpretation, and
clarification: the fruits of interpretive praxis and deeply transformative
psychospiritual commitment. Such a life project is grounded in the development of the authentic, the mindfully contemplative self. Neither of
these tasks is easy. Awareness and unawareness play their flip-flop games in
the process, while uncoordinated words and gestures tell their diverging
tales. In a kind of sacramental action spirituality weaves meaning and
being together in one ritualised achievement. It gestures beyond itself
and in so doing unmasks itself, weaving ambiguity and ambivalence into
the tapestry of life, revealing its indeterminacy and incompletion even in
the very act of evoking real presence and concrete existence.

## CONCLUSION

The reality of a poem lies in its reciting; the reality of a spirituality lies
in its living. The challenge for both is to achieve an open legitimacy, a
fruitful credibility. For the Christian, the mystery of spirituality lies in
the encounter with a living Word that gives birth to a living spirituality,

and in the birthing fulfils itself in a creatively responsible life danced giftingly to the full. Both poetry and spirituality act like webs of meaning that glisten with mist-made dewdrops in the early-morning sun. They show us something real; they allow us to see things we might never have noticed; they set the scene for our breath to catch at the awesomeness of the ordinary; and both craft a living synthesis that has passion and vision as its ally. Both discover in the imaginative use of root metaphors a field guide for a finite being seeking beyond self. Both poetry and spirituality seek beyond social control, seek to move beyond the known to the as-yet unknown, open to a new vision of things. Both poetry and spirituality open the doors to the vitality of vibrant dance; then, echoing discord and a humbler, less ecstatic mood, they pivot into a Job-like proneness to silence on a hill of ash and shards (Job 2:7-8). And they help us to reconnect with the rest of the created universe: with butterflies and rivers, with trees and oceans and shooting stars.

## THEMES AND QUESTIONS FOR FURTHER REFLECTION

1. Explore your understanding of the multilayered nature of spirituality as experience of and response to life in all its ways and all its contexts.
2. Explore what it means for you to encounter uncertainty, bewilderment, suffering, alienation, darkness, mystery, awe, depth, and insight in the dynamic rhythms of spiritual journeys and experiences.
3. How responsive are people to the challenges of bringing together heart and love, soul and spirit, mind and action, freedom and the limits of freedom, commitment and integrity, insight, intuition and awareness with their consequences in developing a spirituality?
4. How do people become poets and prophets, makers of metaphor, bearers of possible worlds?

## FURTHER READING

James Martin, SJ, *Becoming Who You Are: Insights on the True Self from Thomas Merton and Other Saints* (Mahwah, NJ: Hidden Spring, 2006).

NOTES:
1. See Han F. de Wit, *The Spiritual Path: An Introduction to the Psychology of the Spiritual Traditions.* Translated by Henry Jansen & Lucia Hofland-Jansen (Pittsburg, PA: Duquesne University Press, 1999).
2. See John Cottingham, *The Spiritual Dimension: Religion, Philosophy and Human Value* (Cambridge: Cambridge University Press, 2005) 140.
3. ibid. 3.
4. See Leszek Kolakowski, *Religion* (South Bend, IN: St Augustine's Press, 2001) 165.

5. See John D. Caputo and Michael J. Scanlon, eds, *God, the Gift and Postmodernism* (Bloomington and Indianapolis, IN: Indiana University Press, 1999) 1–4.

6. See Valerie Lesniak, 'Christian Spirituality: Definition, Methods and Types' in Philip Sheldrake, *The New SCM Dictionary of Christian Spirituality* (London: SCM Press, 2005) 1–6.

7. See for example, Benjamin B. Page, ed., *Marxism and Spirituality: An International Anthology* (Westport, CT, London: Bergin & Garvey, 1993).

8. Pierre Teilhard de Chardin, *Building the Earth* (Wilkes Barre, PA: Dimension Books, 1965) 5.

9. See Richard Kearney, *Poetics of Imagining: Modern to Post-modern* (New York: Fordham University Press, 1998) 149. See also Thomas L. Martin, *Poiesis and Possible Worlds: A Study in Modality and Literary Theory* (Toronto, Buffalo, London: University of Toronto Press, 2004).

10. See Steven P. Schneider, *A. R. Ammons and the Poetics of Widening Scope* (Cranbury, NJ and London: Associated University Presses, 1994) 71–103.

11. See Don E. Saliers, 'Beauty and Terror' in Elizabeth A. Dreyer & Mark S. Burrows, eds, *Minding the Spirit: The Study of Christian Spirituality* (Baltimore & London: The Johns Hopkins University Press, 2005) 303–313; Mark S. Burrows, '"Raiding the Inarticulate": Mysticism, Poetics, and the Unlanguagable' in ibid. 341–361.

12. See J. M. Bernstein, 'Confession and Forgiveness: Hegel's Poetics of Action' in Richard Eldridge, ed., *Beyond Representation: Philosophy and Poetic Imagination* (Cambridge: Cambridge University Press, 1996) 34–65 at 34.

13. Denise Levertov, *Selected Poems*. With a Preface by Robert Creeley. Edited and with an Afterword by Paul A. Lacey (New York: New Directions Books, 2002) 164.

14. See Rebecca S. Chopp, 'Theology and the Poetics of Testimony' in Delwin Brown, Sheila Greeve Davaney, & Kathryn Tanner, eds, *Theologians in Dialogue with Cultural Analysis and Criticism* (New York, Oxford: Oxford University Press, 2001) 56–70. See also Linda S. Maier and Isabel Dulfano, eds, *Woman as Witness: Essays on Testimonial Literature by Latin American Women* (New York, Frankfurt, Oxford: Peter Lang, 2004). On the role of testimony in Jewish Holocaust theology see Melissa Raphael, *The Female Face of God in Auschwitz: A Jewish Feminist Theology of the Holocaust* (London & New York: Routledge, 2003).

15. See John S. McClure. 'The Way of Love: Loder, Levinas, and Ethical Transformation through Preaching' in Dana R. Wright and John D. Kuentzel, eds, *Redemptive Transformation in Practical Theology. Essays in Honor of James E. Loder* (Grand Rapids, Cambridge: Eerdmans Publishing, 2004) 95–115 at 101.

16. For a technical and scientific discussion of spirit and psyche see Daniel A. Helminiak, *The Human Core of Spirituality: Mind as Psyche and Spirit* (Albany, NY: State University of New York Press, 1996). For a psychological discussion of soul see, for example, Wolfgang Giegerich, *The Soul's Logical Life: Towards a Rigorous Notion of Psychology*, 3rd revised edition (Frankfurt: Peter Lang, 2001); Thomas Moore, *Care of the Soul: A Guide for Cultivating Depth and Sacredness in Everyday Life* (New York: Harper Collins, 1992).

17. See Mark A. McIntosh, *Mystical Theology: The Integrity of Spirituality and Theology* (Oxford: Blackwell Publishing, 2005) 143-145.

18. For a discussion of these issues see David Tracy, 'The Uneasy Alliance Reconceived: Catholic Theological Method, Modernity and Postmodernity' in *Theological Studies* 50 (1989) 548-570.

19. See Andrew W. Hass, *Poetics of Critique: The Interdisciplinarity of Textuality* (Aldershot: Ashgate, 2003). See also Jeremy R. Carrette, *Foucault and Religion: Spiritual Corporality and Political Spirituality* (London and New York: 2000).

20. See Gilles Fauconnier and Mark Turner, *Conceptual Blending and the Mind's Hidden Complexities* (New York: Basic Books, 2002).

21. The term was first used by Gilbert Ryle but developed by Clifford Geertz: see Edith Babin and Kimberly Harrison, *Contemporary Composition Studies: A Guide to Theorists and Terms* (Westport, CT and London: Greenwood Press, 1999) 254. See also Clifford Geertz, 'Thick Description: Toward an Intrpretive Theory of Culture' in *The Interpretation of Cultures* (New York: Basic Books, 1973) 3-30.

## CHAPTER 4

*Learning to Speak Metaphor*

*Metaphors are sensible.*

JACQUES DERRIDA

*Metaphors are built 'on the ruins of the literal'.*

PAUL RICOEUR

## INTRODUCTION

Like a pedigree homing pigeon, poetics leads us to the heart of metaphor. Poetics teaches us that metaphor, the mother-tongue of poetry, is also the mother-tongue of spirituality because metaphors are field guides to depth and mystery. More, metaphor is a privileged locus of spiritual energy and its figurative expression: it helps us engage with and say the unsayable. Metaphors help us to glimpse the profundity of life, catch glints of Spirit, sense the building wave of soul, and imagine the sacred and the holy. Metaphors give us tools to make sense of a world where God is encountered both at the centre and at the edges, in the bright and prosperous places as well as in the arid desert, the dark night, and the dangerous wilderness. Metaphors help us speak about those thin places where the sacred hovers tantalisingly just beyond our fingertips. These are the tip of the tongue places, the stammering places where everyday language refuses its normal fluency and stutters to a stop till a poet's creative imagining gives tongue to metaphor and bridges the gaps into new awarenesses full of surprising discovery.

Metaphors unmask the vampires sucking audacity dry, the things that eviscerate spirit in our day. Deadly in their dark seductions vampires of spirit desiccate dangerous memory, silence the rhythms and melodies of soul, and prevent us from discovering new ways to let Jesus live in the world. Metaphors open avenues back to the light. They help us to explore afresh the spaciousness of soul and the ways of soaring spirit. They help us name the restrictions, the habits of mind that hold us tight in fear, frozen, fettered, unfree. Metaphors teach us how to name the energies and values that heal soul and spirit. They are the balm in Gilead for the tight places that chafe soul and rub spirit raw (Jeremiah 8:22). Metaphors give us a language to explore the awesome relationality of reality. They give us a language to connect to its fluidity and flow. Metaphors allow us space to express the stillness and dynamism of life, its surprises and exceptions. They give us a way to celebrate the potentials of life and the revelations of reality as we seek our full humanity. And metaphors shape the stories we tell of our struggles with the forces of diminishment, depletion and death that masquerade in consumer cultures as freedom and liberation.

Metaphor is the expressive lens through which a particular form of spirituality responds to the invitation and challenge of reality. Metaphor is not meant to be a replacement for faith or for the faith experience it images and narrates. Metaphors help us to adorn the home called faith but they do not substitute for it. Descriptions of faith are not faith, however creative and imaginative they may be just as field guides are not the field, however profound and poetically inspiring their depictions. The life of faith, the spiritually self-implicating expression of the life of faith, the truth that grounds a life of faith is what counts. Descriptions of audacity are not audacity. Descriptions of spirit are not spirit; but they do help us to be open to reality and live. The metaphor is forever a map, never the terrain. In spirituality there is no substitute for life; and yet we do need the power of metaphor, we need maps to give living expression to how and why we live as we do.

## The Power of Metaphor

Spirituality like poetics has to do with metaphors and maps, with quests and their actual human and geographical terrains.[1] Borrowing a phrase from Ellen Davis, spirituality sings in a "vividly metaphorical language that is intensely personal but not private."[2] Metaphor, unfortunately, is as difficult to define as imagination or creativity, domains that lie close to its heart as an agent of creative and imaginative thought. Metaphor endows us with double vision. It appreciates the sensuous image. Metaphor opens doors to imperceptible worlds and lifts the veils that obscure the sacred. Metaphors are starting places for exploring afresh how to be fully human, how to discern the divine in the world. They show us how to find life and lose life and then how to find it again in the wastelands, margins and gaps, in the desert spaces that hint at new-old thresholds crossed now in the visioning company of poets and prophets.

Metaphors are places of lilies (Song of Songs 2:16) where, soul nourished by the Beloved, new songs soar into the winds of Spirit and imagination comes alive in the bits and pieces of a poet's Everyday.[3] Certainly, the language of spirituality has to do with texts and storied histories, and narratives that find expression in a variety of interpretative discourses, but most of all spirituality has to do with metaphor and the ways metaphor constantly seeks life. Metaphors teach us that life has the power to take root weed-like in the no-places of the desert, stopping places in its shifting sands. Metaphors pattern our spiritual reflection. They orient spiritual action. They shape our understanding of what is important or authentic or deep or transformative in spirituality because spiritual narrative is already a metaphorical act that makes incessant self-implicating demands. Through the imaginative use of both simple and complex metaphors, texts, narratives and storied histories generate field guides and maps to orient the human spirit. Metaphors also generate ways of understanding, orienting and evaluating the spiritual journey.

By uncovering vibrant existential structures, metaphor clusters and the field guides they generate help us find uniquely personal ways to focus the life-questioning self-presence and creativity of the human spirit. Metaphors do this even when we have lost track of who we are or who we thought we were supposed to be. Metaphor clusters make fresh and imaginative understandings of life, identity and ethical practice possible. They generate spiritual geographies that help us find our way through the complex worlds of belief and spirit. They mould our perceptions and guide our choices, and they are revealed equally in our acceptances and resistances, as well as our developmental deficits and frozen places. Inner maps also confront us with boredom and its darker blocking cousins, the inversions of depression and despair. They confront us with the places of pathos and grief. Metaphors, too, are known to die when they are disconnected from the wellsprings of creativity and gratitude for life.

Living metaphor suggestively and evocatively sustains spirituality as it seeks to enter deeply into the living trajectory of the human spirit and the invitations whispered on the breath of Spirit. Metaphors are dancers. They dance imaginatively to the music and songs that celebrate the poetic blending of sense, image and sound, and in the dancing make it possible for new rhythms of seeing, saying and understanding to reach harmoniously into new and different places of meaning and insight. Metaphor makes understanding possible by mediating meaning. According to Lakoff and Turner, metaphor has the power to "*create* structure in our understanding of life."[4] Lakoff and Turner argue that metaphor not only has the power to structure experience and thought, it has the power of reason that enables it to borrow patterns of inference that in turn ground our powers of discernment and evaluation.[5] It is not difficult to extend that power to our understanding, construction, orientation and discernment of spiritual life.

The locus of metaphor is not really in language, but in the way we conceptualise one mental domain in terms of another. Cognitive metaphors juxtapose the unclear with the obvious; the transparent *here* helps us to speak of the more mysterious or opaque *there*.[6] This is the source of the power of metaphor to structure and generate new ways of understanding and embracing reality.[7] In *A Midsummer Night's Dream*, Shakespeare opens a poetic window onto the power of metaphor to speak new things into being, to name things anew and give them a place in the world:

> Lovers and madmen have such seething brains,
> Such shaping fantasies, that apprehend
> More than cool reason ever comprehends.
> The lunatic, the lover, and the poet
> Are of imagination all compact:
> ....
> And as imagination bodies forth
> The forms of things unknown, the poet's pen
> Turns them to shapes, and gives to airy nothing
> A local habitation and a name. (V. i. 1–17)

Poets and lovers see more than cool reason ever comprehends. Such is the power and the allure of metaphor in dream and in life. Such is the power of metaphor to transform and transfigure minds.[8] This should come as no surprise since metaphors play a significant part in generating the pre-selected constructs of everyday life, the stock of knowledge that colours and orients our assumptions of reality.[9] Metaphor reveals the language of spirit at its creative best, working to extend and stretch the ordinary powers of reason, entering the spaces of dissonance, dancing in the spaces of incongruity, generating semantic shock and stirring emotional friction in the service of a new, a deeper awareness. Living metaphor always challenges the certainties of cool reason. Living metaphor is on the side of spirit, serving its creativity, focusing its imaginative power to create new worlds and generate new identities.

Sandra Schneiders, echoing Paul Ricoeur, is in no doubt that metaphor is "our most effective access to the meaning of reality at its deepest levels...[it] is an instrument of new meaning, a way of achieving genuine semantic innovation."[10] Almost all non-technical language is metaphorical.[11] Metaphor leads to an expansion of meaning because it is tensive, that is, by simultaneously affirming and denying something it teases the mind to reach beyond the limits of rationality into "newness of thought."[12] The poet Denise Levertov paints an alluring picture of the lightening power of metaphor and its siblings as they wheel beyond literal restraint in her poem *Poetics of Faith*:[13]

'Straight to the point'
        can ricochet,
        unconvincing.

Circumlocution, analogy,
        parable's ambiguities, provide
        context, stepping-stones.

Most of the time. And then

the lightening power
        amidst these indirections
            of plain
unheralded miracle!

### ℂ Source domains of metaphor

The power of metaphor and its related tropes or figures of speech arises from its imaginative and non-literal use of embodied human experiences in what are termed *source domains*, experiences which are then used to build bridges into the more opaque *target domains* we seek to understand and unfold. Reflect for a moment on the source domains or common sources from which metaphors arise: our bodies, health, animals, plants, places, the natural world, building and constructing, struggling and fighting, tools and weapons, practices and technologies, games, economic transactions, eating and drinking, heat and cold, light and darkness, forces, qualities, intensities, spatial movements and orientations, up-down, in-out, left-right. Then reflect on the common target domains of metaphor, the experiences, states and questions towards which metaphors point: emotion, desire, morality, thought, society, politics, economics, relationships, values, commitments, communication, time, life and death, religion and spirituality, events and actions, the divine and the sacred. Now ask yourself questions about your own spirituality. Does it grapple with such themes? Or is it simply an ironic comfort zone, a defensive tool for managing anxiety, a form of relaxing entertainment, a flight from the unpredictable nature of the world, a desert of dead metaphor?

In general, a metaphor arises when a word or image is used to refer to an object, concept, process, quality or relationship to which it does not conventionally refer or when a logical or causal link is made between them. The construction and use of both simple and complex metaphors is essentially pragmatic, grounded in personal reflective or shared communicative need.[14] Simple metaphors generate the mapping that is used in the more complex forms. The 'intensity' metaphor offers an example of metaphor mapping with clear biblical referents: hot-cold, strong-weak, calm-anxious. "Because you are lukewarm, and neither cold nor hot, I will spit you out of my mouth" (Revelations 3:16). "When I am weak then I am strong" (2 Corinthians 12:10). "Be still before the Lord...wait patiently...fret not yourself" (Psalm 37: 7). In spirituality metaphors are used in three main ways: to build or construct spiritual realities, to guide and orient spiritual practices, and to structure, direct and focus future spiritual actions. In so doing metaphors not only connect people to a shared core of fundamental meaning they also provide an inventive framework for non-literal imaginative communication: in meditative practice, for example, references to 'no mind' or 'monkey-mind' are not difficult to understand.

The value of both simple and complex metaphors to spirituality lies in their non-literal, pragmatic, openly thoughtful, imaginative and evocative use. Metaphors are irreplaceable tools in reflective practice and communication. Typical examples of metaphor-definitions in spirituality are: 'spirituality is a journey' and 'spirituality is growth'. Such phrases are patently absurd in a literal sense, but as non-literal, evocative images they open the way to valuable insight into and clearer understanding of healthy spiritual experience and practice. The non-literal nature of metaphor makes it possible to envision spirituality in a variety of different ways: 'spirituality is a pathway', 'spirituality is a living process', 'spirituality is a process of building', 'spirituality is a form of warfare', 'spirituality is a life orientation', and 'spirituality is the manifestation of certain emotional responses' as, for example when Paul encourages Timothy *to rekindle or fan into flame* the divine gift within him (2 Timothy 1: 6).[15]

Such realities point in turn to psychological, mental, mystical, religious, and spiritual states, events, groups, practices, processes and projects, and to an extensive array of related experiences.[16] All of them eventually confront us with the phenomenon of spirit and help us to unfold something of its mystery and its intentionality. They also help us to understand why spirituality is a global need. A clue to the importance of metaphor for the study of world spirituality lies in Lakoff and Turner's identification of both universal metaphors and cultural variations, which help to set the ground for the interspiritual dialogue that is so relevant to world peace in our day.[17] Metaphors help us to identify bridges and affinities as well as differences, tensions, intensities and challenges.

Metaphors that give us a rich sense of the structure of an experience generate helpful maps. For example, metaphors of time make use of motion and space. Descriptions of meditation often use the 'here and now' metaphor. Some metaphors serve an ontological purpose by making use of objects, substances and conditions to expand understanding. Other metaphors serve orientational purposes by making use of spatial references that employ 'up-down' or 'centre-margin' metaphors. Metaphors often serve evaluative and interpretive functions. Examples include references to life ('life let him down'), theory ('the theory opened up new vistas'), inflation ('she had an inflated view of herself'), cancer ('sin is cancer of the soul'), and computers ('we are hard-wired for spirituality but we need the software if we are to engage in spiritual practice'). Yet other metaphors make use of image schemas to describe altered states of consciousness: examples include metaphors that evoke qualities and intensities of mindfulness, attention and awareness, as well as absences and presences, or experiences of break-down and death.[18]

### ℂ The power of root metaphors
Metaphors represent imaginative and creative ways of thinking that anchor, orient, expand and channel perceptions of meaning. They operate on a variety of different levels and can generate knowledge in deeply diverse ways. More specifically, root metaphors identify the pre-understandings that underlie whole discourses. Nor are they closed in on themselves: metaphors are relational. They sing together in creative clusters. Root metaphors provide open frameworks for interpretation; but more importantly, they mould conceptual infrastructures and shape worldviews.[19] Zygmunt Bauman draws attention to the influence of root metaphors on the shaping of whole human societies, their political agendas, and the flow of subsequent historic events. The twentieth century was largely shaped by the 'order-making' metaphor as it sought security. The result in Europe was the rise of the Nazi and Stalinist tyrannies. Postmodern cultures are shaped by the 'deregulation' or 'dismantling' metaphor that has activated the contrary search for new and exciting experiences meant to deliver a constant happiness that comes at the price of order and security.[20] In a similar vein, Donald Gelpi suggests that *experience* itself constitutes the fundamental root metaphor that organises contemporary religious narrative. It is not difficult to suggest that the same is true of contemporary spirituality. In performing its infrastructural task in both religious and spiritual conversation experience is supported by an indeterminate array of influential metaphors.[21]

Metaphors do not appear in isolation. They dance together within ordered systems where metaphorical branches map spiralling ways back to deep yet identifiable roots of the tree of life.[22] Root metaphors shake meaning loose, they provoke new potentials; and their provocative dynamics make creative interactions and open-ended explanations of spirituality possible.[23] In fact, the word *root* itself is a metaphor that points to the deepest concerns and needs of human existence. Consider this definition: the Christian disciple is one who follows Jesus on the way to Jerusalem. Note the three metaphors: way, follow, and Jerusalem (see

Mark 10:32). Note the tension of dynamic movement. The root metaphor 'way' that organises this account highlights the dynamic, vital, living nature of all metaphoric understanding and reminds us that we live by metaphor and need metaphorical literacy to nourish the in-depth spiritual quality and creativity of our lives.[24] The Christian follows a way, is offered a map. According to that map Jerusalem becomes a 'place' metaphor for the paradoxically transformative dynamics of suffering and death, descent, resurrection and ascent. In just this way metaphor helps us to see an authentic spiritual life through different eyes. In just this way metaphor teaches us to sing new songs of transforming grace and dance under the over-shadowing wings of audaciously empowering Spirit.

Metaphors are at once sensory yet ripple with meaning in non-sensory or abstract ways: in Jacques Derrida's terms metaphors are *sensible*.[25] Dancing pregnantly in the spaces between sense and paradoxical non-sense, metaphors map the journey of deification, they trace the path to the centre, they notice what happens at the margins and the peripheries, they react to savage landscapes, they recognise the marginalising power of mainstream agendas, and they give imaginative expression to the good, the true and the beautiful. The vitality of living metaphor is what keeps spiritual discourse alive, connecting it to the sources of life and the realities of life. Metaphor allows spirituality to walk in the world with creative integrity.[26] The vitality of living metaphor finds conscious expression in committed spiritual practice and makes the continuing development of spiritual literacy and matching spiritual growth possible. Living metaphors also have the power to bridge real differences. They have the power to stimulate new potentials, to birth new possibilities, and to open innovative paths to transformed identities in the world.[27]

Root metaphors channel the rhythms that flow from the depths of spiritual-being-in-the-world and spiritual-being-before-God. They not only choreograph the mystical dance, they give narrative and visual expression to the creativity of the human spirit. Root metaphors make imaginative rationality possible because they allow us to comprehend at least in part what we are as yet unable to comprehend in full.[28] The capacity of living metaphor to unfold comprehension and lead it towards a wisdom that never loses its unassuming links to common sense is vital to understanding the mystic's talk of God. It is so easy to forget that a metaphor is and paradoxically is not an accurate description of the Divine Mystery. It is even easier to forget that absolutised metaphors quickly wilt and die. In reference to God, for example, Father/Mother metaphors are always incomplete, and to absolutise either is to replace icon with idol, symbol with sign, the Divine with something of our own crafting. When metaphors are absolutised they betray their imaginative power; they lose their creative force and retreat or die back into mere language. Living metaphors are endowed with the power of verbs: move-ment and change lie at their heart and are their gift.[29] Living metaphors are alive, they sing and dance and resonate in the unfolding of commun-icative and reflexive situations.

According to Paul Ricoeur, metaphors shape interpretive and reflexive practice by openly presenting a conflict between identity and difference in ways that fuse difference into identity. Metaphor allows two energies to come into play, what Ricoeur has described as 'ontological vehemence' and 'philosophical disclosure'. These energies then combine to generate the 'semantic innovations' that for Ricoeur reveal the creative power of language.[30] Attention to root metaphors helps us to explore Christian and other forms of spirituality in ways that are simultaneously open to critical scientific reflection and to a committed embrace of existential values and needs. Living metaphors echo with divine potential; they resonate with the promise of authentic being. But, then, what happens when life and culture expel the creativity of being from the heart of metaphor? What happens to the songs? Where do the rhythms go? What happens to the dancer when the dance is killed? What happens to a lover when the beloved has been eradicated? While it is true that metaphors die and become infertile ground, living metaphors refuse to be trapped behind the bars of fixed meaning. Like symbols, living metaphors are always pregnant with meaning; they permit new possibilities to arise continually from the creative potentials of the human mind. A living spirit finds expression through living metaphor. Dead metaphor suggests a disconnected, unreflective spirit. In Christian spirituality, living metaphor dances with graced empowerment to embrace the challenges of life.

## ℂ Root metaphor and the faith tradition

Metaphor clearly supports the imaginative voicing of faith in human cultures. Within faith-based spiritual traditions, however, it is also important to wrestle with an important question. What in the spiritual tradition controls the structuring and orienting power of metaphor? What structures the structure; what orients the orientation? The answer within Christianity points clearly towards the structuring and orienting force of divine revelation and the Christian faith tradition. Christian spirituality engages with the forces that shape human lives in an explicit context of faith because faith matters profoundly. In spirituality faith plays its own structuring and orienting role in ways that are historically complex: the passion of faith finds expression in a plurality of responsive forms and metaphor clusters. As Paul Avis has noted, it is through metaphor, in company with symbol and myth that we are brought into contact with the sacred, the divine, revelation and God.[31] Metaphors of justification and sanctification, of salvation and holiness, of justice and engagement, of worship and moral integrity are typical examples.

In her poem, *On the Parables of the Mustard Seed*, Denise Levertov teaches us how to see faith through a poet's eye and shows us how a poetics of spirit works:

> Faith is rare, He must have been saying,
> prodigious, unique –
> one infinitesimal grain divided
> like loaves and fishes,
>
> *as if* from a mustard-seed
> a great shade-tree grew. That rare,
> that strange: the kingdom
>
>        a tree. The soul
> a bird. A great concourse of birds
> at home there, wings among yellow flowers.
> The waiting
> kingdom of faith, the seed
> waiting to be sown.[32]

There is a deep wisdom in faith, and metaphor helps to give it imaginative expression, allowing faith to unfold life-giving paths in a postmodern, consumer-driven world. In Christianity, then, it becomes clear that metaphor serves the expression of faith in changing cultural locations. At the same time, however, it is important to recognise that metaphor neither governs nor replaces faith. Again, with Paul Avis, it is important to note that metaphor is not veridical, that is, metaphor does not open a window into reality as such. Metaphor supports a reflection on the impact of objective reality but in a way that is "refracted, dimmed and distorted by the psychological, sociological, political and cultural lenses through which we must inevitably look."[33] Add developmental lenses to that list. Even in the imaginative light of metaphor we continue 'to see in a glass darkly' (1 Corinthians 13:12). Faith-based language may demand metaphor but revealed faith always refuses enclosure within its own metaphoric expression. A metaphor may help us to identify the holy but the holy always refuses to be captured by metaphor because metaphors do not create the objects of either holiness or revealed truth; they express and celebrate them, they neither create nor control them.

The role of a poetics in faith-based spirituality is to make possible the transition from admiration of Christ to a truly performative imitation.

There is no place here for the ironic celebration of the Romantic imagination. The turn to the divine other in faith-based spirituality undermines the Romantic pre-eminence of the self that dominates so many contemporary spiritualities. Christian spirituality is structured by a Christ-centred focus that intensifies the orientation of life in the world. This focus in turn, by shaping the poetics that structures spirituality, controls the way metaphor shapes and orients the understanding and expression of spirituality itself. As a poetic journey through the landscapes of metaphor Christian spirituality celebrates the theological understanding that God poetically composes the world. A fully alive graced spirituality is a divine poem being sung and danced in the world, a poem about truth and justice that has a Christ-shaped rhythm and reconciling audacity. What is at work is the transition from imagining the Christian ideal to practising it. Christian spiritual development is characterised by the transition from reflection on the Christ event to critical application in the world; by its very nature real spiritual development is self-implicating. Christ proclaims and makes transforming love manifest in the world; Christian spirituality continues that existential task.[34]

There is that in metaphor which is intransitive and hence mysterious, beyond metaphor: what metaphor is not, what it can never objectify. There is that in metaphor which always remains beyond the reach of language and image, something apophatic, something paradoxical within and beyond reach. Paradoxical metaphor remains humble even at its most glorious, alert to the peril of its own substituting power where, for example, image replaces the imaged Divinity. Metaphor testifies to the awesomely sacred, but when it objectifies the sacred it reduces the sacred to language and in the reducing violates it. Understood in this light metaphor can help us to 'fan into flame' (2 Timothy 1:6) the passion for a revealed mystery that comes as 'a thief in the night' (1 Thessalonians 5:2); but the mystery always escapes metaphor's attempts to give it totalised expression even when metaphor helps to generate new insights into the contemplation of faith.[35] The faith we contemplate governs the contemplation. Metaphor may allow us to face the problematics of faith today, but it does not resolve those problematics. Metaphor may help us explore and celebrate peace but the objective source of that peace is elsewhere and requires a mind trustingly stayed in God (Isaiah 26:3) because the truth of faith transcends the reductive tendencies of Enlightenment thought: the objective ground of faith remains unutterable, transcendent, no matter how imaginative its metaphoric expression.

No matter how sublime, how rich the descriptions, metaphor can only offer a glimpse, an enticing redescription of a promised land that remains definitively beyond metaphor's purchase. Metaphor promises truth but is not the truth it promises. The 'is' of metaphor is always balanced by its paradoxically simultaneous 'is not'. Metaphor does not endow us with the power to replace the sacred, to replace the truth that sets us free (John 8:32) with our present cultural understandings of the sacred and of truth. But metaphor does endow us with the paradoxical ability to distinguish between idol and icon, and in that space of paradox offers us a path of freedom from intellectual idolatry. Paradoxical metaphor at its best permits a relation to the truth of revealed faith that neither substitutes for that truth nor appropriates its transcendent character. The 'actual' revealed by metaphor can never exhaust the sublimely graced 'possibility' of emancipating truth. The challenge in spirituality is to understand the paradoxical power of metaphor to allow truth to be explored and celebrated without yielding to metaphor the power to seize that truth and appropriate its role. Metaphor is imaginatively poetic, not instrumentally literal. It evokes reality; it does not constitute it. Theology represents faith seeking understanding. However, while metaphor may structure the passionate journey of understanding it ultimately lacks any final authority in the matter. That authority lies elsewhere in the faith community.[36]

Metaphor helps us to keep faith with revelation by helping the person following the Christian path to keep faith alive and open to all the questions and challenges of location and cultural context. It helps the person of faith to keep conscious faith with the faith community. In changing cultural locations metaphor helps us to help faith challenge and subvert what the world holds dear; it helps us live by faith in the reality of a graced encounter with God: metaphor neither governs nor replaces faith or grace. When it is subjected to critical reflection, metaphor helps us explore the reasonableness of faith; it helps us to probe the truth of revelation. When metaphor is brought into the service of revelation the unifying power of faith is uncovered and is seen to unify body and spirit, science and religion, theology and spirituality.

Metaphor unaided, lacking a revealed orientation, displaced from a transformative encounter with grace, is incapable of revealing what God intended to do through the death of Christ. The response to this divine revelation is a graced faith that 'works itself out in love' (Galatians 5:6). Faith and the content of faith determine how metaphor and metaphor clusters unfold creatively in a faith tradition. Just as revelation and faith are necessary to the integrity, wholeness and well-being of a faith tradition and the community that celebrates it, so in the construction of an integral spirituality revelation and faith orient the unfolding of metaphor clusters because creative imagination remains the key to knowing, embracing, expressing and celebrating reality. In spirituality, the role of metaphor is to nourish, to indicate where the heart lives, to choreograph how the ground of passionate commitment dances and sings in the world to a rhythm demanding the audacity of spirit that lets Jesus live in new ways and in new cultural contexts.

### ℂ Spirituality and faith: event-process-relation[37]

There is nothing abstract about Christian faith. It is a dynamic, performative dimension of human experience. Christians generally understand faith as an all-encompassing mode of human response to a self-revealing, self-giving God. Faith is the free, lovingly graced enlightening, structuring and orienting of a believer's whole being-in-the-world. In faith-based spiritualities faith manifests through the performative and transformative dynamics of lovingly free commitment and obedience to a God who is revealed as the gifting Source of freedom-in-love and the healing compassion that is the performance of love. In Christian understandings of spirituality the human performance of faith rhythms to the infinitely more mysterious performance of love that is Trinity. Faith is the vehicle for an intimate encounter in which the deepest longings of the human heart are met and brought to fulfilment. In faith, a gifting Spirit-light glistens in the darkness of the human predicament; light and balm for its tragedies and grief (John 12:46). At the same time, faith remains a complex reality with multiple dimensions and possible meanings.

For example, faith is simultaneously a receptivity and a responsive action (James 1:22-25), an assurance and a conviction (Hebrews 11:1). It is a way of seeing life and a way of making sense of life; it is both cognitive and personal, a knowledge born of love. Faith also names a way of participating in a community of life and love that supports faith life and is always prepared to give an account of its loving hope (1 Peter 3:15): faith remains the template for Christian religious and spiritual practice. In giving an account of its hope, a faith-based spirituality experiences faith as an utterly free, life affirming, lovingly liberating assent to God that is itself anchored in and attentive in real action and practice to God's unconditional gift of total love and grace. Lived in an authentic spirituality, the grace of faith brings newness of life in its train. Such newness is at once engaged and mystical. It is oriented to justice in all its forms; and it is moored in a contemplation before which self-referred illusions of spiritual grandeur hopefully fall into the compost heap of repentant humility. In that falling the freedom that only revealed truth can bring is made known (John 8:32). This gifted freedom sets a paradoxically loving synergy of human and divine freedom in motion that utterly transforms the human person by opening portals to the healing-saving gift of Christ (Mark 16:16).

Faith-based spirituality lives on the threshold of grace: it is ever a graced pilgrimage, a graced way in the heart of the Church and the heart of the world to the heart of God. Nourished and nurtured by grace, faith is the royal road to divine intimacy and divine glory; it is the very basis of Christian mysticism and its contemplation of God's just anger and disappointment at the injustice of the world and God's transformative desire (John 3:36). Faith is a state of alertness to the presence of God; it invites us to live that presence attentively and prophetically in the world. Faith is a graced human act that allows us to touch the divine, to sing love songs together and lift up anthems of praise and worship; but it is not to be confused with passing moments of euphoria, still less with a tired cliché or a dead metaphor. Equally, faith is a challenge, a testing place where dark nights throw down real challenges to freedom and love, challenges that demand committed perseverance if they are to be negotiated with serenity and grace and the Day Star embraced as a lamp for the way (2 Peter 1:19). Not surprisingly faith also challenges us to engage deeply and maturely with the motives of credibility. These motives blossom in the unfolding of awakened human lives and the telling of their stories: William Springfellow and Dorothy Day, Oscar Romero and Edith Stein, Dag Hammarskjöld and Simone Weil (Hebrews 12:1).

Those same motives shine, too, in the lives of women and men who struggle with the elusiveness of God and God's apparent absence in the consumer landscapes that shape much of the contemporary Western world. How many struggle to remain true to what they heard in the faith community (Romans 10:17)? Other motives of credibility come to flower all around us in creation and the cosmos if we have the eyes to see – to see beyond and care for – the complex beauty that surrounds us; yet faith and spirituality continue to flourish in arid places, both urban and rural, and in the faith challenging contexts of ecological crisis and disaster. These are the places where too many of us see too dimly, preferring the safety of the TV screen to face-to-face encounters (1 Corinthians 13:12). But divine revelation itself, as it is received, shared and celebrated in the faith community, remains the privileged place of encounter for the choices women and men of faith make to live lives responsively open to God and responsibly open to and in service in the world. Faith persistently motivates such choices to seek transformative understanding, to engage constantly in the performative journey, and unceasingly to seek a deepening intimacy with God in the gracious light of the Spirit.

Spiritually grounded faith seeks to give an account of its hope in God, its conviction that God seeks a more compassionate, a fairer, more equitable, more just world for us all, a world where people of faith embrace the processes of metanoia that make deep integrity possible. All of this and more is feasible because authentic faith remains markedly reasonable. Authentic faith is constantly ready to face the apparent discrepancies between faith and reason, between faith and science. Mature faith is ever ready to enter into respectful, critical dialogue with philosophy and the natural and human sciences. After all, each of these disciplines in its own way seeks an ever-deepening, increasingly performative understanding of human existence in the cosmos, a quality they share with critically reflective faith. In the service of performative understanding each of these disciplines are themselves challenged to hold diversity and multiplicity in creatively tensive relationship. The believing Christian, contemplating the loving dance of Trinity, is similarly challenged to hold diversity and multiplicity in creatively tensive relationship.

Christian faith is not a determinant, a quality or a possession. It is a gifted encounter with a truth that is at once subjective and objective, inward, outward and upward, something eternal and essential. Faith is an event-process-relation that makes growth towards the other possible, the utterly Other who is revealed as all-things-are-possible (Matthew 19:26), the Other who is the goal of audacious spirit-desire-and-longing. Faith is something other than openness to the metaphorical possibility of infinitude. Faith grounds the graced-openness-and-willingness of spirit that in turn finds form in the structuring and orienting of transformative spirituality. In this light, faith-based spirituality names a graced event-process-relation, a condition-of-possibility that brings the human and the divine together in a synergy that irrupts audaciously into the world.

Such faith is not a reality-avoiding leap into infinitude. By choice, authentic faith takes a stance within the finite. Such faith brings the world-avoiding human leap into infinitude to a stop because authentic faith makes sense only when faced by the challenges of the contingent universe. Faith-based spirituality, too, belongs in the spaces of the finite. When faith is authentic the finite is neither rejected nor lost. By implication the finite world is embraced in faith by a person on a transformative path, a person becoming a new creation, a person with the mind of Christ, an incarnational, incarnated mind, a person who can make a difference in the world because the divine validity of creation has been glimpsed in grace. The validity of all of creation must find performative weight in the real world of human affairs or be proven fictional. And so the performative character of faith becomes plain in an indeterminate array of metaphorical, symbolic, mythopoetic, aesthetic, ethical, religious, and spiritual forms and expressions.

It is at this point that the relation between faith, freedom and creativity comes to the fore. The freedom and creativity of faith manifest themselves in the imaginative capacity to actually construct a better world, a world with a future open to God; and a present touched by the loving wisdom of God and the loving audacity of Spirit-in-the-world. Faith is the space where the human and divine come together in an event-process-relation that is on-going, never completed in the here-and-now: Christian faith consciously and passionately awaits eschatological completion even as it longs to bring that completion about. In the meantime, the human pilgrimage into the heart of emancipating spirituality reveals the performative core of faith-in-love at work in the world. Emancipating spirituality continually uncovers the passionate journey of return to absolute love, to the utterly transformed fullness of human-destiny-in-God. This journey is ever-pregnant with practical implications. So understood, it becomes clear that the faith journey is constantly challenged to transcend the disfigurements and compromises that regularly break out in operative spiritualities, open wounds in the wings of spirit.

Such compromises and disfigurements surface in a challenging range of human contexts: metaphoric, cultural, social, aesthetic, ethical, conflictual, gendered, philosophical, religious, spiritual, ideological, institutional, economic and political. This is by no means an exhaustive list of the locations where faith-in-love visions are compromised, disfigured and lost. The same happens deep within the human heart when contingent reality challenges immature images of life and the divine. In faith-based spiritualities faith, freedom and creativity become axes around which issues of growth inevitably turn, and issues of maturity tend to configure. In the mature faith space where time and eternity, the finite and the infinite dance together, spirit truly comes into creative and transformative play. Spirit does this as an unendingly audacious force that embraces the responsibilities of freedom and, in Christian terms, lets Jesus live in the celebration of dangerous memory. Spirit reminds us that everything is possible in God; and therein lies the gracing source of robust, performative, faith-based spirituality, a spirituality that trusts that the future belongs to God.

### ℂ Working with metaphors in spirituality

A widening range of authors including Bradley Holt, Kenneth Boa, Agneta Schreurs, Mark Holstead, James and Melissa Griffith, Eugene Peterson, Sandra Schneiders, Carol Ochs, Nicola Slee and others highlight the central role of metaphor in spiritual texts, narratives and conversations.[38] The role of root metaphors as ways of thinking about and understanding abstract or mysterious domains is particularly significant in spirituality, not least metaphors that unfold the attractive and energising power of beauty, love, worship and ecstasy. Metaphors of malevolence and evil, of disruptive and destructive powers, as well as the vicious forces of human diminishment and woe also surface through root metaphors and continue to play a considerable role in spiritual conversation and narrative. Metaphors of struggle and warfare, of journeying and climbing, of spiritual pilgrims and tourists, of spiritual vagabonds and holy fools, of ways of ascent and descent are commonly encountered in spirituality. The same is true of metaphors of arrival/birth and departure/death, or metaphors that disclose a radial or spiral structure in attempts to understand and imagine the structural, orientational and developmental dynamics of spiritual lives. Similar embodied experiences underlie metaphors of gazing, of ground and anchor, of mooring and harbour, as well as metaphors of closeness and distance, and related metaphors of rejection, absence, and marginalisation: 'God is absent' and 'God is elusive' are powerful examples of such metaphors today.

In the very act of making metaphor, the conventionality of language is destabilised setting the analogical and poetic imagination free to enter as yet unknown terrains of sacred and transcendental experience. Root metaphor in particular permits us to relocate our dislocated spirits and reach towards newly glimpsed places of deep belonging that keep close company with equally deep places of challenge and disturbance. This paradoxical quality is particularly apparent in the 'life-after-death' metaphor familiar to the Christian eschatological tradition and its 'life/death' variations. The 'life/death' metaphor unfolds in a cluster of other metaphors and their related fields of meaning. These include the 'rebirth' metaphors of baptism and the 'born again' metaphors of adult conversion experiences, the paradoxical 'life-saving/life-losing' metaphors associated with the process of Christian discipleship (Mark 8:35), the 'true self/false self' metaphors that open avenues to understanding contemplative transformation, and the 'Christ/Adam' metaphors that play significant roles in Christian theology. While there is a unitary point of reference ('life/death') in these metaphors, the cluster has many senses that help us to understand the developmental challenges of the spiritual journey.[39]

The 'life-after-death' metaphor projects a future that is seen to be intrinsic to the experience of both human freedom and human consciousness. The metaphor generates a complex world of meanings by contrasting two apparently conflictual fields of meaning. The 'life' metaphor clusters images of breath, spirit, hope, joy, vitality, flow, energy, love, togetherness, community and the like. The 'death' metaphor clusters images of limitation, ending, sorrow, stasis, alienation, loneliness, diminishment, decay, despair and the like. Complex metaphors of this kind introduce a sustained tension because their contrasting clusters clash with conventional experience.[40] It is the struggle with this tension that allows the 'life-after-death' metaphor to generate new meaning horizons for the self, new worldviews, and new ways of living and understanding the meaning of life to the full (John 10:10).

The 'balance' metaphor is another example of this kind of tension. It clearly generates its own tensive contrasts with 'imbalance', 'rebalance', 'fluctuation', and 'see-saw' metaphors. The 'balance-imbalance-rebalance' worlds of meanings are not only expressive of the cosmos and the human place in it, they also have implications for the quality of human interaction with the whole gamut of physical, ethical, psychospiritual, religious and ecological realms and their corresponding fields of meaning. In spirituality the 'tradition' metaphor and the 'naïveté' metaphor trigger similar tensions. The 'fidelity-dissidence' cluster that unfolds the 'tradition' metaphor, and the 'innocence-guilt' cluster that unfolds the 'naïveté' metaphor generate tensions that lie very close to the heart of every spiritual journey. The same is true of the mind-body-spirit cluster in contexts where the elements of the triad are viewed in the light of 'energy system' metaphors. The implications of 'block-wound-antagonism' clusters are not difficult to trace when they are set in opposition to 'heal-care-befriend' clusters, especially when potentials for failure are taken into consideration. The need in committed spirituality for on-going critical reflection, on-going connection to the tradition of faith, and the courage to ask relevant questions can be either strengthened or weakened by metaphors and their interactive fields of meaning. Bland spirituality avoids creative social engagement in favour of uncritical comfort zones populated by dead metaphors.

In spirituality, how we come-to-know ourselves is key to how we come-to-know others: hence the conflicting tensions of 'deep-shallow' metaphor clusters. The process of coming-to-know starkly unfolds the implications of 'commitment-to-awareness' as a foundational metaphor in domains of spiritual growth. The same is true of the co-creative flow of human-divine encounter. In Hebrew and Christian spirituality, the *imago dei* or 'image of God', is a root metaphor. So is the related process of *theosis*/deification. The same is true of the pivotal image of God as Rock (Psalm 18:2, 31) and the images of the Spirit as burning bush, shining face, burning oven, nuptial chamber, lamp, leaven, light and living water.[41] Spiritual discourse is grounded in such clusterings of metaphors. Metaphor allows the spiritual adventure to reveal the full spectrum of embodied human experience. Brian Seaward's imaginative cluster is very contemporary. He imagines the spiritual journey as a flight in an airplane: the bumpy take-offs, the clear blue skies, the colourful horizons, the moments of unbearable turbulence, the unscheduled stops, and more often than not, the smooth landings.[42]

Metaphors in spirituality spread over a wide number of clusters or paired sets that are easily identified:

accord-discord;
balance-imbalance;
birthing-growing;
blessing-cursing;
bright-dull;
chaos-order;
clear and obscure;
contingency and ultimacy;
creative-destructive;
darkness and light;
dead wood and green wood;
dead-alive;
deep-shallow;
departure-arrival;
developing-transforming;
dirty-clean;
dying and rising;
earthly-heavenly;
embodied-disembodied;
erotic-unitive;
face-voice;
fertile, fruitful, barren;
fire and smoke;
front-back;
goals and processes;
grace-destruction;
harmony-disharmony;

heart-mind;
height-depth;
imprisoned-set free;
inner-outer;
in-out;
losing and finding;
loving-hating;
on-off;
oppression-liberation;
part-whole;
play and creation;
presence-absence;
quiet-action;
relational-social;
rigid-fluid/flexible;
sadness-joy;
seeking and finding;
serenity-turmoil;
solitude, loneliness, community;
stages and levels;
still-engaged;
stillness and storm;
strong-weak;
success-failure;
up-down;
value-disvalue;
wayposts, signs, signals.

- height-depth: (in the world of spirituality deep is high);
- journey, path, way, lay-by, dead-end, labyrinth, maze, pilgrimage;
- metaphors of desire: hungering, thirsting, pining, melting, longing;
- mountain, valley, river, sea, desert, pasture, good place-bad place are used to depict spiritual states;
- rescue, redeem, save, justify, teach, heal and empower are used extensively in Christian spirituality;
- sadness-joy; (in the world of spirituality metanoia is joyful-sadness);
- stillness and storm (in spirituality these metaphors ask where is God?);
- success-failure; (in the world of spirituality serenity is success);
- up-down; (in the world of spirituality transformation is up);
- walking, running, climbing, descending, ascending, departing, returning;
- warfare/conflict metaphors: struggling, fighting, wrestling, tempted, victorious, vanquished.

In generating meaning, metaphors employ an array of geographic, ecological, dynamic, and relational experiences to generate windows onto
new and often surprising meaning possibilities. The challenge for the
student of spirituality is to find ways of navigating through the luxuriantly
fertile welter of metaphorical forms revealed in oral and written descriptions of spiritual experience.[43] In such work the relation between
metaphor, metonymy and other tropes is not difficult to trace.[44] Nor is the
welter of root and simple metaphor normally encountered in spirituality
difficult to identify since they draw on a wide range of personal and
collective sensate, cultural, religious, and ecological experiences that are
easy to assemble:[45]

- the human experience of geographic and ecological location:
  journey, path, way, street, mountain, desert, oasis, river, holy
  places, buildings, boundary, barrier, block;
- embodied experiences of dynamic movement: struggle, battle,
  working at, running, seeking, mining, drama, flight, order, chaos,
  power, forces, ascent, descent, pilgrimage, dance, rhythm, time,
  connection, grounding;
- embodied experiences related to life itself: birth, death, infancy,
  growth, transformation, crisis, health, illness, diminishment;
  included here are auditory metaphors (the inner ear) and visual
  metaphors (the inner eye);
- social relations: leader, follower, citizen, self, other, parent,
  sibling, friend, exchange, love, law, danger, fear, risk, enemy;
- metaphors relating to measure: abundance, proportion, increasing,
  decreasing;
- metaphors relating to orientations and directions: centre, periphery,
  up, down, in, out, north, south, turning;
- metaphors relating to shapes: sphere, square;
- metaphors relating to utensils: containers, pots;
- metaphors relating to modes of transport: plane, ship, car;
- metaphors relating to conditions: poor, rich; stop, go;
- metaphors relating to rescue: imprisoned, free; wounded, healed;
- metaphors relating to ultimacy: a warm world, a cold world; eros
  or life instinct and thanatos or death instinct; growth, decay;
- metaphors relating to magnitudes are also encountered: infinite,
  almighty.

Each of these metaphor-clusters, image schemas and pairs map and imaginatively express basic themes in spirituality giving rise to interweaving
experiential images, rhythms and dynamics.[46] Definitions of spirituality

regularly reveal a metaphorical structure. Consider the metaphor clusters in the following definitions:

- spirituality is an adventurous journey through the labyrinth of life in which what is lost is found and what is wounded is healed in the flowing embrace of meaning and love;
- spirituality is knowing when to stand like mountain flow like water.[47]
- mysticism is the ability to swim knowingly in the vast ocean of divine compassion.

The role of metaphor in spirituality is to build bridges, open doors, paint pictures, make connections, challenge and surprise. Metaphor is about relationships and integrations, potentials and limits, ascents and descents, now describing pungent quiverings, then a dim star. Metaphor moves between the familiar and the unfamiliar, the embodied and the abstract, now describing hidden treasure, then the stone of the fear of God. Metaphors guide us through dark places and places where the veil of mystery turns translucent. Metaphor is at work as spiritual experience begins to reveal its bidirectional and double character: flowing between the human and the divine, the secular and the sacred, and the bright and dark aspects of the human self. In spirituality, metaphors reveal more than new understandings or new images. They reveal us to ourselves. Root metaphors challenge the self to relate to its own double nature. Dancing with self-revealing metaphor, spiritual pilgrims are confronted with their own human predicament, vividly depicted in the 'life-death' metaphor. New forms of knowledge, new images rise to confront those on spiritual journeys with states of suspension and struggle. Painful truth begets truthful pain if depth is to discover the way of ascent.

There is another, more technical issue to be faced. When metaphor and its sibling tropes are applied to spirituality it is not always clear whether cognitive or poetic forms of metaphor are at work, whether we are journeying along cooler cognitively grounded paths or image grounded paths bursting with affect and emotion. Are we using metaphor as it is understood by cognitive science or in the more aesthetic terms of narrative poetics? Is there an interplay between them? Is a dialogue between the two at work in spiritual narrative and discourse? A way to answer this question lies in an understanding of Kant's *schema*, an art whose roots lie deep in the human soul. Gilles Fauconnier suggests that the schema actually bridges the abstract and embodied worlds.[48] The schema is the ground on which the metaphor is built precisely because the schema is a structure for organising both our experience and our understanding. Michael Spitzer notes that the schema serves an ordering purpose with the power not only to structure experience but also to generate images that fit concepts.[49]

Spitzer's vision makes it possible to offer a lively metaphorical description of spirituality. Spirituality is an evolving landscape where people dance along a transformative path alive with the rhythms and songs of soul open to the gifting presence of divine Spirit responding actively to the call to change the world. The rich metaphor cluster at work in this description is rooted in the experience of space, motion, journey, engaged service, timing and music. It has both cognitive and poetic referents that structure and orient a powerful affect-laden image full of transformative potential, alive with formative and developmental dynamics. Spiritual narrative also uses metaphor to paint pictures and to evoke image schemas that speak equally to the depths of human desire and to the depths of human discontent. The presence of dreams and visions in spiritual narrative are clear evidence of the power of image and metaphor to impact life and meaning. Powerful metaphors, affect-laden images and dream-visions that contain a challenge, a threat or a call need respectful treatment. The challenge is to allow the imagery to speak for itself and not force it into the straitjacket of theory-driven interpretation. In theory-driven encounters the image is easily subordinated to the word and effortlessly repressed. Images are bearers of understanding, carriers of new stories and new insights. We should delight in the news they bring.

The challenge in spiritual narrative and discourse is to allow what imagery gathers to emerge as meaning. Poetics works with sensuous images and metaphor gives them verbal expression. Both cognitive and poetic metaphor have the power to take us into soft, blurry domains and landscapes that paradoxically allow for a creative interweaving, a choral chanting, a partnered dancing, where orientational and structural schemas are woven into new songs, new modes of liberating awareness that once seen and heard can be given fresh voice.[50] The challenge posed by the new spirituality lies in the paradoxical fruitfulness of dead-metaphor-seeking-revival. Today, lost imagery is finding new life and in the finding makes new-old descriptions of spirit possible. That, too, is part of the world of metaphor: a different way of hearing leads to a different way of seeing. And so a new vision is born from the ashes of the old.[51]

℄ *Root metaphors: imagining masculine and feminine spirituality*
To what extent is spirituality gender blind? To what extent is spirituality gender specific? To what extent is spirituality gender neutral? To what extent is it still possible to explore metaphorical understanding in ways that evade questions of gender difference-in-equality? But then, what is gender blindness if not a metaphor? What is gender neutrality if not a metaphor? How can gender specific spirituality be explored in the absence

of creative metaphor? And what happens to spiritual visions when their rich life-giving arrays of metaphor are reduced to rigid and exclusionary systems? Deadening spiritualities are littered with the bleached bones of dead metaphors. The truth is that gendered experience is structured by cultural metaphors and their respective oppressive or emancipatory resonances.

In the search for authentic spirituality women and men of integrity seek to structure located gendered experience through emancipatory metaphors attuned to culturally different yet equal ways of being and becoming in the world. For example, in the Christian tradition the root metaphor 'the kingdom of God' clusters other images and organises them into meaningful discourse. Typical of this process are complex images of the 'holy man', the 'holy woman', and 'children of God' as well as King and Lord. A spider's web of unquestioning naïveté is dangerous in the face of such complex images. The spiders at the heart of webs of unquestioning naïveté have the power to suck the life out of the best of spiritual intentions. Consider the gender reversal implicit in the 'bridal' metaphor when it is applied to heterosexual men's spirituality. Consider the shock spiritual naïveté suffers when it is confronted by the metaphor of 'heterosexual-man-as-bride'. Then consider what happens when female spirituality is imaged as crazy-wild Dionysiac wisdom set against stereotypical male images of cool, emotionally detached, Apollonian logic. Such divisive contrasts harm the spiritual meaning-horizons of both women and men. And what about the paradox of the wise-holy-fool, that liminal figure who stands in the transitional spaces of culture and spirit? Is it folly to be a wise or holy fool today? Can women be wise-holy-fools? What about the foolishness of Jesus and the women who stood with him to the end and the new beginning? Was Magdalen a wise-holy-fool?

A similar discomfort is at work in relation to feminine God-images. In his conversation with Nicodemus Jesus used a feminine metaphor for spiritual rebirth that images the Spirit as the womb-of-God (John 3:1-7). A feminine God-image is also at work in the 'assiduously searching woman' metaphor in the parable of the lost coin (Luke 15:8-10). Jesus also employed a 'baker-woman' metaphor to image God (Matthew 13:33) before he applied the 'mother-hen' metaphor to himself (Matthew 23:37 & Luke 13:34). Metaphor confronts us with the complex distortions of gender assumptions. A vibrant spirituality needs rich metaphor clusters open to both masculine and feminine energies in order to maintain imaginative contact with the reality of passion and desire, of eros and agape. A simple glance at the *Song of Songs* makes the point that masculine and feminine love needs the other if love is to renew the world. Such love is as strong as death: a gazelle or a young stag dancing on mountains of spices (Song of Songs 8:6-14).

The fundamental root metaphors in gendered spiritualities are imaginatively subtle and complex, but they are quickly if tersely formulated:

- 'the feminine is womb/in/holding'
- 'the masculine is up'.

The energies these companion metaphors identify have given rise over two and a half millennia to richly imaginative and deeply provocative reflections about the nature of human being-in-the-world and the nature of a God who subsumes both sets of energies and qualities (Isaiah 49:15; Acts 17:28). Feminine and masculine metaphors identify the interactive energies that inform integral spiritualities. They also inform the lives of spiritually mature women and men open to the interweaving subtleties of the human spirit, especially when it is confronted by dangerous memory. Feminine and masculine metaphors inform how the affective, sexual, vital, creative and transcendent dimensions of spirituality seek fulfilment.

Feminine metaphor clusters expand on root 'holding' and 'womb' imagery (Isaiah 49:16; Jeremiah 1:5; Psalm 139:13-16) in ways that engage with fundamental relational states, processes, invitations and commitments. Indeed, a shared semantic root links womb to love, compassion, mercy, pity and tenderness.[52] The profound imagery that expresses the 'womb' metaphor in the Hebrew imagination suggests a life-enhancing force that flows from a person's inner depths, a force that is life-giving, nourishing, holding and encompassing. Life-giving and life-restoring echoes of soul and spirit flow creatively from such a richly informed imagination. Consider, for example, Barbara Brown Taylor's metaphor for feminine pastoral care and concern. She speaks eloquently of the 'leaking breast' syndrome.[53] Then consider Symeon the New Theologian's image of humility as the 'womb' in which both men and women 'conceive' the Holy Spirit.[54] In spiritual conversation, many sensual and physical metaphors are common: warmth, energy, flow, growth, nourishment, home-making, harvest. They keep company with metaphors from the natural world: frontier, river, tree, spring and well. So are relational images: father, mother, sister, brother, lover, friend, mentor, midwife, child, stranger, pilgrim, tourist, vagabond and fool. Therapeutic metaphors are also familiar friends: heal, save, renew, restore.[55]

The feminine root metaphor is also suggestive of the intense feeling states that arise deep within the human body in moments of strong intimacy or concern. In this sense both compassion and the appropriate anger that arises in contexts of personal and social injustice are linked in the Hebrew imagination to the womb as metaphor for the incubating quality of deep human interiority. The same Hebrew word pair *rachamim/rachem* activates passionate images of the womb-compassion of Yahweh.[56]

The strength of the feminine root metaphor is its capacity to describe how something new is born from the inner depths of soul, the womb of spirit incubating spiritual life. Soul-womb holds spirit-life until it is ready to be freed into the world singing new songs, sending fiery new rhythms across the artificial boundaries of exclusion and enmity.

The masculine 'up' metaphor tends to have a dynamic outward and upward focus that shines through the military and athletic imagery often encountered in the spiritual narratives written by men. The 'up' metaphor easily leads to the 'spirituality is battle' metaphor (Jeremiah 46:3-4; 1 Corinthians 14:8), which in turn evokes images of violence (Matthew 11:12). As a consequence masculine imagery tends to take on a more blatant, more obviously forceful character than feminine imagery, though the energy of the protective mother cannot be ignored. In patriarchal cultures masculine energy has a more public face. Masculine energy is more obviously ambitious (1 Corinthians 12:31). It embraces upward images of soul journeys more readily than descents into landscapes of pathos where compassionate awareness and understanding is demanded.

In Gregory of Nyssa, for example, the upward metaphor is imagined as a journey from the cave of earthly darkness and deception to the bright promise of divine intelligence. Upward movements are oriented towards the good; downward movements tend towards evil; and because of the natural force of gravity downward evil is easier than upward good.[57] In masculine spirituality, then, upward and downward imagery has implications for operative assumptions about the nature of reality. Spirituality is sometimes imagined as consisting of three interconnected journeys: an upward journey, an inward journey, and an outward journey. The upward journey seeks God; the inward journey seeks the depths of the soul; the outward journey seeks to be of service in the world.[58] What feminine and masculine energies are at work in each of these journeys? How do they interweave? What courage and commitment do they require?

The masculine imagination easily begets imagery of heroic quests and solitary desert or wilderness sojourns, of climbing mountains, of courageous endurance (Hebrews 12:2), of resisting evil (James 4:7), and of overcoming all obstacles placed in the hero's path. Image clusters evocative of struggling, fighting, ascending, overcoming, and conquering are common. Qualitatively ambivalent words like crusader, warrior, knight and soldier regularly occur in spiritual accounts shaped by masculine metaphor. Goal motivation is strong. So is ensuring that the struggle is not in vain (Philippians 2:16). This same imagination is at play in Paul's call to Timothy to fight the good fight (1 Timothy 6:12). It is there in Paul's invitation to the Corinthians to run the spiritual race so as to win the prize (1 Corinthians 9:24-25; see also Hebrews 12:1). The same imagination is at play in Paul's invitation to every Christian to put on the full armour of God (Ephesians 6:10-18), to wear the armour of light (Romans 13:12). In this imagination the word becomes a two-edged sword able to cut surgically through to the hidden depths and reveal secret thoughts and feelings (Hebrews 4:12-13). Masculine root metaphor conjures up robust spiritual images full of confidence and the strength that comes from trust in God (Philippians 4:13).

Where do these two very different energies come together in spirituality? They come together in compassionate action, they inform engaged contemplation, they shape emancipatory spiritualities, they mould integrated spiritual development, they describe mature spiritual relationships and intimacies, and together they resist the dominator and conniver dynamics at work in the world's affairs. Feminine and masculine metaphors and their clusters reveal foundational assumptions about spirituality. Governing root metaphors construct identifiable conceptual networks that are influenced by both cultural and cognitive location. The classic English spiritual text the *Scale* or *Ladder of Perfection* written by Walter Hilton (died 1396) is a well-known example of the combined use of 'ladder' and 'journey' root metaphors.

What is particularly interesting about these two metaphors is their traditional linear or goal-oriented imagery and the positive masculine bias hidden there. Hilton's *Ladder* does engage with the disciple's journey to Jerusalem, a metaphorical destination that brings to fruition the peace traditionally endowed by transforming pilgrimage and engagement with its creative metaphors.[59] But to what extent can Hilton's vision be read in the respectful terms of gender equality-in-difference sought today? A similar question can be put to the governing metaphors in Julian of Norwich's *Showings* and the womb or holding resonances of her anchor-hold. Both works reveal the presence of gendered sensitivities in the way governing root metaphors structure the respective texts. Gender roles – and particularly women's roles as wives and mothers – are always potent symbols of cultural change or cultural continuity.

Even a brief glance at the spiritualities arising in consumer societies demonstrates that gendered imagery remains a compelling symbol in contemporary spirituality; and that opens the way to another matter. Consider the disconcerting gender imagery at play in Ezekiel 16 in the Hebrew Bible. The text seems to be structured around the metaphor of a defeated soldier. Having lost a battle, he then loses his macho identity and is cursed as a woman: 'a weak man is a woman' is the governing metaphor. According to Tamar Komionkowski, what we see in Ezekiel 16 is a reversal of the 'a weak man is a woman' metaphor. Wife Israel is acting like a male and crossing gender boundaries. She has over-stepped the mark in relation to God. Instead of being passive, dependent, and connected only to God, she has become assertive, independent, and nonmonogamous. She has become masculinised and in so doing transgresses culturally located metaphors of gendered order.[60] One gender reversal sets the scene for another, neither of them neutral, neither of them lacking in spiritual pathos, both of them giving rise to provocative questions about attempts to construct de-gendered or culturally collusive spiritualities. Similar reversals are at work in Gospel texts that are structured in the light of the social status of eunuchs, barren women, and children in the ancient Near East.

There is, of course, another side to feminine spirituality and other root metaphors that give it very different expression. Even Jacob's ladder (Genesis 28:11-19) may be re-imagined as a connective metaphor; but it remains difficult for a man to completely ignore the metaphor's phallic credentials. As Carol Ochs has noted, women's spirituality tends to be informed by mothering and relational metaphors that conflict with linear or goal-oriented journey metaphors precisely because strong mothering and relational experiences favour process over destination.[61] The challenge for contemporary spirituality will be to respect the different ways metaphors sing of masculine and feminine modes of being-in-the-world, of appropriately located feminine and masculine ways of being and becoming. Here is the challenge for contemporary spirituality in its dance with gendered metaphors, particularly the 'spirituality is a journey' metaphor given its dominance in spiritual narratives and definitions.

To what extent can the journey metaphor be re-imagined in a gender-respectful way? To what extent can the journey metaphor be re-imagined as an open-ended caring and relational process that embraces the promises of wholeness singing in lives that are struggling to let Jesus live in a marginalising, secular world? To what extent can the journey metaphor engage with the real challenges of dangerous memory and the victims of injustice and oppression, especially the women and children sold into sex slavery? To what extent can the journey metaphor step aside from the compromising comforts of cheap grace and sing a song of integrity in an unjust world? The audacity of spirit needs to be nurtured by many metaphors if it is to develop a capacity to confront the many branching challenges of a dangerous world that is ready to exterminate species, pollute rivers, and destroy the forests that are the lungs of the planet. We need wise metaphors to confront us with our destructive foolishness. We need wise-holy-fools in the places of crosses.

## CONCLUSION

According to Paul Greenhalgh, 'metaphors are mediums which help development.'[62] Metaphors do this by providing imaginative access to 'frozen aspects' of the personality and suggesting ways to unfreeze them. The implication is that in psychospiritual contexts metaphor literacy is linked to stages of development and that stages of psychospiritual development constrain imaginative expression. Human development shows no linear progress; it is open to distortions and deformations. By implication the metaphors used in spiritual conversations will bring to the surface a range of constraining issues that impact psychospiritual development. Metaphors assist developmental processes because metaphors are portals to the soul: they make an appropriate invitation to grow possible because of the versatility of their symbolic imagery.[63] Metaphors open windows to the soul. They help us to identify the fetters that hold it in thrall. They help soul to reconnect to the music of life. Freud's favourite metaphor for psychoanalysis was 'psychoanalysis is archaeology of the soul'. Spirituality is the soul's way of life.

In spiritual conversations the freedoms and oppressions of soul come to the surface. What happens next will depend in large measure on a person's facility with metaphor. That facility in turn will influence the expression of the frozen or unfrozen, fettered or unfettered imagination at work in people's lives.[64] Metaphor reveals the soul's language, a language of process and paradox; a language of intimacy. Metaphor is above all the language of mystical knowing, serving unfettered adult imagining, giving soul the freedom to sing new songs of wholeness and the Living God, songs that suggest gracious illumination in the light of Spirit.[65] Through metaphor spirit learns to dance before the Eternal Eye without minnow-mind darting away from the divine gaze. Like development psychologies, the new spirituality seems to have more in common with jazz, with its openness to individual and group improvisation, than to a fixed musical score with no room for personal intervention.[66] Can faith-based spiritualities sing to both kinds of music and let Jesus live to different rhythms? In either case we all need audacity of spirit.

THEMES AND QUESTIONS FOR FURTHER REFLECTION
1. Explore the role of metaphor in spiritual conversation.
2. Can you identify the metaphors you and your friends use to give expression to your spirituality?
3. If you follow a faith path in your spirituality: how do you understand the relationship between faith as a divine gift and its working out in love in the world? Explore the role metaphor plays in faith contexts.
4. The interplay of feminine and masculine metaphors is everywhere in contemporary and historical spirituality. Can you recognise their influence in your spiritual vision?

FURTHER READING

Barbara Brown Taylor, *Leaving Church: A Memoir of Faith* (New York: HarperCollins, 2007).

NOTES:

1. For a discussion of the role of maps and quests in the study of spirituality see Wade Clark Roof, *Spiritual Marketplace: Baby Boomers and the Remaking of American Religion* (Princeton, NJ: Princeton University Press, 1999) 3–45

2. Quoted in William P. Brown, *Seeing the Psalms: A Theology of Metaphor* (Louisville, London: Westminster John Knox Press, 2002) 3.

3. See Patrick Kavanagh, 'The Great Hunger' in *Selected Poems*, ed. Antoinette Quinn (London: Penguin, 1996) 28.

4. George Lakoff and Mark Turner, *More than Cool Reason: A Field Guide to Poetic Metaphor* (Chicago and London: University of Chicago Press, 1989) 62.

5. Ibid. 64–65.

6. See Zygmunt Bauman, *Postmodernity and Its Discontents* (Cambridge: Polity Press, 1997) 132.

7. George Lakoff, 'The Contemporary Theory of Metaphor' in Andrew Ortony, ed., *Metaphor and Thought*. Second Edition (Cambridge: Cambridge University Press, 1993) 202–251 at 204.

8. See Stuart M. Tave, *Lovers, Clowns and Fairies: An Essay on Comedies* (Chicago: University of Chicago Press, 1993) 17–18.

9. See Zygmunt Bauman, *Postmodernity and Its Discontents* op.cit. 8–9.

10. Sandra M. Schneiders, *The Revelatory Text: Interpreting the New Testament as Sacred Scripture*. Second Edition (Collegeville, MA: The Liturgical Press, 1999) 29.

11. Ibid. 123.

12. Ibid. 139.

13. Denise Levertov, *The Stream and the Sapphire* (New York: New Directions Books, 1997) 31.

14. See Andrew Goatly, *The Language of Metaphors* (London and New York: Routledge, 1997) 107–136.

15. See Timothy G. Reagan and Terry A. Osborn, *The Foreign Language Educator in Society: Toward a Critical Pedagogy* (Mahwah, NJ: Lawrence Erlbaum Associates, 2002) 56–58. See also Zoltán Kövecses, 'The Scope of Metaphor' in Antonio Barcelona, ed., *Metaphor and Metonymy at the Crossroads: A Cognitive Perspective* (Berlin and New York: Mouton de Gruyter, 2003) 79–92; Reidar Aasgaard, *My Beloved Brothers and Sisters: Christian Siblingship in Paul* (London and New York: T & T Clark International, 2004) 23–33.

16. See Zoltán Kövecses, *Metaphor: A Practical Introduction* (New York: Oxford University Press, 2002). See also George Lakoff and Mark Johnson, *Metaphors We Live By*. With a new Afterword (Chicago: The University of Chicago Press, 2003).

17. George Lakoff and Mark Johnson, *Metaphors We Live By*, op.cit. 274.

18. See Zoltán Kövecses, *Metaphor* op.cit. 29–40.

19. See Richard Harvey Brown, *Social Science as Civic Discourse: Essays on the Invention, Legitimation, and Uses of Social Theory* (Chicago and London: The University of Chicago Press, 1989) 52, 96–97. See also Adele E. Clarke, *Situational Analysis: Grounded Theory after the Postmodern Turn* (Thousand Oaks, London, New Delhi: Sage Publications, 2005) 39.

20. See Zygmunt Bauman, *Postmodernity and Its Discontents* op.cit. 16.

21. See Donald L. Gelpi, *The Gracing of Human Experience: Rethinking the Relationship between Nature and Grace* (Collegeville, MN: The Liturgical Press, 2001) 282.

22. See Erik Ringmar, *Identity, Interest and Action: A Cultural Explanation of Sweden's Intervention in the Thirty Years War* (Cambridge: Cambridge University Press, 1996) 72.

23. See Dan R. Stiver, *Theology After Ricoeur: New Directions in Hermeneutical Theology* (Louisville, London, Leiden: Westminster John Knox Press, 2001) 106–110.

24. See Kelly Bulkeley, *The Wilderness of Dreams: Exploring the Religious Meanings of Dreams in Modern Western Culture* (Albany, NY: State University of New York Press, 1994) 149.

25. Jacques Derrida, 'White Mythology: Metaphor in the Text of Philosophy' in *Margins of Philosophy*. Translated, with Additional Notes by Alan Bass (Chicago: The University of Chicago Press, 1982) 207–271 at 209.

26. See Karl Simms, *Paul Ricoeur* (London and New York: Routledge, 2003) 128–130.

27. See Mats Alvesson and Kaj Skölberg, *Reflexive Methodology: New Vistas for Qualitative Research* (London, Thousand Oaks, New Delhi: Sage Publications, 2000) 89–92.

28. See George Lakoff and Mark Johnson, *Metaphors We Live By* op.cit. 193.

29. See Kelly Bulkeley, *The Wilderness of Dreams* op.cit. 149.

30. See Mary Gerhart & Allan Russell, *Metaphoric Process: The Creation of Scientific and Religious Understanding*. With a Foreword by Paul Ricoeur (Fort Worth: Texas Christian University Press, 1984) 105–106.

31. Paul Avis, *God and the Creative Imagination: Metaphor, Symbol, and Myth in Religion and Theology* (London: Routledge, 1999) vii.

32. Denise Levertov, *The Stream and the Sapphire* op.cit. 66

33. Paul Avis, *God and the Creative Imagination*, op. cit. ix

34. See Joel D. S. Rasmussen, *Between Irony and Witness: Kierkegaard's Poetics of Faith, Hope and Love* (New York, London: T & T Clark, 2005) 12, 58, 80, 108 and 173.

35. See ibid. 6.

36. See for example Gary Sherbert, 'Frye's Double Vision: Metaphor and

the Two sources of Religion' in Jeffrey Donaldson and Alan Mendelson, eds, *Frye and the Word: Religious Contexts in the Writings of Northrop Frye* (Toronto, Buffalo, London: University of Toronto Press, 2004) 59–80. See also Peter Sharpe, *The Ground of Our Beseeching: Metaphor and the Poetics of Meditation* (Cranbury, NJ: Associated University Presses, 2004).

37. What follows developed in conversation with Arnold B. Come, *Kierkegaard as Humanist: Discovering Myself* (Montreal & Kingston, London, Buffalo: McGill-Queens University Press, 1995). For other direct influences see Craig R. Dykstra, 'No Longer Strangers: The Church and its Educational Ministry' in Jeff Astley, Leslie J. Francis and Colin Crowder, eds, *Theological Perspectives on Christian Formation: A Reader on Theology and Christian Education* (Leominster & Grand Rapids: Gracewing and Eerdmans Publishing, 1996); Eileen Flynn, Gloria Thomas, *Living Faith: An Introduction to Theology*. Second edition (Lanham and Oxford: Sheed & Ward, 1995); Jeff Astley and Leslie J. Francis, eds, *Christian Perspectives on Faith Development: A Reader* (Leominster & Grand Rapids: Gracewing and Eerdmans Publishing, 1992); Daniel L. Migliore, *Faith Seeking Understanding: An Introduction to Christian Theology*. Second Edition (Grand Rapids/Cambridge: Eerdmans Publishing, 2004); Peter Drilling, *Premodern Faith in a Postmodern Culture: A Contemporary Theology of the Trinity* (Lanham and Oxford: Rowman & Littlefield, 2006); Robin Gill, 'The Practice of Faith' in Gareth Jones, ed., *The Blackwell Companion to Modern Theology* (Malden, MA, Oxford, Carlton: Blackwell Publishing, 2004) 3–18; David Willis, *Clues to the Nicene Creed: A Brief Outline of the Faith* (Grand Rapids/Cambridge: Eerdmans Publishing, 2005).

38. Bradley P. Holt, *Thirsty for God: A Brief History of Christian Spirituality* (Minneapolis, MN: Augsburg Fortress, 1993); Kenneth D. Boa, *Conformed to His Image: Biblical and Practical Approaches to Spiritual Formation* (Grand Rapids, MI: Zondervan, 2001); Agneta Schreurs, *Psychotherapy and Spirituality: Integrating the Spiritual Dimension into Therapeutic Practice* (London and Philadelphia: Jessica Kingsley Publishers, 2002) 85–122; Mark Holstead, 'How Metaphors Structure Our Spiritual Understanding' in Cathy Ochs and Clive Erricker, eds, *Spiritual Education: Literary, Empirical and Pedagogical Approaches* (Brighton and Portland: Sussex Academic Press, 2005) 137–153; Eugene H. Peterson, *Eat This Book: A Conversation in the Art of Spiritual Reading* (Grand Rapids and Cambridge: Eerdmans Publishing, 2006) and *Where Your Treasure Is: Psalms that Summon You from Self to Community* (Grand Rapids, MN: Eerdmans Publishing, 1993); Sandra M. Schneiders, *The Revelatory Text*: op.cit. 27–63; Carol Ochs, *Women and Spirituality*, Second Edition (Lanham and London: Rowman and Littlefield, 1997); Nicola Slee, *Women's Faith Development: Patterns and Processes* (Aldershot and Burlington: Ashgate Publishing, 2004). See also Jerome W. Berryman, 'Play as a Means of Grace' in Cathy Ochs and Clive Erricker, eds, *Spiritual Education*, op.cit. 80–93.

39. See Richard L. Mendelsohn, *The Philosophy of Gottlob Frege* (Cambridge: Cambridge University Press, 2005) 27–40.

40. See Mary Gerhart & Allan Russell, *Metaphoric Process* op.cit. 121–140.

41. See Basil Krivocheine, *St Symeon the New Theologian: Life – Spirituality – Doctrine* (Crestwood, NY: St Vladimir's Seminary Press, 1986) 405.

42. Brian Luke Seaward, *Stand Like Mountain Flow Like Water: Reflections on Stress and Human Spirituality* (Deerfield Beach, fl: Health Communications, Inc., 1997) 47.

43. See Alice Deignan, *Metaphor and Corpus Linguistics* (Amsterdam and Philadelphia: John Benjamins Publishing, 2005) 98–99.

44. Ibid. 53–74.

45. See for example, Kelly Bulkeley, *The Wilderness of Dreams*, op.cit. 19–23; Leslie A. Baxter, 'Root Metaphors in Accounts of Developing Romantic Relationships' in William Dragon and Steve Duck, eds, *Understanding Research in Personal Relationships: A Text with Readings* (London, Thousand Oaks, New Delhi: Sage Publications, 2005) 87–98. See also Richard Harvey Brown, *Social Science as Civic Discourse* op.cit. 90; Agneta Schreurs, *Psychotherapy and Spirituality* op.cit. 85–122 ; Cathy Ochs and Clive Erricker, eds, *Spiritual Education: Literary, Empirical and Pedagogical Approaches* op.cit.; J. Mark Halstead, 'Metaphor, Cognition and Spiritual Reality' in David Carr and John Haldane, eds, *Spirituality, Philosophy and Education* (London and New York: Routledge Falmer, 2003) 83–96.

46. For an in-depth review of metaphor see René Dirvan, Ralf Pörings, eds, *Metaphor and Metonymy in Comparison and Contrast* (Berlin/New York: Mouton de Gruyter, 2003).

47. Brian Luke Seaward, *Stand Like Mountain Flow Like Water*, op.cit.

48. Gilles Fauconnier, 'Analogical Counterfactuals' in Gilles Fauconnier and Eve Sweetser, eds, *Spaces, Worlds, and Grammar* (Chicago: Chicago University Press, 1996) 57–90 at 60.

49. Michael Spitzer, *Metaphor and Musical Thought* (Chicago and London: Chicago University Press, 2004) 60–76.

50. See Margaret Chatterjee, *The Language of Philosophy* (The Hague/ Boston/London: Martinus Nijhoff Publishers, 1981) 45–61.

51. See Paul Ricoeur, 'Meta-phor and Meta-physics' in Zeynep Direk and Leonard Lawlor, eds, *Jacques Derrida: Critical Assessments of Leading Philosophers.* Volume I. (London and New York: Routledge, 2002) 197–212.

52. See G. Johannes Botterweck, Helmar Ringgren and Heinz-Josef Fabry, eds, *Theological Dictionary of the Old Testament.* Translated by David E. Green. Volume XIII (Grand Rapids and Cambridge: Eerdmans Publishing, 2004) 437–458.

53. Barbara Brown Taylor, *Leaving Church: A Memoir of Faith* (New York: HarperCollins, 2007) 66.

54. See Basil Krivocheine, *St Symeon the New Theologian*, op.cit. 265.

55. See for example Nicola Slee, *Women's Faith Development*, op.cit. 65–66.

56. See Andrew D. Lester, *The Angry Christian: A Theology for Care and Counseling* (Louisville, London: Westminster John Knox Press, 2003) 37–39.

57. See Alden A. Mosshammer, 'Gregory's Intellectual Development: A Comparison of the Homilies on the Beatitudes with the Homilies on the Song of Songs' in Hubertus R. Drobner and Albert Viciano, eds, *Gregory of Nyssa: Homilies on the Beatitudes: An English Version with Commentary and Supporting Studies* (Leiden, Boston, Köln: Brill, 2000) 359–388.

58. See R. Paul Stevens, *Liberating the Laity: Equipping All the Saints for Ministry* (Vancouver, BC: Regent College Publishing, 2002) 161–164.

59. See Christopher Howse, ed., *Comfort* (New York, London: Continuum, 2004) 4–7.

60. S. Tamar Komionkowski, *Gender Reversal and Cosmic Chaos: A Study on the Book of Ezekiel* (London, New York: Continuum Books, 2003) 28 and 128.

61. See Carol Ochs, *Women and Spirituality*, Second Edition (Lanham and London: Rowman and Littlefield, 1997) 148.

62. Paul Greenhalgh, *Emotional Growth and Learning* (London and New York: Routledge, 1994) 140.

63. Ibid. 140–142.

64. See John J. Shea, *Finding God Again: Spirituality for Adults* (Lanham, Oxford: Rowman & Littlefield Publishers, 2005) 10–12, 75–79.

65. Ibid. 96–97.

66. See Patrick Bateson, 'Behavioral Development and Darwinian Evolution' in Susan Ovama, Paul E. Griffiths and Russell D. Grey, eds, *Cycles of Contingency: Developmental Systems and Evolution* (Cambridge, Mass: MIT Press, 2001) 149–166 at 157.

CHAPTER 5    *The Shifting Meaning of Words*

*We are drifting towards the mystical,*
*the esoteric and the hermetic.*

SETTING THE SCENE

This chapter explores more fully the meaning of the word *spirituality* as it is used today both within and beyond Christian usage, not least because we are entering an era of interspiritual dialogue that requires a more nuanced understanding of the word and the ways it helps us to name a vast and rich dimension of human experience and creativity. This will necessitate an approach that is simultaneously descriptive and technical. The technical moments will be intentionally brief, a kind of excursus or digression concerned in the main with the nature of definition. The descriptive mode, the kind of poetics of the possible we have already encountered, is intended to craft persuasive images of the spiritual world and its dancing invitations. The descriptive mode is also intended to generate an opportunity for conversation and personal reflection on the dynamic breadth and depth of spirituality, its contextual nature, its revelatory potential, and, especially in the Christian sense, its vision of God's vast lovingness of being and the invitation to open our spirits to soar on its uplifting currents in an epiphany of lovingly transformative meaning (1 John 4).

Two factors shape the criticality of the approach to be taken. The first is grounded in the implications of Johann Baptist Metz's powerful image of *dangerous memory* for an emerging spirituality, a theme we will return to later in the book. Following the horrors of the twentieth century a spirituality grounded in the human capacity for self-transcendence responsive to some ultimate meaning horizon – even God – is suspect on at least two grounds: the damage the twentieth century did to visions of the person as irreplaceably unique, and the subordination of ethical responsibility to the ambitions of power. The second factor concerns the challenges the postmodern represents to those whose spirituality is shaped by the desire to let Jesus live through the ethical lifestyle choices they personally make in postmodern, consumer societies. Both of these factors demand great audacity of spirit because, in Marie L. Baird's terms, the times challenge us to uncover anew a spirituality that springs from the ethical consideration of the other, which celebrates the other as the sacred ground of authentic self-emergence as a responsive and responsible being. [1]

In all of this I am struck by the interplay of two groanings echoing each other in counterpoint: the groaning of the cosmos seeking completion, and the groaning of human interiority in the throes of Gifting Spirit birth (see Romans 8:22 & 23). Spirituality is where their songs converge in an innovative life project birthed in the joy of rekindled wonder and the awesome challenge of ethical responsibility (see 2 Timothy 1:6). Imagine the spiritual life as an ethical dance with the utterly other, a transformative attending to the shared undersong of the inner and outer worlds, allowing life to move to their life renewing rhythms, their challenging beat. [2] Imagine spirituality as an invitation to dance like David before a God, an Other who beckons those who dance into a future beyond imagining, but a future easily misunderstood, as Micah's wife misunderstood. Imagine that spirituality has to do with the ways we navigate the channels and challenges of life, the ways we flow with and honour or baulk at and ill-use the self-other-cosmos-God relation. Imagine spirituality as the place where soul force, awakening flows of deep promise and desire, meets the limitless promise and desire of the Holy One, the Other, who calls us more fully into holy being, to become one with Their dance of life.

Then imagine spirituality in terms of a life resonating to cultural strains that favour a kind of nomadic wandering guided by a highly individualistic vision blind to the compromises demanded by the forces of history. Imagine the audacity of spirit needed to evolve a vibrant spirituality in a milieu where the basic landmarks of trust, mutual confidence and hope have been hopelessly obscured. Then try to imagine spirituality in terms of concrete life in the world where being and doing is all of a piece: where spiritual being is self-implicatingly made visible in ethically-grounded spiritual doing. Imagine spirituality as the encounter with the true self newly birthed in a lovingly transformative encounter with a God who comes through the other and difference, an Other-God who makes it impossible for me to rest in my own self-constructions and their defensive illusions of rigid closure. Then remember that spirituality disturbingly arises in embodied encounters with the other and the different, that it is meant to call us out of our protective bubbles and free us from our imprisoning cocoons. Does Jesus come alive in those moments of disturbance? Is the disturbance of otherness the ground for audacity of spirit?

Imagine spirituality as a journeying in the realms of history and politics, realms where the demands of economics and technology, of liberation and oppression, of creativity and the seductions of extremity and the wreckage of lives play out their games. Reflect on the spiritualities of imperfection, the spiritualities that have to learn how to deal with wreckage and failure; think of 12-step spiritualities; and contemplate spiritualities of woundedness, the kinds of woundedness that tenaciously hold bodies and memories and relationships in thrall.[3] Imagine the audacity of spirit such spiritualities demand. Imagine the courage a spirituality of shared weakness, of shared honesty and the acknowledgment of mutual vulnerability requires. Imagine a spirituality whose very strength is the recognition of weakness, whose ground is a flawed space honestly acknowledged, a spirituality that finds in mutual weakness a source of collective support and encouragement. Acknowledged weakness is the organic humus of self-transcendence and the fullness of humanity.

Then imagine spirituality as an invitation to dance towards a boundless future, a divinely bright spark sparkling in a darkness that simultaneously structures and challenges hope. Spirituality also confronts us with a seeming impossibility gifting the present with the chance to become; that shows us the way beyond; that invites us within; that calls us to the more and the deep in every single aspect of life; that refuses rigidity. Try to glimpse the promise of spirituality in every shimmering aspect of beauty, truth, and goodness; in every expression of unity and diversity; in every attempt to express love of life; in every attempt to grapple with transcendence; and in every troublesome facet of the human predicament: thematics demanding libraries. Then reflect on the search for the traces of God, traces that are difficult to define or pin down, but traces nonetheless that echo with promise and invitation: spirituality, after all, is the space where soul is enacted and spirit challenged to embrace reality audaciously, the space where soul dances and spirit sings to the beating rhythms of existence before the face of the Other, before the face of God.

## WHAT IS SPIRITUALITY?

What is spirituality? Despite the word images I have just painted, this is not an easy question to answer. Quite simply, the wild profusions and proliferating connotations of the word *spirituality* are fast outstripping the lexicon! And while spirituality has been explored throughout human history as a fundamental aspect of what it is to be human, in the contemporary milieu there is disagreement not only about its definition but also about its origins, functions and importance.[4] Nor is Christian spirituality an exception to this growing diversity, a diversity arising out of different theologies, different cultures, different histories, and different geographies, for all that there is a shared commonality rooted in the interweaving themes of faith, grace, person and God. Then add to the mix the different theories of anthropology and human identity within the human sciences

and philosophy that implicitly or explicitly influence different authors
and teachers and you will get some idea of the challenge facing present
attempts at definition. Even a cursory review of the literature and
research available will confirm these difficulties. They will also quickly
affirm that there is no agreed cross-disciplinary or universally acceptable
definition of our subject, and that the specific meaning of the word itself
has become remarkably elusive and vague.[5]

No single definition, description or image will in fact encompass the
spiritual revolution that is currently underway in Western cultures. No
definition could be exhaustive enough or omnicompetent enough to do
the contemporary phenomenon – or its study – full justice. This problem
has been recognised for more than a dozen years now.[6] The reasons for it
are not difficult to identify. For example, what is the point of departure
in seeking to define spirituality? If it is the self, how is the self to be
understood: as autonomous or as part of a community? If it is self-
transcendence, how is such transcendence to be understood and against
what horizon of meaning? If it is interiority, what is the role of action and
life in the world? If it is a life project in the world, is the project
individual or communal? What role do practices, literacies and discourses
play in defining a life project? Is the starting point prayer and meditation,
and their contribution to resiliency in times of crisis or bereavement? Is
spirituality to be defined as a characteristic of human being, and if so
what constitutes its nature and coherence? Is it a motivational characteristic? Is openness the key, or is transpersonal participative consciousness
the benchmark? What about the interplay of such polarities as freedom
and dependence, solitude and society, personal experience and social
reform, inner life and social activism, and what about conservative and
liberal preferences?[7] The problem is that the very choice of a starting
point runs the risk of setting polarising forces in motion, and generating
the suspicion that each starting point is a shaping element in a more
complex definitional field.

The areas of life subsumed under the term spirituality and their diverse
interpretations have become far too differentiated and fragmented today
to admit of a single, concise, universally agreed description or definition,
even within Christianity. Again, spiritualities develop in particular
historical and cultural milieus, and are cross-cut by a wide range of
particular social, linguistic, political and religious forms that complicate
definitional strategies. On the other hand spirituality today deals with
areas of human experience that were once common religious concerns but
are no longer matters of theological engagement, the very issues that for
David Brown are vital to the re-enchantment of the world.[8] The result is
a wide variety of expressions, traditions, practices, literacies, discourses
and questions. Today they include a broadened sense of the sacramental:

body and food, health and well-being, music and dance, ritual, landscape art, architectural styles, town planning, gardening, sport, the eclectic, participative activities, and pilgrimage. Add to these the shadowed presences of war, conflict, devastation, oppression, exploitation, crime, and the changed world of experience all of these and more suggest.

The creativity of Spirit is encountered in the world as place when life and all of creation, in all their forms and expressions, are experienced as the expansive generosity of God; a generosity that is uncovered in an indefinite array of signs, whispers, rhythms and traces, human and otherwise. Spirituality emerges as human experience emerges, and this intimate link raises serious challenges for attempts to define spirituality. Here are two examples of definition: contemporary spirituality is a mode of meaningful action in the world nurtured by spiritual practices; or, spirituality consists of the practices through which beliefs are expressed within a particular community of faith. Both definitions focus on practices, but a burden of ambiguity still remains. What kind of action? What array of practices? What kind of balance between inward and outward concerns? What specific beliefs? What community of faith? Why does the first not mention faith at all? How is the person to be understood? Each of these questions is important. They reveal how definitional ambiguity may serve a useful purpose precisely by raising the need for clarifying questions.

A wide variety of changing motivations, expressions, traditions, practices, literacies, and discourses impacts and shapes the living contexts in which spirituality is encountered and lived in the contemporary West, and they raise other questions about the definition of spirituality today. These socio-cultural contexts and milieus are on the increase as Western society, under the all-pervading influence of consumerism, becomes more individualistic and fragmented. Not only are questions of modernity and the postmodern implicitly and explicitly encountered in attempts to arrive at a definition of spirituality, issues of a philosophical, theological and interreligious nature also arise. What happens, for example, if we decide to explore spirituality as a way of listening deeply to God? What themes inevitably arise?[9] Even if we try to consider spirituality at its most basic and suggest that it has to do with approaches to the mysteries of life, its meaning and purpose, and its relations to the sacred, a work of exploration still remains to be done.[10] Even if we consider spirituality as a field or constellation of specific practices related to a way of talking about God, about deep transformative process, or ultimate meaning, or a life project, blurred edges and ambiguities will still remain.

What follows in this chapter is a series of illustrative fragments, pieces of a jigsaw intended to draw a picture of the lush and luxuriant profusion of cognitive, affective and behavioural expressions of spirituality presently in bloom in the contemporary West. An awareness of this luxuriance seems vital to a critical appreciation of what is happening in Western spirituality today. These are first-order descriptions: they are concerned with spirituality itself, how it is experienced and expressed at first hand. They are intended to suggest the expansive array of issues, levels, focal points and blurred edges that dance together and shape postmodern spiritual experiences and definitions of spirituality. They are also intended to unfold something of the first order spiritual concerns that move people to personally significant transformative action. First-order descriptions help to identify the breadth and depth of the spiritual world confronting contemporary seekers. First-order descriptions also confront those who seek to step beyond narrow self-interest, who desire to respond to the creative urges of the human spirit. In particular, first-order descriptions challenge those who desire to respond with grateful hearts to the divine call to climb the spiritual mountain where life is embraced to the full along a liberatingly meaningful and healingly transformative inter-individual path that embraces all of creation.

## DESCRIBING SPIRITUALITY

The person on a genuine spiritual path immediately encounters a challenge. In the present consumer culture this challenge involves stepping away from self-centred living to favour engagement with the transforming of reality in its relational, social, spatial and ecological expressions. In such a process, egocentric worldviews are confronted and new, ego-transcending reasons for being in the world are allowed to arise and trigger demands for increasingly radical change at the personal and social level. Spirituality is first of all about being aware, transcendentally aware. As such it requires a consistent personal commitment to living an increasingly aware life. Without such commitment a process of personally and socially transforming engagement is unlikely to develop. To be spiritual is to be awake, alert, conscious, receptive to everything that unfolds during the day, waiting openly and listening for that which is more than self and transcends self.

### ℭ Awareness and unawareness
Unawareness, particularly unawareness of myself, how I inhabit and relate to reality, of the conditioning impact of my history and memories, and of the consequences of daily life choices, generates spiritual blindness, an inability to distinguish between emancipatory and limiting spiritualities. How easy it is for those who have sunk into a consensual, conformist sleep to embrace an illusion that seduces the unaware into paths of counterfeit transcendence. Authentic spirituality, grounded in a maturing awareness, moves in the direction of deep-seated transformation. False spirituality moves in the direction of self-delusion, disguising

resistance to change; it sacrifices and scapegoats the other in the service of uninterrupted and undisturbed personal comfort and advantage.

Authentic spirituality names a state of reflective awareness leading to action in the inner and outer domains of life and connectedness on this planet. It entails recognition of the forms of personal and social transcendence embraced by the particular mainstream consensus prevailing in a particular society, the view of the world shaped by power elites and the consequent order that they impose to their own advantage. In such sociopolitical and economic contexts it is all too easy for folk to collude unconsciously with a range of principalities and powers that hold them in spiritual bondage. Authentic spirituality confronts cultural conditions that militate against and marginalise soul-song and spirit life.

In a culture of consumption, authentic spirituality represents a sign of contradiction, the challenge to embrace a counter-cultural stance in favour of a better world. The exact consequences of such an aware choice are difficult to predict, but they will be the lived price of spiritual and ethical integrity. Genuine spirituality becomes more demanding in a consumer society where everything is valued principally in self-referred stylistic, fashionista, monetary and material terms. In such contexts genuine spirituality takes thought, demands reflection, and invites change. It is self-implicating and self-transcending. A life characterised by little thought, by an absence of critical self-reflection, colludes unquestioningly with the unexamined life and its socio-cultural location. Spirituality suggests that every life is worth examining. Choose and embrace the consequences.

Spirituality happens in spaces where self-indulgence crosses the path of self-transcendence, when moments of graced change, palpable metanoia moments, become tangible and difficult to ignore. Spirituality confronts contexts built on oppression, rooted in exploitation, grounded in unilateral visions of material success, whose horizon of meaning is deception and a lie. Authentic spirituality is nothing short of a reflective journey through self-constructed wildernesses to the place where true life is at last revealed. The desert is the place where spiritualities paradoxically bloom. This is a journey through discernment and knowledge, through insight and a changing heart to the place where it becomes clear that Lady Wisdom is our most powerful friend in the effort to break free of self-deception and the mesmerising blandishments of Dame Folly.

### ☾ The desert
The desert is a place, a solitary place and a meeting place, a focal point, a harsh place of nature counterpoised to the harsh spaces of the human city, mirroring the ruthless places of the human heart. It is a place where identity shifts like the wind-blown sands, a place of tempting and a place

of victory over evil (Matthew 4:1–11), a place of purgation, dry bones (Ezekiel 37:1–14), and of fear driven out by a transforming love encountered in the vastness of silence (1 John 4:18–19). The desert is a place of contemplation, a paradoxical space where silence speaks to those who learn to listen to the silence, a place for listeners. Life is hidden there and the waters of life and the dryness all around. There are no commodities there and no commodification; and so religion and spirituality can find their purity, and goodness can find its way. The desert burns away the illusions we harbour. That is why we avoid it and its significance for as long as we can.

The desert is a between place and so a God-space, a space for a Wild God and unpredictable, a place for seekers who truly seek beyond the tame and the predictable, beyond the sham and the shallow. The desert makes a theology that is fully alive, a spirituality that whispers wisdom with the wind: they find their voice when their voices have been scoured and swept away. The desert is a basic place and what is most basic is rediscovered there, the rest swept clean, clean away, till all that is left is the world within, that other desert where the contraries of experience fall and in the falling reveal another truth, another presence, the presence of an Other, and the experience that becomes real in a shifting place, a place of deep de-centring and the extreme encounters with the sand and the sun and the burning of divine encounter, and self-discovery and participation in that encountering.

### ℂ A project, a work in progress

Spirituality is an activity, a work in progress, a laying of foundations for a building that will last. Spirituality is about the preparation of the ground and the gathering of appropriate supports. It is also about the quality of the gifted practices and the gracious materials used interiorly and exteriorly in building a life: gold, silver, and precious stones or wood, hay and straw; the former better able to stand the tests of time, the latter easily ravaged, swept away, destroyed (1 Cor 3:12). Spirituality is a self-implicating and self-revealing work, a craft that becomes manifest in the builder's style of life and transcendent connectedness. Spirituality is a response to the call to seek out and find the contemplative path for which we are made, the path to divinely promised transformation.

Spirituality is about the call to rediscover our true nature as men and women made in the divine image and likeness. Spirituality in this sense subsumes a profoundly original human characteristic, something natural to us, something for which we seem to be neurologically hard-wired,[11] something that tells us who we really are and who we are meant to be in the world and the glorious difference each one of us can make. Spirituality speaks of a call to uncover and unfold our original but lost state of gifted blessing, to take hold of it, live it intensely for the sake of all, for the sake of peace, for the sake of the cosmos, for the sake of the trajectory of human history, human dignity and liberation. This is nothing short of human deification and that is what makes the difference for those willing to grasp hold of it with both hands and walk unselfconsciously with God.

Spirituality emerges in spaces where differences converge, differences that demand a new kind of dialogue and have the potential to shape human experience in new and repeatedly startling and previously unimagined ways. Spirituality comes into view where deeper experiences are explored, especially when they give rise to competing and contrasting images of the human person and human destiny and their dialogue with the divine. Spirituality surfaces where personal visions and capacities for relationship converge with deep questions of meaning, especially in contexts of struggle and doubt. Spirituality opens up in spaces where the demands of the other, and the divine Other so often hidden behind them, open up and confront our life projects.

Spirituality arises in the spaces of human affectivity, especially when affectivity is confronted by questions of the transcendent and God, and where feelings of dependence on the transcendent and God begin to flow and play and dance and make their own transpersonal and transcendental demands. Spirituality becomes visible when we confront the challenge to get beyond the point where we see God as some sort of parent-figure whose task is to alleviate our pain and insecurity, or shield us from the very realities of life that most demand responsibility and maturity. Spirituality is there where we find the courage to go deeper into the mystery of life. Spirituality begins to evolve when we realise that we humans have to choose the path we will walk, the rising path to enlightenment and wisdom, or the slippery slope to destructive barbarism.

### ℂ Expressing spirituality

Spirituality comes into view when people inwardly begin to struggle with language and ways to give conceptual and narrative expression to affectivity, the emotions and feelings that break beyond self-interest and begin to construct an integral spiritual identity. Spirituality becomes apparent when we try to understand and give an account of our confrontations with the limitations of existence, with the life-defining questions of ultimacy, of suffering, of betrayed innocence, and death in all of its expected and unexpected forms, its apparently just and unjust forms. Spirituality is potentially present when prior worldviews or frames of reference are found wanting, in times of crisis or in moments of disorienting dilemma, the pivotal marker moments that demand deep change, where vague or superficial adjustments to the consensual world no longer work or count.

Spirituality demands a new conceptual framework, a new way to say and think and feel about life in all its diversity, and imagine where it is ultimately going. Spirituality responds to the need for a self-implicating idiom that allows us to identify, reflect on and explore our deep, orienting attitudes to and our evaluations of life: our deep orienting experiences, our deep orienting beliefs, especially those that challenge us to stay open to the invitation to live a transformative life, dancing joyously to its music, delightedly singing its songs. Spirituality is the space where we explore the grammar of belief, the vocabulary that shapes our living stories and our relationships, the dialogues and conversations that have the emotional power to connect us with all of reality.

Spirituality is revealed in the kind of language, or metaphor, or imagery we use to move beyond ourselves. It shapes a space of encounter, a rendezvous with creativity and presence that finds expression through many different transformative practices: prayerful and meditative postures and rituals; reflective reading of texts, poetry, literature; engaging with art; exploring music, dance, and stillness; creative writing and journaling; and all of them intended to make self-transformation and self-transcendence possible. Spirituality allows and alerts us to lean towards mystery as we dance in the fluctuating middle ground of reality where boundaries grow thin and the presence of another, hidden, world flirts with us and signals its presence. Spirituality happens where the rhythms of mystery break through our defences and resistances, our blindness to things of soul and spirit, our deafness to the still, small voice, and allows us to glimpse new possibilities in ten thousand hidden places.

### ⟨ Seeking depth and transcendence

Spirituality becomes apparent in the places where the deep, the mysterious, and the wonderful begin a new song to a new rhythm as they weave a new vision of reality. The truly spiritual is deep: deep in its invitations and proposals. The truly spiritual is deep in implications and its unexpected impacts on our lives. It is wonderful in its awesome transformative potential when we choose to enter the freedom of its gracious synergy. It is mysterious in its refusal to be reduced to or trapped in linguistic constructs. It is an idiom that transcends idiom, a root metaphor that becomes a portal to the unsayable. It is mysterious in its capacity to burst free of every alphabet and every image that seeks to contain it.

Spirituality is mysterious in its rhythms and timings, in its stillnesses and silences, its capacity to bring thought to a stop. Spirituality is mysterious in its unexpected turns and its moments of sudden erasure when words and images are checked and stilled and gaps opened in busy awarenesses trying to maintain a language-based hold on reality. We fear the depths of spirit, and so we use spirituality like a guiding thread through the deep labyrinth. Unfortunately we also use the guiding thread of spirituality to draw us back to familiar reality and its recognisable sounds and contours. The profoundly spiritual challenges us to let go of our guiding strings of familiar words and images, let go of our unthinkingly automatic patterns and processes, and risk the other and the different that we inevitably encounter as we seek depth. The spiritual beckons us beyond all that is familiar and invites us to enter spaces that may not be said but may be experienced deeply and wonderfully in the heart, in the soul's core, carried on the wind-lifting wings of spirit.

Transcendence lies at the heart of spirituality, an essential dimension that is built into our very nature as human beings endowed with the gifts of imagination and reflexive thought and speech. Transcendence tells us that speech, the capacity to reflect and imagine, to give expression to the potential self, is simultaneously a bridge beyond the narrow confines of the conscious self, a bridge to the non-self, to the other, to difference, to the hidden, the mysterious and the Ultimately Unsayable. The transcendent quality of spirituality means that it rejects claims that there is nothing beyond language. It rejects claims that we are inevitably locked into domains constructed of ideas or picture words alone, a closed world of words built of arbitrary sounds, cacophonous worlds in which any experience of authentic inner life experienced in felt stillness is ultimately denied. Spirituality finds in such claims distinct traces of category error, confusing stillness with meaninglessness, an error compounded by a lack of common sense. Spirituality stands for inwardness and outwardness and for the transformatively rich potential of lived, reflexive experience of the transcendent. In particular, spirituality stands for the sound-stilling mystery of lovableness and love, of compassion and the gift of healing change.

## THE SOFT EDGES OF CONTEMPORARY SPIRITUALITY

In the contemporary West, spirituality has evolved into an intensely suggestive yet mercurially elusive word with soft, drifting, nomadic, often vague, varied and itinerant edges that refuse closure. Sometimes usages of the word activate a sense of warm aliveness, sometimes a sense of generic abstraction. Sometimes it is used by default, sometimes intentionally. Sometimes it is used with a sense of quiet discipline and commitment, and sometimes with a sense of vibrantly expressive enthusiasm and passion. But the point of focus of the term could be anywhere on a broad spectrum ranging from deeply religious commitment to faddish lifestyle considerations in a consumer-driven environment. Such factors help us to understand why the term *spirituality* has become so fluid in contemporary usage. As the word is applied across traditional, modern and postmodern contexts, not all of which are compatible with differing religious horizons, a robust internal flexibility becomes necessary. And then there is the question of social commitment, social roles, social change, and the living of spirituality in a world of action.[12]

Today spirituality ripples across a widening pool of applications and appropriations. In the West this is happening in an increasingly complex, pluralist society where Christianity still continues – under pressure – to provide the principal socio-religious location. Given the prevailing pragmatism and the seemingly endless creativity of bricolage, spirituality also seems to be endowed with a never-ending supply of sources, resources, horizons and applications. Even as a search for the sacred spirituality remains multidimensional, especially when the range of practices and beliefs, and the contextual influences of cultural location are taken into account. This becomes more obvious when the emotional and feeling-toned dimensions of spirituality are brought into the discussion. All of this means that taken-for-granted, unexamined meanings are suspect in conversations about contemporary spirituality. For example, while spirituality certainly has to do with ultimate questions about life and death, and our uneasiness about their answering, it also has to do with passion and the passionate life.[13] In Rolheiser's terms, spirituality has to do with our inner fire and how we channel it in our lives.[14]

⌈ *Passion and other elements of the spiritual landscape*
Forces like the fear of death, grief, pain, suffering and tragedy become part of the spiritual landscape as we struggle to make some sort of sense of them. A spirituality – indeed a theology – that does not struggle with these questions but rationalises, evades or resists them is suspect. But a spiritual landscape that excludes the all-encompassing passions and desires of humanity, our capacity for passionate love, joy, wonder, awe, trust, gratitude, humility, patience, reverence, wisdom, compassion, commitment, courage, justice, is sadly lacking in what makes life worth living. These glorious passions, sometimes dark and painful, sometimes bright and breath-taking, are also the stuff of spirituality. They keep on resurfacing as insistent challenges to human integration. In Jewish and Christian terms, they celebrate the ability to walk fully alive before God in the land of the living (Psalm 116:9). In such a light there is nothing vague about life, even if the living sometimes falls prey to ambivalence, conflict and uncertainty. Even then the emerging consensus suggests that spirituality is for people who want to be more fully, more passionately alive. The problem is in unpacking what passion and aliveness really mean in actual contexts and situations.

Beauty, wholism and a renewed sense of community also evoke a sense of life and passion. So does being real, having integrity, and going beyond pretence. So do the ordinary passions of every day, not least the passion to survive life's challenges and tragedies with some degree of humanity and love intact. The very ordinariness of everyday spirituality enhances its capacity to bring about local change and sometimes even global change. Spirituality always hints at and flirts with change because ultimately spirit manifests through the forces and dynamics of personal and social transformation. Spirituality always touches the forces that shape human identity and responsibility in the world; and it always invites contact with the forces that engender and generate authentically creative and liberating lives. Spirituality not only points to depth and the congruent experience of reality, it also dances with value and meaning, with aesthetic and moral value. But above all it learns to sing about the meaning of life, of humaneness, and of the promise of the cosmos.

The word *spirituality* is also used of awareness, of intentionality and choice, of the nature and uses of freedom, of justice and its ways, and the use and abuse of personal, social and natural resources; and it is deeply concerned with the kind of world we are building today. At its best, spirituality seeks to respond to humanity's deep pain, pain that so often arises in response to exploitive socio-economic and socio-political forces, practices and ideologies, and the alienations they activate. The spiritual also evokes the human potential for creativity, a defining capacity of what it means to be human. And today it takes on increasing importance in the lives of rising numbers of people, secular and religious alike, as they confront the dominance of the materialism, consumerism, individualism and the conspicuously value-free greed of the times.[15] Spirituality confronts us with our contemporary slaveries and idolatries.

### ℂ *Identifying common images and descriptions*

The word *spirituality* conjures up many different images and themes. It connects us to many different theories and disciplines, including theology, psychology, philosophy and the social sciences. Psychotherapies, including psychoanalysis, are reconnecting with spirituality.[16] Medicine has begun to focus more attention on the links between spirituality and health.[17] The result is a new flow of secular definitions to place alongside those with a religious or traditional origin. This explosion is paralleled by an expansion of other understandings guiding individuals who have chosen to walk self-defined spiritual paths. To take the conversation forward it will be helpful to reflect for a moment on a typical summary list of thirty-three such understandings drawn from a list of several hundred I have noted over the past few years during conversations with people in spiritual guidance or psychotherapy contexts, in conversations during retreats or seminars, and from participant research. No attempt has been made to prioritise items; in fact the list is sorted alphabetically. The summaries that follow are offered to illustrate the breadth of images, emphases and descriptions the word *spirituality* now embraces.

- A deeply felt sense of connection or unity with the universe.
- A more alive, more realistic, more receptive, more creative, humbler self.
- A more coherent, value-led life.
- A more embodied, natural, holistic, organic, ecologically responsive way of life.
- A more humane way of living that facilitates and honours uniqueness.
- A thoughtful, more loving and compassionate life.
- Breaking free of illusions about oneself.
- Building a better, fairer world.
- Choosing a path of well-being and well-doing.
- Confronting the forces of injustice and exploitation.
- Cultivating a significant form of human intelligence.
- Cultivating a still-point from which to live fully.
- Developing a significant form of human literacy.
- Embracing life-changing practices.
- Embracing self-transcendence in the encounter with the other.
- Embracing the natural world and living lightly on the planet.
- Finding a way beyond the egocentric, self-referred lives we live today.
- Learning how to live in harmony with God, nature, and all that is.
- Learning to listen, really listen to life.
- Living a soul-based life.
- Living compassionate, respectful lives.
- Managing spiritual distress.
- Noticing the gifted nature of life, its blessing and renewal.
- Seeking the kingdom within, seeking depth.
- Seeking to encounter God's limitless aliveness.
- Seeking union and oneness.
- The encounter with Spirit.
- The inclusion of normally excluded human qualities (embracing the passionate life).
- The search for balanced wholeness.
- The search for deeper, more sustaining, more balanced values to guide life.
- The search for the sacred, for ultimate reality.
- The search for the true, the deepest self.
- The task of re-enchanting the everyday.
- Transforming consciousness.

Taken at face value such descriptions seem trouble-free and entirely laudable. At the very least they show us that spirituality is an abundant, multidimensional reality focused clearly on life. But life has its shadowed aspects and often the spiritual view does not name or shies away from the whole truth about the unpredictability of life. This problem becomes more acute if personal or group spiritualities lose their grounding in the affairs and issues of every day. Spirituality demands awareness of contrary and contradictory, what is incomplete and alien to conventional life. It also demands awareness of the things that distort and disturb our preferred happy-clappy, childish visions. How often is spiritual and religious language trapped at the level of primary school vocabularies and literacies? Spirituality also demands action. Stripped of its self-implicating social and personal morality, spirituality is revealed as a caricature, a gross falsification, a form of cant, a recreational drug, a connivance and a collusion with the forces of diminishment and oppression. Spirituality reminds us that alienation is not a natural law; nor are anti-spiritual structures and systems. These are themes that re-echo in this book.

### ℂ A useful imprecision

Clearly, then, the word *spirituality* is already used in reference to an expanding range of human and cosmic phenomena. The price is the serious cut back of its capacity to convey precise meaning, a watering down that becomes crystal clear when we begin to look closely at what is actually happening in the West. Although Christianity remains a force in the world of public faith in this part of the world, given the absence of evidence to the contrary I tend to concur with John Drane's intriguing intuition that what he has designated the *new spirituality* is increasingly likely to affect the lifestyle beliefs and practices of growing numbers of people.[18] I prefer Drane's suggestion to Christopher Partridge's option for an entirely new word, *occulture* (from *occult* and *culture*), to name the contemporary spiritual scene, although I accept its descriptive accuracy.[19] Preferred nomenclature aside, both researchers agree that a spiritual paradigm shift is in full swing.

These are further reasons why, in a world of plural visions, finding an agreed definition of contemporary spirituality has become well nigh impossible. And yet, precisely by becoming a vague umbrella term lacking precision, the word *spirituality* is able to embrace the diversity and difference demanded of it today. Precisely by being vague and ambiguous the word is able to serve an almost endless variety of functions. It can encapsulate types and kinds of spirituality. It can name sub-traditions within the world religions – and their alternatives. The term *spirituality* can also embrace the personal choice of styles, modes and manners of life, with all the nuances, gradations, and shades of opinion such choices imply. As we attempt to understand the variety and variability of meanings that have encrusted the word *spirituality* today we are further confronted by the extent to which new applications and appropriations serve the purposes of neo-conservative and neo-liberal socio-political, socio-religious, socio-cultural and socio-economic movements and ideologies alike. Authentic spirituality is consistently confronted by cultural conditions that militate against the audacity of soul-song and spirit life and seek to limit its innate freedom.

## ⦅ A spiritual revolution

It is also clear that we are facing what David Tacey in Australia, and Paul Heelas and Linda Woodhead in Britain have aptly termed a spiritual revolution.[20] The meaning of this revolution is not fully clear, but the term fittingly baptises the present situation. There is little doubt that spirituality looks set to represent the emergent form of religiousness, but present indicators suggest that this is occurring in a form that marries it well to the workings of a consumer society.[21] The commodification of spirituality in a market-driven environment, its manipulation by consumerist tendencies, its mercurial fuzziness and murkiness, and the glowing fascination it seems to hold for mounting numbers of people raise serious questions about the fundamental quality of contemporary expressions of spirituality. At the same time, spirituality is never static even when it seems to serve a status quo: it always conceals the promise of change. Spirituality is integral to life, and so it seeks out spaces in which to come alive and blossom. On the other hand, spirituality is touched by many opposing tensions not least those of conservation and transformation, and the paradoxical tendency to preserve values while engaging in the quest for change.

The audacity of spirit keeps on surprising us. It refuses to be controlled, subjected to routine, and domesticated. It refuses to be crystallised or to serve the needs of logical definition alone. In approaching an understanding of contemporary spirituality, then, it is important to understand the dynamic nature of spirit: in the form of what sociologists call charisma and theologians refer to as charism or grace, it keeps on setting itself free in the world as a transformative force that is once again confounding our modern processes of logical rationalisation.[22] Spirit is now revealing itself as a powerful vehicle for the transformation of contemporary identity precisely because of its capacity to transcend routine bureaucratisation, legalisation and domestication processes. Quite simply, spirit refuses to be reductively systematised even though it can be ignored, blocked and resisted.

At the same time, it is important to recall that charismatic action of the kind intended here threatens power elites precisely because it empowers persons to embrace change. Spirit retains the capacity to become a unique source of embodied empowerment and transformation revealed in the changing and dynamic fields of spiritual and social practices. We know it by its fruits. Spirit blows in from the margins; it crosses boundaries and borders and sets change in motion, unsettling personal and social assumptions and identities in the process. Read the stories of Nicodemus and the Samaritan woman in the Gospel of John chapters three and four for provocative examples of the potentially subversive power of spirit. Because spirit/Spirit is not the sole, patented property of any individual it easily evades routine and soars freely like the wind for which it is named. Spirit is innately versatile, generative of change; and in the processes and practices of change it reveals a potentially revolutionary form of shared consciousness and relation that continually arises in the relational spaces where the human spirit, the spirit of the times, and the Holy Spirit converge and dance.

Spirituality is always challenged to attend to the signs of the times and learn to sing new songs for new worlds. Those who speak of a spiritual revolution and the re-enchantment of the West are speaking of just such a gift arising in highly secularised spaces regardless of the surprise to the unobservant and the inattentive. In fact, history indicates that spirituality has always dynamically responded to what is distinct and unique about different contexts and to the complexities of personal and social situations and locations. It has always dynamically refused imprisonment. Spirituality responds to and reveals the spirit of the times. As value-free forms of consumerism and materialism take on increasingly global importance, they increasingly represent major socio-religious, socio-spiritual and socio-ethical challenges. In such contexts spirituality signals an invitation to take seriously who we are and where we are as we face the intimidating seductions a consumerising world offers.

Spirituality is encountered today at a crossroads where it is challenged to make a powerful choice: to become a sign of contradiction and even begin to embrace a counter-cultural stance, or to embrace consumerisation and go with the market flow. This taking of a cultural position becomes more complex in a consumer society that commodifies everything including spirituality.[23] As Thomas Ryan has noted, selling to the false or alienated self is simplicity itself with whole industries catering to its every need.[24] Commercialised spiritual practices – religious tourism is a typical example – are everywhere on the increase.[25] The problem is that when spirituality is successfully commodified spiritual consumers risk becoming ever more dependent on the rules of the marketplace in responding to their spiritual desires and needs.[26] Set this in the context of the common-place libertarian opinion that it is all right for people to pursue bad habits provided that no one else is harmed, and the potentials for illusion become rapidly apparent.

When this happens to spirituality, when being a spiritual pilgrim becomes culturally popular; when spirituality begins to show market-driven signs of re-awakening, or re-enchantment, or even revolution; when these changes occur in contexts where links to a living religious or spiritual tradition are treated with suspicious scepticism, or lost, or repudiated, or severed, or parasitically used and repackaged; then, being spiritual can easily become the new face of a market-driven cultural conformism. When that happens it becomes even more painfully challenging to seek integrity, to become a sign of contradiction, and in the process be made someone small and despised (Psalm 119:41). In the end, spirituality is about freedom, not the happiness or satisfaction of the false or alienated self. But in the dangerous transitional spaces between individual freedom and socially alienating self-satisfaction there is no shortage of complexity or potential for decadence.

¶ *Shaping forces*

Appreciation of the significance and meaning of lives and actions arises from the interpretation of just such particularities, challenges, complexities and potentials. This means that language, history, and the events, shifts, beliefs, practices, literacies, discourses and transformations that characterise culture, as well as the specifics of real people's lives in real places, shape the themes, values, and expressions of spirituality. This raises the question that lies at the heart of this chapter. What are the principal forces that shape the meaning and influence the usage of the term *spirituality*, and its associated expressions *spiritual* and *mystical*, since they share a similar genealogy.[27] As we shall see, the word *spirituality* has a long history,[28] but it locates us in a complex and uncertain arena today because of the shifting and at times arbitrary meanings attributed to the term.

For example, I might describe spirituality in terms of light and fire, and target those images on soul, spirit, mind, heart and life. In a Christian context such metaphors point immediately in the direction of the Holy Spirit and the world of grace. In Christian experience it is the light of the Spirit that seeks to fill and heal all the dark spaces in our lives, minds and hearts. In this way, spirituality may be described as a light that longs to shine out in our lives as our souls and spirits are transformed, set on fire in a transforming blaze that generates a radically new heart-centred understanding. However, the same metaphors may be used in a very different theological or philosophical or even personal contexts and the discourse will be utterly changed.

We simply cannot presume that the word *spirituality* has a fixed meaning today, even when we agree that it names something innate and creative, that it identifies our human disposition to a fuller life, or our longing for a deeper, liberating truth. We still have to attend to the details and the drift of meaning. By way of example, in order to understand the problem more fully, reflect on the phenomenon of multiple religious and spiritual belonging that is more and more common today. Reflect on the omnipresent processes of bricolage, making use of whatever is to hand in the construction of spiritualities today. Then ask yourself what really happens in your own search for spiritual meaning and purpose: where are your sources, where do your practices come from, and how congruent are your perceptions?

Where are the borders of the spiritual today? Is it a territory, a domain of discourse, a psychological space, a health resource, a commercial product? Is it a blend of all of these and more? What discomforts does journeying to one or other of these spaces imply? There are other questions. What of exile and the spiritual wastelands, the places of isolation, alienation, of depravity or decadence? What of the contexts of excess and waste? What of a world where spiritual meaning has fled to the edge spaces, the intersections and the margins? Or what of a place of fads chasing each other in diminishing circles of increasing meaninglessness? Or is spirituality simply about perspective? Or is it about reality? Or again, is it about function? When you are finished with those questions, ask more. If I experience reality, how am I to interpret my experience? What lenses shall I use? Am I interpreting words in the belief that I am interpreting an experience? Is knowledge something of the whole person or simply of the mind? Is it embodied? Is it enough merely to report experience, to count experiences? Is that spirituality? What about tacit spirituality? What about the personal unconscious, the social unconscious? What happens when they intersect with the sacred unconscious? How do I account to myself for what I know or think I know when the words I conjure with change their shape and point in different, often contradictory directions? Buying what a culture approves of and organises takes little thought, neither does self-gratification when spirituality, which ought to take thought and demand self-implication, is the product desired.

THE PRESENT FUZZINESS

That there is no consensus, no single agreed definition of the word *spirituality* in contemporary spiritual literature and conversation is due in no small measure to late modern and postmodern influences on contemporary Western society, a subject we have already examined. Factually, the meanings, connotations and linkages of the word *spirituality* have undergone major shifts over the last thirty years. This is clearly evident in the way varying usages of the word have invaded ever-widening sets of contexts. It is now employed in an expanding range of new roles, a clear example of which is the debate about the presence of spiritual and religious discourse and training in counselling, psychotherapy and health contexts,[29] or concerning the presence of spirituality – however understood – in organisations, business, and the world of economics.[30] The same is true of the world of higher and adult education.[31] As a consequence, the academic study of spirituality is rapidly evolving across a range of disciplines, each with its own definitional needs.

As Wesley Carr has noted, the pervasiveness of the broad range of beliefs deriving from the *New Age* mood or milieu is an excellent example of the current complexity and diffuseness of usage.[32] The themes confronting researchers and practitioners of spirituality have increased dramatically: the individual and the cosmos, quantum physics and human personality, the inner and the outer worlds, the new Gnosticisms and Paganisms, the new mysticisms and the turn to hermetic magic, religious pluralism, the interest in Oriental and Aboriginal practices and philosophies, the burgeoning of ecological concerns, the interest in Western Esotericism and Theosophy. These and many more are all now linked uncritically under the singular, undifferentiated umbrella of contemporary spirituality. The result is an increasing diversity and imprecision of meaning that has been evident for most of the last decade.[33] What does this fuzziness tell us about contemporary consciousness regarding things spiritual? What has happened to make the word spirituality so popular and attractive over the last thirty years or so? How did it become the expansive, slippery, fuzzy, mercurial, murky, glowing, soft, passionate, catch-all term it has become today? The search for answers to such questions challenges us to reflect on the socio-cultural changes that are making them possible.

There are two other reasons why the word *spirituality*, and related words such as *spiritual*, *mysticism* or *mystical*, locates us in a complex, shifting and uncertain arena. In contemporary usage the word *spirituality* has the capacity to surface alternative meanings and values in spaces from which a sense of the sacred or the transcendent, or the politically humane have been exiled and excluded. This is particularly evident in contemporary secular and consumer societies where highly individualised libertarian principles tend to dominate. Even in such contexts the word maintains a mysterious magnetism for people who seem to be ill-at-ease with themselves, searching for answers to their feelings and intuitions of disturbance and lack. The second reason is much more obvious. The clue lies in the origins of the word. Trying to pin down the meaning of spirituality today seems so much like trying to pin down the wind in all its moods and colours and scents, its gentleness and stillness, and its roaring stormy power. Spirituality follows spirit, and spirit goes everywhere, blowing where it wills.

## TOWARDS A THEMATICS

Spirituality is generally associated with a particular way of life characterised by certain themes that are held to be spiritual. It is also associated
with fields of practice that are equally held to be spiritual. Both act as
horizons. It is at this point that complexity enters and reveals spirituality
as the multifaceted reality it has become in the last ten years. Consider
the following summaries.

First, consider the Divine, the sacred and the holy; understandings of
eros and agape; and forms of love and intimacy. These three also include
questions of religiosity, knowledge, spiritual and theological literacy,
and faith or belief; questions related to grace, divine energy, deification,
union with God, and transformation; themes related to qualities and forms
of awareness, insight, inspiration, enlightenment, illumination, and altered
states of consciousness; issues related to desire, motivation and devotion;
questions related to spiritual direction, accompaniment and healing;
themes related to paradox, transcendence and metanoia; themes related to
the tragic, to the contingent, and the limiting of both self and others;
issues of harmony, balance and self-redefinition; and theories related to
spiritual and faith development, intentionality and motivation. Questions
of wholeness, openness, authenticity, commitment and communication
also arise.

Associated practices include inner or soul work, a range of reflective
modalities including critical self-reflection, journaling and reflective
reading, art, dance, and music; forms of theological reflection and praxis;
various forms of discursive and non-discursive meditation, prayer, worship,
and ritual; approaches to liturgical and sacramental celebration; pilgrimage; approaches to self-care and well-being, to supportive empowerment,
and ways of dealing with stress, anxiety, sorrow, tragedy, and grief;
gender-based practices; family-based practices; communal and group
practices; and many forms and expressions of conscientious ecological,
economic, political, religious and social engagement. Practices that
support an integral understanding of the human-environmental nexus are
also significant. These qualities and practices then intersect and interact
in a wide variety of personal, communal and institutional contexts,
structures, experiences and expressions. Thus, the basic themes of spirituality begin to surface. They reveal spirituality above all as an existential
reality with profound implications for the meaning of life and a hope for
the future. The impact of world events is also significant.

Key words used in contemporary spirituality tend towards the
humanistic. They include such words as: attitudes, availability, awareness,
balance, change, comfort, community, compassion, connectedness, contemplative, creativity, detachment, encounter, engagement, experience, flexibility, forgiveness, fulfilment, godliness, good deeds, grace, growth,

healing, holistic, hope, human, individual, integration, listening, love, mind, openness, patience, peace, personal journey, prayer, presence, psyche, quest, reality, reconciliation, relationship, search, self, self-lessness, serenity, service, silence, solitude, soul, spirit, stillness, transcendence, trust, wonder, virtue. Words pertaining to Christian theology, particularly those relating to God, Trinity, Jesus, the Spirit, and the Divine presence also arise, as do words pointing to more traditional devotional practices.

These lists suggest that the word *spirituality* sings to the heart of our humanity and our desire for connectedness and reconnectedness to self, others, nature, and God. It also dances along a path of personhood and transcendence that allows it to draw on inner resources and strength. Connecting with the Divine presence is important here. The lesson is that spirituality is pregnant with the power and energy to evoke and support a more humane, more creative, more caring, more compassionate mentality and mode of being-in-the-world. There is a growing hunger for spirituality everywhere in both traditional and new forms. This is so because the word *spirituality* speaks of and embraces the whole of human life and responsibility on this planet. It identifies a way of understanding and embracing life in ways that prove difficult to define or measure. It reaches into the depths because it is evocative of the innermost being and rich potential of every person, and has the capacity to engage with every level of human experience and relationship.

Spirituality has to do with many things at many different levels of human life, but most of all it has to do with the shaping and moulding of a life project, its lifestyle and its relational, social and planetary responsibilities. It has to do with the forms and styles and structures of life, how we humans function in the world. It has to do with the restlessness of life, its enslavements and freedoms, its illusions and realities, its addictions, oppressions and emancipations. It also has to do with deeper needs and their ever-deepening satisfaction. Spirituality has to do with the power to shape a real life, an ethically responsive life not a sham, a life unfolding in integrity and responsiveness to Something More. Reflect, for example, on the increasing political significance of the word today. Notice how spiritual authenticity is increasingly measured and tested by its capacity to motivate a whole society to care enough about the impact of humanity on the world to look beyond our own personal and national concerns. Then ask yourself some very pertinent personal questions.

Spirituality becomes apparent in the places where the deep, the mysterious, and the wonderful converge: deep in its potential impact, wonderful in its awesome transformative potential, mysterious in its refusal to be trapped in linguistic constructs. It becomes evident in rhythms and timings that cannot be easily said but can be experienced deeply and wonderfully in the heart and soul. All it takes is audacity of spirit. At the same time, spirituality needs to be attentive to a subtle trap: the nostalgia for a stability rooted in a golden past that never existed outside of a fantasy about the human condition, an Eden of innocence that never existed in our human time. Talk to those who have suffered; indeed, remember your own dangerous memories of pain and loss. When we are open to them these conversations quickly teach us that casual or dismissive notions of individual lives cut no ice. The true enemy of all things spiritual is an enforced silence that is afraid of meaning. Spirituality seeks out real words, words that heal and liberate. True words are offspring of spirit whispering the audacity to shake off fear's paralysis and embrace life in all its amazing birthing messiness. Or is stability just the disdainful paralysis of nostalgia?

### ☾ Dancing and singing

Soul-song does not really need words; it can be paradoxically sung in silence, danced in stillness. It is enough that the singer knows that there is a song, that the dancer knows that there is a dance, a making of silent music, a dancing without visible movement, an embodying of spirit. Such a song is intimate, soft, lilting the fullness of promise. Such a dance is subtle, gracious, full of power. Such an embodying personifies life itself. The tragedy is that this glorious promise is weakened, actually weakened by neglect. Such a song is shy but seductive, loving, companionable. Such a dance is flirtatious, alive, inviting. Such a life is creative, resourceful, imaginative, capable of remaking the world. Together they reveal depth and beauty. They give the human spirit an undertone of shape, a pulse of rhythm, a divinely enamoured life-beat rhythm. They beckon towards loyalty and trust. They call for commitment to the Singer of the Song of the Cosmos, the Cosmic Dancer leaping down, the Filler of the void, the Embodier of true humanity, the invisible Giver of the gift of life.

Such singers and dancers evoke the story of the gifted livingness of all creation. Such embodiments set hearts a-beating. They spin life into unforeseen, almost invisible spaces, spaces to be filled with life and treasured, held fast. Soul-song and spirit-dance have the power to reveal life in its purest, most real, most embodied sense. The singer and the dancer follow its hints and flirts and traces, and in the following allow them to be made flesh. They are the restorers of an *imago dei* (divine image) that reflects God back to God, and back to the cosmos and in so doing their singing and dancing re-enchant it. In so doing they reveal spirituality as a path to re-creation, to lucidity of life. They utter a remaking to a different stamp, created all over again, refashioned divinely to the divine imprint, and rebirthed as true selves, truly selved, saved from isolating alienation.

In this sense spirituality is a path to a second creation, a lovingly re-creative re-creation, giftingly re-made as beloved persons, re-embodied re-enchanting re-enchanters.

Spirituality reveals us as more than pilgrims, immigrants, refugees, exiles, or people avoiding existence. We are revealed as citizens, sojourners in an uncluttered land. Uprooted from the place of illusion, yes, but replanted in a place of springs, like olives in sacred ground (Psalm 52:8), sifted and remade like rebuilt ruins or replanted gardens. In such a world fragmentation is overcome in singleness of heart and richness of spirit. We become walkers in a path of light, the old alienations and diminishments consumed in a fire fuelled by divine zeal. The now becomes a source of delight and new music soars as shackles fall away and binding patterns grounded in darkly distorting ways dissolve as deliverance, compassionate deliverance, takes hold. As creative spirit spirals between both our inner and our public living echoes of renewed life murmur in the unfolding chapters of our personal stories.[34] As it develops, spirituality points in the direction of a caring balance, an ethical connectedness to the totality of life in the cosmos. Most of all it inhabits the spaces where our life stories mysteriously and joyfully, painfully unfold, places touched by the whispered breath of spirit and the often resisted and silenced rhythms and sounds of soul, promising healing and transcendence.

Resistance to spirit often takes the form of dullness and heaviness of mind and heart. It blocks the turning and seeing that spiritual renewal and deliverance from diminished and depleted forms of life endow. The Hebrew Bible offers some intriguing images of spiritual resistance. It paints evocative word pictures of foolishness and senselessness. It describes states of fat, stubborn, and rebellious hearts, of heavy ears and closed eyes that refuse understanding and thwart its attendant healing (Isaiah 6:10; Jeremiah 5:21). Similar images are found in New Testament depictions of hardened hearts, blind eyes, deaf ears, forgetfulness and dull senselessness (Matthew 13:15; Mark 6:52 & 8:17–18). Their significance for escapist spiritualities is self-evident.

At the very least, then, spirituality suggests victory over fragmentation and resistance. It surfaces the search for the rich promise of transforming awareness. Regardless of how we understand it and its cognate terms, from an existential point of view the reality of spirituality continually resurfaces in the humbling ordinariness of everyday life, illuminates it and makes it a place of extraordinary encounter. Spirituality is lived out in the dance of human relationships, and grounded in the dramas and contingencies of human existence in the world as it is, and it is a horizon for understanding ethics of care and ethics of justice.[35] Authentic spirituality dances with affective moral awareness attuned to the whisperings of heart and soul.

Such awareness makes audacity of spirit possible, connecting it to deep roots of moral and spiritual courage.[36] Such awareness makes dangerous memory possible in spaces where Jesus needs to live in caring lives; such awareness is a space where generative empathy and contemplative listening blossom and release transforming balm. Creative spirituality is lived out in the world of commonplace dramas and grounded in the normal relationships that make up everyday human life. It is an antidote to the dead weight of a society suffering memory loss but does not know it, a society simultaneously losing its memory and its God in a haze of unrecognised superficiality and disregarded pathos. Deeper desire sets creativity in motion in the world of the spirit. The spiritually discerning join the dance.

THEMES AND QUESTIONS FOR FURTHER REFLECTION

1. Identify the impact of the present profusion of spiritualities in people's lives.
2. Do you listen to the songs that converge deep in the human spirit?
3. How pivotal is the role played by a sustained commitment to awareness in the struggle for authentic inner and social freedom?
4. Identify the places in personal and communal lives where the transformative audacity of spirit is most needed.

FURTHER READING

Thomas Ryan, *Four Steps to Spiritual Freedom* (New York/Mahwah, NJ: Paulist Press, 2003)

NOTES:   1. Marie L. Baird, *On the Side of the Angels: Ethics and Post-Holocaust Spirituality* (Leuven-Paris-Dudley,MA: Peeters, 2002) 73; see also 80–88.

2. The term undersong is from Ralph Waldo Emerson. See Peter B. Price, *Undersong: Listening to the Soul* (London: Darton, Longman & Todd, 2002) 1.

3. See Ernest Kurtz and Katherine Ketcham, *The Spirituality of Imperfection: Storytelling and the Search for Meaning* (New York: Bantam Books, 2002).

4. See Kwok Pui-Lan, 'Porous Boundaries: Eclecticism in Emerging Spiritual Practices' in *Spiritus: A Journal of Christian Spirituality* 7 (2007) 1, 82–85.

5. The work of scholars such as Walter Principe, Sandra M. Schneiders, Bernard McGinn, and Mary Frohlich in exploring the issues involved in defining Christian spirituality is indicative of the problems that are encountered in this debate. See their respective contributions in Elizabeth A. Dreyer & Mark S. Burrows, *Minding the Spirit: The Study of*

*Christian Spirituality* (Baltimore & London: The Johns Hopkins University Press, 2005). See also Philip Sheldrake, 'What is Spirituality?' in Kenneth J. Collins, *Exploring Christian Spirituality: An Ecumenical Reader* (Grand Rapids, MI: Baker Books, 2000) 21–42; David Tracy, 'Recent Catholic Spirituality: Unity Amid Diversity' in Louis Dupre and Don E. Saliers, eds, *Christian Spirituality: Post-Reformation and Modern* (New York: Crossroad, 1989) 143–173; Cheslyn Jones, Geoffrey Wainwright and Edward Yarnold S. J., eds, *The Study of Spirituality* (Oxford and New York: Oxford University Press, 1986); Daniel Helminiak, *The Human Core of Spirituality: Mind as Psyche and Spirit* (Albany, NY: State University of New York Press, 1996); Michael Downey, *Understanding Christian Spirituality* (New York/Mahwah, NJ: Paulist Press, 1997); Declan Marmion, *A Spirituality of Everyday Faith: A Theological Investigation of the Notion of Spirituality in Karl Rahner* (Louvain: Peeters Press, 1998); John Drane, *Do Christians Know How to Be Spiritual? The Rise of New Spirituality and the Mission of the Church* (London: Darton, Longman & Todd, 2005). Regarding cross-professional applications see Lucy Bregman, 'Defining Spirituality: Multiple Uses and Murky Meanings of an Incredibly Popular Term' in *The Journal of Pastoral Care and Counseling* 58 (2004) 3, 157–167; Lyren Chiu et al., 'An Integrative Review of the Concept of Spirituality in the Health Sciences' in *Western Journal of Nursing Research* 26 (2004) 4, 405–428; A. M. Unruh et al., 'Spirituality Unplugged: A Review of Commonalities and Contentions, and a Resolution' in *Canadian Journal of Occupational Therapy*, February (2002) 5–19; A. M. Unruh et al., 'Spirituality in the Context of Occupation: A Theory to Practice Application' in Matthew Molineux, ed., *Occupation for Occupational Therapists* (Oxford: Blackwell Publishing, 2004) 32–45; Robert Giacalone and Carol L. Jurkiewicz, eds, *Handbook of Workplace Spirituality and Organizational Performance* (Armonk, NY and London: M. E. Sharp, 2003); Jay A. Conger & Associates, *Spirit at Work: Discovering the Spirituality in Leadership* (San Francisco: Jossey-Bass, 1994); Peter Van Ness, *Spirituality, Diversion and Decadence: The Contemporary Predicament* (Albany, NY: State University of New York Press, 1992); Jeremy Carrette and Richard King, *Selling Spirituality: The Silent Takeover of Religion* (London and New York: Routledge, 2005); Len Sperry, *Spirituality in Clinical Practice: Incorporating the Spiritual Dimension in Psychotherapy and Counseling* (Hove and Florence, KY: Brunner-Routledge, 2001); Jorge N. Ferrer, Foreword by Richard Tarnas, *Revisioning Transpersonal Theory: A Participative Vision of Human Spirituality* (Albany, NY: State University of New York Press, 2002); Leigh Eric Schmidt, *Restless Souls: The Making of American Spirituality* (New York: HarperSanFranciso, 2005).

6. See J. Matthew Ashley, 'The Turn to Spirituality? The Relationship Between Theology and Spirituality' in *Christian Spirituality Bulletin* 3 (1995) 2, 13–18 at 13.

7. See Leigh Eric Schmidt, *Restless Souls: The Making of American Spirituality* op. cit. 255-256.

8. See David Brown, *God and the Enchantment of Place: Reclaiming Human Experience* (Oxford and New York: Oxford University Press, 2006) 5-36.

9. See Frederica R. Halligan, *Listening Deeply to God: Exploring Spirituality in an Interreligious Age* (Mystic, CT: Twenty-Third Publications, 2003).

10. See for example, Alfred Adler, *What Life Should Mean to You* (London: George Allen & Unwin, 1980) and Viktor Frankl, *Man's Search for Meaning* (New York: Praeger, 1959).

11. See David Hay, *Something There: The Biology of the Human Spirit* (London: Darton, Longman & Todd, 2006) 172-187.

12. See for example Gregory C. Stanczack, *Engaged Spirituality: Social Change and American Religion* (New Brunswick, NJ and London: Rutgers University Press, 2006).

13. See for example, Elizabeth Dreyer, *Passionate Spirituality: Hildegard of Bingen and Hadewijch of Brabant* (New York/Mahwah, NJ: Paulist Press, 2005).

14. Ronald Rolheiser, *Seeking Spirituality: Guidelines for a Christian Spirituality for the Twenty-first Century* (London, Sydney, Auckland: Hodder & Stoughton, 1998) 6.

15. See for example, Robert C. Solomon, *Spirituality for the Skeptic: The Thoughtful Love of Life* (Oxford: Oxford University Press, 2002); Benjamin B. Page, ed. *Marxism and Spirituality: An International Anthology* (Westport, CT & London: Bergin & Garvey, 1993); Eugene H. Peterson, *Christ Plays in Ten Thousand Places: A Conversation in Spiritual Theology* (Grand Rapids, MN and Cambridge: Eerdmans Publishing, 2005).

16. See for example, David M. Black, ed. *Psychoanalysis and Religion in the 21st Century: Competitors or Collaborators?* (London & New York: Routledge, 2006); F. LeRon Shults and Steven J. Sandage, *Transforming Spirituality: Integrating Theology and Psychology* (Grand Rapids, MI: Baker Academic, 2006); Len Sperry, *Spirituality in Clinical Practice: Incorporating the Spiritual Dimension in Psychotherapy and Counseling* (Philadelphia, PA & Hove: Brunner-Routledge, 2001).

17. See for example, Gary W. Hartz, PhD. *Spirituality and Mental Health: Clinical Applications* (New York, London, Oxford: The Haworth Pastoral Press, 2005); Caroline Young and Cyndie Koopsen, *Spirituality, Health, and Healing* (Thorofare, NJ: Slack Incorporated, 2005); G. Frank Lawlis, PhD. *Transpersonal Medicine: A New Approach to Healing Body-Mind-Spirit*. Foreword by Larry Dossey, MD. (Boston and London: Shambhala, 1996).

18. John Drane, *Do Christians Know How to Be Spiritual? The Rise of the New Spirituality, and the Mission of the Church* (London: Darton, Longman and Todd, 2005).

19. Christopher Partridge, *The Re-Enchantment of the West: Alternative Spiritualities, Secularization, Popular Culture and Occulture*. Two volumes. (London, New

York: T & T Clark, 2004 and 2005) volume 1, 62–183 and volume 2, 207–278. For a history of esoteric spirituality see B. J. Gibbons, *Spirituality and the Occult: From the Renaissance to the Modern Age* (London and New York: Routledge, 2001).

20. David Tacey, *The Spirituality Revolution: The Emergence of Contemporary Spirituality* (Hove & New York: Brunner-Routledge, 2004); Paul Heelas & Linda Woodhead, *The Spiritual Revolution: Why Religion is Giving Way to Spirituality* (Oxford: Blackwell Publishing, 2005).

21. Vincent J. Millar, *Consuming Religion: Christian Faith and Practice in a Consumer Society* (New York & London: Continuum International Publishing Group, 2004).

22. See Raymond L. M. Lee and Susan E. Ackerman, *The Challenge of Religion after Modernity: Beyond Disenchantment* (Aldershot: Ashgate, 2002) 19–31.

23. See for example, Jeremy Carrette and Richard King, *Selling Spirituality: The Silent Takeover of Religion* (London and New York: Routledge, 2005); see also R. Laurence Moore, *Selling God: American Religion in the Marketplace of Culture* (Oxford: Oxford University Press, 1994); Peter H. Van Ness, *Spirituality, Diversion and Decadence: The Contemporary Predicament* (Albany, NY: State University of New York Press, 1992).

24. Thomas Ryan, *Four Steps to Spiritual Freedom* (New York/Mahwah, NJ: Paulist Press, 2003) 54.

25. See for example Dallen J. Timothy and Daniel H. Olsen, eds *Tourism, Religion, and Spiritual Journeys* (London and New York: Routledge, 2006).

26. See Thomas Ryan, *Four Steps to Spiritual Freedom* op. cit. 196.

27. For an overview of the genealogy of mysticism see L. E. Schmidt, 'The Making of Modern "Mysticism"' in *Journal of the American Academy of Religion* 71 (2003) 2, 273–302.

28. See Bernard McGinn, 'The Letter and the Spirit: Spirituality as an Academic Discipline' in Elizabeth A. Dreyer & Mark S. Burrows, eds, *Minding the Spirit: The Study of Christian Spirituality* (Baltimore: The Johns Hopkins University Press, 2005) 25–41 at 26–29.

29. See P. A. Kahle & J. M. Robbins, *The Power of Spirituality in Therapy: Integrating Spiritual and Religious Beliefs in Mental Health Practice* (New York: The Haworth Pastoral Press, 2004).

30. See C. Elliott, 'A Spirituality of Economics' in J. F. Cobble, Jr. & C. M. Elliott, eds, *The Hidden Spirit: Discovering the Spirituality of Institutions* (Mathews, NC: CMR Press, 1999) 103–108.

31. See Elizabeth J. Tisdell, *Exploring Spirituality and Culture in Adult and Higher Education* (San Francisco: Jossey-Bass, 2003).

32. W. Carr, 'Can We Speak of the Spirituality of Institutions?' in Cobble & Elliott, *The Hidden Spirit*, op. cit. 109–117 at 109–110.

33. See B. J. Zinnbauer et al. 'Religion and Spirituality: Unfuzzying the Fuzzy' in *Journal for the Scientific Study of Religion* 36 (1997) 4, 549–564.

34. See Philip F. Sheldrake 'Christian Spirituality as a Way of Living Publicly: A Dialectic of the Mystical and the Prophetic' in *Spiritus. A Journal of Christian Spirituality* 3 (2003) 1, 19-37.

35. See for example, P. L. VanKatwyk, *Spiritual Care and Therapy: Integrative Perspectives.* (Ontario: Wilfrid Laurier Press, 2003) 1-39.

36. See Richard M. Gula, S. S. *The Call to Holiness: Embracing a Fully Christian Life* (New York/Mahwah, NJ: 2003) 84-87.

## CHAPTER 6

*Forces of Meaning and Shaping:*
*The Landscapes of Spirituality*

*The answer is blowing in the wind, the wind of God*
*making circles on the primal waters.*

## INTRODUCTION

In this chapter the principal concern is to trace the meaning and shaping of contemporary spirituality. Our initial task is to reconnect with the origins of the word *spirituality*, to trace its early genealogy and draw contemporary lessons from it. There is no need to delve too deeply here into the wide variety of historical developments that have shaped the notion over more than two and a half millennia: that work has been done elsewhere.[1] Our problem has to do with the meaning and shaping of the word as it is subsumed into the contemporary world, captive to its consumer impulses and its therapeutic culture. In the consumer multiverse serious rifts between spirituality and theological or religious convictions on the one hand, and socio-political commitments on the other, are to be expected. The reasons are straightforward enough. In consumer worlds the word *spirituality* can refer to almost anything. Consumer worlds favour a vague airiness, a level of banality, a kind of anaemic unreality in things spiritual, deriving in large part from the often underdeveloped and shapeless nature of people's spiritual desires and yearnings.[2]

This unreality becomes more complex when the problem of undifferentiated awareness is encountered in spirituality. In an undifferentiated world distinctions do not exist, so that popular pieties, civic and religious doctrines, and spiritual practices drawn from a variety of sources sit happily together, undistinguished one from the other. In a recent piece of fieldwork one of my doctoral students interviewed a person who had no apparent difficulty putting atheism, frequent Marian pilgrimage, and regular Evangelical Church attendance together as a lifestyle choice. The rationale? Identity requires grounding in a tradition. This blissful state of patchwork indistinction must change when critical reflection and its distinctions enter the scene. Then tensions and resistances can and do arise. When the outer supports for religion and morality prove unreliable or are badly shaken by events and philosophies, an inward turn is to be expected.[3] The present tensions around the links between religion, religious practices and spirituality are a case in point.

In contemporary usage spirituality has become a container or signpost word appealing to other signifying words to unearth its vast potential and reveal the innumerable assumptions and expectations people project on to it, especially in consumer locations populated by socially disengaged people ignoring the interweaving challenges of meaning, value and mystery. In this process the word *spirituality* also serves a cultural task, bringing together arrays of proposals discovered in arrays of very different contexts and locations. Today the term spirituality is applied to a variety of disparate concepts, expressions, feelings, emotions, practices, discourses, structures, forms, schools, relationships and engagements. It is made to span the gap between systemworlds and lifeworlds, seemingly comfortable in both, but meaning different things in both. Such usage clearly demonstrates that contemporary spirituality represents neither a unitary trend nor a single alliance.

Contemporary Western spirituality is a loose bundle of contrasting and contesting concerns, desires, and interests sharing a largely postmodern cultural milieu that favours an inward turn. The social and cultural contexts in which we live today in the West confront us with a wide range of potentials and possibilities. They are easy to summarise.[4] The following is a suggestive list of approaches to spirituality that are readily discernible in the contemporary West:

- The turn to psychospirituality and complementary therapies.
- The turn to age-specific and developmental spiritualities.
- The turn to individuated and autonomous spiritualities.
- The growth of undifferentiated bricolage-based/patchwork/toolkit spiritualities.
- The turn to the East and to inter-spirituality as resources for spiritual practices.
- The new-gnostic interest in inner-work technologies.
- The turn to emancipatory spiritualities.
- The turn to humanistic spiritualities.
- The turn to pragmatic spiritualities.
- The turn to holistic spiritualities.
- The turn to African and Latin American spiritualities.
- The turn to quantum discourse in spirituality.
- The turn to esoteric and occult practices.
- The rediscovery of desire, eros, and embodiment in spirituality.

- The turn to goddess spiritualities.
- The turn to gendered spiritualities.
- The major turn to ecological and cosmological concerns in spirituality.
- The turn to creation-based and creational spiritualities.
- The turn to aboriginal spiritualities.
- The favouring of autonomous spirituality over institutional religion.
- The turn to spiritualities of feeling.

The complexity of this state of affairs, even granting degrees of overlap and indistinction, becomes even clearer if we take the link between spirituality and beauty as an example. Different kinds of beauty, human and natural beauty, the beauty found in art, music, poetry, literature, and craft-work for example, are capable of grounding multiple associations with arrays of spiritual feelings and desires. Architects, painters, sculptors, poets, musicians, mystics and creative writers try to communicate values taken from human experience and give them creative form.[5] A similar observation is applicable to their efforts to wrestle with geography, space and time and create, as it were, music and images to live by; spirituality shares this desire to shape spaces to sing and dance in, and practices to guide us through the flux and flow of life. Spirituality is a fine example of the ways in which spatial practices – pilgrimage, holy wells, sacred places are typical examples – and the messages they communicate become central to emancipatory social action.

Compare wilderness and desert spiritualities with well-to-do urban and well-being or prosperity spiritualities. Spatial context predicts the kinds of social action that are characteristic of the people who live there. Compare township or inner-city spiritualities to monastic spiritualities. Reflect on the differences between urban and rural spiritualities. Then wonder about the impact of education and career on spirituality. Ponder the spiritualities of concrete jungles and savage landscapes; of landscapes of intellectual and physical disability; of landscapes of loss: cultural loss, job loss, identity loss, the loss of tradition or home, the loss of hope, the losses of abandonment, betrayal and tragic death. Rifts and discontinuities flow in and through them all and reveal the transitoriness and unpredictability of fragile lives. These forces in spirituality have their left and right versions and their ideological losses of integrity.

Today the word *spirituality* has also become amenable to the divergent demands of both instrumental reason, which is control and task-oriented and is focused on a goal, and communicative reason, which is culturally and socially oriented and has an integrative focus. Spiritualities shaped by the forces of modernity show the signs of instrumental reason. They tend to be instrumental, rational, goal-oriented, focused on action, interested in technique. Spiritualities grounded in the postmodern milieu try to overcome the separations and rifts of modernity. They bring to the surface processes that favour integration, that wrestle with coincidences of opposites in the search for non-duality.[6] For some, spirituality is an object to be consumed and used, often in devaluing or parasitic ways. For others, it is something to be lived and expressed, something to be warmly valued.[7]

For some, spirituality is driven by the desire for a specific social status and the social validation it brings: 'I am spiritual, but not religious'. For others it refers to a humbler, more grounded form of disciplined, integrative practice. For some, spirituality is acutely private and subjective. For others it has manifest social and planetary implications. For some, spirituality is patently self-referred. For others it makes clear other-directed ethical demands. For some, spirituality is very private. For others it moves them towards explicit human community. For some, spirituality is severed from religious linkages. For others such linkages remain important to the coherent public and social expression of personal spiritual commitments. The following is another suggestive list of understandings of spirituality that surface typical expressions of spirituality in the contemporary West:

- A way of life and purpose.
- A way of relationality and connectedness.
- A way of committed awareness.
- A religious way.
- A sacred way.
- A Gospel way.
- A way of grace.
- A way of consciousness.
- An esoteric way.
- An integrative, holistic way.
- A way of healing.
- A liberational way.
- A prophetic way.
- A humanistic way.
- A transformative way.
- A way of social commitment.
- A way of peace and justice.
- A way of nature and (panentheistic) consciousness.
- A way of discipline and practice.
- A way of inner-work techniques.
- A way of the spirit in the world.
- A way of engagement and activism.

Consequently it is difficult to know what spirituality means with any precision until clarifying questions are asked and helpful answers given. It is difficult to identify how spirituality functions in different personal and social settings, times and landscapes. Is spirituality hidden away in some private corner or socially revealed? Is it something for which apologies must be made or something audacious? This is a major reason why first-order definitions, those that are immediate and uncritical, tend to become ambiguous; even when we try to distinguish between authentic and potentially pathological spiritualities our distinctions are likely to be contested. In contemporary usage, then, the word *spirituality* has become a confusing carrier of multiple, often hazy meanings that are open to misuse and uncritical selectivity.[8] It is very easy to leave assumptions that orient approaches to contemporary spirituality completely unexamined.[9] Much the same may be said about models of spirituality. Where do we go for an answer to this dilemma? The answer, it seems, is blowing in the wind, waiting for us to pay heed to its intimations and acknowledge its empowering voice.

## A Brief Genealogy

To uncover the original meaning of the word *spirituality* we must return to the Bible and to the Hebrew and Christian origins of the concept. The word *spirit*, which lies at the heart of the word *spirituality*, stands for the Hebrew *ruach*, which occurs three hundred and eighty-nine times in the Hebrew Bible. It is a word that is difficult to describe, define or confine in English translation. Much the same may be said about its cognate term in Greek, *pneuma*. The root meaning of *ruach/pneuma/spirit* confronts us with powerful and rich imagery focused on the wind, breathing and breath, and moving air – words that suggest invisible but profoundly dynamic, vital forces that spill over into creative and transformative action.[10]

The Hebrew concern was quite unequivocal. *Ruach* addresses the way God enters and impacts the world. Right at the start of the Book of Genesis God's Breathing touches the formless, the dark and the deep and a world emerges. God's Breathing touches clay, and human life emerges. *Ruach/Spirit* is creative power at its most divine. In the Hebrew imagination there is no split between the physical and the spiritual world; there is one reality and the Divine *Ruach/Spirit* is blowing through it all. *Ruach* has a two-fold reference: it names the human life force, but it also names divine power at work in the cosmos. In consequence, spirituality is the landscape of Spirit, the place of encounter with divine power. Spirituality is also the landscape of human life in its deepest, most liberated, originating sense. Where reality is, Spirit is; where life is, Spirit is; where Spirit is, divine power is at work.

In the New Testament *pneuma* and *pneumatikos* refer respectively to the Holy Spirit and to the state of being spiritual, a technical term for Christian existence: the Christian is spiritual/*pneumatikos* (1 Corinthians 2:13–15), Christian goodness is spiritual/*pneumatikos* (1 Corinthians 9:11), and the gifts that empower Christian living are spiritual/*pneumatikos* (1 Corinthians 14:1). In the originating Christian usage, to be spiritual/*pneumatikos* is to be one with the Spirit of Jesus (1 Corinthians 6:17); where the Spirit is, there is utter freedom (2 Corinthians 3:17). The original sense of the words *spirit/spirituality* is clear: they create an image of a dynamic, empowering, gifting, enlivening force that is utterly divine. They simultaneously name a Spirit-gifted way of living in and relating to the world and all that is. Unfortunately, that early clarity became clouded over time as dualistic splits were set in motion that further complicate our present difficulties: soul–body, spirit–matter, inner–outer, freedom–necessity, private–public, dualist–holist, experiential–theoretical, and a host of related moral, personal, social and historical concerns.[11] It is time to return to the Source and listen to the Wind.

What is most at stake for spirituality in these originating images is the clash of two ways of life: one receptive to the Divine Spirit, the other resistant; one moved by and expressive of the creative and emancipatory concerns of spirit, the other attempting to control it for self-referred or exploitive reasons. Such concerns raise a pivotal question: is spirituality – and by extension authentic religiosity – meant to be a world-maintaining or a world-shaking force?[12] The metaphor of the wind suggests that spirituality is meant to become a world-shaking and a world-remaking force, especially when it is read against the background of the Hebrew creation story. Understood in this light, spirituality has to be about more than establishing a personal identity or social status quo. It has to be more than self-referred. We are talking about the energy to construct far more than an individual life project; in spirituality we are talking about the energy that created a world.[13] Similar challenges are implicit in two familiar contemporary triads: *mind-body-spirit* and *body-soul-spirit*. Taken at face value they seem to be empty of world-shaking, world-constructing force, favouring a more privatised and individualised turn; but that is because we have inherited an impoverished concept of spirit and many do not know what an experience of Spirit is meant to do.

The words *spirit/spirituality* are evocative of a creative, life-giving force moving over a deep and dark primordial void, and echoing a creating word: Let there be! There are other ancient echoes in the word spirit. It is reminiscent of the Gaelic *Sidhe* who were known as the people of the Wind, hinting at primordial forces invisibly riding the whirling winds, swirling the leaves of autumn, and making their unseen presence felt in our inner and outer landscapes, no matter how savage.[14] Spirit is the liberating wind of God disturbing our spiritual lassitude, our seemingly safe, comfortably undisturbed lassitude. When we stay close to the originating metaphor it is clear that spirit points to life, energy, and vitality: life-giving, whole-making, life-enhancing, world-making creative and emancipating power. Where spirit is alive so also is creativity, emancipation and hope, because spirit/breath/wind/air finds its way everywhere, especially into domains of human limitation and failure, of absence and exile, and the places of alienation and tragedy. When its whisperings are heard and attended to, spirit stirs up new ways of living, inspires new and audacious responses to the challenges of history and politics.

In fact, spirit and spirituality constantly evoke tones of creativity, emancipation – *healing-saving* in the classic Christian vocabulary, connectedness, relationship, and social engagement. These themes have taken on an almost synonymous ring in contemporary spirituality. They constantly remind us that spirit is transformative of its very nature. Spirit is there when people deal with the forces that diminish or block or make them turn away from life, or that crystallise as elemental forms of threat, dread, anxiety, vindictiveness, destructive anger, and fear in all its most morbid forms and expressions. Spirituality as a form of living characterised by creative and emancipatory expression and engagement demands involvement and self-implication because it means that a person or a group has, in the face of history, decided to ride the wind and not just think about it or listen in an abstractly disengaged and disinterested way.

## ENGLISH USAGE

Movement of the words *spirit, spiritual* and *spirituality* into the vernacular languages in Europe began in the middle of the thirteenth century, coming into English from the French. Movement into Middle English occurred over the course of the fourteenth and fifteenth centuries. In English, *spirituality* translates earlier Latin words, the adjective *spiritualis* and the noun *spiritualitas* that in turn translated the Greek *pneumatikos* with its links to *pneuma* and the Hebrew *ruach*. Care needs to be taken here, however, for it is not clear that the Latin and Greek share the same meanings, or that the English unerringly connects us to ancient experiences. Linguistic assumptions need to be handled with care. The Greek certainly has a broad range of references including weakened secular uses and ambiguous allusions dating across the centuries from the Stoics to St Augustine and beyond.[15] That said, the meaning of the Latin *spiritualis* (spiritual) tended to remain quite stable in its reference to the spiritual core of Christian existence, holding in focus the central role of the Holy Spirit.

By the time the word *spirituality* entered vernacular use in English a range of meanings had begun to emerge. While subjective, inner-life meanings began to dominate, the word was also used in more humanistic and political contexts. When we first meet the word *spirituality* in sixteenth-century English it not only carries the original meaning but it also gave expression to abuses of spiritual authority and power. From this starting point the meaning of the word gradually moved towards the naming of inner dispositions, inner states of soul, and interior exercises. In this context it is interesting to read Mary Frohlich's recent piece on the significance of critical interiority to the academic study of spirituality.[16] With the turn to interiority, especially in the contemplative tradition, the connection of spirituality to personal practices of piety and devotion soon followed, mainly through the work of writers in the Catholic tradition. However, the emphasis on the interior life of the individual began to take centre stage and so helped prepare the way for the privatisation of spirituality that marries so well with the contemporary turn to individualism and personal consumption as shaping forces in contemporary spirituality. In this way the foundations were laid for the present breadth and gradation of meanings the word *spirituality* has acquired in contemporary English.

The origins of modern usage emerge first in France in the latter part of the seventeenth century. Modern English usage starts much later. In France, the word *spiritualité* was used in two contrasting ways at this time, first as a way of describing a personal, affective relationship with God, and then as a reproach against Quietist writers of the time. Madame Guyon's work (she died in 1717) strongly identified spirituality with the interior life of the individual soul, but the mode of practice, with its emphasis on pure love, led to fears about the neglect of engaged charity. The problem concerned – and to an extent still does – what Michel de Certeau has described as maps of intentions, maps of the inner world.[17] Modernity has made the danger of an inner–outer split all too real in contemporary spirituality, and the theories of the human person play a significant role in determining what happens. If such theories split and privilege interiority over sociality the rift continues.

Usage of the word *spirituality* languished during much of the eighteenth and nineteenth centuries. However, at the beginning of the twentieth century the use of the word became popular again, first in France and then in England. Development of usage was slower in English than in French and did not become popular until the 1960s. Since then its confident use has exploded. However, the influence of a parallel English usage dating from the latter half of the nineteenth and early twentieth century should also be noted. This sets the meaning of spirituality in an Indian context in opposition to perceived Western materialism. This use is particularly evident in the orientalising turn promoted by modern Theosophy under the influence of Annie Besant, Alice Bailey and others.

This turn has been particularly influential in the New Age milieu and helped to prepare the cultural ground for the contemporary propensity to set spirituality and religion in opposition to each other.

The array of meanings given to the word *spirituality* today, then, is quite recent in Western languages. Even in the early 1980s the confident use of the term spirituality was quite new.[18] The popularity of the word and the breadth of meaning attributed to it have grown steadily over the past fifty years. It was accompanied by the turn to psycho-existential and socio-cultural emphases that became typical of spirituality in this period. The turn to psychology already had a history by the 1960s. At that time Louis Bouyer, editor of *History of Christian Spirituality*,[19] had already recognised the links between spirituality and psychology even though he was more concerned by the dangers of reductive psychologism. Thomas Merton had already signalled the need for a turn to psychology in his *Sign of Jonah*, published ten years earlier in 1953.[20]

During the 1960s, the word *spirituality* came to centre stage in Christian contexts in the effort to find a route to meaning and practice that would bypass the crisis that was beginning to emerge in the mainstream Churches. In this context it is interesting to note that the published papers of a major conference held in Durham in 1967 with the title *Spirituality Today* show no agreed way of defining spirituality.[21] Since then, in contemporary Western cultures, interest in spirituality has spread 'luxuriantly'.[22] It seems that the lack of agreement on a definition of spirituality at Durham in 1967 was a harbinger of things to come; success seems as far away as ever.

## Emergent Manifestations and Questions

The very popularity of the word *spirituality* presents its own challenges and ambiguities. In the West today, does the word retain anything of its originating power and creativity? How much of its Hebrew and Christian origins does the word *spirituality* actually retain? Is contemporary usage thoroughly de-traditioned? Has the word been successfully domesticated? Does spirituality reveal soul hungering for life and meaning, or is spirituality a successfully commodified object shaped to serve nothing more than personal gratification and comfort? Even then the resonances and contours of the word *spirituality* are coloured by the psychosocial histories of speakers or writers, their assumptions and habits of mind, their cultural and linguistic frames of reference, as well as their expectations and agendas. Other factors include their personal religious experience or lack thereof, including experiences of being either helped or hurt by clergy or other religious people. The trend towards more privatised and more individualistic understandings and expressions of spirituality has continued to grow, a symptom of modernity and the

either/or visions that made the tyrannies of the twentieth century and
their horrors possible.

## Other influences

Whatever the case may be, the impact of groups of highly active seekers
who rejected traditional religion has also played a significant role in
shaping contemporary usage. The traditionally close interaction between
spirituality and theology has been attenuated and replaced by a linkage to
positive and transpersonal psychologies and contemporary theories of the
autonomous self. Simultaneously, as institutional participation declines,
the link with religion has become increasingly problematic, tense and
conflicted, as Sandra Schneiders has noted, though it is also important to
recognise that the separation of the goals of religion from the goals of
spirituality is a typically contemporary phenomenon.[23] Add to this the
findings of Robert Wuthnow's study of post-1950s American spirituality.
He offers a typology of spirituality that I believe applies well in other
Western societies. This typology distinguishes between three different
time-related expressions of spirituality.

The first, identified with the 1950s, is called *a spirituality of dwelling*. It
names a spirituality with firm religious and cultural linkages that offered
a place of stability in an increasingly uncertain world. The second,
identified with the 1960s and 1970s, is called *a spirituality of seeking*, as
people crossed traditional spiritual and sacred boundaries in the search for
something more individually satisfying. It is during this period that the
phrase 'spiritual, but not religious' became popular. Wuthnow's third
form is more recent and contemporary. It is called *a spirituality of practices*
and offers something of a more disciplined, more focused approach than
its immediate predecessor. It also favours depth and the setting aside of a
regular time and place for spiritual practice. Links to the world's
religious and faith traditions are also being re-forged.[24] Who is to say
what will come next? The attempt to understand fully the nature and
meaning of spirituality, as well as its relationship to religion and
mysticism, remains a work in progress.

The emergence of the new spirituality raises other important questions.
Christopher Partridge's work is particularly helpful in understanding
this process and in outlining its principal characteristics and challenges.[25]
Does the rise of new spiritualities represent a trivialisation of religion or
does it represent a genuine resacralising of the Western mind? The
problem here is the definition of religion in traditional terms, an approach
that no longer works given the sharp decline in traditional religious
forms of practice, particularly in Europe. At the same time, definitions of
spirituality are equally problematic, especially when they are inflected
by reaction to negative images of traditional religion. The implications are

obvious. In a world where traditional religion has drastically declined, where its discourses and literacies are considered irrelevant or are effectively absent, where detraditioning has led to a measurable loss of religious language and literacy, revivalist notions of religion, or processes of accommodation with postmodern culture, or forms of retrenchment are unlikely to aid resacralisation. In some parts of Europe the traditional Christian milieu appears no longer strong enough or has become so abstract that its replacement by discourses that are actually in tune with contemporary Western thought forms, ideas and practices is no great surprise. This is particularly so in locations where optimistic secularising and sacralising trends dynamically interact and support each other.

What about chosen as distinct from traditional religion? That runs the risk of conforming to processes of privatisation in a world that already wants to relegate religion to the purely private sphere. Theologically it also runs the risk of idolatry: people creating divinities to satisfy their own personal needs. What about a chosen spirituality? As a form of bricolage or patchwork spirituality, piecing together strategies for spiritual living from a range of different sources, it may represent a strength precisely as personally chosen in a process of continually renewed choice. But such an approach also represents a break with the past and with the spiritual wisdom of an ancient tradition, and so a potential loss of way. Such is, however, the nature of the new spirituality. Of its very nature it is personally chosen and constructed. It is continually composed and recomposed in terms of changing personal needs and experience. Precisely as chosen the new spirituality is both personal and malleable, open to continuing change in response to changing circumstance and location. It may have no set doctrines, but it does have an identifiable methodology and a rich reservoir of related beliefs and practices.

The new spirituality has changed as popular culture has changed and as changing identities seek structural conformity with new operative belief systems. A radically different popular culture has a formative impact that is diminishingly Christian. The sacred–secular tension is itself undergoing change as postmodern thought forms bite. The new spirituality is attuned to a more liberal, more democratic, more individualistic secular reality. It is principally concerned with prosperity, with life enhancement, with well-being and a healthy lifestyle, influenced by consumer visions of the world. It rationalises doctrinal belief and adopts a more permissive stance in the search for happiness and the realisation of personal potential. To what extent is such a spiritual landscape open to prophetic-political or mystical-prophetic understandings of spirituality? At the same time indicators of ecological, political, public, and being-in-doing spiritualities are close to hand. The same is true of concerns about consumer ethics and support for less exploitive modes of commodity production such as those related to the fair-trade movement. There is also evidence of a turn to focal practices that highlight non-technological human action.[26] These represent valuable contributions.

In looking at the new spirituality as an expression of popular culture, ambiguity is never far from the surface. Is the new spirituality a focus for social action, a spiritualised escape mechanism, or merely an interesting topic of conversation for the dinner party or talk radio? Or, as Tom Beaudoin suggested, is *popular culture* the new bible for a new spirituality?[27] Or is Gordon Lynch's *clubbing spirituality* closer to the mark?[28] Or are we in fact dealing with the spiritual face of a post-religious, post-Christian, post-human culture? Yet, in all of this there is evidence of a search for meaning: even fragmentary meaning, often found in unexpected and unlikely places, can offer some basis for hope. The contemporary is certainly a spirituality that seeks embodied experience. But it is also a spirituality that is challenged to look beyond the superficialities of a consumer milieu and its latent narcissism in which persons remain the sources of themselves. There is need here for a deeper, more authentic humanism; but whether that can be recuperated by free-form spiritualities serving the needs of a superficial culture is an entirely different question.

## Loss of Memory

What the new spirituality transmits is not belief but a way of doing or practising spirituality, a way of living spiritually in terms of a key image, or aspects of a tradition, or multiple traditions. As they blend they tend to take on the form of a soft, different, undemanding orthodoxy open to holistic visions. In the new spirituality the holistic milieu is real; and while it is personal it is not always selfish. Some cohorts of the new spirituality encourage personal responsibility and are concerned about the impact of spiritual voices in the public sphere. The personalisation of spirituality does not by definition preclude social responsibility or the attempt to influence public policy and ethics in a range of areas. Reflect on issues to do with fair-trade and the injustices and exploitations that are so characteristic of world commodity markets. The coffee trade is a typical example. Unfortunately, there is also ample evidence of what Bonnie Miller-McLemore portrays as the new spirituality's parasitical relationship with Christianity and Judaism, a relationship that edits out the prophetically demanding bits that have to do with social justice, concern and the common good.[29]

We are confronted by a catastrophe of memory that seeks to exclude prophetic Christianity and an ethic of social solidarity from any role of positive influence; an amnesia that even forgets that it is serving a rampant secularist techno-economic agenda. Memory has always had profound implications for spirituality: it reminds us to remember who we are. Memory helps us to understand that we are part of something bigger than ourselves. It colours our sense of identity and belonging. Memory touches our experiences of presence and loss. It connects us to all the fundamentals of human existence. Memory shapes our struggles not only to remain consciously aware but our struggles with God as well.[30]

Without memory how can spirit, creative imagination, destiny, energy, being or the transcendent be made accessible and transparent, or located as a significant moment in a long history? In a world of limited and limiting angles and perspectives how are we to grapple with spirit if memory is stolen? In the absence of dangerous memory how is spirit to find the audacity to engage in historically meaningful personal and social change? How are we to grapple with the dangerous memory of even the recent past and ensure that its horrors and tragedies do not happen again? A spirituality that backs away from such challenges reveals its self-referred shallowness. Loss of memory is the key to understanding much of what is emerging in consumer spirituality today. Indicative of this risk in new spirituality discourse is the way two trajectories are arranged to converge. In constructions of the new spirituality the personal-subjective intersects the spiritual-optimistic, becoming very attractive in the process.

In general, then, the new spirituality encourages eclectic, individualised forms of spirituality that make no absolute claims, have no central leadership, subscribe to no sacred text, require no creedal formulae. The new spirituality is typically open to exploration, experimentation, and spiritual journeying: engagements grounded in personal interest and authority. Yet concealed in all of this a basic religious impulse remains. Present evidence suggests that the new spiritual impulse is turning away from traditional Christianity towards a more amorphous, almost magical, somewhat mystical self-spirituality. Nevertheless, a vague religiosity continues to exist that reveals some Christian values alongside a range of heterodoxies made possible by the information revolution and the growth of religious pluralism.

## Spiritual Landscapes: Memory and Imagination

Landscapes are repositories of cultural and religious memory: mountains, hills, deserts, valleys, wildernesses, rocks, forests, abysses, cliffs and massifs, wet and dry places, pools, oases, wells, streams, fens and marshes, lonely places, caves, groves, bright places and places of shade and shadow, high places, low places, flora and fauna; they all become carriers of memory, stirrers of imagination and carriers of the holy. Memory is framed and nurtured by landscapes. Landscapes frame and nurture experiences of many kinds, even if the meaning of such memories and experiences are contested. As source domains of metaphor, landscapes inspire our constructions of reality, people our dreams and frame our bravest imaginings. Natural landscapes and spiritual landscapes overlap. They are natural elements in the spiritual dance.[31]

We bring personal, social and religious imagination to landscapes, a sense of place, a cultural and religious awareness that we have our being in landscapes; and so meanings arise there, imaginative meanings and dialogical identities to give them expression. We discover who we are in landscapes; we discover history; we discover purpose; we discover narratives and tell stories, and in the telling tell ourselves into new existences. Public lives unfold in public places. Landscape reminds us that spirituality is essentially relational, a celebration of connectedness and location in spatial and human terms. Landscape reminds us that spirituality is and always has been about more than the human person's private inner world.

Landscapes are the natural environments of stories and storytellers, of poets and mystics, sinners and saints: they constantly confront us with difference and diversity, with the seemingly firm and the ever-flowing, with boundaried and unbroken vistas, with otherness and the strange. We encounter life in landscapes; we encounter spirit there, too: we wrestle at Jabbok fords (Genesis 32:22–31) and cross the paths of whales (Jonah 1:17). Incarnation happens in a landscape and so does covenant. Jesus was tested in a wilderness (Mark 1:12–13) and walked the land, wending a way to destiny. On the west side of a wilderness, at a bush aflame (Exodus 3:1–12), Moses found holy ground and his life's meaning; he spent forty years in a desert, receiving a moral code on a mountain in a cloud. Landscapes are part of our most sacred memories and stories.

We climb Tabors, we slumber in Gethsemanes, we seek out holy islands searching for the sacred: Ionas and Lindisfarnes and Lough Dergs. Every country has their counterparts. Landscapes are inescapably part of our spiritualities and our religions and our search for deeper lives. Landscapes teach us about startles of starlings whirring upwards, harebells ringing in a roiling wind. Landscapes bring us to flowing waters and weeping willows, tide-pools full of tiny life, and tidal basins that become meeting places of salted and unsalted stories, thick like butter on fresh-baked bread. Landscapes remind us that in the deepest affairs ritual is more potent than reason: ritual and a sense of place honouring memories of loss and pain – dangerous and holy ground. Landscape teaches how to stand in such places. Our Hebrew religious forbears knew that holy ground sanctified what was upon it: things and people. We have the sense of holy ground because we have a sense of encounter with divinity there: places touched by the Holy One. In holy ground we are reminded of God's concern for the world, of God's presence there. Making mud from spit and dust Jesus healed a blind man

(John 9:5–7). We need the earth to heal us to God's creative presence.

Holy ground connects us to landscape-as-theology, as God-Word: a Bethel marked by a stone, a boundary-place where human-space and God-space meet and invite a dangerous wrestling (Genesis 28:10–22). Landscape connects us to flows of immanence and flows of transcendence and their interweaving dance.[32] Where spatial holiness and spatial spirituality is lost the power of landscape to minister to us is also lost, and with it our sense of the impact of landscape on our language and metaphor structures. The new spirituality challenges us to rediscover the spatial nature of sacred experience. Contemporary theology has essentially forgotten place and space and ground, has largely forgotten landscape, caught up as it presently is by the forces of time and history. In embracing historical consciousness we have forgotten spatial consciousness and with it our ancestral sense of responsibility for the earth.

Ellen Ross has made a helpful distinction between six expressions of holy ground in the Christian tradition with specific reference to women's spirituality and experience.[33] The first is drawn from the Hebrew tradition and identifies the land itself as sacred presence. The second identifies historical places as sacred presence; the third identifies created space as sacred place; the fourth is a subset of the first and refers to what she has described as landed eruptions of the sacred; the fifth identifies space as apocalyptic presence; while the sixth addresses the figural nature of the sacred. In the first, the relationship to God happens through the land as symbol of divine presence, and sacredness is invested in the land itself. The *Book of Ruth* is an excellent example of this usage.

In the second, place acquires the sense of the sacred through historical events that connect believers to the divine in a process where imaginative identification plays a major role. Pilgrim sites are typical of this model and represent places touched by the salvation tradition and its implications for healing and transformation. There are echoes of incarnation in this representation because such places represent the possibility of connecting to salvation-enabling events. The third refers to places that have been specifically created and ritually invested with a sacred character. The fourth refers to discontinuous but sometimes dramatic identifications of the divine perceived in the land. The experience of Margery Kempe is an overlapping example of Ross's second, third and fourth models.

The fifth is set in train by experiences of bondage and freedom where physical and spiritual experiences occur in parallel. This form is evident in slave narratives where bondage characterises the real world, while freedom characterises the spiritual. The natural world acts as a divine simile or metaphor of judgement. In the sixth type the landscape provides imagery that gives expression to the relationship with the divine. Consider, for example, a voice crying in the wilderness (Matthew 3:3;

John 1:23; Isaiah 40:3), or a woman at a well (John 4:4–26). The goal is a spiritual map for a spiritually meaningful life in the real world. In suggesting this typology Ross draws attention to the ways in which land, historical place, humanly created space, figurative space and the reality of transcendent and otherworldly space interweave to create way marks for the spiritual journey.

Unfortunately, we have largely forgotten lived space; we have forgotten its implications for meaning, relationship, sociality, spirituality, religion, politics, embodiment and the earth itself. We largely ignore how we represent landscape and place, how we live in landscape and place, the practices we bring to bear on landscape and space, how we configure the sacred, and the implications these have for our religious, spiritual and theological sensibilities and sensitivities. Place becomes a place of practices: religious buildings are an example: they emerge to make religious practices, rituals and ways of life possible. Reflect on places of pilgrimage; they too are places of practices: places and practices and representations full of theological and spiritual implication. Reflect on entrances and exits as metaphors. Reflect on paths and roads and ways as metaphors. Reflect on spiritualities of ascent and descent, and spiritual levels and stages, for example; notice how they are grounded in spatial representations that are themselves grounded in experiences of place, space and landscape.

Think of the wealth of spatial representation in spiritual writing: gardens and springs, gates and mountains, seas and downhill roads to places like Jericho (Luke 10:30). If the spiritual significance of landscape remains unrecognised and unaffirmed, not taken as real, we risk defining spirituality in purely subjective, individual and inward terms. This is the major reason why a turn to landscape and the earth as holy is so important to spirituality today. We need to rediscover space and place and their implications for a fuller, more coherent worldview. We cannot actually transcend landscape, no more than we can transcend history, or ignore interiority. Our narratives celebrate them all. We need to rediscover how to celebrate our spatial location, how to enter spatial consciousness and touch the holy in the landscape.

Where time, space and the human situation meet, there, meaning surfaces. There, spirit is alive, rhythming differently, attuned to God's making-word still echoing in the wind of Spirit, remembering that we are God's field, the fruit of God's husbandry and God's building, full of the promise of life (1 Corinthians 3:9). Spirit is about life, about listening, hearing, seeking, finding, knocking, opening, looking, gazing, stilling, leaping beyond human goals to the reasons, the heart and soul reasons, for living and going on living in the face of predicament, horror, tragedy and contingency. Spirit is about the things we cannot control, precisely because spirit rhythms differently, responds to time differently; but Spirit song is always met in landscapes and spaces, even by captives on the banks of foreign rivers (Psalm 137).

Landscapes are full of stories, stories of skittering butterflies, bright colours flashing; buzzing insects on hills glorious in their purple heather robes; peregrinating geese hooting their way north along invisible roads; roaring lions and bleating lambs creating images of an impossible peace; dusty plains sprinkled with sparse grasses and scratchy sands, sprinkled with scattering leaves on a low wind; starlight, moonlight, blazing sunlight hinting at an altered awareness in a shifting of shadows; elderberry blooms and rosehips, herbs that heal and herbs that kill, trees and bees and sibilant sounds; rags on hawthorns by holy wells; memories, inscapes made visible by medals in pools, an unsullied splendour thrown like a blossoming mystery on the land: a kind of radiant liturgy, a hint of landscaped Eucharist gifting an unfolding universe.[34] Landscapes are full of echoes of what was and what is, echoes wondering 'what happens next?' lest it all vanish in the wintry gusts of a darkening evening and a hush of birds. None of us forget the places where ecstasy touched us, or tragedy, or the holy, or the dark: and that is as it should be.

Everything happens in landscapes and spaces, the landscapes of nature and the spaces of spirit: birth, the living, the dying, the creating, the destroying; praying and the forgetting to pray, worshipping and the refusing to worship; the making and the unmaking of commitments, the loving and the hating; the approving and the contesting, the best and the worst. Even when we are exiled and living nomadic postmodern exist-ences, even when we are in non-places and experience dis-placement, landscape is part of it all. They all unfold somewhere. Even then we seek a home, a place to be, a place to dwell, a place of domestication, a place of connection and participation, a place of comfort and security. Without landscape there is no place, no home, no connectedness, nothing to read incarnationally, nothing for the analogical imagination's integrating vision and the capacity of contemplation to originate something new, something beautiful in the land.

Landscapes are full of the power of place and the power of the memories of place. They are theatres of memory and possibility, theatres of prophetic promise generating futures in the dreaming, the dreaming of the land and the dwellers on the land. Natural landscapes entwine with cultural landscapes and spiritual landscapes, touch them and shape them, shape and hold their glad and bitter memories and the heritage of ancestors. Place is landscape and memory, memory littering natural, cultural and spiritual landscapes with private and public meanings, some large, some small. Landscapes have political resonances, too. Think of centuries of monks, nuns and hermits going out into savage landscapes to find God and in the going making landscapes sacred. The tragedy today is their switch to tourist venues and their packaged products sold in visitor centres tastefully contoured: transformed into simulacra, empty images of themselves under the power of the postmodern sign, memories without meaning beyond the snapshots of moments soon forgotten.

But then the categories of perception have always had the power to create different readings of the natural world. Can the contours of landscape in spirituality be satisfactorily mapped? But that begs another question: what is the nature of landscape consciousness? What were the monks, nuns and hermits really doing when they sought their savage spaces? What sort of imagination was at work? What sort of satisfaction were they seeking? What is it that links our nature-sensitivity to ideas of the sacred and the holy: what alerts us to holy ground? In the Celtic tradition, what generates thin places where the divine breaks through? What is it in the Hebrew imagination that fills landscape with divine breath? Such questions remind us that our omissions of landscape from our definitions of spirituality will always be problematic: a grave omission. Spirit moves over the face of the world. Spirit plays in the interplay of light and darkness; and Spirit moves through the land. Then reflect: what impact does my landscape, my place of dwelling and connectedness, have on my spirit, on my living spiritually, on my soul-based search for life to the full? What effect does my inner landscape have on my outer dwelling, and relating, on my seeking and my practising? How does the place where I dwell shape or hinder my spiritual search? And how do I shape or hinder it?

## HISTORICAL FORCES: THE ENLIGHTENMENT AND ROMANTICISM

Two great movements in recent European cultural history have influenced the emerging understanding of the word *spirituality*: the Enlightenment, and its antithesis Romanticism. In the fourteenth century a loss of confidence in the human mind had begun a movement that led to the dominance of practical reason. Knowledge became linked to domination, and thus was set in train the loss of transcendence and the sense of the sacred we see all around us today. The mediaeval worldview collapsed, modernity with its emphasis on scientific rationalism was born, and we inherited a disenchanted world.[35] Three questions immediately come to mind. Is to know to love or to dominate? In grace traditions is God to be loved or dominated? In consciousness traditions is enlightenment to be humbly received or dominated? The answers are pivotal to our understanding of contemporary spirituality and the challenges it faces in a disenchanted, desacralised world. But that world raises another question. Do we have the spiritual awareness to discern what needs to be done and the audacity of spirit to do it?

The Enlightenment is the major shaping force in recent Western cultural history. It lies beneath the turn towards the individual, towards logical analysis, scientific method, scientific reductionism, and pragmatic naturalism. But it has also bequeathed us a narcissistic restlessness, a fascination with material success, the sovereign ego, materialism and secularism. The Enlightenment portrayed religion, piety and the spiritual as a betrayal, a lie, a transitory element soon to be swept away by the dominant powers of human reason; its worldview is incompatible with and inimical to religion and religiously informed spirituality. Enlightenment thought broke down the unified religious-metaphysical world that preceded it into three domains of knowledge and reality. The first is defined as the natural-objective world, which is the domain of science and instrumental reason, giving us objective truth. The second is the social and intersubjective world, which is the domain of politics and ethics understood through pragmatic reason, giving us normative rightness. The third is the subjective, individual world, which is the domain of art, religion, and spirituality approached by aesthetic and expressive reason, giving us sincerity.[36]

In this worldview spirituality is at best sincere, possibly edifying, but essentially empty of meaning in any rational or scientific sense. Spirituality and religion are placed in the same context as superstition and irrationality, however well meaning, and at worst alongside dissociative states indicative of functional mental disorder. Modernity is a cold house for spirituality, especially when it seeks a public voice. What is at work is the empirical colonisation and subjugation of the spheres of human value and meaning. The political ramifications are immense and readily discernible in Western societies.[37] There is another danger. The turn to the subjective and the individual exacerbates the risks of self-reference: self-absorption, self-inflation, and spiritual materialism where spirituality is narcissistically consumed for self-referred reasons. Spiritual narcissism has become a reality on the spiritual landscape precisely because of the embrace of modernist reductionism. The result is the blocking of the processes that support authentic integration and spiritual maturity.[38] Regardless of what Gregory Stanczak describes as modernism's reign,[39] the feeling that spirituality has something important to do with the practice of everyday living has endured and is widespread all across the world.

In the late eighteenth and nineteenth centuries, the core rationalism of the Enlightenment produced a strong philosophical and literary counter-reaction. Hard rationalism was opposed by a softer, nature-based antithesis known as Romanticism. Romanticism is antithetical to the Enlightenment if for no other reason than that it pitted heart and creativity against cold logic, single-minded intellectualism, and the supremacy of technological reason. Romanticism called for a return to nature, an affirmation of the innate goodness of the human person and the recognition of the corrupting force of modern science and commerce. It lauded heroic individuals, affirmed creative genius, and praised democracy as the way forward for all. Traces of the conflict between these two opposing forces in Western culture are still with us today, most obviously in the new spirituality. While Enlightenment thought has had a continuous effect until recently, Romanticism has had a wave-like history that was particularly strong in the eighteenth and nineteenth centuries and again since the 1960s. Romanticism viewed spirituality as a legitimate carrier of knowledge, and it sought a creative engagement with the social world. The implications for the emerging understanding of spirituality are not far to seek.

Romanticism sought a realistic view of the natural world, a view that was at once organic, ethical and spiritual; its contemporary heritage is visible in the radical turn to ecological and creational spiritualities that shape much of the present interest in things spiritual and ethical. A study of Romantic spirituality will surface most of the themes that characterise the new spirituality. However, the Romantic approach to things spiritual runs the risk that popular enthusiasms always provide for the emergence of shallow, immature spiritualities. Recent, more holistic approaches have begun to recognise the need to bring both creative metaphor and reasonable accounts of the world and our place in it together in a way that recognises the danger of splitting creativity from cognition in any form of human activity especially those concerned with the human person as a knowing, ethically reasonable and creatively responsible agent. This suggests an interesting way forward for contemporary spirituality.

## TILLICH AND LUCKMANN

Lucy Bregman has drawn attention to two significant twentieth-century influences that have had a shaping impact on expressions of contemporary spirituality. The first has to do with Paul Tillich's work on faith and ultimate concern, and the second has to do with Thomas Luckmann's work on implicit or invisible religion.[40] For Tillich, faith has to do with whether persons are concerned with or indifferent to the nature of ultimate reality: a delightfully ambiguous phrase that replaces much traditional religious language.[41] He wanted to reach beyond conventional or traditional understandings of faith, to find a way out of its growing alienation from contemporary life. He wanted to point towards a greater reality that sustains individual lives and leaves traces in our individual experiences in ways that make a transforming difference. For Tillich faith is an act of the total personality that gives us back to ourselves, changed.[42] In his account of faith Tillich has given us one of the major twentieth-century images for the new spirituality: the encounter with ultimate concern. As finite beings we are confronted by the spectre of non-being, death and the potential for absurdity. The decision of faith is made possible and is finally explained by this unique confrontation. Faith and the question of meaning arise in the same experiential space; they express the central act of the human mind.

Spirituality is what happens when the dilemma of ultimacy and its personal and social implications are at last confronted. By claiming that ultimate concern is a universal human phenomenon Tillich opened the way to a more inclusive understanding of the orienting focus of contemporary spirituality.[43] He also pinpointed apathy and misplaced spiritual enthusiasm as the great twin dangers to spirituality itself, dangers activated by confusing preliminary and ultimate life concerns.[44] According to Tillich, if a person is really desperate about the meaning of life, then the seriousness of despair itself becomes the expression of the meaning in which that person is still living. In this very experience of separation, that person encounters the presence of the divine.[45] It is not difficult to see in the new spirituality evidence of the dangers Tillich noted, not least in the popular enthusiasms that have blossomed into the fuzziness currently associated with the word *spirituality*.[46]

Thomas Luckmann's thesis is that the problem of individual existence in society is essentially a religious one.[47] He held that the social processes that lead to the formation of self-identity are concerned with the construction of a universe of meaning that transcends biological nature. In this sense, religion – and by implication, spirituality – is a constituent part of being human. Religion is present in non-specific or implicit form in every socialised person and in all human societies. It is part of the human condition. Luckmann anticipated the emergence of an increasingly de-institutionalised and private form of religious identification in contemporary Western society alongside persisting Church membership. The implication for the burgeoning interest in spirituality is the emergence of a religious or spiritual identity that is not churchly, not denominational, not sectarian, but largely autonomous, capable of selecting private meanings, even when such a project is culturally reconstructed through and around themes with, for example, Christian origins. What is becoming increasingly evident is the implicit nature of the core of personal beliefs and practices that sustain an individual and provide guidance, a sense of direction, and/or a sense of belonging within secular society in postmodern times.[48]

Tillich's and Luckmann's work pointed clearly in the direction of a softly boundaried catch-all concept; but neither Tillich's humanistic faith nor Luckmann's implicit religion caught the popular imagination the way the word *spirituality* has done. Nevertheless, their ideas lie close to the heart of the new spirituality. What we are witnessing today is the convergence of a variety of cultural, philosophical, theological, anthropological and sociological trajectories that cleared the ground for the emergence of spirituality first as an innately human, largely private force, and second as an endlessly elastic term that works in ways that humanistic understandings of faith or appreciations of implicit religion failed to do. Today the word *spirituality* not only acts as a substitute for religion when that word is held to be too determinative and public, but also locates a private space for what theologians and sociologists once called personal religion, or faith in Tillich's sense, or invisible religion in Luckmann's sense.[49] Both Tillich and Luckmann confront us with a profoundly spiritual question: What is the meaning, purpose and value of life in the light of the apparent failure of religious and humanist discourse?[50] If Bregman is right, the efforts to define contemporary spirituality in ways that ignore powerful socio-cultural forces are doomed to failure. We face a seemingly open-ended process.

### DIVERGING PROCESSES AND THE BREADTH OF MEANING

What, then, can we say about the meaning of the word *spirituality*? That precise answers are difficult to frame should now be plain. There are clear social and historical reasons why spirituality in the postmodern context should demonstrate a soft, mercurial quality that eludes the kind of rationalistic knowing that requires precise, logical definitions. In fact, the variegated and inconsistent ways in which the word is presently conceptualised seem to be a major reason for its wide success. According to Bernard Spilka, the precise imprecision of the word has been embraced with a passion.[51] However, we are also confronted by other trajectories of divergence and difference that have deep historical roots and are relevant to the present discussion. The divisions within Christianity, first between Rome and Constantinople and then at the Reformation and since are moot points in this long historic process.

A divergence was also growing between theology and spirituality within Western Christianity. Hints are visible in a range of distinctions that emerged both in theology itself and between theology and spirituality. Examples are easy to identify. Reflect for example on the distinction traditionally made between asceticism and mysticism. Reflect on the twelfth-century turn to spirituality brought about by the work of Richard of St Victor and others who belonged to that school. Theological trends set in train by Abelard at Paris at the same time also contributed to the strained relationship between spirituality and theology. Something similar can be said about the *devotio moderna*, the new devotion, in Germany and the Low Countries. By the time the Counter-Reformation was in full flood, the gap between spiritual or mystical theology and the speculative theology of the time was seriously underway.

No less than Yves Congar has noted that the spiritual works of such influential figures as John of the Cross and Teresa of Avila, Ignatius of Loyola, Francis de Sales and Jane de Chantal show the development of spiritual languages and resources that had little in common with the language and resources of their theological contemporaries.[52] My admittedly provisional hypothesis here is that the trajectory of divergence between spirituality and theology already at work within Western Christianity must be considered in critical approaches to the situation that confronts us today. There appears to be a process at work that parallels the way changes in speculative theology prepared the ground for the Enlightenment: a trajectory of divergence is embedded in the history of spirituality as it has evolved over the best part of a millennium. Today, spirituality has become multilocal, multivocal, multidimensional and multilayered – in short, a highly complex reality that requires academic study in its own right. It is also a complex reality to be approached with humility and a beginner's mind, one that understands the complexity of the spiritual world and approaches it with awe and reverence.[53]

## From Divine Spirit to secular experience

What happens when elements of a religious tradition are used abstractly or parasitically, or themes and practices are disembedded from religious traditions of origin for personal or commercial reasons?[54] We began this chapter with the Hebrew and Christian origins of the word spirituality. We conclude with a vision that has become increasingly secular, that favours experience over belief, and the personal search over congregational allegiances.[55] In secular contexts *religiousness* has been endowed with a much more restricted, negative, institutional, traditional and frequently pejorative aura, that depicts religion as a hindrance. On the other hand, *spirituality* has achieved a much more highly personal, open, subjective, experiential and glowingly positive yet increasingly elusive tag. Formerly interchangeable, the two terms are more likely today to be contrasted and placed in opposition one with the other, though statistical and other evidence does not seem to support the clean break some draw between the two terms.[56] Very little work has been done to assess what people actually mean by either term. If spirituality is denied sacred reference, is it still meaningful? If a sacred reference is unnecessary, is there any difference between spirituality and psychology? Does the concept of spirituality add anything new or different to discussions of the meaning and purpose of life in non-religious or specifically therapeutic contexts? The spiritual dance is wider than we think.

THEMES AND QUESTIONS FOR FURTHER REFLECTION

1. How would you identify your spirituality? Is it a world-maintaining or a world-shaking force?

2. Have you ever been touched, touched in your soul, by the transforming power of Spirit? How would you describe that to another person?

3. Does your spirituality reveal soul hungering for life and meaning, or has spirituality become a consumer object shaped to serve nothing more than personal gratification, security and comfort?

4. Identify the social and cultural forces that are presently shaping your life and your patterns of response or reaction. Can you identify them with any clarity?

FURTHER READING

Jane Kopas, *Seeking the Hidden God* (Maryknoll, NY: Orbis Books, 2005).

NOTES:

1. For a history of the term see Declan Marmion, *A Spirituality of Everyday Faith: A Theological Investigation of the Notion of Spirituality in Karl Rahner* (Louvain: Peeters Press, 1998) 1–40; Jeremy Carrette and Richard King, *Selling Spirituality: The Silent Takeover of Religion* (London and New York: Routledge 2005) 30–53.

2. See L. Gregory Jones, 'A Thirst for God or Consumer Spirituality? Cultivating Disciplined Practices of Being Engaged by God' in L. Gregory Jones and James J. Buckley, eds, *Spirituality and Social Embodiment* (Oxford: Blackwell, 1997) 3–28 at 4. See also Belden C. Lane, *Landscapes of the Sacred: Geography and Narrative in American Spirituality*, Expanded Edition (Baltimore and London: The Johns Hopkins University Press, 2001) 9: here Lane quotes Josef Sudbrack.

3. See Richard Viladesau, *Theology and the Arts: Encountering God Through Music, Art and Rhetoric* (New York/Mahwah, NJ: Paulist Press, 2000) 93 & 128.

4. For a brief discussion of some of these see Valerie Lesniak, 'Contemporary Spirituality' in Philip Sheldrake, *The New SCM Dictionary of Christian Spirituality* (London: SCM Press, 2005) 7–12.

5. See David Harvey, *The Condition of Postmodernity: An Enquiry into the Origins of Cultural Change* (Oxford: Basil Blackwell, 1989) 205–206.

6. See Ann W. Astell, 'Postmodern Christian Spirituality: A Coincidentia Oppositorum?' in *Christian Spirituality Bulletin* 4 (1996) 1, 1, 3–5.

7. On questions of value see for example Morris B. Holbrook, ed., *Consumer Value: A Framework for Analysis and Research* (London and New York: Routledge, 1999).

8. See Douglas Burton-Christie, 'Spirituality: Its Uses and Misuses' in *Spiritus: A Journal of Christian Spirituality* 7 (2007) 1, 74–76 at 75.

9. See Philip Sheldrake, 'Spirituality and the Integrity of Spirituality' in *Spiritus: A Journal of Christian Spirituality* 7 (2007) 1, 93–98.

10. See for example, D. T. Olson, 'A Breath of New Life: Old Testament Reflections on the Spirit of God and the Leadership of Human Communities' in Cobble & Elliott, *The Hidden Spirit*, op. cit. 9–15, at 9–10.

11. For more on the genealogy of the word *spirituality* see Bernard McGinn, 'The Letter and the Spirit: Spirituality as an Academic Discipline' in *Christian Spirituality Bulletin* 1 (1993) 2, 1, 3–10; Josef Sudbrack, 'Spirituality 1: Concept' in Karl Rahner et al., eds, *Sacramentum Mundi: An Encyclopedia of Theology*, volume 6 (New York and London: Herder and Herder, 1970) 147–153; Lucy Tinsely, *The French Expressions for Spirituality and Devotion: A Semantic Study* (Washington: The Catholic University of America Press, 1953).

12. See for example Joseph Rotblat, ed., *Towards a War-free World: The Annals of the 44th Pugwash Conference 1994* (Singapore, River Edge, NJ, London: World Scientific, 1995) 154–155.

13. See for example David Morgan, *Visual Piety: A History and Theory of Popular Religious Images* (Berkeley, Los Angeles, London: University of California Press, 1999) 10–12.

14. See for example Vicki Mahaffey, *States of Desire: Wilde, Yeats, Joyce and the Irish Experiment* (New York, Oxford: Oxford University Press, 1998).

15. I. Hausherr, *Spiritual Direction in the Early Christian East* (Kalamazoo: Cistercian Publications, 1990) 30–44.

16. Mary Frohlich, RSCJ, 'Critical Interiority' in *Spiritus: A Journal of Christian Spirituality* 7 (2007) 1, 77–81.

17. Michel de Certeau, *The Mystic Fable: The Sixteenth and Seventeenth Centuries.* Volume One. Translated by Michael B. Smith. (Chicago and London: The University of Chicago Press, 1995) 170.

18. Simon Tugwell, *Ways of Imperfection* (London: Darton, Longman & Todd, 1984) 8–9.

19. Louis Bouyer et al., *History of Christian Spirituality*, 3 volumes, (London: Burns & Oates, 1963–1968). See also his *Introduction to Spirituality* (London: Darton, Longman and Todd, 1961).

20. Thomas Merton, *Sign of Jonah* (New York: Doubleday, 1953). See in particular 8–9. This emphasis can be traced back in English to the work of William James.

21. Eric James, ed., *Spirituality Today* (London: SCM, 1968).

22. L. E. Schmidt, 'The Making of Modern "Mysticism"' op. cit. 276.

23. Sandra M. Schneiders, 'Religion vs. Spirituality: A Contemporary Conundrum' in *Spiritus: A Journal of Christian Spirituality*, 3 (2003) 2, 163–185.

24. Robert Wuthnow, *After Heaven: Spirituality in America Since the 1950s.* (Berkeley, CA: University of California Press, 1998).

25. Christopher Partridge, *The Re-Enchantment of the West: Alternative Spiritualities, Secularization, Popular Culture and Occulture.* Two volumes. (London, New York: T & T Clark, 2004 and 2005). See for example volume 1, 8–59 and volume 2, 1–20. See also Gordon Lynch, *After Religion: 'Generation X' and the Search for Meaning* (London: Darton, Longman and Todd, 2002); David Hay and Kate Hunt, *Understanding the Spirituality of People Who Don't Go to Church* (Nottingham: University of Nottingham, 2000); Jeanne Hinto, *Changing Churches: Building Bridges in Local Mission* (London: Church House Publishing, 2002).

26. See Meredith B. McGuire, 'Mapping Contemporary American Spirituality: A Sociological Perspective' in *Christian Spirituality Bulletin* 5 (1997) 1, 1, 3–8.

27. Thomas M. Beaudoin, *Virtual Faith: The Irreverent Spiritual Quest of Generation X* (San Francisco: Jossey-Bass, 1998).

28. Gordon Lynch, *After Religion: 'Generation X' and the Search for Meaning* op. cit. 69–89.

29. Bonnie J. Miller-McLemore, *In the Midst of Chaos: Caring for Children as Spiritual Practice* (San Francisco: Jossey-Bass, 2007) 108–111.

30. See for example Mark Dooley and Liam Kavanagh, *The Philosophy of Derrida* (Stocksfield: Acumen Publishing, 2007) 1–19.

31. My reflection on this theme has been influenced by a variety of authors, especially Dolores Hayden, *The Power of Place: Urban Landscapes as Public History* (Cambridge and London: MIT Press, 1997); Chris Fitter, *Poetry, Space, Landscape: Towards a New Theory* (Cambridge: Cambridge University Press, 1995); Gaston Bachelard, *The Poetics of Space* (Boston: Beacon Press, 1994); Philip Sheldrake, *Spaces for the Sacred: Place Memory and Identity* (Baltimore and London: The Johns Hopkins University Press, 2001); Richard D. Nelson, *Raising Up a Faithful Priest: Community and Priesthood in Biblical Theology* (Louisville, KY: Westminster/John Knox Press, 1993); Belden C. Lane, *Landscapes of the Sacred: Geography and Narrative in American Spirituality*, Expanded Edition (Baltimore and London: The Johns Hopkins University Press, 2001); Werner Kuhn, Michael Worboys, Sabine Timpf, eds, *Spatial Information Theory: Foundations of Geographic Information Science* (Berlin: Springer-Verlag, 2003); Kim Knott, *The Location of Religion: A Spatial Analysis* (London, Oakville, CT: Equinox Publishing Ltd, 2005).

32. David Brown, *God and the Enchantment of Place: Reclaiming Human Experience* (Oxford and New York: Oxford University Press, 2006) 84.

33. Ellen Ross, 'Diversities of Divine Presence: Women's Geography in the Christian Tradition' in Jamie Scott and Paul Simpson-Housley, eds, *Essays in the Geographies of Judaism, Christianity and Islam* (New York: Greenwood Press, 1991) 93-114.

34. See Hugh O'Donnell, *Eucharist and the Living Earth* (Dublin: The Columba Press, 2007).

35. See J. J. Bacik, *Spirituality in Transition* (Kansas City: Sheed & Ward, 1996) 7–36.

36. See Jorge N. Ferrer, *Revisioning Transpersonal Theory: A Participative Vision of Human Spirituality*. Forward by Richard Tarnas (Albany, NY: State University of New York Press, 2002) 22–34.

37. For a detailed discussion of the impact of modernity on conceptualisations of spirituality see Jorge N. Ferrer, *Revisioning Transpersonal Theory*, op. cit. 15–70.

38. Ibid. 34–39.

39. Gregory C. Stanczak, *Engaged Spirituality: Social Change and American Religion* (New Brunswick, NJ: Rutgers University Press, 2006) 9.

40. Lucy Bregman, 'Defining Spirituality: Multiple Uses and Murky Meanings of an Incredibly Popular Term' in *The Journal of Pastoral Care and Counseling* 58 (2004) 3, 157–167.

41. Paul Tillich, *Dynamics of Faith* (New York: Harper & Row, 1957).

42. Paul Tillich, *The New Being*. Introduction by Mary Ann Stenger. (Lincoln and London: University of Nebraska Press, 2005) 38–39.

43. See David Carr and John Haldane, *Spirituality, Philosophy and Education* (London: RoutledgeFalmer, 2003) 116–126.

44. See Andrew Wright, *Spirituality and Education* (New York: RoutledgeFalmer, 2001) 11–12.

45. See Paul Tillich, *The Protestant Era*. Translated by James Luther Adams (Chicago: University of Chicago Press, 1948) xv.

46. See Lucy Bregman, 'Defining Spirituality' op. cit. 161–163.

47. Thomas Luckmann, *The Invisible Religion: The Problem of Religion in Modern Society*. (New York: Macmillan, 1967).

48. See Lucy Bregman, 'Defining Spirituality' op. cit. 163–165.

49. Lucy Bregman, 'Defining Spirituality' op. cit. 157.

50. Andrew Wright, *Spirituality and Education* op. cit. 13.

51. Bernard Spilka 'Spirituality: Problems and Directions in Operationalizing a Fuzzy Concept.' Paper presented at the APA annual conference, Toronto, Canada, (1993) quoted by Zinnbauer et al. 'Religion and Spirituality: Unfuzzying the Fuzzy', op. cit. 549.

52. Yves M-J Congar. *A History of Theology*. Translated and edited by Hunter Guthrie (Garden City: Doubleday, 1968) 166.

53. C. Jones, G. Wainwright, E. Yarnold, *The Study of Spirituality*, 4th Impression. (London: SPCK, 1996) xxii.

54. See Vincent J. Millar, *Consuming Religion: Christian Faith and Practice in a Consumer Culture*. (New York: Continuum, 2004) 88–94; A. M. Unruh et al. 'Spirituality Unplugged', op. cit. 5–7; P. A. Kahle & J. M. Robbins, *The Power of Spirituality in Therapy*, op. cit.

55. M. J. Mahoney & G. M. Graci, 'The Meanings and Correlates of Spirituality: Suggestions from an Exploratory Survey of Experts' in *Death Studies* 23 (1999) 521–528.

56. See Zinnbauer et al. 'Religion and Spirituality: Unfuzzying the Fuzzy',
op. cit., 552–563. See also M. A. Mc Coll, 'Muriel Driver Lectureship:
Spirit, Occupation and Disability' in *Canadian Journal of Occupational Therapy*
67 (2000) 217–228 at 220.

## CHAPTER 7

*Recuperating Soul*

*How can we live without nurturing soul,
without awareness of our true being?*

INTRODUCTION

We live in an expanding universe in which the origins of life can be dated back 3.8 billion years. The stuff we are made of comes from the fusion fires in the stars: carbon, oxygen, nitrogen, phosphorus, and hydrogen that comes from the Big Bang itself. Everything in the universe is startlingly interconnected. We are born of the stars, part of a galactic ecology, touched by the long history of the universe. The cosmos is implicit in who and what and how we are at the deepest levels of our being. Soul, too, has cosmic significance. It is part of the flow of creation and creativity, cousin to the primordial fire, fruit of the Divine Spirit hovering over the waters of life. If not, we live in a soulless universe, strugglers against definitive despair, living lives that are less than fully alive. Something of a communion is at work in cosmic history, a communion, a rhythm and a dance that helps us to open up to the word *soul* and the future hope it reveals, and the sense of meaningful purpose.

This sense of cosmic communion also helps us to recover the notion that we are not just things, however wonderful: we are living beings, carriers of life in a vast universe where our people share a short history of only about 130,000 years, a period in which we have radically altered the planet, no more so than in the last one hundred years, years when we also lost contact with the meaning of soul and everything good, thoughtful and moral it represents. Soul is a word about communion and unity, a word about the interactive forces of life, of being in communion and relationship, something touched by the Breath of Life and the beautiful livingness of being. Soul names what happens when life is breathed into a world and living, acting beings emerge into the sun. [1]

Soul is not a word that is popular in the human or therapeutic sciences today, one of those rich words displaced in the desire to secularise knowledge. It is a word that has been drastically marginalised; but the marginalising of soul has had serious consequences for our understanding of what it really means to be a human person. Its removal razed a long history. By marginalising soul, we have also marginalised our awareness and knowledge of our own essential human being – that part of us that is in communion not only with earth and nature, myth and mystery, the transcendent and the divine, but also with everything that is involved in the common struggle for a real, essential self: a self with a true appreciation of life and being. Without soul we have lost contact with our creaturely origins and our transcendental destiny; we fail to recognise our very being, not only as the source of life, but also as the source of our deepest healing, the healing that flows from the depths of life itself. Soul helps us to understand the homeliness of life and the rhythms of welcome, receptivity and hospitality so vibrantly depicted, for example, in the meditations of Julian of Norwich.

Without soul and the innate, mysterious dignity soul implies, where is the ultimate significance of the human person to be found? How is ultimate significance, the significance that blocks and restrains human exploitation, to be given to the human person and all other living beings? The absence of soul in spirituality as elsewhere leaves more than a gap in language; it leaves a gap in our understanding of the depth and dignity to be accorded to each individual regardless of personal circumstance, ethnicity, gender, age, or religion. Without soul there is no adequate view of what a person, what a living personal being actually is. Without soul the person is little more that a social fragment, a statistical rather than a profoundly spiritual and deeply mysterious reality. Without soul all other living beings become fair game for human exploitation and greed: the evidence is worldwide.

What kind of depth can be given to words like individual, person, self and their variations and synonyms without soul? How can an essential understanding of self emerge without reference to soul? How can we talk at depth about the corruptions of the essential self without reference to soul? How can we talk about the potential self without reference to soul? Soul contains within it the whole semantic range of self words. Most importantly soul accords ultimacy to the essential self, something easily damaged or lost as it struggles to survive in a cold, commodifying, fragmenting milieu. In what follows in this chapter I want to explore soul, but I also want to affirm its centrality to spirituality today. I want to affirm the necessity of soul and its ultimacy, its fragility and its need. But most of all I want to affirm its mysteriousness and the ease with which the word soul can take us beyond conventional and consensual thinking about the human self to the deep levels of passionate, affective living; to the substratum of life itself and its awesome destiny. Soul goes to the very depth of what it means to be a human being; it goes to the very depth and complexity, to the founding rhythms and intricacies of our felt-sense of being alive, real, able to respond to and dance as richly unique individuals in the real world. Soul takes us on paths that are deep and sacred, spirit paths that make human selves, paths that are rich in their ordinariness and necessity.[2]

## SOUL: A BRIEF HISTORY

Soul is a dappled word filled with colourful meanings that surface in an almost indeterminate array of contexts and a history of usage spreading back beyond Ancient Greece and, through Old Testament influences, to the Ancient Near East. It is there we look for answers to two questions: the nature of soul, and why the recuperation of soul is so important to an understanding of contemporary spirituality. Soul has had a difficult time in the twentieth century, especially in the human and medical sciences. This has not been helped by a reluctance in theology over much of that time to engage with soul: its interests had turned elsewhere. The result is that soul has become an equivocal, uncomfortable word in both science and theology and we are now in a situation where, if it is considered at all, soul has become something largely ephemeral, something easy to disregard as we grapple with issues of power, and gender and emancipation.

At the same time, we face a revolution in the neurobiological sciences with implications for our understanding of every aspect of life, from conception to death. Unfortunately, science and philosophy, particularly the philosophy of medicine, have not kept pace with each other at a time of exponential scientific growth. Mind studies avoid the word soul as unscientific; the neurosciences, and neurobiology in particular, paint a new picture of mind, showing millions of nerve cells carrying electro-chemical impulses regulated by genetic factors interacting with the environment. Psychiatry tends to identify consciousness with mind in distinction to soul; mind is open to empirical study linked to neurobiology. Soul is not. Genetic medicine, stem-cell research, and the possibilities of human cloning are typical of diverging opinions and approaches grounded in different understandings of mind–body relatedness that are then projected on to the relationship between consciousness and soul and raise questions about them. Herein lies the core of a debate that has immense implications for contemporary spirituality. This is a debate about two paradigms: the mind–body paradigm and the soul–consciousness paradigm; and to make matters sharper still, this is happening at a time when the very existence of soul is contested. Which path shall contemporary spirituality follow? Soul is, after all, a philosopher-poet's word: a seed-word in stardust meant to blossom in moments of rich and glorious creativity.

## Greek Origins

The modern view of soul with its eschatological and psychological characteristics derives in large measure from the Greeks.[3] They have given us the concept of *psyché*, which we have received as *soul*.[4] In the Western philosophical and religious tradition it is clear that soul originates in Greek culture and philosophy, more especially in the work of Socrates, Plato and Aristotle. *Psyché* is an extremely rich and complex concept, one of the truly great achievements of Greek thought. *Psyché* is a very ancient concept, the product of development whose roots are blurred by the mists of time. However, it came to its defining meaning some 2,500 years ago in a turn that represents a true cultural revolution. Allusions to soul in early Greek writings point to a worldview that is strange to us today, one we no longer understand. They were sometimes noble often barbaric times moving to very different ideas and ideals from ours. What the Greek story does is bring us face to face with the nature of human consciousness and sustained efforts to find its embodied human location.

In developing their understanding of soul the ancients noted the connections to speech and so sought a body-base for consciousness. They linked it to the midriff and the diaphragm and air, but especially to something vaporous called the *thymos* in the Homeric tradition, perhaps breath; perhaps even the lungs and breath. It is possible that *thymos* originally meant smoke and only later took on the meaning of thought or purpose. The Homeric tradition presents us with two kinds of soul, the free-soul representing individual personality that manifested itself in fainting spells and death, and the body-soul or *thymos* that manifests itself in urges and emotions.[5] In the Homeric tradition, *psyché* is imaged as a larva, lacking the capacity for intentional action, or as an image of death hinting at the interplay of being and non-being, connotations that never fully disappear from soul discourse and are graphically depicted in contemporary understandings of soul-murder.[6]

Over the centuries *psyché* gradually absorbed the meanings of *thymos* and eventually came to stand for the psychic totality of the human person as a whole; especially when connections were made with motion and perception, concepts that come to the fore in Aristotle.[7] Thinking and everything associated with it was naively deemed to arise from the perceived organs of speech, and early connections were made to feeling, emotion, desire and action. In effect, life is alertness and activity, and the aim of soul is the good life; movement, sensation and knowledge become the faculties of *psyché*/soul.[8] Our ancestors came to a clear understanding of mind in its primal wholeness. Mind is mind as a whole, not just as a locus of conscious thought as it is often taken today.

These early metaphorical meanings underwent change with the rise of Orphism, the development of philosophy, and the rich imagery emerging in Greek lyric and tragic poetry. Sappho's metaphor of bittersweet love is an enduring example of the creative imagination at work at that time, and of the link between poetics and philosophy. Sappho's image is interesting for a number of reasons, not least because of its powerful depiction of a foundational threshold experience where inner and outer forces meet. Personified in Sappho (Plato's tenth Muse), Greek lyrical poetry helped to draw attention from the outer to the inner dimension of experience: it made it possible to conceive of and explore inner space; and so enigma, paradox and ambiguity emerge as potential characteristics of soul. The person is no longer a puppet of the gods: the dawn of the modern ensouled individual is near to hand, and the concept of psychological depth we appreciate today is coming to birth. Soul generates the unified, organic person that is about to emerge.[9]

The real revolution in thinking begins with Socrates and his student Plato and their play with the concept of an inner world: interiority. *Psyché*/soul: here is the concept they used to make the connection, one that has remained stable in its essential meaning ever since: soul emerged as the principle of life and true self.[10] In Europe and the West generally, the word *psyché* has been interpreted through a Christian lens for more than 1,600 years, but it does not name a Christian discovery: the word predates Christianity by centuries and had achieved its high meaning by the time Christian thinkers accepted it as a pivotal term in their spiritual and theological reflection. It had already played a crucial role in the evolution of spiritual thought in Greece. *Psyché*/soul made it possible for them to speak of a dimension of identity and personality imaged as real rather than a vague something made of atmospheric vapours or forces. This notion took time to spread to all classes, but spread it did to become a founding postulate of Greek and later European civilisation.

In this process, *psyché*/soul took on qualities of sensibility and consciousness: the person became a thinking being capable of interiority and ethical decision-making, the centre of moral responsibility in society, something uniquely and infinitely precious. This is more than a semantic change in the meaning of a word: this change transformed the cultural experience that followed. Building on the work of the Sophists, Socrates was able to initiate a radical turn. The key question in Greek philosophy changed from the cosmos in general to the human person in particular. Socrates made it possible to identify a new principle of unity: the *psyche*/soul as intellectual and moral consciousness. Interiority has come into its own: Plato makes it clear that self-care requires self-knowledge, and self-knowledge is knowledge of the *psyché*/soul. The grounds for what we now know as psychoanalysis and well-grounded spiritual accompaniment are firmly laid in this mode of thinking: the beauty and wholeness of any person is in the soul and it is the *psyché*/soul that needs to be released, healed, uncovered, integrated.

This is especially clear in Book 9 of Plato's *Republic* where we actually encounter analysis of the soul, of the unconscious as it is revealed in dreams. Not surprisingly, much that we find in contemporary psycho-therapy and in the psychoanalytical worldview has Platonic roots. In Plato, *psyché* has three expressions: the concupiscible (appetites), the irascible (anger), and the rational. The first is imaged as a multicoloured beast with a ring of many heads of animals, some gentle, others savage, but all relevant to particular desires. The second is imaged as a fierce lion, while the third is given a human face. We are a unity, yes, but a unity that includes wild and savage propensities needing management: the beast and the lion need to be brought into agreement in the service of reason and reasonableness. The state of harmony between all three is named justice, a justice expressed through moderation, courage, and wisdom.[11]

It is not difficult to see in Plato's turbulent vision the origins of the Freudian id and the Jungian shadow, and the recognition of the dark and disturbing forces of the individual and collective human unconscious. Plato saw virtue as revealing the state of health of the soul in terms of the good and the beautiful. But he also saw vice, the ugly and the evil, as the disease of the soul. In virtue, the divine is revealed; in vice, our animal nature. Human happiness requires the health of both body and soul; it requires a harmony between them, true music. It is not difficult to suggest that the formative and transformative tasks of spirituality arise in not dissimilar contexts: soul-work even here is about the discovery and making of the true self, the discovery and flourishing of the potentials of the self.

For Aristotle, soul represents the form and movement of the body. He identified kinds of soul corresponding to kinds of life – vegetative, animal, rational – and granted immortality only to the last; the lower faculties (sense, memory, imagination) are forms of the body and die with it. Intellect is the key to understanding soul for Aristotle: soul is made visible in the intellective functions. Within Aristotle's thought, trans-cendence plays an important role, as does the notion of goal in human self-realisation: the human search for self-realisation is a transcendental search in love for the Beloved. This happens in a play of *physis* (nature) and *eros* (aspiring love). It is against the background of *physis* that the body-soul unity emerges as inseparable. Soul is the principle of living things, manifest in a hierarchy of life-functions and psychic powers or poten-tialities: soul is a life power, the cause of our being alive, the source of all our expressions of life, the explanation of all living functions. The person's task is to bring all of these powers and potentialities into play, make them actual.[12] This is the basis of soul-work. Yet soul's goal remains divine.

In contemporary terms, Greek thought suggests that without self-action, without self-manifestation, without relationality and commun-ication with self and others soul cannot be fully realised.[13] This suggests that abstraction be avoided in real soul-work: soul-work must stay as close as possible to the movements of life so that transcendence may be found in immanence. This in turn means staying as close as possible to affectivity. There is a second implication for contemporary Western understandings of soul-work. Soul is the place where God finds God's image: the essence of soul surfaces as a divine operation through which God fills the soul. In terms of traditional Western spirituality, this is the gifting light by which soul does what it does, by which it becomes real; and all of this within the round of embodied life.

Life, dynamically moving life, remains the paradigm of soul. In terms of spirituality the implications are clear. Soul-work and soul-praxis are interactive with all of life; they are the tasks of a person seeking to live life as dynamically and as fully as possible. Spirituality is the field of practices in which soul is brought fully into the world of embodied reality: soul is dynamic and emerges in the dynamics of living, of being and doing, that shapes every aspect of the personal self. Understood so, even stillness is an utterly dynamic state of soul precisely because stillness reveals life-embracing eternal return to the core, to the beginning, to the essence of being. These active elements of soul-work and soul-praxis will be more fully fleshed out as we explore the Hebrew tradition.[14]

## HEBREW ORIGINS

Ancient peoples had a possibly holistic, certainly synthetic and stereo-metric view of life, a grasping of things in their totality, an expressive rather than a conceptual view of the world. This unitary vision is something we desperately need to recover today in a world of fragments and pieces lacking depth, lacking any great sense of connection to the cyclical nature of life and the power and inevitability of the eternal flows of return that so often bring us to therapy and spiritual accompaniment seeking soul care. The ancients viewed soul – *nephesh* in Hebrew – not only in expressively embodied ways that included body secretions and vapours, but also in ways that involved touch, contact and hints of what we would describe today as 'contagious magic'. Nor was soul restricted to the limits of the body. It extended into personality, character, identity, relationships and even into the things a person used. In the ancient records, there are intriguing allusions to the dream-soul, the animal-soul, the bird-soul and even the external-soul: the semantic range is full of adventurous possibilities whose meanings and potentials are now long forgotten and easily misunderstood.

The ancient Hebrews shared this worldview; hence the range of, to us, often elusive meanings they tied to *nephesh*/soul and the body-based origins of such ideas. At the very least, they intended a psychophysical unity, where links to breathing and aliveness are close to hand. Then came the step to conscious life and the creation of a totalising view of the person-in-relation, a view that recognises soul in the whole reality of life and in its passing, even if such clear-cut distinctions have a contemporary rather than an ancient ring. We are still confronted with *nephesh*/soul as indicative of a comprehensive view of sentient life in its cognitive, affective and conative or behavioural fullness in an indeterminate range of personal, physical, natural, social, and emotional contexts and conditions. This is particularly the case with the whole gamut of uncensored desires that surface in the Hebrew biblical texts. *Nephesh*/soul, then, refers not only to physical life but to all the physiological, psychic, and psychological phenomena manifested in a living body.

If we base our exploration of the word *soul* in Old Testament studies, then the originating text in Genesis 2:7 (with linkages to Genesis 1:20, 21 and 24) becomes our starting point. Soul emerges within a creative drama in which a creature made of the stuff of the earth is infused with the breath of life so that it becomes a living, breathing being. In the Hebrew, *nephesh* and *nepheshim* refer to living creatures that breathe. In this foundational text, soul/*nephesh* does not name a part of a person; it names the whole living, concrete, creaturely, breathing being as such. Of the seven hundred and fifty times the word *nephesh* appears in the Hebrew Bible, the vast majority are translated by *psyché* in the Greek Septuagint translation, usually with a pre-Platonic meaning mirroring Hebrew rather than Greek concerns.[15] What is important here is the humanistic reference of *nephesh*/soul that reveals a sense of the human capacity for self-relatedness and the perception of life as a profoundly joyful rhythm. *Nephesh*/soul is the fundamental life force.[16]

The Hebrew Bible does not present us with a unified anthropology. Semitic thought, expressed in dynamically expressive images, is stereo-metric. This means that it brings different, even contrary aspects of reality together in a vibrant synthesis, one that is foreign to our dualistic ways of thought and understanding today. In this worldview, aspects always have the capacity to express the whole. The vision is aspect-based and creative, imaginatively expressive rather than conceptually definitive. Words such as *heart, soul, spirit, flesh* are everywhere in the biblical tradition and are often used interchangeably in the Hebrew, especially in Hebrew poetry with its fondness for verbal parallels. Psalm 84:2 with its references to soul, heart and flesh filled with spiritual longing, and Proverbs 2:10 with its references to wisdom coming to the heart and knowledge coming pleasantly to the soul offer typical examples of this vision. The same is true of the use of stereometric imagination in Psalm 6:2–4; note the flow of ideas: I – my bones – my soul – I. The working of a unitary imagination is crystal clear.

Stereometric thinking or harmonising presupposes a synthesis of the whole person with specific reference to movement and doing: soul surfaces in the movement and in the doing. The well-known text in Isaiah 52:7 about the feet that bring good news in the mountains is typical of this mode of reflection: what is truly beautiful is the pulsating movement associated with the feet, its vibrancy and vitality and its sense of verve and life, of soul. Viewed stereometrically, key words like soul are endowed with a marvellous range of meanings that include capacities, characteristics, modes and vitalities: the whole range of things that tell us we are alive and what it means to be human. The word soul as we usually understand it today is clearly not a close translation of the Hebrew *nephesh*/soul. In our minds, soul is too strongly linked to the narrower Greek tradition and so we have difficulty with the luxuriant range of living possibility the Hebrew word evokes. The Hebrew imagination takes in the whole vitality of life when it encounters the notion of soul: however we live, we live soul.

Hebrew images of soul began with intuitions about the neck, the throat, the gullet, the maw: the organs for breathing and eating. These led to intuitions about hunger and need, about want and greed, about fragility and danger. From this imaginative intuition the move to a metaphor for the self, for the whole person as a living, relational, unitary being is an easy step. In the process, *nephesh*/soul continues to refer to craving, yearning, pining, striving, wishing, hungering, thirsting, longing, and above all to desire, but in the sense of vitality rather than suspect libidinous forces to be sublimated and dominated to serve ego-centred needs. In the Hebrew sense, the many modes of desire just listed are spirited forces proclaiming life in all its wild unpredictability. The linkage between these profoundly human forces and *nephesh*/soul is particularly obvious to anyone who reads the *Book of Psalms*.

The reference to desire is significant for a second reason: it reveals *nephesh*/soul as a principle of living action, full of the desire for life. Reflect on the command to love God in Deuteronomy 6:5. It points to the living force of desire, a desiring love full of vitality and longing that embraces heart, soul, and strength: the whole person. There is an organicity to this vision that is difficult to connect to today: we are alarmed and sometimes shocked by that kind of totalising desire and so our spiritual lives are deeply impoverished. Instead, the Hebrew soul is imagined as the seat of the whole range of spiritual experiences. There are those full of Samson-like power and those replete with Jonah-like refusal and grudging cooperation. Others echo subtly to a still small voice. Others still include experiences of abandonment and betrayal, alienation and suffering, and even bitterness and the desire for vindication and bloody revenge. References to such desires are very clear in the psalms of complaint and lamentation.

*Nephesh*/soul expresses an accurate image of concrete human existence rather than some remote ideal. The Hebrew soul pictures a real person in real relationships, who suffers and rejoices, falls ill and longs for healing, lives life in all its ups and downs, its joys and its dangers, and finally falls prey to death. This is a real picture, not a romantic evasion, and today as never before soul needs realism and a sense of defiance in the face of adversity and injustice. We can touch something of this sense of soul in the African-American insight: echoes and intuitions of victorious endurance in hard times. There is something of it in the psalmist's weeping thirst for God and vindication by the rivers of Babylon. There is something of it in our cries and groans, in our laughter and our shouts of affirmation: soul finds expression through the throat and the voice as we give vent to its desires and longings, to its rhythms and moods, to its songs of jubilee and the wailing lamentations that refuse silence: lamentations that must soar into the cosmic night and demand attention and completion. The murder and loss of soul is also evident in the silenced voice, the deadened affectivity, the shadowed existence.

The Hebrew vision of soul confronts us with a synthesis of aspects of a unitary person-in-relationship seeking wholeness and seeking God. The vitality of the soul in such a conception reaches beyond the contours of the body; it forms and shapes every aspect of personality and informs even the spoken and the written word as it reaches out to the Divine as the soul's portion and object of hope.[17] But we cannot run away from the fact that soul-wound and soul-murder also imply a seeking that is easily derailed and damaged by narcissistically wounded and dysfunctional family systems, depraved social forces, and the abuses of power. If soul raises images of desire, desire in its turn raises images of potentially devastating power and domination. Soul is not neat: it is impacted on by energy vectors that can and do generate states of fusion and separation: unbounded states of passivity, irrationality, and submission on the one hand, and rigidly boundaried states of agency, rationality and domination on the other. These are states utterly lacking in humane pleasure and delight, in the mutual recognition of the other. The innate intentionality of soul that fosters the relationality intrinsic to the Hebrew tradition is missing.

The meanings associated with *nephesh*/soul may be summarised in three referential categories, all of which reveal and reinforce an image of a complete soul–body unity.

- Reference to a breathing, vital, living being (see Leviticus 17:11; see also Genesis 9:4 and 19:7). It refers in general to concrete human life, creaturely life; though very rarely it has been used to indicate a corpse (Lev 19:28).
- Reference to a range of psychological states, for example impatience (Numbers 21:4), bitterness (2 Kings 4:27), hatred (2 Samuel 5:8), sadness (Jonah 2:7). It is also linked with the heart (Deuteronomy

6:4–5), is seen as the seat of the mind (Deut 4:9), is associated with appetitive functions (Deut 23:24), and above all desire (Exodus 15:9).

- Reference to an individual, to a precious, beloved person, or self (Exodus 21:30; 2 Kings 1:13; Psalm 23:3; 63:1).

*Nephesh*/soul is never used in contrast to body (*bashar* in Hebrew). The ancient stereometric way of seeing the world would have resisted the contemporary forms of conceptual thinking that pit soul against body. The Hebrew interest is dynamic and synthetic rather than dialectical and dualistic. That contrast enters Western spirituality through the influence of Greek rather than Hebrew thought. The Hebrew usage confronts us with the undifferentiated psychosomatic anthropology that was common in the ancient Near East and is still evident in many aboriginal traditions today. We need to regain its vitality if we are not to drown in a commodifying world of peer-driven consumption of de-souled bodies that are open to every kind of exploitation and manipulation, not only in the sex industry, but in so many other aspects of commerce and life where living bodies are harvested for their parts.

In the ancient Hebrew tradition the body is imaged descriptively rather than conceptually in ways that underpin an underlying holistic or stereometric image. Beauty is expressive, active; it is not based on a perfect, idealised form, the trap we fall into today. Beauty is in what someone does rather than in some abstract form against which they are measured. The body is physical but the physical is celebrated, open to healing, to wellness and the erotic. In its very physicality, in its physical well-being, the body bespeaks the divine, just as in its brokenness it bespeaks the diabolical. The body also celebrates and brings together many other aspects and expressions of the whole: goodness and the spiritual, the inner and the outer, the individual and the other. In fact, despite the imagery in Psalm 8, for the Hebrew sages the human was not generally seen as superior to other creatures: all bodily life is short, threatened by dangers, weakness and fragility: and death is the great equaliser.[18]

At the heart of *nephesh* is a world of desire and need that only God can fully satisfy, something to which the mystical tradition stands as witness. This is a desire and a need that has the capacity to shake a person to the core, become a kind of driving torment (Psalm 6:3). Such needy, boiling desire bespeaks interaction and the welter of deeply felt forces that are the stuff of real life. In the Hebrew imagination *nephesh*/soul confronts spirituality with the desiring nature of creaturely life, the space where every spiritual quest begins, and the space where so many spiritual dreams are often lost and shattered. On the other hand, *nephesh*/soul does not support the contemporary vision of the sovereign, isolated individual even if there is a juridical reference to the individual as *nephesh* in Hebrew legal usage. In the Hebrew world the postmodern isolated individual was inconceivable: the person is always a person-in-relation.

There is no basis here for the individualistic vision of the kind that is rampant in the late-modern and postmodern milieu, nor is there ground for the radical disengagement from social responsibility now so common with its wildly diverging and fragmenting spiritual expressions: and its implications for emotional, psychological and spiritual health. It is also misleading to search for a theoretical account of the human person in the Hebrew Scriptures, or of the body-soul relationship. There simply is no biblical equivalent of Plato's *Phaedo* or Aristotle's *De Anima* or the many other technical writings on human anthropology that followed down the centuries and have informed Western spiritual and religious reflection. Nor is there even a strict equivalent in Hebrew for the Latin *persona*, the Greek *prosopon*, or the English *person*. The closest is *living-being*, the phrase that probably most accurately translates *nephesh*.

The implications for contemporary spirituality are clear. In the light of the Hebrew imagination neither soul-work nor soul-praxis is a turn to something individualistic, fragmented, isolated, or private. Far less is soul-work or soul-praxis about an inward turn defensively or autistically cut off from the world of the other and the human predicament. Nor are soul-work or soul-praxis about the narcissistic lifestyles so many live today. Soul-work and soul-praxis are about being fully alive, lively, concerned, relational, committed, empowered, whole-hearted, social, capable of passionate living, passionate service and passionate mutuality and receptivity. In this sense, spirituality is about a robust life-affirming, world-engaging, receptively involved stance: the holy is found here and now in the ordinary realities of every day. There is no split between the sacred and the secular, the personal and the social, as we would sometimes like to have it in order to protect our self-referred lives.

## TOWARDS A CHRISTIAN VISION

The Hebrew tradition teaches us that we are concrete living beings, part of the creaturely world in which we live. Grounded in an understanding of *nephesh*/soul, spirituality – and spiritual accompaniment – is intended to support a holistic style of life, a mode of realistic, concrete living that embraces life to the full. That means embracing the bright heights of divine encounter and the dark valleys of death and destruction. It means embracing earth and history, the wounded, desiring, needy-greedy self, and the wounded/wounding neighbour. The person is an indivisible whole, a radical unity that belongs to this world, challenged by the realities of this world. Reflect for a moment on the example of Jesus.

What his life shows us above all is how to confront suffering, how to enter into and share the suffering of others. He never teaches the avoidance of the human predicament, or defensive flight from its challenges and difficulties. He teaches engagement, even critical engagement, but engagement nonetheless.

Jesus challenges us to enter right into the messiness and unpredictability of human reality in all its forms. He teaches us to confront and struggle with the forces of human and creational diminishment: these are pivotal challenges for Christian spirituality. Jesus also teaches us that there is a palpable danger to spiritual realism in a misplaced compassion that seeks to remove suffering or at least evade responsibility for it by blaming it on God, or nature, or others. That path reveals an unreality, a defensive reality. The human predicament is real and most of it of our own human making; there and there alone the spiritual adventure surprisingly unfolds. There in the human predicament is the dance floor, and the rhythms, and the music, and the drama; there is the song of victory and the grieving lament: spirituality is found where real life happens and beckons and challenges and threatens. It is there at a joyous birth, it is there in the wreckage of a tsunami. It is a call to holy ground and to the seed-kernel where a divine image awaits a wise gardener who will nurture its journey to God: after all, in the Christian tradition we are invited as ensouled beings to grow up in every way into Christ (Ephesians 4:15). In Christian terms, soul is nothing less than the image and likeness of Wisdom, that is, of Christ.[19] Soul-Wisdom is the ground for the emergence of the true, the contemplative self.

In the New Testament *psyche* has complex overtones connecting it with life, with self and selfhood, with God, and with eternal life. Soul is utterly priceless (Matthew 16:26). Dedicated to God it acquires a special character (1 Peter 1:22; 4:19); it becomes anchored in God and can be abandoned to God's care (Matthew 16:25).[20] There are several texts in the New Testament that have profoundly influenced reflection on soul in Christian spirituality. These include Peter's reference to the hidden person of the heart with the imperishable jewel of a gentle and quiet spirit (1 Peter 3:4), Paul's invitation to put on a new nature created after the likeness of God (Ephesians 4:24), his reference to the spiritual person (1 Corinthians 2:14–15), to a treasure in earthen vessels (2 Corinthians 4:7), to an infilling with all the fullness of God (Ephesians 3:19) and to a house not made with hands (2 Corinthians 5:1). Then there is Matthew's treasure hidden in a field (Matthew 13:44) and John's image of a dwelling place for God (John 14:23).

In the early tradition, the strict link between soul and body is maintained, a link especially noted in the Orthodox tradition. Two texts in particular stand out: the term spiritual body (1 Corinthians 15:44) and glorious body (Philippians 3:21). It is clear that a synergy exists between soul and body that means quite simply that the human body is also on a journey of spiritual transformation, precisely because soul and body form a radical unity. The spiritual life transcends soul and synergistically incorporates every dimension of life, transforms it and glorifies it. Life is the key word, even when it is described as a life hidden with Christ in God (Colossians 3:3), or an inner life that is daily renewed (2 Corinthians 4:16). This is a life that grows into the full measure of the stature of Christ (Ephesians 4:13). In this sense, then, soul becomes a root metaphor that maps the authenticity of a life lived to the full, fully open to the transcendent, to the Divine.

Soul names the human capacity to be touched and reached by the Divine, the pivotal metaphor of the immeasurable capacity for communion with life, a life leaning towards an eschatological reality – the ultimate destiny of humankind and the world – with profound implications for history and all that is in the present moment. In all of this, the image of the human person as a psychophysical unity with a spiritual dignity, a human person called to spiritual well-being, is clearly drawn. There is a marvellous image of this in the Book of Job. It imagines God as a cheese-maker, making us like cheese, pouring out the milk and letting it curdle, covering us with skin and knitting us together, making us a living spirit (Job 10:10–11). What a marvellously poetic, accessible image of God! But the human image is just as accessible: an image of human materiality, fragility, limitation, finitude, death; factors we humans share with everything else in the cosmos.

Genuine spirituality provides no basis for arrogance; it calls instead for integrity in the face of human weakness, inconsistency, limitation. Soul names the living breath of being, it opens portals to a vast interconnectedness; it creatively responds to the rhythms of the dance of life. But it also remembers that we all come from the same ochre-coloured clay and that we all return to it in our time. In the meantime, we practise hospitality: we try to be open to the stranger and the enemy, to planetary and cosmic reality. We try to be practical about love: of self, of the other, of all that is, and God. We learn to share who we are: people alive, people of innate dignity, people with a sublime destiny, yet fragile people needing tenderness, yearning for love and the encouragements of love.

Over its long history Christian spirituality has developed a rich understanding of soul, the product of deeply reflected experience and contact with many cultures. One of the more evocative summaries of soul is usually attributed to the twelfth-century monk, Alcherus of Clairvaux, a follower of St Bernard. The text has also been associated with St Augustine, Hugh of St Victor, Isaac of Stella and William of St Thierry, among others.[21] The work is essentially an eclectic compilation of quotations and paraphrases from earlier authors that are evocative of the wholeness, dignity and fullness of human life. The importance of the text lies in its influence on later thought and the fact that it opened up discussion by introducing new ideas and systems of thought. It represents the contemplative psychology and anthropology of the time and seeks to refine the terms used there, and interestingly there are clear references to the medical knowledge of the time.

Of major concern in Alcherus's work is a discussion of the powers of the soul as these manifest in and through the body which it vivifies and enlivens, creating and preserving a unity of being.[22] According to McGinn, the overall tone of this treatment is practical and pragmatic: self-knowledge and understanding of soul are seen as key to self-knowledge, even though soul is and remains mysterious. At the same time, self-knowledge also demanded body knowledge. The two went hand in hand. Personal unity is affirmed even in the face of the logical dualism that understandings of the spiritual nature of the soul seemed to suggest. The medieval writers were alert to the problems of dualism but were loathe to let logic have the last word on the human person. One of the ways of avoiding logical dualism was to see the person as a microcosm containing both spiritual and material levels of reality. That is the path Alcherus chose. Writers like Alcherus were aware of the challenge of dualism and dealt with it imaginatively and poetically: they were suspicious of dialectical methodologies and refused to be contained by their dualistic logics.[23]

Alcherus's work also evinces the analogical and symbolic mentality prevalent at the time. The compilation paints a picture of a body–soul unity of great profundity. In the language of the time, the soul represents the human capacity for goodness and openness to love, truth, liberty, beauty, happiness and blessing. Soul also represents the thirst for eternal life and the capacity to welcome the divine presence. Above all, soul represents the centre of life understood as a spiritual journey in which the contemplative depths and heights of human existence are explored. The gift that Alcherus and the Cistercian tradition of the time give to us is an understanding that self and self-knowledge bespeak a soul-body unity and a spiritual-material microcosm of immense beauty.

In Christian spirituality, the link with a metaphysical understanding of soul that suggests that soul is endowed with simplicity (the soul is indivisible, irreducible) and autonomous existence is maintained. That is, soul is understood to be something wondrously vital in and of itself, something gifted with the capacity to transcend death. But Christians also believe in the resurrection of the body. Both are equally valued, because they are elements of our unitary being in the world. This is an analogical, not a dialectical relationship. Remember Alcherus's microcosm?

Christian spirituality is fundamentally called to glorify God in the human body, not just in the human soul (1 Corinthians 6:20): it is innately embodied. Both body and soul are understood in profoundly religious terms: they dance in unity before God in the world. They both represent what it is to be divinely made. They both have a future. When we say that the soul is the spiritual principle in the innermost depths of the human person, we are not devaluing anything: instead, we are valuing a profound vision of life.

When we acknowledge that the soul is directly created by God, we are acknowledging a gift: we are endowed not only with the divine image and everything that precious gift entails in terms of the trajectory of human development and destiny, but also with the possibility of graced communion and love-graced connectedness with God. To say that soul lies at the heart of the Christian understanding of the spiritual life and mysticism is not to belittle or marginalise body: both lie together at the heart of the human capacity for transcendence. We are rejoicing in the ensouled capacity for loving mind and intelligence, for loving insight and wisdom, and for wise and loving relationality. Our ensouled being is the portal of freedom, a freedom imprinted in the divine image that lies at its core. Eros is of body and soul. It is the basis of unity and union. It is the opening to agape, divine love. Soul-work is a work of freedom that opens the way to ever-deepening love as eros and agape meet and dance new life into being.

Properly understood, Christian spirituality is open to all of these characteristics of soul, weaves and knits them all together, finds ways to give them creative, loving and emancipatory expression. Christian spirituality is all about an utterly embodied soul-praxis: soul-awakening, soul-caring, soul-discovering, soul-exploring, soul-loving, soul-making and soul-nurturing, factors that make spirituality both a discipline and an adventure. Spirituality is about the dance of soul and the work of soul in the world as inward and outward forces leap more consciously to the loving cadences of creativity. We cannot grasp the ways of spirituality without the power and the light of the soul. We experience the divine through the soul setting hearts aquiver, roiling desire for connection across unexplored thresholds. In a sense, soul is the organ of all things spiritual, but not in any kind of disembodied sense. The ancient dance of *Eros* and *Psyche* continually unfolds in the background, beating to the rhythmic promising of *Agape*. The longing for divine agape-love is always there even when it is ignored or is left to function tacitly in the backrooms of the mind; so is the painful reality of soul-conflict and the hurting soul returning to loss and dreaded absence.

In the Hebrew and Christian traditions of mysticism, soul is a pivotal aspect of creation: today we would say that soul represents essential spiritual energy, the very stuff of spirituality and life, indeed the foundational stuff of all reality and the cosmos. Another helpful metaphor is to see soul as a force-field, a field of magnetic energy that recognises no limits, no boundaries, and is intimately linked with matter: giving it form, giving it its primordial pattern. A third way is to link soul to patterns and rhythms of rebirth, the paschal patterns of dying and rising rooted in the Easter story, and the changing states of being we experience as we shift between moribund, melancholic states and states of vibrant life: soul, after all, is the seat of sensitive life and sensitivity tracks trauma and joy, sickness of soul and the joys of life to the full. We live to the pulses of soul, to its simplicity and unity.[24] We are after all the stuff of stars, made of Eden's winds and the breath of the Creator. Soul links us to these primordial origins and empowers us to dance to a bigger music than individuality alone can capture, a music that originates in the life-giving irruptions of Creative Love.

Soul and love: sibling forces in their timelessness and their unbounded energies, full of creating, healing, emancipating power. Can soul and love be confined by the limits of the conscious mind? Or as the Zen koan asks, is the moon on the water? There is enigma and paradox here, an invitation to engage in a different vision, to become a poet of the spirit. Soul and love both speak the language of imagination, they both respond to beauty, they both see through and beyond appearances, they both recognise thin places and holy ground where the sacred is only a heartbeat away, just there, just beyond our fingertips, right here where we stand. They both respond to the mysterious call of a starry night, a blood-red sunset low in the sky, a startled bird, a bumbling bumble bee defying gravity, the whispering gurgles of streams on rocks breathing in the oxygen of life: a sense of eucharist making eternity present, nature's liturgy. Soul and love respond knowingly to the mysterious; they find ways to go deeper, to let mystery unfold and dance through our embodied, our creational existences.

Soul and love are at home in the enigmatic and the paradoxical. They enter and are challenged by the complex and baffling play of enigma; they encounter, explore and embrace the contraries that teasingly play within the push and pull of paradox. They reveal questions of attunement, a capacity to dream into things, an intuitive connecting, a letting go of assumptions and preconceptions, an embracing of the symbolic and the metaphoric, an entering of contemplative space, a deepening movement away from ego and its concerns, its often brittle and easily shattered concerns; but too much shattering hardens, even if the hardening does not always lead to discomfort and the need for change.[25] Soul and love know the landscapes of pain: they emerge in the flows and rhythms of emotional and expressive embodiments: they permeate the body.[26]

Soul and love live at the edges of logical thought; they live where poets live and artists, who glimpse beyond the reach of the mind's fingers and controlling thoughts. Such spirituality is not about mind knowing, but soul and love knowing; different knowledges from different places peeking beyond the mind's veils and illusions to something purer, something less inhibited, something more open. Soul and love: the spaces where we meet God and learn afresh what it means to be fully human: divine image meeting the Divine and entering the dance of transformation and healing. Change begets change; cadence begets cadence. Energy fields expand with use. They expand as soul and love teach us to imagine beyond our limits, the limits of anxiety and stress and their hormonal impacts.[27] The powers and virtues of soul and love grow over time and as a result of long practice. Soul and love teach us to embrace life, they teach us about being profoundly in communion with the totality of human existence, they teach us about different ways to be aware and conscious, they gift us with the courage to become contemplative, and serenely look reality in the face.

Contemplative consciousness is of the soul, is of love, and God draws soul and love like honey draws a bee. There is no place here for vinegar, though bitterness must be confronted. Be drawn beyond the surfaces of things – that is the key to soul-work and soul-praxis; be drawn and learn to love more deeply, to live with great delight in each moment knowing how perfect the moment is for love's energies to flow, to ripple up and down the layers of consciousness and across the arenas of suffering and pain. Love's energies are as deep as soul, as complete and as simple. Love and soul know how to live in many realities because they know the truth that brings true freedom: they hear God in the voice of the universe, they hear and they see the seeds and fruits of incarnation everywhere.[28] Soul and love know how to negotiate the worlds of action and physical reality; they know how to negotiate the worlds of speech and emotion, of sensual and sensuous reality where emotional literacy plays its vital role. The language of soul and love is not cerebral, but it is always clear in its own way, always more deeply tuned, always sensitive to the turnings of self before God. Learn to discern.

Being comfortable in this space of feeling, being free to laugh or cry, is foundational to spirituality, which is nothing less than what happens when soul meets God in God-given love, when human spirit and Divine Spirit dance the cadences of lovingly re-birthed existence to the rhythms of deepening vision. This is what it means to be in Christ, to be touched by the light, life and love of God. Like any dance, this new life has its rhythms, its process, its needs of space and time. Give time to it if the meaning and purpose of life is important; give space to the sacred in it, and integrity: this is the spiritual life. Soul and love are at home in the worlds of integrity and character, in the worlds of ethical response and congruent value: spirituality is also about how we choose to live and the light that enlightens soul and love. Soul and love lead us to the core, to the living-loving essence of being: they seek unity and union, they seek oneness and communion. Give it time: soul and love are ultimately concerned with awareness, a unified awareness, a gracious awareness, an awareness of the Divine will and grace, of *theosis* and *one-ing* with God. This is pure gift, pure endowment. Wait patiently for it. In the end, soul-life is not just about you or me: it is about healing the world.

## A Poetics of Soul

Trying to describe soul is like trying to describe love: it is a task for poets and saints, a task for those with the imagination to see beyond divisions and fissures and rifts and regressions, and encounter a hidden beauty, to see a wonderful microcosm of the human and the divine in another person. The comparison is deliberate because where soul and love meet, living-being creates rhythms and dances in the world. Both have to be experienced before they can be described: but neither their elusiveness nor their subtlety make them unreal or an illusion. Our inability to pin them down is part of what they are: messengers of mystery. When love and soul come together and embrace the rhythms of life, at the very least they sing of something profoundly valuable: when love dies, soul shrivels. When soul is murdered, love is fractured and diminished. Love and soul interweave together, they spin newness as they spiral in an eternal return to the unity of being. Both have to do with the invitation to intimacy, to participation in God and God's Triune dance of Oneness. That is the contemplative path to true beatitude: soul and love, soul-in-love and love-in-soul coming to a new knowing of Love, like cherry blossoms raining petals in the sun after a spring shower. That is why rape is so horrendous: it murders soul and shrivels life, robs them of vivacity.

It is probably true that the human soul, like love, is still a largely uncharted mystery, whether in spirituality, theology, psychoanalysis or depth psychology, but we desperately need its symbolic power today as we seek the way to life and the love that can remake the world. The other option is the dark, downward spiral to destruction. While it is true that in many ways soul represents what is most unfathomable and indeterminate about us, our capacity to approach it depends on the level of consciousness, love, commitment and reflective interest we bring to it. Soul's linkage to the deepest levels of spiritual well-being is simultaneously ancient and new, simultaneously desirable and challenging. Can soul ever be fully known; can its deep inner workings ever be fully known? On the other hand, how can spirituality be unfolded, how can it exist, without the loving light of the soul? How can spirituality be understood if the vibrant life-giving, love-stirring force of soul is ignored or marginalised? How can spirituality exist without an awakened soul lovingly opening to enlightenment? How can human depth be lovingly plumbed without a sense of soul-depths? How can deep meaning be lived and integrated without the love-energies that arise from the depths of soul?[29]

Down the centuries, soul has been described in a wide variety of ways. For Plato, soul is the source of all change and transformation. Aristotle underlined its essential and enduring character. Plotinus understood soul to contain the body and give it existence. For Gregory of Nyssa, soul is always implicated in contingent matter and bodiliness.[30] Thomas Aquinas named it the first principle of life. Aelred of Rievaulx described the utter simplicity of the soul. William of St Thierry celebrated its profound mysteriousness. Isaac of Stella saw the soul made visible in the body and through the body. For Dame Julian of Norwich soul is the source of light and movement. Ralph Waldo Emerson names soul the wise silence to which every part is related. For René Descartes, soul is reason. For Rudolf Otto, soul is a presence that releases feelings of mystery and marvel. Walt Whitman embraced soul as the exquisite realisation of life. For Bishop Berkeley, the soul always thinks. Gary Zukav depicts soul as a process of conscious creativity.[31] For psychologist James Hillman, soul is the seat of calling, character and destiny.[32] For analytical psychologist Wolfgang Giegerich, it is soul that makes authentic psychology possible: ideas as well as the soul need therapy.[33]

What is common to all of these very different descriptors of soul? first is the direct linking of life and creativity, and then the emphasis on reflective thought and transformative healing. Qualities of creative, cherished, connected, reflective and joyful living reveal the healthy presence of soul. Soul shines in innovative approaches to life problems, it underpins life orientations, it finds expression in such qualities as authenticity, autonomy, decency and compassion, sensitivity, and is there in all actions that express integrity and ethical courage. Soul is there when love finds meaning even in suffering and tragedy. Soul names the deep, integral source of human life, its essence and its deep inner workings. Soul is the first principle of life: when life is embraced, soul is embraced. Soul-discovery means that a richer lifeworld is being created: one that gives expression to a new state of affairs that is in a delightfully paradoxical way at once always actual and always possible and always sparkling with the lights of love.

Spirituality needs soul because soul names the precondition for complete and healthy existence in the world, the precondition for meaningful and creative lives. Soul-life has to be discovered and its wide hinterlands explored if individuation and its in-depth meaning-making potential are to unfold. In spirituality, soul-praxis and its critically reflective processes of soul-discovering, soul-exploring, soul-making, soul-holding and meaning-making confront us with images and feelings, ideas and practices, coherent memories, fragmented flashes and hints of a half-forgotten past fleetingly remembered, elements of sacred tradition and story, the tragic and the dark, the joyful and the bright, and their impacts in the present as something new seeks to blossom in the world, as unity of being struggles into existence seeking its time in the sun. Soul is a many-faceted gem of great price.

In this sense, spirituality may be described as the lovingly creative experience of body–soul life; the process of lovingly holding soul in conscious experience and learning from it how to live imaginatively in the unpredictable world of contingent reality, flowing with its surprises and disappointments. Of course, such a definition requires a commitment to the appropriate quality of awareness and a readiness to carry it through in a practical, creative and disciplined manner. Soul-discovering, soul-exploring, soul-making and meaning-making are each essential elements of a well-founded spiritual anthropology (from the Greek *anthropos*, a human being): the exploration of what it means to be fully human, fully alive, fully open to truth and love. A developed spiritual anthropology will reflect on such issues as our relationships with the universe, the make-up of the human person – including questions about spirituality as a human trait or characteristic, questions about human motivation, questions about the human task and human destiny, questions about human practices, questions about human behaviour and activity, questions about value, questions about compassion and empathy, questions about time, history and ultimacy, questions about the Source of being, and questions about the human relationship with God.

Soul glimmers and reveals its dappled glory in all of these questions as we struggle to discover who we are and take our place lovingly in the universe before God. We are not whole persons in the absence of soul, nor are we whole when soul is ignored, marginalised and alienated as is so often the case in contemporary consumer venues and their love affairs with the superficial, the fragmentary and the ephemeral. We become bearers and carriers of melancholy, that ancient symptom of soul-sickness. An integral or holistic view of the person is incomplete, wounded, flawed, without clear reference to soul, without healing contact with soul-love.

Soul and body allow us to affirm two aspects of the human person: they allow us to affirm our body-nature and our soul-nature as a single reality. Their inseparable relationship also allows us to affirm interiority and intimacy as foundational aspects of individuality and relationship; and they allow us to connect spirituality to reason and reasonableness, to anchor the authenticity of spirituality there. The union of body and soul allows us to recuperate soul as energetic, active in and through thought and love as thought and love become lived performance. Healthy soul reminds us of the depths of our human nature, depths to be sought and discovered in soul-work and soul-praxis. Body and soul together invite us to affirm the intimacy and uniqueness of each person, beings at once mysterious yet communicable, relational, social, discovered in mutual dialogue. Soul invites us to affirm the infinite value of the human person in a way that sees a glory and a mystery beyond the limits of embodiment.

If we take this holistic point of view into the world of twentieth-century psychology, some of the difficulties to be faced in understanding soul-encounter, soul-discovery, soul-making, soul-nurture and soul-work become more apparent. Psychology was originally understood as the study of soul, a focus psychology shared with poets, mystics, philosophers and theologians. In the late nineteenth and early twentieth century, that understanding was rapidly replaced by medical-mechanistic models growing out of a positivism concerned to desacralise the discipline and so allow it to be called a modern empirical science.[34] This was particularly the case in English-language psychology and is only too clear in the English translations of Freud's work where the word *Seele* (the German for soul), which Freud continued to use to do justice to the more mysterious dimensions of the human person, was reductively translated as mind and disconnected from soul (*Seele*).[35] *Psyche*/soul was thoroughly secularised, and soul was viewed at worst as a vestige of primitive superstition and at best the product of hit-and-miss philosophising.[36]

Something similar happened in medicine. A major criticism of twentieth-century medicine is that it lost sight of the person. The body first became the object of a diagnostic gaze and then became a manipulable object. In the process, personalising words got lost. We became 'it' and were treated like an 'it'. Persons essentially disappeared and became bodies to be examined, explored, measured and corrected. The opposite was happening in spirituality: in caring for the ensouled person, the body was lost to sight, was devalued, seen as dangerous to soul. The dialectics of modernity have not been good to either body or soul. These dialectical processes reveal another enigma, another paradox: we humans have this marvellous capacity to lose things. If we are not losing souls, we are losing persons, and if we are finding souls and persons, we run the risk of losing bodies and planets. In this strange world of losses we need a stereometric or holistic imagination, one that holds seeming opposites equally in view.

In the twentieth century, we lost so much. We lost so much of ourselves. We lost vital sets of relationships and what in-person relationships have to teach. It is so easy to lose sight of 'me' and forget 'it' and lead a partial existence, a half life in a half world. There are so many reasons why such amnesia occurs. In his intriguing book on bioethics, Allen Verhey suggests several. Dualism is one. In following Rene Descartes' philosophical vision the soul was detached from the body and associated with things like immortality and rationality, things free and independent of the body: interesting ideas and very influential with many important people, but not a complete vision of the stuff of life. Where is all the messy stuff? Where are the needs and desires, the pain and the passion, the mortality and the melancholic apathy, the unfreedom? Where is body and its gloriously limited implications? Is body really nothing more than Descartes' *res extensa*, something purely physical, purely material? I can find no basis for such thinking in the ancient vision of life, of unified, unitary life. We need to be critical of visions that allow body to be exploited, treated as manipulable matter; and we need to re-envision our spiritualities and our ecologies, our economics and our technologies, view them in a different light, one that has some sense of soul, some sense of unity, some sense of depth.

Verhey suggests that positivism is another explanation of our losses, something grounded in Auguste Comte's vision of positive progress through science. But is human progress the same as scientific progress? Is there truly no space for theological and philosophical reflection and insight? Knowing you and knowing me must not be reduced to pieces of scientific data and science's reductive capacity to distort how we take responsibility for ourselves and all that is. The present nuclear debates are a case in point. Is it all right for us to depersonalise and disembody for dualist and positivist reasons? Do I have a body or am I embodied? Do I have a soul or am I an ensouled living being, a unitary embodied soul – ensouled body where both body and soul are simultaneously and intensely present to each other, indistinguishable in living reality? In the end what makes me a person is crucial: if I am not sure what a living person is, how can I demand respect for persons? Person is, after all, pivotal to spirituality.[37]

As we conclude this chapter some reflections grounded in the thoughts of Otto Rank suggest themselves. By explaining the unconscious in terms of reality, by making it an object of scientific self-observation and objective understanding, Freud and those who follow him take the human soul seriously for a moment and then deny it. By recognising the unconscious, Freud acknowledged the soul, but by explaining it materialistically he reductively denied to it the force of spirit. But the unconscious contains more than remnants of memory: it contains elements that belong to soul and bring spirit to light. Even as psyche, soul is more than either brain function or sublimated drives: brain is just one instrument on which soul-themes play, and sexual libido is only one manifestation of soul. Much of psychology defies explanation precisely because modern science does not have the last word on soul: the best, the most meaningful dimensions of human subjectivity – soul – remain beyond its reach. The mystery, the subjectivity of the human person, needs more than science if it is to be unfolded: it needs poets and artists and musicians, and singers and dancers as well. Psychology is important, so is neuroscience, but they do not have the last word on soul. Spiritual values remain as a challenge. Soul does not need to be reinvented to fit the biases of an age; it remains a vital force in all things living and as such a force that refuses to be ignored.[38]

THEMES AND QUESTIONS FOR FURTHER REFLECTION
1. How do you understand soul? Do you recognise that your soul is as big or as small as you are yourself?
2. Identify your vision of life and reality. Is there place in that vision for the adventure of soul, or is your vision too narrow to embrace all of life and creation?
3. Identify the forces that enhance you and the forces that oppress you. How aware of them are you? Where do you meet them?
4. List the ways soul refuses to be ignored.

FURTHER READING
Paul K. Fehrenbach, *Soul and Self: Parallels between Spiritual and Psychological Growth* (New York/Mahwah, NJ: Paulist Press, 2006).

NOTES:  1. For an overview of cosmology see Denis Edwards, *Breath of Life: A Theology of the Creator Spirit* (Maryknoll, NY: 2004) 7–15.
2. For a discussion of these founding issues see Richard K. Fenn and Donald Capps, eds, *On Losing the Soul: Essays in the Social Psychology of Religion* (Albany, NY: State University of New York Press, 1995).
3. See Jan Bremmer, 'Soul: Greek and Hellenistic Concepts' in Mircea Eliade, ed., *The Encyclopaedia of Religion*, Volume 13 (New York: Macmillan Publishing Co., 1987) 434–438.
4. For a detailed exploration of the origins of psyche-soul see Richard Broxton Onians, *The Origins of European Thought: About the Body, the Mind, the Soul, the World, Time, and Fate* (Cambridge: Cambridge University Press, 1951).
5. See Jan Bremmer, 'Soul: Greek and Hellenistic Concepts' op. cit.
6. See Leonard Shengold, *Soul Murder: The Effects of Childhood Abuse and Deprivation* (New Haven: Yale University Press, 1989).
7. See F. E. Peters, *Greek Philosophical Terms: A Historical Lexicon* (New York: New York University Press, 1967).
8. Nikolaos Bakalis, *Handbook of Greek Philosophy: From Thales to the Stoics. Analysis*

and Fragments (Victoria, BC and Crewe: Trafford Publishing, 2005) 44
& 150.

9. For a discussion of these issues see Daniel Chapelle, The Soul in Everyday
Life (Albany, NY: State University of New York Press, 2003) 19–22. See
also Catherine Maxwell, The Female Sublime from Milton to Swinburne: Bearing
Blindness (Manchester and New York: Manchester University Press,
2001); Ellen Greene, ed., Reading Sappho: Contemporary Approaches (Berkeley,
Los Angeles, London: University of California Press, 1996); Laszlo
Versényi, Man's Measure: A Study of the Greek Image of Man from Homer to Sophocles
(Albany, NY: State University of New York Press, 1974).

10. Bernard McGinn, ed., Three Treatises on Man: A Cistercian Anthropology, with
an Introduction by Bernard McGinn (Kalamazoo: Cistercian
Publications, 1977) 2.

11. Nikolaos Bakalis, Handbook of Greek Philosophy, op. cit. 133–135.

12. See Jiyuan Yu, The Structure of Being in Aristotle's Metaphysics (Dordrecht:
Kluwer Academic, 2003).

13. See Constantine Cavernos, Modern Greek Philosophers on the Human Soul:
Selections from the Writings of Seven Representative Thinkers, 2nd Revised and
Enlarged Edition (Belmont, MA: Institute for Byzantine and Modern
Greek Studies, 1987).

14. See Jean-Marc Narbonne, Wayne J. Hankey, Levinas and the Greek Heritage,
and, One Hundred Years of Neo-Platonism in France: A Brief Philosophical History
(Leuven-Paris-Dudley, MA: Peeters, 2006).

15. In English translations the use of the word soul occurs much less
frequently than either nephesh or psyché because of a preference for
contextualised meanings and contextual synonyms.

16. On the Hebrew concept of soul see in particular H. Seebass, 'Nepeš' in
G. J. Botterweck, H. Ringgren, H-J Fabry, eds, Theological Dictionary of the
Old Testament, Volume IX (Grand Rapids: Eerdmans Publishers, 1998)
497–519.

17. See Aubrey R. Johnson, The Vitality of the Individual in the Thought of Ancient
Israel, 2nd Edition, (Cardiff: University of Wales Press, 1964).

18. See Sylvia Schroer and Thomas Staubli, Body Symbolism in the Bible,
Translated by Lynda M. Maloney (Collegeville: The Liturgical Press,
2001).

19. See Bernard McGinn, ed., Three Treatises on Man: A Cistercian Anthropology, op.
cit. 59–60.

20. See Geddes MacGregor, 'Soul: Christian Concept' in Mircea Eliade,
ed., The Encyclopaedia of Religion, Volume 13 op. cit. 455–460.

21. The text is entitled De spiritu et anima (Concerning Spirit and Soul). For an
introduction and translation see Bernard McGinn, ed., Three Treatises on
Man: A Cistercian Anthropology, op. cit. 181–288.

22. Ibid. 229.

23. Ibid. 87–89.

24. See Michael Eigen, *The Sensitive Self* (Middletown, CT: Wesleyan University Press, 2004) 36–61.

25. Ibid. 138.

26. Ibid. 173–174.

27. See Joseph Chilton Pearce, *The Biology of Transcendence: A Blueprint of the Human Spirit* (Rochester, VT: Park Street Press, 2004) 234.

28. See Tomaš Spidlik, *Prayer: The Spirituality of the Christian East*. Volume 2 (Kalamzoo: Cistercian Publications, 2005) 158–168.

29. See for example, Murray Stein, *Jung's Map of the Soul: An Introduction* (Chicago and La Salle: Open Court Press, 1998; seventh printing 2004) 60.

30. See Sarah Coakley, *Powers and Submissions: Spirituality, Philosophy and Gender* (Oxford: Blackwell, 2002) 165

31. Gary Zukav, *The Seat of the Soul* (London: Rider, 1990) 175–189.

32. James Hillman, *The Soul's Code: In Search of Character and Calling* (New York, London: Bantam Books, 1997) 10.

33. For the debate in analytical psychology see Wolfgang Giegerich, David L. Millar, Greg Morgenson, eds, *Dialectics and Analytical Psychology: The El Capitan Canyon Seminar* (New Orleans: Spring Journal Books, 2004). See also Wolfgang Giegerich, *The Soul's Logical Life* (Frankfurt: Peter Lang, 2001).

34. William James, for example, dropped the word soul from his *Principles of Psychology* published in 1890.

35. See Daniel Chapelle, *The Soul in Everyday Life* op. cit. 3–4. See also Bruno Bettelheim, *Freud and Man's Soul* (New York: Vintage Books, 1984); Donald Capps, 'Enrapt Spirits and the Melancholy of Soul: The Locus of Division in the Christian Self and American Society' in Richard K. Fenn and Donald Capps, eds, *On Losing the Soul: Essays in the Social Psychology of Religion* (Albany, NY: State University of New York Press, 1995) 137–169 at 138–146; Otto Rank, *Psychology and the Soul: A Study of the Origin, Conceptual Evolution, and Nature of the Soul* translated by Gregory C. Richter and E. James Lieberman (Baltimore and London: The Johns Hopkins University Press, 1998) 81–91.

36. See Donald Moss, 'The Scientific and Philosophical Context of Humanistic Psychology' in Donald Moss, ed., *Humanistic and Transpersonal Psychology: A Historical and Biographical Sourcebook*. Foreward by Stanley Krippner (Westport, CT: Greenwood Press, 1999) 12–23 at 17; J. Harold Ellens and Donald E. Sloat, 'Christian Humanistic Psychology' in ibid. 167–191 at 170.

37. See Allen Verhey, *Reading the Bible in the Strange World of Medicine* (Grand Rapids, Cambridge: Eerdmans Publishing, 2003) 68–98.

38. Otto Rank, *Psychology and the Soul: A Study of the Origin, Conceptual Evolution, and Nature of the Soul* op. cit.

## CHAPTER 8

*Spirit, Soul and Prayer*

> *Where do we encounter soul and spirit?*
> *They meet in the worlds of prayer.*
> *Thus does the song of spirit begin to soar,*
> *whirling and dancing on the world's winds.*

## INTRODUCTION

Spirituality names the life-long process of becoming a fully human, fully compassionate person, fully embodied, culturally, politically, spatially and temporally situated, fully alive and active, and present to all that is: a life open to awe and wonder. Christian spirituality does all of this in a process of becoming fully engaged with God, with brothers and sisters, in a Christian community compassionately open to the world and its realities and predicaments. Spirituality has the capacity to break us free from egocentric concerns. It turns us towards the other, generates a spirit of discerning openness. While spirituality has always had an inward vector it has also had an outward, transcendent vector that impacts on both culture and religion. In fact, Mortimer Ostow has suggested that spirituality provides the emotional force that supports and sustains interest in and commitment to religious practice and that it has had, however indirectly, a shaping role to play in all cultures.[1] Certainly, links between religion and spirituality remain, even in postmodern contexts.[2] Spirituality touches every aspect of human life.

However, in recent usage, the rich meaning of spirit, like the meaning of spirituality, has become increasingly blurred, narrow and unclear, not least because of contemporary trends in philosophy and psychology, as well as spirituality and theology.[3] This has had much to do with reductive linkages made between spirit and mind on the one hand, and spirit and subjectivism on the other. We need to recuperate earlier concepts of spirit, particularly those that sustain intuitions of creative inspiration and dynamic movement, as well as the vision of spirit as the animating principle of life. From the Christian point of view, soul and spirit converge in interacting domains of prayer, meditation, worship, and contemplation: in John of the Cross's terms, walking in fields of silent music. In this chapter we are going to explore the nature of spirit, and the convergence of soul and spirit in the world of prayer.

### SIMONE WEIL: SPIRIT AND LOVE

Even against the background of the horrors of the twentieth century, it is in spirituality that we experientially glimpse the possibility of a love with the power to transform history and the politics and ideologies that shape it. This happens because spirituality has the capacity to discover Spirit at the heart of a divine dance that simultaneously transcends and acts within the particularities of place and time and, in so doing, sets the human spirit free. This discovery places Spirit dynamically at the heart of spirituality. It also shapes how the human spirit is itself understood, how it is made to be drawn into a unifying dance of loves, eros and agape, finite and infinite, an upward and a downward embracing, spiralling new ways of life, new ways of experiencing life into being. In Simone Weil's terms, spirituality and Spirit confront us with a divinely transforming love radiant with the harmony, equality and perfect joy of a God who needs our cooperation precisely in order to be present in the world as Spirit. In Christian terms, through the interweaving dynamics of soul and spirit, we are gloriously made to discover and grow in God's gracing presence. We are made to receive a loving, liberating power that is gracious and nourishing, transforming and uplifting. By our consent we become transparent to Divine Love and discover what it means to be made in God's image and likeness.[4]

It is in this radiant space where soul and spirit dance audaciously to a divine undersong that the dilemma of personal worth finds its resolution. In this radiant space, everything sterile, vain, diminished and diminishing in the human story meets healing and liberation. As ego is transcended, the past falls away and seeds of future promise bud and blossom and bear fruit and grow, spiralling newness.[5] It is in such a process of consent, in this radiant body–soul–spirit space, that spirituality begins to understand the whole web of relationships that constitutes life in the world. As we meditatively, reflectively, contemplatively dance in this radiant space, we begin to glimpse the deep nature of human spirit finding expression in a vision of human life called to engage lovingly with God in all the pathways of the world. It is love arising from the bright wellsprings of spirit that alone makes it possible to glimpse a crucified God in spaces of tragedy, suffering, and in every imaginable horror.

For Simone Weil, love is not simply about a point of view. It is much more a question of action, a way of acting towards others and the world, a way of acting towards God that reveals human spirit finding the capacity in love to respond to Divine Spirit, even in disastrous and monstrous circumstances. There is a depth of spirituality here, a mystical insight that requires time and reflection to be fully grasped. This is a matter of a love grounded in experienced faith, not philosophy – and Weil was a philosopher – even though philosophy helps us to unfold its mysterious logics. This is a love capable of the complexities of faith, a faith capable of the complexities of love in the real world we inhabit every day: a question of consciously operative belief not explanation, of love in action accounting for itself. Such is the true awakening of spirit.

Spirituality is a question of a faith to which free consent has been given; it is not a metaphysics. Within the Christian tradition, Spirit generates spirituality and in so doing suggests the possibility of transcendental creative purpose. This purpose, as it is grasped, permits faith itself to become embodied in the world, open. As a construction, spirituality, even at its most theological, cannot be categorised outside of faith and love as they flourish and grow in the world. We are simultaneously bearers of a natural and a spiritual history. Spirituality allows us to see our lives in the light of a love that brings a new freedom and openness into play. The deep origins of spirituality lie in the embodied relationship with Spirit that spurs the human spirit on and makes everything possible.[6] What about the spirit of justice and truth? Not surprisingly, that too for Weil is fundamentally a question of the attention of love. Love is the quality that allows a spirit seeking justice and truth to reveal beauty; for in the contemplation of beauty, human desire is transformed into love. Everything that grows from love shines with the radiant glow of beauty, and this bright beauty reveals the essence of the human spirit.[7] This bright beauty, this communication of creative light, reveals the truth of spirit unfolding as a vibrant reality in the world.

## A POETICS OF SPIRIT

The postmodern world challenges spirituality to maintain a balance between membership in a highly rational culture and the flourishing of spiritual awareness.[8] What, then, is spirit? There are many ways of answering this question. For example, David Hay's work reveals the individuality of spirit in contemporary accounts of spiritual experience.[9] Spirit has also been described as a vast ocean abundant in its gifts of connectedness and healing. It shows us how to become our truest selves as it reconnects us to the Source of life. Spirit is evoked in our deep need to experience the wonder-making, heart-leaping transcendent beauty of the world, to see the world with different, more than aesthetic eyes. The worlds of narrative, music, poetry and art are full of examples of such unique moments of communication and contact with the transcendent possibility of spirit. These moments have major implications for our usually small, self-referred visionings and their ties to immediate embodied and social needs.

We are part of a process that continually opens up the possibility of new life. The question for spirituality and spirit is: what generates this new life? The answer is Spirit, the Holy Spirit, revealed in a flow of continual creation in openness to the future and its purpose. The human spirit is revealed in experiences of beauty and in their capacity to evoke moments of awe-filled stillness and timelessness. The human spirit is there in the energy that touches people's voices and faces when they share such experiences, in the refusal to allow them to be trivialised, or restricted, or cynically mistreated. Every spiritual mentor or soul-friend has witnessed and been touched by such intensity and its transformative potential.[10] The human spirit is revealed, not so much in the awe and wonder such experiences trigger, but in the deeper, more tacit need for the experience itself. Touched by grace, the spirit is drawn upwards with the power of love towards the transcendent. Rudolf Otto famously explained such experiences in terms of the *mysterium tremendum*, the transcendent mystery that inspires reverential awe and trembling before its overwhelming splendour.

We also need to recognise that spirit is as common as life itself, or the wind and moving air, the breathing for which it is named. The human spirit is so normal that we often fail to recognise its power, just as we fail to acknowledge the wind or life itself unless they turn violent and set destructive forces to work. The same must be said about spirituality and its ordinariness: just like life, wind and breath, what is extraordinary about spirit and spirituality is their absence from a life, not their presence. Their inspirational role is foundational to human life, their capacity to motivate individuals and communities. As inspiration, spirit comes in plural forms. It is at work in poets, musicians, artists and prophets, in the simplest acts of gratitude and humour, as much as in acts of courage and great sacrificial love. Spirit takes on a guiding role in lives that seek its inspiration precisely because inspirations imply directions that shine in joy and sorrow.

But the human spirit is also revealed in experiences of disgust and the causes of disgust. Spirit is revealed in the weaknesses of the flesh and in the more sordid expressions of our animal natures, and the hostile forces that shove spirit into the dark recesses of the human mind. The undersong of the human spirit cries out against our own self-betrayals, the tendencies to exorcise spirit from life, to leave spirit and its reasons lying unused: a censored reason crying for us to confront our true natures and the results of our actions. Evidence of this cry of disgust is there in *Hamlet*, in Nietzsche, in the cry of the poor, it is there every time we shudder with fear and disgust at the evidence of what human brutality can do and is doing. It echoes in the shuddering cry of the planet rejecting what we are doing to it. Philosopher Michael Gelven has even suggested that this disgust, this refusal of one-sided living, is the origin of spirit. The human spirit is revealed in our reaching out beyond ourselves because disgust is not an argument; it is a mode of being.[11]

The human spirit, and with it human spirituality, is paradox: it emerges because of a conflict that is embraced. Spirituality, and with it spirit, is grasped in its refusal to be grasped; it is understood precisely in its refusal to be grasped or understood: there is in spirit a knowing and a not knowing. It exposes what makes us ignorant of ourselves; it confronts us with what is greater than ourselves: spirit connects, spirit bridges, it moves beyond self, it transcends self.[12] Spirit refuses to be locked into the parameters of the self, the phenomena that occur in the first person singular in the inner landscape: the mental landscape that constellates around the ego and leaves everything else in the dark lands of unawareness and the sleeping mind. Spirit is about openness and the courage to be open, the courage to be awake, especially to the mystery of our own origins and destiny.

In a garden, awaiting betrayal, Jesus reminded Peter that spirit is willing but flesh is weak (Matthew 26:41). Like disgust, flesh, too, is a mode of being, a kind of somnolence, a landscape of limitations that tends to favour the self. Spirit is also a mode of being, surfacing the kind of wakefulness and watchfulness the fullness of life demands. Without the watchful and wakeful disgust of spirit, its protesting refusal of a half life, without the passionate cry of refusal and negation it entails, life risks becoming nothing more than a shadowy representation of its own potential, a deadening somnolence going nowhere: spirit rescues us from the nihilism that whispers to our soul that life is pointless, that human values prove worthless.[13] Spirit refuses the false boundaries of a self-referred world; spirit transcends these boundaries and brings with it the passion and courage to join the flow of ego transcendence and bring a whole other mode of existence into being.

The human spirit confronts us with the paradox of creative passion; it moves to the rhythms of music; it has energy, melodic character, the capacity for intricate harmony and inventiveness. Just like music, spirit has resonance; it evokes memory, it challenges integrity, it reveals sincerity and beauty, and it can bring the healing of pain. At the same time, it is capable of the big and the small, the fast and the slow, the public and the intimate. And like music it is evocative of time and eternity, of heaven and hell, of serenity and an anger that is not always just. The human spirit is also capable of discord and destruction when its ways are perverted and turned in darker, hostile, vengeful directions. Spirit is there in human dignity, in the honest expressions of human freedom, and in the appropriate as well as the inappropriate uses of power. When spirit encounters Spirit, we are challenged to acknowledge mystery and invited to be enrapt, drawn into spaces of wonder and the cadences of awe. Spirit teaches us that we are redeemable, capable of the adventure of transformation. Ideally, when we encounter spirit we encounter the ability to laugh at ourselves and our self-important attitudes.[14]

What is spirit at its most essential? Michael Gelven makes three suggestions: nearness, transcendence, and gratitude. Nearness means that the I becomes We and the I-It becomes I-Thou: spirit makes nearness possible. Transcendence is a more difficult word because of its many philosophical uses, but its meaning keeps us grounded in this world. It helps us to see the difference between states of being. Noble and ignoble, spiritual and crass are good examples: spirit transcends the crass and the ignoble, it embodies and situates us differently in the world; it changes the modalities of being in the world away from ego and its narrow, often vindictive and self-referenced concerns. In so doing, spirit makes prayer possible: it allows us to go beyond ourselves, to move away from self and entreat justice.

Gratitude is the opposite of betrayal. Gratitude means that I am glad I exist, that in some sense I have been blessed, that I have been loved, that I have worth. The human spirit helps me to understand that life is bestowal, and as something bestowed has meaning. The bestowal of life means that you and I matter, that love is present, that caring is present as part of existence itself: spirit tells me that my life is a favoured, a gracious modality of being, something that evokes gratitude. In nearness, transcendence and gratitude lies the autonomy of spirit; and in that autonomy lies the possibility that spirit is not always good: thus spirit reminds us who we really are and our lives and our choices tell the story.[15] The challenge is to discern the spirit that moves us in a given situation: Holy Spirit or fragile spirit, alert spirit or somnolent spirit?

Ignoring spirit proves unsustainable if only because the impact of spirit knows no bounds. It is always indicative of freedom. Freedom is both a disposition and a desire of the human spirit. Spirit surfaces as a lightness of self-contained freedom when we choose a good path. It blossoms into love and justice and in so doing transforms the essence of human consciousness into something that shines inwardly with contemplative beauty. The freedom of spirit revealed in the consent to love lies at the heart of human freedom and defines and describes it. The same is true of Christian freedom: Christ set us free for freedom, not slavery (Galatians 5:1). The challenge to spirituality is to live this lightness and freedom, this love and truth, this embrace of justice at every level of human relationality and sociality.

Poets know that spirit is a 'how' word: it makes life imaginatively intelligible, generates a horizon of creative understanding, and reveals spirit as ground and culmination of the human odyssey. However, the human spirit is not a tool: it is the central inspiration of the whole of life and, in every moment of its living, makes life beyond the alienated self possible. It sets the potential self free to blossom. Spirit is an experiential concept and the best language for it is experiential language, especially when experience is understood in terms of such forces as inspiration, relationality, and the encounter with wonder. Spirit is experienced in all the dimensions of human existence. Many words hint at its vast experiential range; words like thought, feeling, loving, touching, testing, hurting, resisting and many others. Experience of spirit tends to be cumulative, open to discernment and decision precisely because its traces are found in the bright and the dark aspects of life, in the green valleys and the dry stretches of the desert and the wilderness. Above all, spirit is relational; it flows in relational patterns generating interweaving bonds of love. Its milieu is communion and its way is the way of invitation and appeal, the way of influence and attraction, the way of synergy where combined efforts are greater than the parts, and the dance of synergy with Spirit.

Authentic spirituality encourages us to reclaim the possibility of unity. Within that unity, soul makes me alive; spirit enables me to be alive in God (Romans 1:9). Spirit names the human dimension capable of relating to the Divine Spirit; it is the domain of action of the Holy Spirit; it is that part of us that reaches out and up to God, becomes the channel of divine life, and opens us up to transpersonal reality: spirit dances with Spirit into a whole new mode of understanding of what it is to be alive in the world before God, graced to be one in spirit with the Spirit of the Lord (1 Corinthians 6:17). On its own, *psyche*/soul cannot do full justice to the human person, regardless of the findings of contemporary psychology. We are more than soul can say; we are incomplete without spirit and its capacity to plumb our very depths, to scale the heights of transpersonal possibility: spirit lets Jesus live (Galatians 2: 20).

St Paul understands soul as the source of human life, and spirit as the source of spiritual life. These are references to dimensions of a unitary being. When we set inner life and outer existence against each other, we split the human person. When soul and spirit are set against each other, we arrive at an even more distorted and distorting view of the human person. Spirit reminds us that we are not alone, that we are part of something greater, that we are relational and social beings capable of life to the full, that we are capable of spiritual heights and spiritual depths. Without spirit and its self-transcending energy, soul energy can be easily subverted to serve the wounded and wounding demands of the false, alienated, isolated, fragmented self. Spirit reminds us that we are receptive beings, capable of being awakened to the transforming power of the Spirit of

God. The energies of body, soul and spirit converge in the world of prayer and in the world where prayer is made flesh.

## DIVINE SPIRIT AND HUMAN SPIRIT

Christian spirituality does not float free of the wonderful story of God's dealings with the world even when disgusting subtexts of human corruption rise to the surface. Christian spirituality is about the good and the bad in us; it challenges us to open our fallible lives to the fragrance of God-knowledge and become the aroma of Christ's loving offering to God in this world of often brutal and conflicting forces (2 Corinthians 2:14-15). To live with Spirit is to breathe out fragrance (Ephesians 5:2), a fragrance that is unfolded as loving compassion given integrity in openhearted self-giving. Fragrance evokes an attractive threshold experience, a bringing of inner and outer realities into harmony. Fragrance images an alluring harmony that has direct relational and social implications. In the Hebrew tradition, the holy is depicted sensually as perfume of great subtlety. The list is extensive: aloes and myrrh, calamus and cinnamon, saffron and nard, balsam and honey, apple blossom and attar of roses, dark musk and the lightness of the lily flower with the whispers of swallows' wings and hints of rich spices from the East.[16] The Divine Spirit is a perfumed, fragrant, enthralling, transforming presence. There is something here of the interplay of eros and agape: the Spirit attracts spirit as a gracious fragrance carried on the soft breezes of Divine Love. And the Spirit comes to the land within and the land without like the return of the jonquil flower and the hum of the turtle dove; scents and bird chants carried on dawn winds as shadows flee and dew-glistening blossoms break their fast in the light of the returning sun.

It is interesting to note that contemporary interest in both the human spirit and the Holy Spirit is unfolding at a time when the secular turn is at its height, especially in Europe.[17] We are confronted by an intriguing counter-cultural turn, a true sign of the times calling loudly for audacity of spirit. What is at stake is nothing less than the integrity of our own meaning and healing, processes that begin in the loving embrace of Spirit, in the re-birthing into freedom that Spirit brings to spirit. In this transforming relation, our spirit is empowered to bring truth in love to the world. The Spirit broadens the horizons of spirit.[18] The Spirit enfolds us in gracing love and in so doing invites us to participate fully in the creational dance of our own transformation.[19]

Spirituality means bringing this all-embracing invitation, the freedom and lightness and love and justice of transformed spirit into the world. Spirituality allows transformed spirit to breathe and live. Spirituality restores spirit to the whole gamut of human affairs and challenges us to walk lightly through people's lives, walk lightly and lovingly and caringly on the planet itself. Spirit teaches us simplicity of spirit, the simplicity of a mind and heart transformed by grace, a life turned towards God, a life responding lovingly to the movements of the Spirit in the inspirations and intuitions of the unfolding moment. To be spiritual is to be moved by the Spirit to walk lightly, to walk with prudential foresight in ways that evoke ethical freedom and love, and a justice that heals and frees in an encounter with a Truth shining with the Beauty of healing-saving love. To choose otherwise, to choose the dark path, is all too easy, and its outcomes all too evident in human society.

We need Spirit-to-spirit inspiration, this wind-like stirring of inquiry and wonder if authentic spirituality is to blossom in our worlds of contesting voices. We need Spirit if we are to find our way in the spaces where call and mystery converge. We need Spirit to find our way in the movements that call us in new directions, and we need Spirit to help us follow the deeper, more mystical movement into Divine mystery. Then we need to discover that the Spirit also works in the messy and often conflicted conditions of everyday human life. The polyphonic action of grace, the multi-contextual work of the Spirit, the multi-layered flow of transformation, all suppose the reality of human nature and its fallibility. It is the nature of the Spirit to work something wonderful from all our apparent chaos and resistance.

To be spiritual is to become lovingly conscious of our own freedom to dance in the freedom of Spirit. To be spiritual is to become aware of the meanings and obligations of freedom and the choices that allow the Spirit to orient our histories in a love that lets beauty glisten and glow in the darkest of places. Thus does the song of spirit begin to soar, whirling and dancing on the world's winds. Spirituality is a work of art, spirit the canvas, and Spirit the gifting artist. Awareness of Spirit makes a lighter existence possible. It allows us the freedom to attend lightly to our aims, desires, needs, interests, passions, personalities, and talents and the actions to which they give rise. Spirit also empowers us in freedom to look closely at our corruptions and hostilities, and our capacities for relational, social and planetary destruction. It frees us to shine the light of truth into our diminishments and illusions and find ways to break free of the domination they exercise over our present lives and commitments, the diminishments they cause in ourselves and others. Freedom evokes the necessity of choice. The principle of freedom is one thing; the choices that make it real in love and justice are another. That is why the Spirit also calls us into the healing domains of metanoia.

Encounters with Spirit arise in the space between willingness and wilfulness. When we are willing, we are drawn towards the Source. When we are wilful, we evade the Source, and the challenge of the Source. We fill our minds with pleasing images and comforting thoughts.

Then we discover that the contemplation of this breath-taking Beauty, this imageless, wordless Source is sidelined by the imagination, and our inability to yield control: ego does not want to go there lest it die; and so defensive imagination divertingly saves us from encounter with our ego limits and fears, with self-losing dynamics.[20] Active choice confronts us with these dynamics and leads us where defensive imagination would not wish to go. It is not easy to learn that authentic spiritual enlightenment so often comes through the liberating gift of unknowing.[21]

In spirit embraced by Spirit we encounter the paradox of existence. Finite freedom encounters infinite freedom. This is the graced space where engaged and interested contemplation and mysticism find the key to a new lightness, a new and loving humbleness of being and action that is transformative of its very nature; transformative of the contemplative and the mystic, and transformative of the world because of the rippling influence of authentic transformation. Do not let glib imagination lead you astray from this transformative task because the re-birthing of spirit in love is not easy. A poetics of spirit bespeaks a life-long spiralling journey into the beautiful truth and goodness of love. According to Simone Weil, God's silence compels us to an inward silence.[22] Spirit draws us beyond private interest: it draws us into spaces where sensitivity to context and sensitivity to encounter teaches us to be open to difference and the changes that such sensitivities demand in an unpredictable world.[23]

To consent in love to Spirit, to engage freely in Spirit-led historical solidarity with all that is, draws us into God, draws us into the flowingly creative graced energy of creator God revealed in the utterly free, utterly unselfish, utterly liberating self-emptying act of Jesus of Nazareth: out-pourers of Spirit, givers of loving freedom in a paradoxically spiriting dance of piercing beauty and healing truth (Philippians 2:5–8). As we are rendered powerless before God, so we are enabled to bloom and bear fruit and scatter seed in the world in increasingly explicit ways, wildfire mustard-seed ways (Matthew 17:20). But we need the inward gaze, the silent gaze into the heart of stillness if this is to occur on any scale. We need to sit at the edge of the abyss. We need time to experience and walk through the lovingly intimate silence of God. We need to face our fear of it. We need to discover that it is good to wait in silence, good to sit in solitude and silence, to examine our path (Lamentations 3:26, 28, 40). This is Spirit work, this inward–outward gaze that has such political, such historical, such personal and communal consequences. This is the abyss from which spirituality emerges into the world as the human spirit is honed in the secret ways of love and silence, as we learn to let Jesus live.

The tragedy is that we find ways to block the soaring Spirit. We block our ears to Spirit song. We insulate our hearts against Spirit winds that are meant to blow freely though every facet of our existences, lifting our spirits and birthing us afresh. Choices have consequences, some of them perplexing and unexpected, and choices grounded in force and fear have the power to sweep spirit away, turn spirit into a thing. Jesus teaches us that true spirit is twice born and that the second birthing takes place in an ungrasping self-emptying that has nothing to do with force or domination, or collusion with either. Jesus teaches us about a finding in a losing, a living in a dying, a striding ahead in a following behind, an embracing of law in the freedom of spirit, in an obedience to love that is the epitome of spiritual freedom. The simple truth is that a coerced spirit is a shamed spirit. That is why every spirit, every soul cries to be delivered from the confusions and devastations of corruption. Only love finds the way through and beyond devastation and corruption: love that is unafraid of silence and is nurtured and watered in stillness to bear fruit in life.

The more nobly we do these things, the more closely we reveal the image of God. In living a soul-based life, spirit resonates to the loving awareness that is at work; spirit is the basis of the contemplative stillness, the loving stillness in which a profound knowing takes place, a recognising and an embracing of the True, the Good, and the Beautiful. Spirit-led, Spirit-gifted-consciousness gifts us to share in an unalienated awareness that sets us vividly free in the breakthrough of a contemplative self that sees now with the eyes of Spirit. Contemplative spirituality is thus a transformative immersing in the lightness and simplicity of Spirit. It is the portal to unalienated unselfish knowing, to a space of boundless possibility whose sorely tempting enemy is a dulled, alienating, apathetic, melancholic indifference. The contemplative spirit is gifted with the love that sees through such indifference and its corrupting torpor. The contemplative spirit finds, lost treasure-wise, the capacity to step beyond the debasing thrall of torpor. That is why we can speak of an engaged spirituality that is truly, compassionately free, and of a spirit glowing with the fruits of kindness. Obedience to Spirit is, after all, liberating obedience to the source of life.

An authentic spirituality teaches us to risk the ways of Spirit obedience and find there an unthought-of fullness and lightness of being. There is nothing here of a legalistic piety or a rigidly defensive devotion. Authentic spirituality transcends such self-defensive postures and recognises them for what they are: diversions on the path of love, lay-by existences confused with reality, a resisting and a deserting of the Spirit of life. The Spirit brings a vibrant, fruitful unity to life not a sealed-off existence protecting a dull abstraction, a fictional life frightened of freedom in an illusion of reality. None of these things can be comprehended or actualised outside of spirituality, outside of the graced action of the Spirit. Genuine spirituality is always borne on Spirit wings, lifted aloft on Spirit wind, sung with the breath of Spirit, spun in the twirling dance of Spirit. Spirituality is spirit breaking free of an unconsciously deadened life and its tacitly distrustful compromises.

Genuine spirituality uncovers spirit taking hold of Spirit-formed conviction. True spirituality uncovers engaged love attuned to the cycles of creation and sabbath, of work and wonder, and worship in spirit and the luminous truth of love. Real spirituality is spirit lovingly realising its graced potential, giving expression to its true creative genius. Spirituality is not just a question of an ideal, however laudable; it is a question of real activity in real situations: Spirit draws us into an engagement with all of reality. Spirituality grows progressively, subsuming in its development each earlier phase of life as Spirit leads onwards towards the light. It is not in the nature of Spirit merely to lie dormant and leave creation untouched; though Spirit may be driven away and spirit left for dead. Spirit germinates, fosters new life, disturbs complacency, roils the stagnant waters of unexamined motives, and stirs up the embers of life, ever seeking to produce new life and the fruit of new life.

That is why spirituality is ultimately subversive of conventionality and seeks a better, more just, more honest, more loving way forward for society and the world. Spirituality reveals a life that stands freely and subjectively in conscious cooperative relation to the Spirit's life-giving action in the world, freely responding to the Spirit's gift to the world, the gift of freedom and love and light and life, the gift of hopeful time and the dazzling promise of eternity, the Spirit's natural element. There is no basis here for any spirit-matter split, no basis here for a rejection of nature: Spirit encounters us in the sensible world of embodied reality. Remember, Christian spirituality dances with a radiant Word made radiant flesh even in the brutal darkness of the Cross.

### LIFE: THE SONG OF SPIRIT

In a way that is highly relevant for spirituality, Yves Congar acknowledged the priority of a living theology of the Spirit. He understood that a living spirituality of Spirit flows from the spiritual vitality of personal and communal experience. He also recognised that we are persons in communion. He taught that a vibrant theology of the Spirit, a theology alert to its spiritual responsibilities, would be characterised by the dynamic interweaving of anthropological (about people) and ecclesiological (about the faith-community) poles. Any kind of disjunction between these two expressions of spirit and grace has no place in an authentic theology of the Spirit.[24] And yet evidence of just such a disjunction is clearly apparent in contemporary moves to sever the link between spirituality and religion. The challenge posed by Congar's vision of Spirit is contemplatively to imagine the implications of a Spirit-gifted human communion, a Spirit-gifted desire to sing a creative paean of prayer and life, a rapturous song of people enlivened by the Spirit in the dynamic interactions of personal, ecological and social lives.[25]

This represents a subtle, complex, life-long task. The Holy Spirit is the Spirit of Divine Wisdom. To live spiritually is to live according to the Wisdom of the Spirit, and therein lies the challenge. The Book of Wisdom enumerates the qualities of Divine Wisdom in some detail (7:22–30). The Divine Spirit is the designer and fashioner of all things, all-knowing, intelligent, holy, unique, manifold, subtle, dynamic and agile, clear and incisive, pure, distinct, invulnerable, kindly, loving the good, keen, irresistible and unhampered, beneficent, humane, steadfast, sure, tranquil, free from anxiety, all-powerful, all-surveying, penetrating every dimension of existence, sent by God, the aura of eternal light, the outpouring of God's glory, the brilliantly shining mirror of God's working, the radiant image of God's goodness, the force of renewal, the maker of friends of God and prophets, more beautiful than the sun and stars, omnipresent. There is a lifetime of reflection and transformative action in this account. To be spiritual is to love Lady Wisdom dearly, to do justice, to love kindness, to live wisely and well in the world, and walk humbly and consciously in the bright ways of the Spirit (Micah 6:8). Spirituality is a portal to a transformed life, a place of continuing reflection, a doorway to a life committed to unfolding the Spirit's loving mystery, a recurring invitation to rekindle and fan into flame the personal and communal gift of God that is the Spirit (2 Timothy 1:6).

We cannot let Jesus live and release his springs of living water into the contemporary consumer wilderness without the creative presence and wisdom of the Spirit. Without the Spirit we will never understand the dangerous memory that grounds our Eucharistic celebration and its emancipatory implications for the world in which we live. Our concern is the living implications of the mystery of Spirit-led deification, the transforming *theosis* that is the fruit of the Spirit's transforming presence. This is the spiralling process that renews us utterly and makes us new creations (Revelations 21:5), truly daughters and sons made one with the whole cosmos in the Son (Ephesians 1:10). Nothing in this process eclipses our humanity or our freedom. We are invited to cooperate freely in a synergy whose principle is the Spirit, a cooperative process in which our deepest human needs and longings are progressively met: we discover that we really are God's field, God's building, temples of the Holy Spirit (1 Corinthians 3:9). The mystery of the Spirit is the mystery of the transformation of human life, an innately spiritual mystery precisely because we are made in the image of God and cannot fully know ourselves apart from God.[26]

A spirituality that walks in the ways of Spirit is joyful, graced, communitarian; it involves ongoing and active cooperation with the Spirit.

We rediscover that we are no longer strangers and sojourners in a foreign land; we remember our Spirit-crafted dignity as citizens of God's household, holy temples in the Lord, dwelling places for God in the Spirit (Ephesians 2:19–21). We realise that we are persons in communion, made for transpersonal encounter.[27] We are persons, not just isolated individuals valued only for their capacity to consume goods and services in a commercialised world, valued only for their usefulness as producers of profitable goods and services. As persons, we are capable of love, relationality, freedom, uniqueness, divine participation: we are capable of mystery. When we are individually and communally open to the grace of the Spirit, our lives inevitably open to the spiritual disciplines of prayer and meditation, and so ethical practice and contemplation flourish, dancing together hand-in-hand. The spiritual gifts of faith, hope and love unfold, and the fruit of the Spirit matures.[28] Prayer is the way forward; contemplative prayer is where the music soars and the new song sings itself deep within us, moving us rhythmically towards God and the other, towards God and the world of which we are a part.

There is another side to a reflection on a living theology of the Spirit, a reflection grounded in the recent turn to relationality. When we speak of the dance of the human spirit and the Divine Spirit, when we speak of the inner music that supports and carries that dance into the world, we are speaking relationally. However, we need to do this in a way that recognises how easy it is to place the human and the Divine against each other in ways that undermine radical images of mutuality, cooperation, participation, and union. From the human side there is a dying to be considered, a dying to the demands of the alienated human ego, a dying into the death of Christ (Romans 6:3–11). There is a radically trans-formative process to be taken into consideration (Colossians 1:29), one that has no place for voyeuristic or addictive consumption of comforting spiritual goodies. Life in the Spirit has to be able to give an account not only of the processes of self-discipline, but of the dark night, of spiritual crisis, and of spiritual emergency if it is to have any kind of developmental rigour or integrity. There is another aspect to this: Christian spirituality as life in the Spirit is also about the process of becoming self-implicating sharers in the divine nature (2 Peter 1:4).[29]

## THE FRUIT OF THE SPIRIT

Life in the Spirit gives a self-implicating account of itself by actively and consciously walking in and progressively cultivating the *fruit of the Spirit* (Galatians 5:22–23). Fruit: another word to conjure with alongside fragrance. A Christian spiritual life achieves creative harmony to the extent that the fragrant fruit of the Spirit characterises its responses to inner and outer provocation and challenge. The fruit of the Spirit bespeaks the conscious choice of a life rich in the vigorous spiritual qualities of Christ, a choice between two opposing ways of walking in the world.[30] The characteristics of the other, dark way are clearly listed by Paul (Galatians 5:19–22) and are just as clearly at work in contemporary consumer society. We face a dilemma and a choice: the choice of how to live in the world, and the dilemma of choosing what spirit to walk by in the unfolding events and challenges of life.

A life rich in the fruit of the Spirit is a dynamically alluring life, an appealingly fragrant life, a convincingly attractive and provocative life, lived out in the realm of the Spirit. Paul explores this life through nine words organised in three sets with love at the beginning and self-control at the end. Taken together, these three-word triads unfold a vision of human perfection and completion in the grace of the Spirit. It is a life characterised by the active presence of graced love (*agapē*) that opens the way to a joy in life that then becomes a peace-making, non-divisive force for good. The fruit of the Spirit is eminently practical, touching and changing the deepest levels of human character and personality. The practical nature of the fruit of the Spirit becomes self-evident when love, joy and peace are recognised as irreplaceable facets of a dynamic mode of relating inwardly and outwardly to self, others and God. This new relational mode is grounded in a grace-empowered and a grace-supported awareness that chooses to deal with all the vagaries of existence in humanising and Spirit-led ways.

Love, joy and peace are relationally completed by a rainbow of other affirmative qualities: patience, kindness, goodness, gentleness, and self-restraint; while faithfulness to Christ protects against all forms of inner and outer deceit. These love-based qualities, and others like them identified in the new Testament, not only flesh out what a Christlike life looks like in practice; they name robust and creative forces that not only heal and bring completion to countervailing passions and drives, they also constitute a basic life stance, ways of responding creatively and compassionately to all the contrary forces in personal and social life. A life characterised by such qualities is different, counter-cultural, and in some ways even subversive of the consumer culture we have built for ourselves, a culture of imbalances, inequalities, and invisible exploitations: invisible, because the exploited ones are usually far away and out of sight. Fruit grows fragrantly to the extent that we live lives that actively *remain* in Christ (John 15:5).

Here is a third word to bring into play alongside fruit and fragrance: *remain* is used ten times in John 15. The process of remaining in Christ, with its clear echoes of authenticity, commitment and fidelity, represents a powerful challenge in a world that undermines consistency, congruence and loyalty, while supporting inconsistency, fragmentation and indifference.

The essence of Christian spirituality is defined by an active and culturally tangible process of remaining in Christ that is made manifest in a fruitful, fragrant life open to the transforming grace of the Spirit. In order to understand this process, the contemplative imagination finds ways to live the imagery of the vine and the branches in John's gospel. In order to grow in a life embodying fragrant fruit, it is necessary to remain organically connected to Christ like branches on the living vine: branches pruned and cared for by the Spirit in and through the challenges, difficulties, and transitions of life. What is at issue is the stripping away of dead and unfit wood: the addictions, habits, attitudes and diminishments that bind and impoverish the human spirit.

In his Letters, Paul identifies many of the shaping traits of fruitful and fragrant spiritual lives. The first is his beautifully poetic celebration of love and the qualities of love (1 Corinthians 13) that flow from being in Christ, the fruitfully fragrant love that is the very soul and spirit of genuine Christianity. All other worthwhile affections and passions flow from a love that longs for the fruitful completion of what is good, and true, and beautiful. Such are the loving affections and passions that flow together and make prayer possible. There is no place here for the hatreds, resentments, aversions, angers and unforgiving choices that resist love. Love multiplies itself and flows into the world of relationships as a dance that first reveals patience and then kindness: love is a harmony of a tranquilly patient kindness and a serenely kindly patience. There is no place here for the discordant notes of selfish arrogance, conceit, dismissive rudeness, resentment, or jealousy: love calmly favours what is right.

In the fruit of the Spirit, we are gifted and empowered according to the mind of Christ and in the freedom and holiness of Christ to deal appropriately not only with our own moodiness and negativity but also with the wide range of people and circumstances we perceive and experience as difficult (Galatians 5:22–23). In the healing flow of the fruit of the Spirit, projections are recognised and taken back, blame is set aside, love is embraced. Opening to the fruit of the Spirit, then, is basic to the development of a truly Christlike personality. But the fruit of the Spirit must be consciously chosen and practised if its different facets are to shimmer and refract love in the world and so become integral to our identity: if we live by means of the Spirit, then we walk in the world freely following the ways of the Spirit (Galatians 5:25); and the ways of the Spirit are always the ways of love and the integrity of love.

There can be no deep intimacy, no deep unitive knowing without love, love progressively freed from the dross of self-referred illusions and self-serving infatuations and desires. Without love even the greatest eloquence, the deepest understanding and knowledge of things, the most powerful miracle-working faith, the most radical choice of poverty, or even the desire for martyrdom ring hollow. Add to this rich vision Paul's invitation to reflect deeply on whatever is true, honourable, just, pure, lovely, gracious, excellent, and worthy of praise (Philippians 4:8); and his invitation to his community to adopt a relational style shaped by love, a style that is compassionate, tender, kind, meek, patient, forgiving, grateful, encouraging and helpful, a peaceful relational style grounded in the forbearance and harmony of love (Colossians 3:12–17). There is no end to what love can do, to the fragrant fruit it can nourish and bring into being. Love is holy because God is love and divine love is a self-giving love, a love that saves and heals (1 John 4:8 & 16). To live in such love is to live in God in whose eyes each one of us is precious, and honoured, and loved (Isaiah 43:4).

There are many examples of fruit-bearing lives in the history of Christian spirituality. They represent many different and courageous ways of remaining attuned to the mind of Christ in the realities of very different lives and times. However, the basic strategy has always been straightforward: we first come to know Christ, and then we learn and unfold what it means to be Christlike, to let Jesus live. In his Letter to the Philippians, St Paul identifies two such people and offers them to us as models, Timothy and Epaphroditus: Timothy, a leader genuinely seeking the welfare of others (Philippians 2:4, 2:7 and 2:25); Epaphroditus, a sick man putting his life at risk for others (Philippians 2:8 and 2:30). Then there is Tabitha, a woman who never tired of doing good or giving in charity (Acts 9:36); or Mary and her sister Martha, images of engaged contemplation and faith (Luke 10:38–42; John 11:1–12:8); or Euodia and Syntyche who, despite their personal disagreements, laboured side by side with Paul (Philippians 4:3); or the city woman, Mary of Magdala who is mentioned in all four gospels, friend and follower of Jesus, first witness to the resurrection. The list accompanies us down the centuries even to our own days.[31]

### ℂ Holiness and God

The fruit of the Spirit models and anticipates the future. The process is to participate in the graced shimmering of the faceted beauty of Spirit fruit as situations act like prisms and reveal their rich-hued spectrum, a beauty mothered by Lady Wisdom. Choosing to do this with awareness can be a risky business in a world that acts very differently: lives can be lost when power elites are disturbed. Each facet of Spirit fruit is sacred and reveals holy ground, the very place that allows soul to unfurl, spirit to spiral creatively and expand responsively into the world as it is. In the Christian tradition, the word that best describes this process is *holiness*. Holiness is not a comfortable word today because of the cultural baggage that has accumulated around it. Holiness names a process of participation in that sphere of existence where God's gracious power is unleashed into every level of human existence in the world, taking gendered form in the lives of women and men. Holiness is also mirrored in a range of other human characteristics: spiritual literacy is one, sexuality is another, and social role and status is a third. Each of these in turn becomes a context through which the Christ-life is revealed, explored and lived. We do not make ourselves holy; we are made holy through participation in a divinely driven process: we become holy because the Holy One has touched our lives.[32] Spirituality is what we do; holiness is what God does in us, and therein lies the mystery of holiness.

According to Donna Orsuto, holiness is God's project to bring people to share in the life of Christ in their everyday lives.[33] It is essentially a gift to people who are the primary context of its expansive realisation, even though holiness is also given spatial meaning: holy ground, sacred space. Holiness is the transformative expansiveness of God's self-gifting faithfulness in action in real human lives. In Rowan Williams's terms, holiness is God's endurance in the face of humankind's historic refusal to walk in the way of God.[34] Holiness is the graced quality of a life open to the Holy One, walking through the Spirit in the way of Christ, and thereby participating in the life of the Holy One. Holiness is what allows a person to see contemplatively through distracting appearances. It translates in practice as an expanding concern for the most vulnerable, a trait that is especially important in a world of uncaring globalisation. Holiness learns to recognise holiness in the other, including other religions, other spiritual paths. Today, holiness expands to include care of the earth, the Holy One's good gift, precisely because holiness expands to include everything that is in God's embrace. In that sense holiness is engaged contemplation, an active attitude of performative prayer that truly becomes the expansion to every aspect of life of the liberating joy of gratitude, wonder and praise.[35]

Holiness is a work of God because God alone is holy and because the Holy One is in our midst (Hosea 11:9), and is glorious in our midst (Isaiah 12:6). Holiness is a God-path and, regardless of age or level of human development or maturity, we call people who walk cooperatively with God along this path holy because of the grace of the Holy One alive in them, radiating warmly and amazingly through them. Holiness is what the Holy One is doing among us; it is God-quality shining through our lives, the Holy One acting expansively in and through us. Holiness is pre-eminently a God word, a word that names God, a word that can be defined only in terms of the being, action and relation of God. It is the word through which we come to know and acknowledge God. If we do not know God as awesomely holy, we do not know God at all: *Holy God, Holy Mighty One, Holy Immortal One, have mercy on us!* Holiness tells us that God is merciful, close, and active among us. Prayer helps us to discern the Holy One: to discern and open up to God as creator, saviour and sanctifier. Prayer is important because holiness implies integrity and compassion, and a sense of exquisite justice that opens the way to life and peace for all (Romans 8:1–6, 15–17, 22–23, 26–29).

Holiness is a covenant word: the Holy One is the Holy One of Israel. Holiness is a relational word, a word that names a Holy One who chooses and invites us to be a part of a people who are holy because God is holy (Leviticus 19:2). All other applications of the word to people and places are derivative of this foundational meaning. Holy places and holy people reflect the light of God as it refracts and sparkles in the dance of creation towards divine perfection on its journey of return to the Source. All of created reality has this potential to unveil the light of the Holy One. This is especially true of the soul with its graced capacity to reach out lovingly to all of existence and treat it all with respectful kindness. Hatred is the suppression of holiness and the forgetting of God. In the context and content of our lives, the foundation of holiness is found in the realisation that the unity and inter-relatedness of all is found in the active presence of God in the cosmos.

Holiness calls for the full integration of our humanity, of all our abilities and talents, even our weaknesses, in the service of unconditional love. In this sense, holiness has social, relational, ecological, political, economic, theological, religious, spiritual and institutional implications, and compassionate, healing love is its test. The test of a Church's institutional and interpersonal holiness is the test of its compassionate and healing love, and the way to it is a humble spirit of institutional – and clerical – metanoia, a capacity for continuing self-critique and critical self-evaluation: that is what prophecy is and what prophecy does. Churches and faith communities need structures that mediate the Holy Spirit in love, in kindness, gentleness and self-control: not in harshness, not in domination, and certainly not in emotional or sexual abuse. Holiness chooses the former and rejects the latter. Holiness brings everything together in the wholesomeness of love and, for the Christian community, Trinity is the only model. Prophetic holiness demands that we judge ourselves from the point of view of the margins. Therein lies the true risk of holiness: an openness to the other and the different, an openness to authentic transformation, an openness to the Spirit who makes it happen through our assent.

Holiness is the basis of a divinely expansive openness to all that is, and if we are to live lives touched by that expansive openness, then holiness must be rediscovered and its gift embraced even in capitalist and consumer societies desperately in need of the gentle touch of a compassionate God. Otherwise, hatred will lead to more brutality and more of its horrors.

Holiness is on the side of life, on the side of soul and spirit; it allows us to glimpse true universality and beckons to us to embrace it. Our task is to fan the embers of holiness into the living fire of love: human holiness is a commitment in life to be ablaze with the life of Christ and the Christlike quality of life that reveals holiness as the heart of existence. The Christian task in a postmodern, secular world is to carry the torch of holiness with self-implicating integrity and love. At heart, every prayer is a cry that the Holy One expand holiness in the heart of the world; free holiness from its suppression and imprisonment in the human soul and allow it to become the ground of everything in our spirituality, and all our social and relational actions. That is the path of joyful love, the path to a nobler, more equitable world. Holiness, after all, is nothing less than participation in the life and love of God, the place where the fruit of the Spirit continually blossoms and blooms in the liberty of God.

Holiness unfolds in freedom. It responds creatively and progressively to the changing nature of the times, the sensitivities and needs of the times. Attentive textual analysis makes this plain.[36] The essence of Christian liberty is the freedom to put on the mind of Christ in the world and live by it. Christian liberty is the freedom to live and walk and remain in love (John 15:12) as we choose to live lives anchored in love, and allow that life to find multi-faceted creative expression: we are called not to the dullness of slavery but to the brightness of freedom (Galatians 5:1). In the fruit of the Spirit, we let go of self-conceit, we leave aside provocative behaviours, we flee envy (Galatians 5:26): we allow our lives to be actively pruned so that we may bear much fruit, much creative and whole-making fruit in love (John 15:8); and the journey of prayer, the journey into contemplative prayer, is a privileged place for the pruning: expert pruning in times of dormancy and in times of growth.

## Prayer: Between Image and Metaphor

According to Maximus the Confessor, to pray is to be insatiably satisfied by the Inexhaustible One. According to Thérèse of Lisieux, prayer is a surge of the heart, an inward gaze, a cry of recognition and love that embraces both trial and joy. Spirit teaches us to reach insatiably beyond ourselves. This is another way of saying that in prayer we discover who we truly are, we intensify what it is to be alive in the world. In contemplative prayer we discover what it is to be known by God, a discovery that takes us into places where language quickly proves its inadequacy. Contemplative prayer takes us into places where stillness and silence speak volumes about love and the trust that holds loving relations in being, and the transformed consciousness that is the place of Spirit. The Spirit attracts us into a place, a Trinitarian place, where person and relation take on infinitely different connotations, connotations of a Unity beyond all imagining, an apophatic place of profoundly transforming significance, a place for the mystic and the prophet and those who have learnt to trust and then to surrender. Prayer teaches us that to move outside ourselves is an essential part of a transcending progress into a softer, more honest, more liberating self-awareness.

Prayer is the space where soul and spirit insatiably converge in the transforming fire of the Divine Spirit (Zechariah 13:9); and there is no hiding from the Spirit, not even on the wings of morning or under the cover of deepest darkness (Psalm 139:7–12). Soul and spirit play their parts in the interweaving worlds of prayer and meditation, and in their rich metaphorical and imaginative world. When I sit down to pray, the first person I consciously meet is myself; and then I meet the speckled state of my desire. The extent to which my life is self-referred and self-anchored will determine what is likely to happen next: a movement towards depth or a return to the safe shallows, the seemingly safe shallows of distracting convention. Prayer has to be constantly rediscovered as a movement away from self, a movement away from the predictable patterns of self-referred living and all the things that support self-referred living. To pray is to enter a world of self-transcendence in a conscious move towards others, the world, and God. To pray is also to enter a world of image and metaphor that opens vistas into the ways prayer brings our whole being, body, mind, heart, soul and spirit into the dance of life, into a transforming flow of divine healing and convergence.

The tradition of prayer is full of images and metaphors. Prayer is a harbour, an anchor, a staff, a treasure, a refuge, a reason for joy, a cause for delight, a source of wisdom, a chance for encounter, a strong wall and rampart. Prayer is spiritual sight, the way to spiritual insight. Prayer is as indispensable to the soul as water to a fish; prayer is the natural environment of spirit. Prayer is the very breath and the very light of the soul, its spiritual food and drink, nourishment brought to it on the wings of a spirit at prayer. Prayer is a weapon for a spiritual hunter, a mirror of self-knowledge, an aid and necessity for spiritual union, a relational contract. Prayer is the search for humanity's original freedom and blessing, the entry to self-transcendence, the return to a lost presence, the invitation to rediscover the original frankness of speech before God, the recognition of a profound human need.

Prayer is the entry to the Holy of Holies, a portal to the Spirit who is the soul of the soul, a way of renewal in Christ, a path to an ever-more-complete participation in Trinitarian life. Prayer is sitting at the gates of paradise, swimming in the vast ocean of divine love, walking along paths of life eternal, climbing the holy mountain. Prayer is the celebration of being with God, finding a home in God, touching the expansive holiness of God, bowing down in reverential awe before God, giving God glory and honour and praise. Prayer is an arena of grace, an arena of healing and deliverance, an arena of awareness and commitment, an arena of light and glory, an arena of utter transformation. Prayer is a return to the Source, opening the whole of life itself to the healing and transforming embrace of divine mercy: *Kyrie, eleison me* – Lord, mercy me, change every aspect of my life and personality.

Prayer is a place of epiphany, a place of ultimacy, a place of transcend-ence, a place of otherness and difference, a place where face is transformed in glory like the face of Moses. God, passing him by, presses him into a crack in a rock (Exodus 33:22) and transforms him: we intuit God after God has passed by; we see God only from behind, at the limits of our imaginative horizon. Prayer is an invocation of the Name that contains all. God's Name is recursive: it continually returns to itself, repeatedly touches the very depths of our being in its returning, begins to repeat itself in our minds until, like a stream of living water, it has drenched us through and through. Prayer is a longing, a pining, and a thirsting that arises from the dry places of soul, the weary stretches of spirit. In prayer, we begin to identify the broken cisterns we have made that hold no water; we acknowledge the ways we have turned away from the fountain of living water (Jeremiah 2:13). We become foolish makers of broken cisterns when, in the name of an illusory self-sufficient autonomy, we cease to pray. Prayer is a surge of the heart towards the well of living water, that wonderful place of rest and healing (Psalm 62:1).

Prayer is a place of worship, an acknowledging of the Holy, the Awesome, the Merciful, the Beautiful: of Sacred Splendour. To worship means to move away from self and self-love. Worship means shifting psychospiritual groundedness from self to God: when that grounding shifts, the focus of awareness changes. The veil between earth and heaven thins and sacred space beckoningly appears from the depth of God, as Spirit makes ritual and symbol, movement, language and gesture sparkle with the fire of new life. In such moments, the Divine undersong takes hold of soul-song and spirit-dance and soars through the whole of creation seeking antiphonal response and loud acclamations, alleluias rising like incense (2 Samuel 6:14–15). Why hold back in fear? Put on holiness and cross the threshold into the space of worship. Sing to the Lord. Declare God's glory (Psalm 96:1; Chronicles 16:23–30). Enter the sea of divine love. Swim in the river flowing from the temple door (Ezekiel 47:1–12). Risk being out of your depth. There is healing for the wounded heart there, and with the healing comes a gifting to sing new songs to God (Psalm 40:3).

Prayer is an act of the whole personality responding to the call to divine intimacy and its call to a challenging prophetic task (1 Samuel 3:1–18). Prayer is a discipline of entering the presence of the thrice holy

God, the Triune God, an awesome practice if truth be told. It invites us to reflect on that ancient Trinitarian prayer, the *trisagion*: Holy God, Holy Mighty One, Holy Immortal One, have mercy on us! In prayer we are challenged to plumb the Living Springs of Holiness. Prayer is joining Jesus when he cries out, 'Yes, Abba!' And when he cries out, 'Why have you abandoned me?' Prayer is entering by the narrow gate, letting go of whatever would block entry. Prayer moved by spirit is a creative thing full of rhythm and music, movement, gesture, cadence and posture: a living iconography of the body. Prayer is a gathering up of life's fragments, allowing them to be drawn into the impossible beauty of God.

Prayer is perfume for the spirit, a sweet nard, an aromatic sachet of myrrh-balm, and the Beloved a fragrant spray of henna blossoms in a fruitful vineyard (Song of Songs 1:12–14). Prayer is desiring to be with the One whom my soul loves, tracing the tracks of his flocks, seeking intimate pasture where his tent is pitched (Song of Songs 1:7–8). Prayer is a welling up of desire, so is meditation and the range of reflective practices that seek the mind of Christ (1 Corinthians 2:16): a complex goal at the best of times, but impossible without the graciously fragrant presence of the Holy Spirit. Prayer, meditation, and reflective practices, each in its own graced way, uncovers the fine point of soul as it reaches its crescendo in the gift of contemplative union and lets its symphony soar on alleluias and the high praises of God (Psalm 149:5–6).

Prayer is also a struggle with dryness, distraction and doubt. At such times, prayer means struggling to put one foot in front of the other along the right path (Psalm 23:3). The core problem is the escapist tendencies of a time-travelling, shape-shifting mind, a monkey-mind that is evasive and skittish by its own psychological nature. The healing comes when in prayer our soul experiences the vision of Psalm 99:3. Adonai is holy! Adonai is great and terrible! Praise Adonai! Is it any wonder that the inexperienced mind wants to run away? Prayer truly begins at such unitive moments when the deep chasm that lies between us and God is bridged in the empowering of Spirit. Such prayer brings us into liminal spaces, to the edges of our conscious worlds, to places where imagery and language fail and silence becomes our only recourse (Job 40:4). The task then is to keep watch at the edge, remain steadfast, continue, and be thankful (Colossians 4:2).

Praise is music to the soul's ears, the expression of the spirit's joy: where hope abounds praise soars (Psalm 71:5–8). Praise is difficult because it is a complete movement away from self-interest. It is a movement beyond self and self-consciousness. Praise is a sacrifice to God, the fruit of lips that acknowledge God's name (Hebrews 13:15). Prayer is a refusal to shrink away from the challenges of life, be they inner or outer challenges: through prayer we make life our own and take responsibility for it. Prayer is performative: its cognitive and affective dimensions are completed in action and enactment. There is a long tradition that links prayer and performance: the praying, and the doing promised in the praying. In some forms of prayer, the link is obvious; liturgical prayer makes it quite clear. In liturgy, the prayer is the action, the ritual the performance: the Eucharistic prayers make Christ present; in the sacrament of reconciliation, the prayer of absolution is the act of absolving.

In other forms of prayer, too, the same link is to be respected. To pray for justice contains a call to act justly; to pray for compassion is to act compassionately; to pray for peace is to become a peacemaker; to pray for healing is to become in some sense a healer, however wounded and uncertain, at least a carer, a compassionate one, a listener, a supporting presence. The performative nature of prayer makes the converging of soul and spirit evident in the transformative creativity that is set in motion: the empathy and understanding, the forgiving and reconciling, the caring and the supporting, the welcoming and the liberating, the discerning and the walking. The performative nature of prayer is there as action in praise of God, in the ethical quality of a life engaged with God. The performative nature of prayer is there in the contemplative quality of a life listening to the echoes of God in the depths of the world's pain, in learning how to act in favour of the world's soul and its saving emancipation. It is there in the contemplative quality of lives becoming holy ground, living stones, sacred spaces open to the gifting of new life.

More importantly, the performative heart of prayer is in the setting aside of time for it; time to pray, time to meditate, time for ritual and sacrament, time for deepening awareness, time for God: time for Wisdom to come alive within and set ripples of change flowing in the rhythms of the world. The worth of prayer is in the doing of it, not in thinking about it or even in planning to do it. The worth is in the performance. If prayer has worth, it flows into and becomes visible in the doing, in the myriad practices that give it expression. If not, then nothing happens. Is nothing happening? What are you doing? Prayer is not a wish; it is a deed: a life-embracing life-changing deed. Do you do it? The worth of a life is in its living, the worth of a life of prayer is in the changed living it delivers into being like a skilled midwife: and prayer is learnt and grows strong in the doing and the living, it grows with exercise and discipline as all worthwhile things do.

The word performance is used here as an action word: verbs are performative, they are action words. To say that the worth of prayer is in the performance confronts us with prayer as a verb, as living action. Prayer is to be lived: it is about acting justly, loving tenderly, walking with integrity in the world before God, self and others. The saying of prayers out of duty or obligation is not really what prayer is about. Prayer is a free choice built on the conviction of its necessity in a life attending to God and the human predicament. Prayer not felt as a need, a life-changing, world-changing need, has missed the point. The spiritual worth of prayer whatever its form is in the lives it changes. Prayer is a choice, a statement of intent, a choosing to honour the sacred dimensions of existence and enter the domain of God; it is a longing and a choosing to dwell consciously and explicitly for a time in thin places, entering the courts of the Lord (Psalm 84:2). In prayer, we welcome God, we keep company with God, and God's Spirit weaves love songs and wedding dances with ours that rise to the heart of Trinity. Prayer is taking a sunbath in the warm glow of divine love.

Prayer is an exalting of God grounded in the integrity of honest self-knowledge and self-awareness. It is aware of the vast gulf between God and us and understands that the crossing of the void is God's gift to us in Christ. The Spirit lifts us through it on wings of quiet prayer. Prayer, after all, is the recognition of God's holiness and supremacy, a stepping along God's way, a turning towards God's tracks in human history and in all created reality. Prayer is a responding to the unique grace God has given to each one of us, the new name on a white stone, the new, the secret, identity hidden in God (Revelations 2:17). Prayer is the accepting of this name, the honouring of it and the growing into it, letting it come alive in the worlds in which we live: relational, social, creational, spiritual. In the final analysis prayer is a matter of justice.

Prayer is an encounter with wonder, transcending the cloud of unknowing, walking in paths of silent music, glorying in a bright unknowing, seeking with the heart and will, breathing with the lungs of spirit, knowing that all manner of things will be well, calling on God with a loving heart, serving a hidden God. Prayer is above all entering into Trinitarian love: in the Spirit gazing on God with the eyes of Christ, growing in the fidelity of a Moses or a Julian of Norwich holding a single-minded focus. According to Theophane the Recluse, prayer, as the lungs and breathing of the spirit, serves as the barometer that measures the rise and fall of spiritual awareness and commitment. Remember that in the Hebrew Bible the barrenness of the land was always a spiritual barometer of Israel's fidelity and faith, just as our spiritual barrenness is a measure of ours. Prayer is a measure of our true core value.

Prayer is lungs, breath, barometer; its absence signals spiritual morbidity. The lesson is clear: without prayer the human spirit suffers and falls prey to infirmities that soon touch the other domains of being. Prayer is spiritual self-care, the way to spiritual well-being.[37] The challenge in prayer is to chant with the psalmist not only that we are wonderfully and awesomely made, but also that we are known utterly by God as wonderfully and awesomely made (Psalm 139:14). Prayer allows us to plumb the healing depths of such a loving knowing. Embracing it in prayer sees our spiritual barometer set fair. Prayer is the dance of a Christlike life: dance it well in the Spirit and let your spirit sing, rejoicing as you weave your way into the heart of God (Philippians 4:4).

### Appendix: The Etymology of Spirit

The terms that establish the meaning of the English word *spirit*, the Hebrew *ruach*, the Greek *pneuma*, and the Latin *spiritus* share a double-edged reference to wind and breath, like spirit's sibling word, *soul*. This etymology gives the word spirit two metaphorical meanings that are clearly evident in the Hebrew Bible. The first, to do with the wind, evokes images of suddenness and power, Spirit touching people's lives and empowering them for great tasks in the history of Israel. This usage answers the question: what makes ordinary people capable of great and charismatic tasks as judges and prophets in Israel? Something similar is at work in the lives of great artists (Exodus 31:1–11). The second has to do with living, life-giving breath. It evokes vibrant images of life and intimacy: what makes us living, breathing human beings; breath-spirit is our central living reality either as individuals or communities. The most vivid story about it in the Hebrew Bible is found in the vision of the dry bones in Ezekiel 37: breath came into them and they lived.[38]

In the Hebrew Bible, the word *ruach* (spirit) appears three hundred and seventy eight times and is translated in the Greek Septuagint translation as *pneuma* two hundred and seventy seven times. The word means breath, wind, air, the life principle. It also describes a human disposition, emotion, mood, thought, inclination or determination; and it names the Spirit of God. It is noteworthy that the other Hebrew word for breath, *neshamah*, is also translated by *pneuma* in the Greek. What is clear is that the Greek Septuagint translation of the Hebrew Bible mirrors Hebrew rather than Greek usage. However, in Greek usage, *pneuma*/spirit was gradually used metaphorically to indicate spiritual reality, and then, in Stoicism, *pneuma* was applied to God. Thus *pneuma* has both divine and human referents: the Spirit of God and the human spirit; and there are human references to soul, mind, and conscience. The *pneuma* references to God include the creation of the cosmos, the relationship between God and the world, and the relationship between God and humankind.[39]

The New Testament shows us how the anthropological and theological uses of *pneuma* continued to emerge.[40] This is particularly evident in St Paul's understanding of the human person. As well as soul (*psyché*) and spirit (*pneuma*) with their overlapping meanings, Paul pairs four other overlapping terms that complete his understanding of the human person: body (*soma*) and flesh (*sarx*), mind (*nous*) and heart (*kardia*). Body represents the human person as an embodied, interactive being; flesh represents the world of human limitation, including ethical limitation. References to mind remind us that we are thinking beings; and heart reminds us of our inner being, that we are capable of true depth. Paul also writes of the human person embodying natural life (*soma psychikos*) and spiritual life (*soma pneumatikos*) (1 Corinthians 15:44; 1 Corinthians 2:14–15).[41] In one of his blessings, Paul interestingly brings spirit, soul and body together in ways that show us the nuanced vision of the human person at work in his worldview (1 Thessalonians 5:23). By implication, when spirit and soul are marginalised from our thinking about ourselves, we radically impoverish our human self-understanding.

*Soma* (body, used fifty times) and *sarx* (flesh, used ninety one times) are the dominant pair in St Paul's writing. *Soma* names created human kind and embodied existence: it provides the social and ecological basis of Christian spirituality. Accurately understood as one dimension of humanity among others, this broad view of body prevents spirituality from becoming dualistic. *Sarx* is a more complex, controversial term in Paul's usage. The meaning of the word ranges from the stuff of the body to a condition of hostility to God. The spectrum of meaning includes the stuff we are made of, human relationships and needs, weaknesses and limitations, imperfections and corruptions, and the potential for complete hostility to all things spiritual. However, *sarx*/flesh is not to be separated from embodied human personhood or set against it for the simple reason that all Paul's words are descriptive of the unitary human person. They are 'I am' words not the 'I have' words of common English usage: I am my body, I am my flesh and all it entails, I am my mind, I am my heart, I am my soul, I am my spirit, I am my desires, I am my weaknesses, I am my limitations, I am my abilities. I am all of them and more than them.[42]

These three pairs of words help us to understand that we are spirit and nature and that nature is the realm of our freedom and responsibility, the space where we encounter necessity: the necessity of nature itself in all its forms to be cared for and protected. Body is our way of being heart, mind and soul in nature and society. There is nothing here that conflicts with the meaning of spirit. The problem of the human predicament does not arise with either body or spirit; it arises with the drama of the human struggle for power and knowledge and the power that knowledge brings. What is then revealed is a cunning, exploitive, other-diminishing intelligence engaged in a deceptive search for a life without limits: without nature, without others, without God. Hostility to spirit, a lack of sensitivity to its needs and conditions, is not surprising in such contexts and encounters: power has a price and alienation is its currency. The horrors and tyrannies of the twentieth century point accurately in just such a direction.[43]

The challenge for spiritual accompaniment or spiritual therapy arises today when the self-referred needs and claims of *sarx*/flesh, its fragilities and hostilities run counter to the self-transcending needs and conditions of *pneuma*/spirit; or when the self-referring needs of *kardia*/heart run in similarly opposing directions. Imagine what happens when the claims and needs of the alienated ego are added to such a potentially volatile mix: the symptomology of spiritual crisis is close to hand. It is to resolve this complex of opposing forces, needs, states and conditions that the dark night experience begins to unfold. Within this dark and painful process, the potential oppositions between *sarx* and *kardia* to *pneuma* are gradually healed and dissolved and an integrated union forged. Paul's vision is not dualist as so many commentators on Western spirituality seem to think as they embrace an Oriental turn. The standard dualism of body and soul we are accustomed to in the West derives from Aristotle rather than Hebrew or foundational Christian thinking. On the evidence, Paul's analysis belongs firmly within the unitary vision of his Hebrew antecedents.

## THEMES AND QUESTIONS FOR FURTHER REFLECTION

1. Do you experience the Creative Spirit active in life? What evidence have you?
2. How does the Creative Spirit challenge self-referred stances? Identify the ways people respond to or resist the forces of creativity.
3. Identify the other significant forces that move people. How do they open people to the holy and the sacred?
4. What evidence suggests that people's lives are authentically touched by the holy and the sacred?

## FURTHER READING

Donna Orsuto, *Holiness* (London and New York: Continuum, 2006).

NOTES:
1. Mortimer Ostow, *Spirit, Mind, & Brain: A Psychoanalytic Examination of Spirituality & Religion* (New York: Columbia University Press, 2006) 2, on spirituality and religion see 52–111.
2. Brian J. Zinnbauer et al., 'Religion and Spirituality: Unfuzzying the Fuzzy' in *Journal for the Scientific Study of Religion* 36 (1997) 4, 549–564.
3. See Wolfhart Pannenberg, *Toward a Theology of Nature: Essays on Science and Faith.* Edited by Ted Peters (Louisville, KY: Westminster/John Knox Press, 1993) 151.
4. Diogenes Allen and Eric O. Springsted, *Spirit, Nature, and Community: Issues in the Thought of Simone Weil* (Albany, NY: State University of New York Press, 1994), 41 and 73–76.

5. See Simone Weil. *Waiting on God*. Translated by Emma Crauford. (London: Routledge and Kegan Paul Ltd, 1951) 150–152.

6. Diogenes Allen and Eric O. Springsted, *Spirit, Nature, and Community: Issues in the Thought of Simone Weil*. op. cit. 82–91.

7. See Siân Miles, ed., *Simone Weil: An Anthology*. Edited with an Introduction (New York: Grove Press, 1986) 72.

8. David Hay, *Something There: The Biology of the Human Spirit* (London: Darton, Longman and Todd, 2006) 53–75.

9. Ibid. 69.

10. See, for example, David Hay, *Something There* op. cit. 89–90.

11. Michael Gelven, *Spirit and Existence: A Philosophical Inquiry into the Meaning of Spiritual Existence* (Notre Dame, IN: Notre Dame University Press, 1990) 6.

12. See ibid. 22–44.

13. See ibid. 7.

14. See ibid. 47–178.

15. See ibid. 202–264.

16. See for example, *Song of Songs* 2: 1–3; 4: 13–14; 5: 1; *Esther* 2: 12; *Exodus* 30: 23; 34: 28; *1 Kings* 10: 10; *Isaiah* 35: 1. See also *Matthew* 6: 28; *Luke* 12: 27.

17. See Edith M. Humphrey, *Ecstasy and Intimacy: When the Holy Spirit Meets the Human Spirit* (Grand Rapids/Cambridge: Eerdmans Publishing, 2006) 1–10. See also Steven G. Smith, *The Concept of the Spiritual: An Essay in First Philosophy* (Philadelphia: Temple University Press, 1988); Michael Welker, ed., *The Work of the Spirit: Pneumatology and Pentecostalism* (Grand Rapids/Cambridge: Eerdmans Publishing, 2006); Michael Welker, *God the Spirit*. Translated by John F. Hoffmeyer (Minneapolis: Fortress Press, 1994); Kathryn Tanner, 'Workings of the Spirit: Simplicity or Complexity' in Michael Welker, ed., *The Work of the Spirit* op. cit. 87–105; Denis Edwards, *Breath of Life: A Theology of the Creator Spirit* (Maryknoll, NY: Orbis Books, 2004).

18. See *Redemptoris Missio*, 28–29.

19. See Denis Edwards, *Breath of Life* op. cit. 50–65.

20. See Gerald G. May, *Will and Spirit: A Contemplative Psychology* (New York: HarperSanFranciso, 1987) 1–21 & 52–68.

21. Ibid., 124.

22. Simone Weil, *The Notebooks of Simone Weil* Translated by Arthur Wills (London: Routledge, 2004) 282.

23. See John Polkinghorne, 'The Hidden Spirit and the Cosmos' in Michael Welker, ed., *The Work of the Spirit* op. cit. 169-182. See also his *Faith in the Living God: A Dialogue* (London: SPCK, 2001) 97.

24. Elizabeth Teresa Groppe, *Yves Congar's Theology of the Holy Spirit* (Oxford: Oxford University Press, 2004), 3–4.

25. Ibid. 13, 172.

26. Ibid. 9–10, 85–92.

27. Ibid. 112–113, 132–135.

28. Ibid. 150–151, 169.

29. See F. LeRon Schults, *Reforming Theological Anthropology: After the Philosophical Turn to Relationality* (Grand Rapids/Cambridge: Eerdmans Publishing, 2003) 88–91. See also Stanley J. Grenz, *Reason for Hope: The Systematic Theology of Wolfhart Pannenberg.* Second Edition (Grand Rapids/Cambridge: Eerdmans Publishing, 2005) 131–132.

30. See Frank J. Matera, *Galatians* (Collegeville: The Liturgical Press, 1992) 198–212; James D. G. Dunn, *The Theology of Paul the Apostle* (Grand Rapids/Cambridge: Eerdmans Publishing, 1998) 661–665; David S. Dockery, 'Fruit of the Spirit' in Gerald F. Hawthorne, Ralph P. Martin, Daniel G. Reid, eds, *Dictionary of Paul and His Letters* (Downers Grove, IL & Leicester: InterVarsity Press, 1993) 316–319.

31. See Charles B. Cousar, *Reading Galatians, Philippians, and 1 Thessalonians: A Literary and Theological Commentary* (Macon, GA: Smyth & Helwys, 2001) 161–163.

32. See for example, John Webster, *Holiness* (London: SCM Press, 2003).

33. Donna Orsuto, *Holiness* (London and New York: Continuum, 2006) 9.

34. Rowan Williams, *Open to Judgment: Sermons and Addresses* (London: Darton, Longman and Todd, 1994) 136.

35. See Donna Orsuto, *Holiness* op. cit. 181–206.

36. See Irene Visser and Helen Wilcox, eds, *Transforming Holiness: Representations of Holiness in English and American Literary Texts* (Leuven, Paris, Dudley, MA: Peeters 2006).

37. See St Theophane the Recluse, *The Spiritual Life and How to be Attuned to It.* Translated by Alexandra Dockham. Second Edition (Platina & Forestville, CA: St Herman of Alaska Brotherhood, 1996).

38. See T. J. Goringe, *Discerning Spirit: A Theology of Revelation* (London: SCM Press, 1990) 4–6.

39. Marie E. Isaacs, *The Concept of Spirit: A Study of Pneuma in Hellenistic Judaism and its Bearing on the New Testament* (London: Heythrop Monographs, 1976) 1–64, 150–156.

40. See ibid. 65–145.

41. See Donald J. Goergen, OP, *Fire of Love: Encountering the Holy Spirit* (New York/Mahwah, NJ: Paulist Press, 2006) 1–17

42. For a considered overview of Paul's terminology see James D. G. Dunn, *The Theology of Paul the Apostle* op. cit. 51–78.

43. See Clifford J. Green, *Bonhoeffer: A Theology of Sociality.* Revised Edition (Grand Rapids/Cambridge: Eerdmans Publishing, 1999) 197–203.

## CHAPTER 9

*Mapping Definitions of Spirituality*

*The map is not the terrain, but ...*

## INTRODUCTION

In a fragmented world producing fragmented identities it is easy to see how a life-subject like spirituality would inevitably provide evidence of a diverging excess of ideas: the emergence of a pervasive postmodern consumer label. The word spirituality has become largely unspecifiable, and the cornucopia of literature offers a superabundance of ideas, images, practices and discourses about our subject, often with little cross-communication between them. The one thing that can be said with certainty is that contemporary spirituality is going through a monumental change that defies definitional consensus. The image of the ancient Tower of Babel comes to mind, such is the bewildering variety of voices competing for attention in the contemporary spiritual forum. A clutter of clammering possibilities, rendered rootless and disconnected from the spiritual, philosophical, religious and creational traditions that gave them birth, confronts us. Critical approaches seeking congruence win few friends in a consumer-led world where underlying spiritual assumptions and presuppositions are rarely identified. Exploring the world of definitions will help to reveal these underlying assumptions and bring some of them at least into the light of reasoned awareness.

## THE NATURE AND TASK OF DEFINITIONS

Dancing with definitions of spirituality requires subtle and imaginative reflection, a contemplative attunement to much that is left unsaid, taken for granted; and never more so than in a time of popular definitional contestation and confusion. Definitions ideally create representative environments within which the primary elements of a spirituality are given imaginatively descriptive and technically precise expression. There is also a sense in which good definitions of spirituality resemble metaphors: both share the qualities of helpfulness and modulation that add something poetic, something almost musical to the spiritual processes, as well as the spiritual situations and goals they are intended to describe or map. Good definitions of spirituality are like good musical scores, open to breadth, depth and subtle tonality. Yet, just as the test of a good musical score is in its performance, so the test of a good definition of spirituality is in its closeness to transformative spiritual experience in real life situations. A good definition is also like an elegant architectural design, the fruit of a precise, well-trained and creative imagination. Again, the test is not in the artistic and technical elegance of the design and its simulation but in the elegance of the building that arises from it, its hospitality to human life and the conviviality and warmth of the living context it provides.

A good definition is also like a good story line. But its creative potential is only fulfilled if the story line develops and comes to life in a book, on the stage, in a musical, or in a film. Good definitions are like precious vines cared for by a skilled and knowledgeable vine-dresser. Yet again, the test is not in how the vines look after their careful pruning but in the fruit they produce and the quality of wine that comes from the fruit, be it a rich and classic blend or an aromatic single varietal. The map is not the terrain. The definition of spirituality is not the spiritual life. Definitions are representations, models, maps of reality. They call for journeyers and seekers, singers and dancers, builders and the crafters of things. And just as maps remain open to dispute, definitions of spirituality remain open to living and creative interpretation.

According to Val Plumwood, definitions of spirituality often harbour interesting confusions.[1] The first has to do with the difference between necessary and sufficient conditions. The second has to do with definitions of spirituality that focus on the sacred and its oppositional vectors. The third has to do with the defining stress on interiority or social engagement. Once it is granted that spirituality is necessary for a full life, the question of its sufficiency to achieve such fullness inevitably arises: necessity is not the same as sufficiency. The question becomes more complex when spirituality is defined in terms of the access to and the pursuit of meaning, value, vision, and deep purpose. Each of these themes raises anthropological, theological and philosophical questions that in turn need to be evaluated for their positive and negative spiritual or world-view potentials. World-denying or body-denying visions are obvious examples. If an approach is taken from the perspective of the human sciences, similar evaluations need to be made precisely because definitions are not value-free or neutral. Is something akin to psychological development intended?[2]

Authentic spirituality has to grapple not just with how spirituality is necessary for a better life; it also has to engage with all the structures and expressions that hinder or block the attainment of a better life. Something similar is necessary when spirituality is defined from the perspective of the sacred because such definitions tend to be oppositional. If we speak of holy or of sacred ground are we implicitly suggesting ground that is neither? This in turn raises the question of how we perceive the sacred or the holy. Are these terms used in immanent or transcendent ways? Does the sacred have this-worldly or other-worldly references? Does transcendence refer to a supreme being, a higher power, God, a greater self, or something more from which a sense of power and meaning flows? Does transcendence refer to the capacity to go beyond egocentric and self-referred perspectives in a move towards wholeness?

Like maps, definitions are about locating key features in a landscape and noting how they are linked. Definitions give us the basic rules for navigating the spiritual life and giving it coherent expression; they focus attention on the essentials and make them public. They situate spirituality in the public sphere. However, in the defining process spirituality risks being rendered abstract; and in a consumer culture this may suggest that spirituality has become a branded commodity, neatly packaged and ready for consumption: not all contemporary spirituality resiliently resists such depersonalising processes. It may also be argued that spirituality, like the true, the good, and the beautiful, or like religion and proper names, or even death, is largely indefinable except, perhaps, on the most basic of dictionary terms.[3] The advantage of a good definition lies in its capacity to name spirituality, identify it, describe it, and call core aspects of it into critical focus. The disadvantage is that even good definitions are tempted to view spirituality as an object removed from the lives of real people.

Good definition lies at the heart of good spiritual discourse; but the art is often bedevilled by circular thinking that takes too much for granted; thus many definitions end up telling us very little. Take this obviously circular definition: *Spirituality is the art of living a spiritual life.* This definition simply claims that spirituality is spiritual, but tells us nothing of what that means. Too much is taken for granted; too much is left ambiguously unsaid. Compare this to environmentalist John Feehan's poetic view of the spiritual significance of the dipper bird and its slow, soft warbling. Feehan writes, "The role of each and every species is not merely ecological, it is spiritual; it is a unique shout of joy, affirmation, worship that no other species can give."[4] The definition of spirituality revealed here is much more informative. Spirituality is intimately linked to how a unique ecological role is fulfilled in a way that softly and uniquely warbles joy, affirmation and worship in places where waters flow and splash and fall. There is an echo here of the great St Basil who held that even inanimate things have received a voice from God, a voice that proclaims the Creator in a single shout; and Basil also invites us to listen to the fish![5]

Spirituality is expressive of our very nature, its landscapes and the life forms that share them with us.

Problems also occur when we use words such as *meaning* or *value* in definitions of spirituality. Too often their references are simply presumed without attending to problems of complexity, or the way use of such words can branch off in different directions, especially when themes of personal or social identity and relationships enter the frame. For example, do *meaning* or *value* refer to facts or interactive experiences in which processes, events and concepts interweave and dance to natural and spiritual rhythms? Or do they respond only to historical facts and private usages? Are they quasi-concepts that make other modes of thought and definition possible? Contemporary spirituality incorporates dynamically subjective dimensions that evade concise, tight, objectifying descriptions. This is an elusive quality spirituality shares with experience. The implication is that spiritual experience has its own rationality, coherence and value, its own claim to truth. Interestingly, the concept *experience* is also a late arrival in Western thought, dating back only as far as Friedrich Schleiermacher (1768–1834). Spirituality and experience are evolving words we need to handle with care lest the search for precision leads to impoverishment and reductionism.[6] For all that, definitions are part of the world in which we live and so we must acknowledge the challenges they represent.

### ⓒ The challenge of quasi-concepts
Quasi-concepts are useful tools when considering definitions of spirituality and spiritual discourse. Quasi-concepts come in a variety of forms: as concepts whose meanings have been destabilised; or loose concepts whose meanings have not yet been stabilised; or broad concepts that are only partially understood from their verbal context; or concepts whose meanings are undecidable; or whose existence has to be presupposed for other things to be understood. *Justice* is a perfect example. How can ethics be constructed without it? *Atheism* is another useful example: its meaning depends on the understandings of theism and religiosity it actually contests and the accuracy of these understandings. The same is true of the concepts *spirituality* and *spiritual*, particularly in postmodern contexts. How many of us fully understand what these concepts actually mean? There are at least two reasons for this: first, neither word can be understood without reference to *spirit* whose existence must be presupposed; second, the meanings of both words are vigorously contested.

Quasi-concepts offer at best partial definitions and descriptions: if there is a storyline it will be either incomplete or non-existent, consisting just of strings of words. When quasi-concepts are used in definitions of spirituality contesting voices inevitably arise because of the incomplete and limited nature of such definitions. Quasi-concepts also name situations where the rhetoric of spirituality replaces engaged action, situations where the spiritual never moves beyond a fine turn of phrase, where there is no self-implicating commitment, and concept is confused with event. Definitions that make uncritical use of metaphors, images, quasi-concepts, and de-traditioned vocabularies whose meanings are in flux and are unconnected to sustained compassionate action may find themselves seeking an elusive goal. People may simply decide that they know what the operative meanings of *spiritual* and *spirituality* are and cease examining underlying assumptions, contentedly and uncritically relying on the links between words and concepts stored in memories, while all the time misunderstanding the essential nature of spirituality and its necessary experiential linkages to creative and emancipatory action.

€ *Spirituality as symbolic and social interaction*
Spirituality also consists of many layers of symbolic and social interaction. Symbolic and social interaction theories are powerful tools for anyone looking at contemporary spirituality. They help us understand that people who engage in spiritual quests are creating meaningful relational worlds for themselves; they are not simply reacting to life, they are engaged in generating what they perceive to be creative alternatives to what is consensually on offer. Interaction theories suggest that meaning systems and social relationships impact self-narratives and the self-definitions, symbolic meaning systems, locations, processes, projections and lifestyles that give them expression. Similar forces are at work in spirituality, especially in contexts where group values influence such dynamics as religious or spiritual disengagement, continuity or engaged action.

Interactive theories are concerned with human interactions and growth, with roles and enactments, and the unfolding of shared and co-constructed social meanings and perceptions; so is spirituality. Symbolic interaction theory views people as proactive, cooperative and influenced by goals. Something similar may be said about spirituality. Spirituality is made up of fields of interactions, but not all of them favour growth and therein lies the challenge: valid tools of discernment are required. Interaction theories are helpful at this point because they help us focus attention on the intellectual, emotional, and non-verbal components and expressions of spirituality, and they are also helpful in drawing attention to questions of experiential intensity and transformational learning, as well as the communication and networking behaviours that increasingly characterise the new spiritualities. Interactive theories also help us to grapple with what is indefinite about contemporary spiritual experiences, interactions and events by focusing attention on evocative images that help us understand what they are.[7]

C *Mapping definitions*

Map is defined here as an explanatory and exploratory model of the inner and outer processes, and the causal and reality concerns of spiritual experience as it emerges in practice. They are normally designed to identify and orient engaged spiritual practice, and to shape critical reflection on them. Spiritual maps come in a variety of forms, some visual, others discursive. Typical visual maps include the *mandorla* (Christian), the *mandala* (Tibetan Buddhist), *medicine wheels* (Native American), and the kabbalistic *etz hayim* or tree of life (Judaism).[8] The Greek labyrinth is another example of a map that is achieving interspiritual and interfaith popularity. Discursive maps are found everywhere in spiritual conversation, formal discourse and writing. From an academic point of view it is important to distinguish between first-order and second-order definitions of spirituality. A good first-order definition will be experientially descriptive and imaginatively engaging, narrated by a person who has had a spiritual experience. A good second-order definition, based on an analysis of first-order descriptions, will be ideally precise.

The difficulty is that spirituality is interpreted through theistic, transpersonal, naturalistic, mainstream, minority, esoteric, contemplative, mystical, transcendental, secular, agnostic, atheistic or monistic lenses. In effect, we need a second map, one that identifies and accommodates the broad spectrum of interpretative lenses that are currently in use and the equally broad range of definitions they generate. What is needed is a tool versatile enough to map a wide variety of definitions across a broad spectrum according to their religious or secular purposes and referents. An essential component of such a tool is a firm statement about the non-neutrality of definitions, models and maps: they are all constructed on the basis of operative assumptions and presuppositions. The proposed map (see p. 271) places hard definitions with precise religious content at one end of the spectrum and hard secular definitions at the other. The spectrum has space for softer, non-religiously and non-secularly specific definitions towards the middle. Here is a summary listing of what might appear on such a map today.

- Theological, biblical or confessional definitions.
- Sociological definitions.
- Definitions grounded in religious studies.
- Psychological and psychotherapeutic definitions.
- Social work definitions.
- Nursing definitions.
- Medical definitions.
- Definitions appropriate to behavioural medicine.
- Definitions grounded in occupational therapy.

- Definitions arising within the world of education.
- Definitions serving the needs of the business community.
- Definitions influenced by Enlightenment philosophy mirroring the modern secular rejection of religion but open to spiritual qualities. Marxist, atheist, and secular humanist spiritualities are examples.

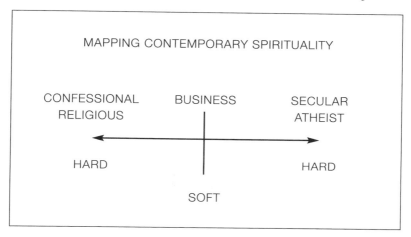

Consideration has also to be given to several other frames of difference.
- Consider softer, more diffuse, first-order colloquial definitions and compare them to the more precise second-order technical definitions that serve academic and scientific purposes.
- Consider definitions that focus on more inward forms of spirituality and compare them to those concerned with the ways in which spirituality is expressed in cooperative communal and public arenas.
- Consider engaged spiritualities and spiritualities that are defined in terms of social, ecological or emancipatory activism.
- Consider the questions raised by the spiritualities of children and adolescents, and those specific to other age cohorts.
- Then consider the potentially narcissistic nature of inner-focused, self-referred spirituality: for example, how is this potential pathology to be identified and measured?

Within confessional contexts further definitional lenses arise:
- Fundamentalist
- Traditionalist
- Conservative
- Critical orthodox
- Critical apophatic
- Liberal

Similar differentiations need to be made at the secular-materialist end of
the spectrum:
- Atheist
- Autonomy-based
- Character-based
- Civic spiritualities
- Culture-based
- Ecological/environmental
- Ethics-based
- Feminist
- Gender-based
- Liberational
- Marxist
- Nature-based
- Non-religious
- Peace oriented
- Prosperity oriented
- Psychologically oriented
- Secular-humanist
- Value-based
- Well-being oriented
- Work-based

Further questions about definitions also arise. How are spiritual
practitioner goals to be taken into consideration? What methodologies
will allow commonalities and differences to be identified and respected?
For example, definitions arising in medicine tend to be more clinical in
focus and more open to rigorous double-blind experiment and measurement
than those arising in the human sciences where quantitative and qualitative
research and measurement methods are favoured. On the other hand, some
of the more interesting work in spirituality today is emerging in business
contexts where efforts to counter alienating work practices by developing
best-practice models is underway, often using ethnographic fieldwork
methodologies. This raises other questions. What role does geographic,
cultural and economic location play in mapping and defining spirituality:
East-West, North-South, rural-urban, poor-prosperous?

Does spirituality have an essential role to play in forging new social
meanings and action-strategies for times of social upheaval and normative
uncertainty?[9] Is spiritual well-being significant in the quality of life of
older people?[10] How are humanity and personhood to be understood
while mapping and defining contemporary spirituality: in terms of species,
or organically, or functionally, or behaviourally, or morally, or psychologically, or sociologically, or theologically, or philosophically? How are

we to understand the impact of personality? How do individuals and groups negotiate connections through the spectrum of spiritual practices, rituals, beliefs, values, and the contexts, spaces and locations where these are celebrated? It seems that in Western contexts today the question 'what is spirituality?' has many different answers arising in many different contexts, and serving a variety of different purposes. In lush fields where many definitions bloom, definitions themselves need to be discerned, analysed and critically evaluated.

In examining a definition it is important to remember that spirituality also represents the construction of a coherent worldview, the creation of a horizon of meaning, a marking of a lifestyle signed by relational consistency and ethical integrity, a search for empowerment and connectedness, a search for a life lived in the presence of God, or a life lived on consistently secular grounds. All of these suggest practices, expectations and expressive behaviours that identify distinct patterns of choice. Such choices will invite potentially creative and emancipatory or lacklustre and restrictive consequences. At the same time, some kind of working or stipulated definition implicitly or explicitly influences every writer and practitioner of spirituality. Students of the subject need to be alert to this and reflect critically on its implications.

## ⊂ Comparing definitions

For example, writing in a theological context, I might wish to define spirituality as follows: *Spirituality is the continuing personal transformation of an individual or group of persons responding to the call of God to live fuller, more ethically creative lives.* This definition is clearly theological and doctrinal with an emphasis on transformation, responsiveness, relationality, social mind-edness and God. Another definition may approach the question from a different perspective: *Spirituality is a stepping beyond the narcissistic self to embrace the transforming Source of life and the personal and social consequences of that liberating and healing choice.* This definition brings a different set of referents to bear, referents that are more obviously psychospiritual and polarised, contrast-ing two forms of human life and two potential outcomes: one potentially pathological, the other healing and liberating.

In the second example, the nature of the Source of life and spirituality is not immediately clear. Are we operating in a graced or in a consciousness tradition? Consider for a moment that the listener follows a consciousness tradition and the one who offers the definition follows a graced path. Identifying and clarifying the layers of meaning and imagery that mould the definition calls for respectful, empathic, contemplative listening. In another conversation the Source could be understood in a naturalistic or theistic way depending on context and a practitioner's expressed or operative assumptions. Whatever the case, reverence is called for: faith in either circumstance represents an active, open, dynamic state reaching out to embrace reality, and in so doing takes on a very personal, very delicate timbre. The faith a person lives by merits a softer, more deferential acknowledgment, especially from those who do not share it.

Nevertheless, both definitions are potentially persuasive. It would be an interesting experiment to bring the two examples together. Each definition brings forth significant themes capable of opening up an array of possible experiences, problems, helps and hindrances, particularities of various kinds, events, processes, images, self and divine representations and the like. On the other hand, each definition is limited and boundaried, location is not addressed; yes, but the full range of potential themes encountered in contemporary Western spirituality is far from explicit, not least the search for meaning and the identification of an unmistakable ethical praxis. There is a related question. Does spiritual tradition have a shaping force today? What impact does it have on the new spiritualities, especially those emerging in seemingly de-traditioned locations? The word *spirituality* names more than ideas; it more significantly refers to what enlivens people.[11] It should not be a surprise, then, that the word *spirituality* is used in all sorts of ways and in a variety of contexts, or that it serves a range of ideological purposes that actively seek to avoid definitional rigour. Once again, it is important to recall that no definition is entirely 'innocent', and that each becomes the bearer of some form of ideological stance that satisfies an author's own purposes.[12]

⸿ *Further challenges*
Apart from what is happening in actual usage, there is another challenge to be faced when considering definitions of spirituality. This challenge has to do with the contours and interests that influence and mould the formulation of definitions themselves. A summary review will adequately highlight the fundamental difficulties. In this regard, it is necessary to identify the disciplinary lens through which a possible definition is approached. Fourteen such approaches to definition surface immediately in a far from exhaustive list:

- Behavioural approaches
- Business approaches
- Cognitive approaches
- Confessional approaches
- Developmental approaches
- Educational approaches
- Formative approaches
- Health and medical approaches
- Inductive approaches

' Interdisciplinary approaches
' Performative approaches
' Psychological approaches
' Social science approaches
' Theological approaches

Each of these approaches, grounded in bodies of experiential practice and knowledge, is challenged by the need to address at least two crucial factors. First, the dynamic nature of spiritual experiences and the related problems of categorisation must be considered. Next, the issue of the kind of definition to be used must be decided. Is it possible to develop a definition capable of doing justice to the range of spiritualities encountered in the Western world? Identifying the most common forms that arise in academic and practitioner circles may serve a useful purpose in approaching this question. I have noted several dozen arise over the years.

Abstract or second-order definitions
Academic definitions
Applied definitions
Blended definitions
Colloquial definitions
Consciousness definitions
Contextual definitions
Developmental definitions
Dynamic co-action definitions (interactive)
Eclectic definitions
Emancipatory definitions
Empiricist (nurture-based) definitions
Engaged definitions
Enlightenment definitions
Esoteric definitions
Experiential or first-order definitions
Formative definitions
Generic definitions
Gnostic definitions
Grace-based definitions
Image-based or poetic definitions
Implicit definitions
Justice-based definitions
Love-based definitions
Medical definitions
Monergistic definitions (e.g. grace-alone or faith-alone approaches)
Mystical definitions

Nativist (innate nature) definitions
Nature-based definitions
New Pagan definitions
Nursing definitions
Occult definitions
Orientational definitions
Phenomenological definitions
Philosophical definitions
Psychological definitions
Religious or doctrinal definitions
Sacred definitions
Secular, atheistic or Marxist definitions
Sexual orientation or gender-based definitions
Social definitions
Soft or diffuse definitions
Technical (e.g. psychological, sociological, ethnographic) definitions
Theological definitions
Theoretical definitions
Tradition-based definitions
Transcendental definitions
Wisdom definitions

¶ *Definitions, material and formal objects*

The question of definition in spirituality has been problematic for a long time now. The point was well made more than twenty years ago by Sandra Schneiders in a 1986 article with the intriguing title, *Theology and Spirituality: Strangers, Rivals, or Partners?*[13] The problems of definition have not improved since then. What makes the task difficult is not only the fact that contemporary spirituality arises in complex cross-cultural, cross-religious and cross-geographical contexts, making it difficult to know how the word *spirituality* is actually being used, its study also engages a broad interdisciplinary approach that requires more than a definition. It requires a structure made up of a set of objectives and a methodology, arrangements that can so easily clip the wings of an audacious spirit and mute the song of soul. In order to illustrate how these ideas work in practice, the tools (material and formal objects)[14] used to clarify what is being studied is explained and then, as an illustration, the approaches taken by four influential writers in spirituality, Sandra Schneiders, Mary Frohlich, Ronald Rolheiser and Philip Sheldrake, are summarised. The material object, the formal object, the preferred methodology and basic definition of spirituality of each author is outlined in brief. The differences and similarities between the four writers are indicative of the inevitable differences of emphasis and interest at work in the whole field.

- MATERIAL OBJECT: This represents the broad, phenomenological domain of a discipline, its primary subject matter; it serves to broadly delineate the field of interest and distinguish it from others. The material object names the domain we study as a well-founded phenomenon: humans experiencing spirituality. However, a broad domain still contains an array of variables and so further precision is required to make study, research and definition possible.
- FORMAL OBJECT: This is what distinguishes one discipline from another. It acts as an evaluative category that identifies and delineates a precise area of interest by limiting the range of issues to be considered. The formal object identifies the specific, intentional aspect of study and its basic horizon (e.g. Christian spirituality). It not only raises what is specific to the course of study, e.g. the inner spiritual experience of grieving parents, it also surfaces the need for and is grounded in specific definitions, methods, and forms of discourse.
- TOPICAL OBJECT: Similar in meaning to *formal object* this term is sometimes used in educational contexts. It has to do with identifying and exploring different components of a theme, particularly its contents, the supportive strategies or practices in use, and a theme's contexts and environments.

For Mary Frohlich the material object, or broad domain specific to the study of spirituality, is constructed expressions of human meaning: the living and concrete human person in dynamic transformation towards the fullness of life. The formal object is the human spirit fully in act: i.e. the core dimension of the human person radically engaged with reality considered in both its contingent and transcendent dimensions. The method she advocates is an action/reflection articulation of spiritual experience based on a principle of critical interiority or aliveness, and she defines spirituality as a matter of full presence with oneself, with others, with the world, and with God: dynamic transformation towards the fullness of life in which interiority plays a critical role. In Christian terms, the fullness of life is defined as fullness of life in Christ.[15]

For Sandra Schneiders the material object of spirituality is clearly Christian. Her broad focus is on the experience of living the paschal mystery of Jesus Christ in all its ramifications: a life project of lived Christian faith. The formal object is experience, Christian experience as such, that is, the study of the spiritual life precisely as experience. Her specific focus is the experience of conscious involvement in a project of life integration through self-transcendence towards the ultimate value a person perceives. The method she has advocated involves interdisciplinary, cross-cultural, interreligious research, and she defines spirituality as living within the horizon of ultimate value.[16]

For Ronald Rolheiser the material object of spirituality is the unquenchable fire of human desire and madness: the complex world of human desire, an ache that can be filled with good or ill. The formal object is what people do spiritually with this desire in a wounding world: the spiritual experience of desire. Once again an interdisciplinary method is favoured. Rolheiser's definition is related to primordial experience. He suggests that we are precisely fired into life with a certain madness and we have to do something with it. We do not wake up in this world calm and serene, having the luxury of choosing to act or not act. We wake up crying, on fire with desire and madness. What we do with this madness is our spirituality.[17]

For Philip Sheldrake the material object of spirituality is also clearly Christian: the whole of human life at depth as it is consciously questioned by revelation and the nature of God; the fundamental human desire to encounter and respond to the sacred. The formal object is living publicly as a disciple: a provocative presence-in-the-world expressed by the classic themes of discipleship (following), and conversion (change). A contemplative, contextual, intertextual, interdisciplinary method is favoured, and spirituality is defined as the self-transcending practice of living publicly as a disciple in the complex world of events.[18]

### ℭ Proliferating definitions

The proliferation of kinds of definitions identified so far in this chapter is another reason why *spirituality* has become a vastly tricky term pointing in seemingly endless directions. For example, spirituality will have religious and non-religious uses, many of them based on a misunderstanding or misrepresentation of the authentic meaning of religion and religiosity. The same is true of secular-humanist approaches, which are also open to bias and misunderstanding. Religious spirituality may also take on life-giving or destructive forms in response to life events.[19] In effect, the word *spirituality* raises a spectrum of concerns that are simultaneously complex and intrinsically equivocal, especially when viewed against the background of rapidly changing social, intellectual, cultural, religious, philosophical, artistic, economic and political realities. The addition of such factors introduces a range of variables that makes the task of achieving a clear definition of spirituality well nigh impossible.[20] The best thing that we can do is talk around it and elicit useful intimations and descriptions in what is a meaning-laden and assumption-driven field.

For example, Neville Symington defines spirituality as a discipline whose goal and organising centre is ethical, the purification of motivation and the recognition of self-deception. True spirituality incorporates the moral, while false spirituality bypasses morality. According to Symington, false spirituality aims to give the self the *feeling* of righteousness without having to act morally.[21] John Fulton and his colleagues Michael Hornsby-Smith and Margaret Norris develop a very different approach. They view spirituality as both a cultural and an organisational reality. Spirituality is linked to the practicalities of human relationships and how they are shaped by forms of organisation and relationships of power, as much as by specific charisma and inspiration. This permits the authors to develop a typology of four forms of spirituality that are developed along two axes, a modern–traditional axis and a mechanistic–organic axis. The former corresponds to cultural concerns, the latter to structural and organisational influences. Mechanistic spiritualities are leader-driven and show a top-down form of organisation and development that tend to become routine once developed. Organic spiritualities are much more flexible, and tend to have an innovative group structure.[22]

Harold G Koenig, David B Larson and Michael E McCullough take quite a different approach. They define spirituality operationally as the personal quest for answers to ultimate questions about life, about meaning, and about relationship to the sacred or transcendent, which may (or may not) lead to or arise from the development of religious rituals and the formation of community. Five broad types of spirituality are then identified in terms of the relationship between spirituality and religion. The authors use Martin Marty's term 'mooring' to describe this relationship. The five forms of spirituality, based on US research findings are humanistic spirituality which shows no such mooring and favours an ethical understanding of spirituality, unmoored pluralist spiritualities which have severed links to religion and serve to blur religious boundaries, moored spirituality Eastern type, moored spirituality Western type I (conservative monotheist), and moored spirituality Western type II (mainstream monotheist). Many of the new spiritualities tend to share aspects of the first three types.[23]

Compare that approach with the result of Holly Nelson-Becker's research. She distinguishes between approaches that define spirituality as a coping resource supportive of self-maintenance; as connection with a power, purpose or idea that transcends the self; as one human dimension among many (bio-psycho-social-spiritual) or as the core essence of the person; and as the motivational and emotional basis for the quest for meaning.[24] Rogene A Buchholz and Sandra B Rosenthal cite other research that describes spirituality variously as shorthand for the deepest urgings and impulses of the human self – what gives meaning and depth to daily life; that identifies spirituality with inner consciousness as the source of inspiration, creativity, and wisdom; as something that comes from within and goes beyond programmed beliefs and values; and as the life force that permeates life and behaviour.[25]

Riane Eisler and Alfonso Montuori take yet another approach. They distinguish between fear-based spiritualities rooted in formative experiences of coldly damaging power-driven domination, and love- or trust-based spiritualities, rooted in formative experiences of warmly supportive love and partnership in families of origin. Clearly love-based spiritualities will be very different to those grounded in fear. Very different practices, literacies and discourses will be clearly identifiable, reflecting very different anchoring and shaping forces. Eisler and Montuori derive their descriptions from attachment theory, more specifically the positive and negative impacts of early experiences of attachment and loss that typically recur in the relational practices that typify later social, gender-based, workplace and religious contexts, especially in the contexts that confront the capacity for authentic human intimacy and warm relationship so relevant to the development of a mature spirituality.[26]

David Moberg suggests that the definitional confusion evident in spirituality may be explained by analogy to what happens in the study of physical life, maturity and health. What these have in common are complex processes of growth and development towards wellness and wholeness, processes in which spirituality represents the integrative dimension. According to Moberg, then, the difficulty is less about definition than about problems of identifying, assessing, and measuring spiritual integration, wellness and wholeness in people's lives. Even a one-line definition of spiritual well-being as the affirmation of life in a relationship with God, self, community and environment that nurtures and celebrates wholeness in contrast to fragmentation and isolation, creates complex problems for those engaged in the assessment and measurement of spiritual wellness. While the number of indicators of spiritual wellness is very large, the results of research usually depend on the narrow range of indicators of spiritual well-being and wholeness included in assessment or measurement scales. Each assessment instrument, then, presumes an operational definition defined by the narrow range of information it seeks. Like definitions, spiritual assessment scales are on the increase. So are problems of interpretation.[27]

In another important piece of work Pam McCarroll, Thomas St James O'Connor and Elizabeth Meakes examined seventy-six pieces of research on spirituality published in health-care literature between 1975 and 1996. Twenty-seven of these articles offered definitions of spirituality that showed little agreement. On analysis, as many as eight definitional themes emerged. Spirituality has to do with meaning and purpose, connection and relationships, God/god(s)/Transcendent Other, the transcendent Self, a vital principle, a unifying force or integrative principle, something personal and private, and hope.[28] Compare these themes to those identified below. Consideration must also be given to more recent questions about definition thrown-up by the turn to deep ecology and the emergence of eco-centric spiritualities, especially when these contest the eco-attentive and eco-responsive dimensions of other spiritual traditions and their ethical concerns: the creational traditions that trace back to the Bible, or to a charismatic founding figure like Francis d'Assisi are typical examples.

Eco-centric spiritualities tend to see the earth as God's body and respond to ecological concerns in that light. There is a big difference between eco-attentive and eco-centric spiritualities. Eco-centric spiritualities tend to move close to pantheism and the veneration and worship of nature. In many respects they take on the character of the nature-based religion associated with New Pagan movements. The distinction between a spiritual ethic that takes ecological issues seriously and a spirituality that engages in nature worship is pivotal to understanding definitions of ecological spirituality. Questions of motivation inevitably arise when definitions of radical green spirituality come up, especially in contexts where Earth-centred belief systems that blur the boundaries between self, nature and the divine are on the rise.[29]

Then there are the conversations about the nexus between science and spirituality; the questions raised by globalisation and the re-emergence/neo-colonial consumption of aboriginal spiritualities; and the emergence of spirituality as a question of individual or cultural expression of gendered identities shaped by processes of spiritual contestation and reappropriation. The re-emergence of esoteric and New Pagan spiritualities further complicates questions of definition by introducing understandings of the construction of contemporary spiritualities as forms of less radical mobile alteration, a product of market production, rather than radical conversion.[30] The task of critical reflection on spirituality is compounded by the fact that the sacred is not synonymous with accepted images of the sacred, and to pretend that conventional images of the divine are the divine reality itself is tantamount to idolatry and a delusion. But those are questions of meaning.

## A Reflection on the Nature of Meaning

Mark McIntosh suggests that meaning is an invitation and an event stipulating enactment.[31] Spiritual meaning is persistently dynamic and contextual, arising in multidimensional meaning-contexts that constantly flow into and overlap each other, and constantly claim living expression. Spiritual and religious meaning also unfolds in prayer, stories, narratives, and texts that typify meaning-events and invite practitioners, listeners and readers to join a dance of meaning. In the dance, new horizons of meaning fuse with those already present and make change possible. Change happens as paradoxes, strange logics, interjections, outcries, yearnings, gaps, negations, concealments, revelations, invitations, commands, prohibitions, moments of surrender and visual imagery engage us in ways that affect self-image by confronting it with a new meaning-matrix alive with transformative possibility. Spiritual meaning acts through reflective processes that shape transformed practices and perceptions. These then make new existential perception possible.

However, it is important to understand that this is not just a question of new concepts or experiences that become secure self-possessions or structuring elements of a new self-identity. Instead spiritual and religious meaning is an invitation to an encounter with something that demands a move away from self, that demands a move towards something less easy to manipulate, towards what McIntosh calls 'a beyond-without-limits'.[32] Spiritual and religious experience is always in some sense encounter-with-other, an invitation to seek more thoroughly, to decipher more fully what this other reveals: a journey through personal uniqueness towards the demand, the obligation that surfaces in the encounter-with-other-and-difference.

Meaning serves an orienting purpose in spirituality; it tends towards depth. Meaning makes its presence felt as understanding and insight; it dances in knowledge, interpretation, and intuition. Spiritual meaning arises in the soul's encounter with God: it arises out of life and the touch of beauty, goodness and truth. It also arises in spaces of absence, of pathos, and tragedy. Meaning is an invitation to enter new possibilities, reflect on new challenges, walk new paths, hear new musics, dance new dances, become spiritually more alert, more acutely aware. Meaning is also there as a motivating force, a partner for intention, a goal and a starting point; it is a horizon, a compass, a navigator's star: without it, how are we to know where we are or where we are going?

Meaning is like a footprint in a trackless waste, hinting at a way to go. It is like the springtime, giving birth to new buds of possibility from the mulch of memory and language responding to the invitation of new experience, birthing new and audacious aspects of spirit. Spiritual meaning arises within and between, and like the wind it crosses boundaries. It is like a good wine or good music: it travels well. Meaning offers solace and comfort, challenge and promise, hope and the possibilities of future growth. Reflection on meaning brings the new understandings that make creative action possible. Spiritual meaning is like a fire preparing a path through the undergrowth, like a lamp in the darkness, a heart-warming lamp and a call to transformation, a glad call to liberating insight leading to renewed joy. Where meaning is absent, it is as if life were surrounded by cloud and darkness, disoriented, distressed; when it returns, it is like lightning lighting up the chaos, striking it down: vision made newly possible.

Meaning is the mirror in which we see life, however darkly; it is the mirror in which we glimpse the divine, however dimly. Without meaning we are rudderless in an ocean of possibility lacking the key to discernment. Spiritual meaning renews life; it lifts us up like the warm updraft beneath a soaring eagle's wings. Meaning empowers us to move and act, to choose and opt for humanising compassion and love. Contemplative meaning pierces the chaos of the lie; it recognises the truth of weakness, allows reconciliation, brings healing acceptance and forgiveness, concedes the lessons hidden in humiliating circumstance, acknowledges the forces of diminishment. Contemplative meaning is generative; it calls forth gratitude, opens prisons, empowers, supports, encourages, motivates. When such meaning is absent, hearts waste away like pelicans in a barren desert; we moan like lonely birds on rooftops. Then, when meaning dawns, the troubles melt away like yesterday's snows, a memory now, the teaching done.

These are all reasons why meaning lies at the heart of spirituality, one of its defining characteristics. In effect, meaning shines in the space between self and the other; it is like the face of God, a carrier of God's loving Word, the New Dawn dawning on us and bringing life to light, lifting a veil. It dances an ethical, caring, responsive, responsible dance that challenges the desire to settle down in a comfortable illusion of spiritual arrival or contemplative depth regardless of whether this dance-of-demand can ever be brought to fulfilment. The meaning is in the dancing, in the practicalities of the encounter. Spiritual and contemplative meaning is located in responsiveness: it surfaces in the move away from self towards the other rather than in propositions that sit still, going nowhere. In this sense, spiritual and religious meaning is dynamic, in movement, oriented beyond the perceiving self. It evokes a conceptual system that makes the mapping of constantly new meaning frameworks possible, that makes new contexts of experience possible where meaning becomes a matrix for living the new. Experience is shaped in the dance of meaning. Meaning enlivens the very practices that make the transformation of experience possible. In the dance of meaning, in its transformative embrace, categories of understanding are transcended, surpassed; new ways of experiencing reality are glimpsed, recognised, and engaged.

Spiritual and religious meaning is transformative to the extent that it is self-dispossessing. The paradox is, of course, that this self-dispossessing constitutes the self as responding responsibly to the other. The meaningful self is revealed as the dynamically and responsibly responsive self, because meaning constantly resurfaces in a dance of self-dispossession and self-realisation. It draws the dance beyond the familiar and the comfortable, towards new patterns, new practices, new understandings that continually point beyond themselves, move beyond present self-constructs. There is no definitive closure in this flow of possibility. If spirituality and contemplation are a journey into meaning, then every point of arrival is paradoxically a point of departure in a spiralling movement towards the more, the other, in the world of concrete particularities and the metaphors that aid the mapping of ways forward into the as-yet unknown.

Spiritual and contemplative meaning is not isolated in a world of well-defined formulae or seemingly finished statements. Spiritual and contemplative meaning surfaces in the unfinished messiness of life itself, in orientations and practices that always have more work to do. It is in this unfinished messiness that meaning events take place. They occur in the glimpses of possibility that emerge in the thin places, in the barely noticed flirts caught out of the corner of an eye that draw us forward differently into difference, invite us to defer deferment. Meaning in such places is open, always yet-to-be-concluded, not to be caught or tamed by a single mode of expression or contained in or coerced into however precise a proposition. Meaning, like God, is at hand, inviting embrace, inviting an always fuller entry into all its implications.

Meaning opens us up to the more; it cannot be fully grasped or said. It always leaves an apophatic space, a moment of aporia, a gap. It dances just beyond our reach in a swirl of excessive and transgressive possibility that finds its way into the very pattern of the stories and texts that we share with others. It is there in the turn of a phrase, a gesture, a tone, a linguistic construction that seeks to honour Divine presence in the human interplay: as finite humans dare to join in the infinite dance of Divine freedom. Spiritual and religious meaning does not look backwards like Lot's wife. It leans forward and reaches for something new: a new divine-human encounter that again and again births a new, a contemplative self into being. Spiritual and religious meaning is an encounter with an empowering force, the push towards a continuingly imaginative spiral of transformation in which gifting meaning opens portals to new possibility, to new meaning.

## A FOREST OF FORMS

Contemporary spirituality is a diverse phenomenon with many voices and many faces, inhabiting many different human and natural landscapes. The task of definition is made more difficult by an explosion of forms of spirituality in recent years.[33] First, consider the newly emerging forms of psychospirituality. These tend to be based on a hypothesis that argues for the fundamental unity of the psychological and spiritual aspects of personhood. This is based in turn on the modern theory of the single unified self and the interactive relationship that exists between structure and direction in human life and the forms that express them. In this view, spiritual activities and experiences are grounded in and supported by psychological processes and vice versa. In effect, both psychological and spiritual well-being are intimately linked. A critical comment is important here. Religious understandings of spirituality are at a disadvantage because of a tendency among health professionals and psychotherapists to prefer secular or reductive and naturalistic understandings of spirituality grounded in a positivism that views religious forms and expressions as too touchy or esoteric or 'unscientific' to consider.

The dialogue between theology and psychology is bedevilled by mis-understandings of each other's methods. This is not helped when these misunderstandings or suspicions of methods harden into ideological stances. This tension is exacerbated by a polarising of individual and institutional perspectives on spirituality that leads to a rejection of institutional religious approaches and the consequent loss or rejection of the sacred and religious origins and dimensions of spiritual life. All of this indicates the active presence of a series of disconnections and gaps between eros and religion, for example, as well as spirituality and religion, subjective morality and social justice, and between secularism and religion. Other forms of spirituality also press insistently for attention. These include the following:

1. *Lay spiritualities*: these represent the earliest and most common forms of spirituality. They configure such themes and experiences as birth, marriage, sexuality, parenting, home, care, relationality, work, death, dying and bereavement. Everyone's life and experience is touched by these experiences in a variety of different ways. Childhood and adolescent spiritualities belong in this domain.

2. *Schools of spirituality*: organised around source experiences and the influential presence or memory and writings of a founding figure, these schools represent other arrangements of forms and expressions, usually related to religious traditions. They characteristically configure such themes as ways and practices, ritual and worship, community and service. They also represent important cultural expressions that stress renewal and transformation as lifestyle options and often represent historical syntheses of spirituality.

3. *Spiritual counter-movements*: are particularly relevant in the contemporary context. These draw together people who contest or reject establishment or mainstream religious, cultural or civic spiritualities. There are many examples. These include such forms as liberation spirit-ualities, feminist spiritualities, marginal and transitional spiritualities, devotional spiritualities, spiritualities of disturbance and challenge (for example, Dietrich Bonhoeffer), political spiritualities that remind us not only that politics has risks, but also that any humane politics has at its core a care for the world and a care for the public realm. Also included are spiritualities of exile and solitude, ecological and

creational spiritualities, gay, lesbian and bisexual spiritualities, prophetic or eschatological spiritualities, ethnic spiritualities, world-embracing and world-denying spiritualities, as well as those involved in the recuperation of mythologies and rites of passage (for example, contemporary male spiritualities).

4. *Other forms of spirituality:* include those grounded in twelve-step programmes, social justice groups, the new Gnosticism, the new Paganism, goddess spiritualities, and Eastern religions. Newly emerging Christian expressions also make their presence felt as do blended forms of spirituality that express multiple forms of belonging.

The result is a lush and potentially bewildering plurality of voices, forms, practices and experiences. Is it any wonder that the definitional problem in spirituality has become so notoriously difficult? However, reviews of definitions reveal sets of shared definitional contours.

### DEFINITIONAL CONTOURS

A review of definitions of spirituality brings into focus a series of constructs and categories that tend to fall into broad thematic groups sharing common features.[34] While all definitions present constructed expressions of human relationality, meaning and belief, they are also challenged to present complex patterns of reflected action or praxis. Comparative research on definitions of spirituality sets in stark relief the absence of consensus and the growing discontinuity in respect to traditional sources. It also indicates the word's radically enlarged purview and its extensive semantic range. On analysis, three triadic sets of definitional contours may be identified in the literature, but not without the complicating impact of tension and conflict.

- The first triad distinguishes between religious, sacred (i.e. not explicitly religious), and secular definitions. Each of these offers interesting first-order (experiential/descriptive) and second-order (analytical) subsets deriving from the different models, methods and normative-prescriptive disciplines used in their composition (for example, theology, or psychology, or ethnography, or history, or sociology, or medicine, or education, or philosophy) and the forms of discourse employed (for example, critical-analytical, comparative, form-descriptive, hermeneutic, specialist-denominational).

- The second triad distinguishes between definitions of spirituality that are clearly theological, those that are clearly anthropological, and those that take a historical-contextual position grounded in the experiential particularities of time and place, with specific reference to the dynamics of language and culture.

- The third triad is an interweaving of three distinctive experiential domains. The first of these has to do with the natural ground of human spirituality as a human characteristic; the second reveals the interactive implications for spirituality of concepts of the sacred and religious doctrines and beliefs; the third concerns the impacts of landscape, location and time on spirituality. What kind of human characteristic is spirituality? How is spirituality shaped by representations of the sacred, or by belief and doctrinal systems? How does landscape shape spiritual experiences? How is time experienced?

## THEMATIC CATEGORIES

Forms of spirituality and the contours of definition in turn draw attention to thematic categories in spirituality. Seven sets of thematic categories are presented here. They offer an insight into the luxuriant possibilities that face those attempting to define spirituality against the background of contemporary experience. All seven are abundantly represented in the world of the new spirituality, indicators of the revolution that is currently underway.

- The theme of *God*, a *Spiritual Being*, a *Higher Power*, a *Super-sensible Reality*, a *Reality greater than the self*, and the related theme of *transcendence and connectedness* to this *Higher Reality* shape the first thematic category. Many such definitions strive for an *inclusive view of the sacred* that avoids traditional or explicit religious references, while others are more obviously influenced by theological concerns.

- The second thematic category highlights *themes of transcendence and connectedness* within the world or the cosmos but *without explicit reference to a higher or divine power*. These definitions may be intra-subjective (coming from the self as it struggles to understand), relate to altered states of consciousness, or to transpersonal levels of knowing that go beyond consensual rationality. They may also refer to experiences outside the normal boundaries of the body-ego and space-time. While these approaches clearly view spirituality in terms of transcendence and connectedness, the precise referents of these two words, while sometimes pointing to something beyond daily experience or the self, are often left unclear.

- A third thematic category focuses on the theme of spirituality as *not of the self*. These definitions tend to describe spirituality as a manifestation of the *spirit*, or the *divine within*, or of a *realm of consciousness beyond the individual*. Some definitions are content to state that spirituality, while an existential domain, is not of the material world. These definitions tend to accentuate the *ethereal*, the *intangible*, the *non-physical* aspects of spirituality, or a vital principle that is contrasted to materiality.

- A fourth category focuses on the themes of *relationality, connectedness, place, social solidarity* and *participation*. These themes are particularly evident in descriptions of women's spirituality, justice and emancipatory spiritualities, business spiritualities, creational-ecological spiritualities, aboriginal spiritualities and spiritualities that emphasise holistic and inter-subjective visions. Such definitions may be either religious or secular in tone and outlook.

- A fifth category focuses on the themes of *meaning* and *purpose* and their *life-shaping significance*. This factor is common to a range of religious, sacred and secular definitions. Spirituality in this category is understood in terms of an individual's construction of meaning, search for purpose, vocation, and choice of direction in life. These approaches often include references to *desire, willingness* and *motivation*. Some configurations focus these themes on the self, for the most part in terms of the core dimension of the human person radically engaged with reality. In many of these approaches the role of the sacred is understood to be secondary.

- Then there is the representation of spirituality as an *integrating force*: many contemporary definitions identify a *force* within the person that has the power to bring about *complete integration and balance*. These approaches understand spirituality in terms of an *integrative energy*, a unifying, vital, inclusive, life-giving force characterised by wholeness, interdependence and patience experienced within occupational, leisure, cultural and relational contexts. This integrating force or energy is depicted as the centre from which all other human activity flows. Typical references are to the truest self, or the innermost self, or the real self.

- There are also complex definitions that combine *multiple themes* such as *transformation, ultimacy, interiority, experience, values, practices and disciplines, choices, outcomes, participation and shared meaning, happiness, praxis, ambiguity, self-implication, socio-political engagement*, and the *dynamic, interactive nature* of spirituality. These tend to be linked to an animating principle of some kind.

This by no means exhaustive list of thematic categories should help us to come to terms with the misty, nomadic, glowing, mercurial, drifting nature of the word *spirituality* in contemporary usage. The list also focuses attention on the contemporary mystification about spiritual matters and the increasing presence of Aboriginal, Asian, African, and Latin American traditions and practices in the mix. The list is also indicative of the tendencies towards bricolage in contemporary Western forms of spirituality, especially at personal and individual levels. Above all, the range of these thematic contours is indicative of the operational usefulness of the contemporary vagueness of the word *spirituality*, and the by-now-celebrated difficulty of reaching consensus on an agreed definition. If you feel called to compose a definition, enjoy the adventure!

## WILLIAM STRINGFELLOW

Writing in 1984 when the word *spirituality* was entering mainstream usage as a useful umbrella term, William Stringfellow identified an amazing list of ways in which the word was already being used. The following paragraph clearly demonstrates how vague and fluid usages of the word have become:

> *Spirituality* may indicate stoic attitudes, occult phenomena, the practice of so-called mind control, yoga discipline, escapist fantasies, interior journeys, an appreciation of Eastern religions, multifarious pious exercises, superstitious imaginations, intensive journals, dynamic muscle tension, assorted dietary regimens, meditation, jogging cults, monastic rigours, mortification of the flesh, wilderness sojourns, political resistance, contemplation, abstinence, hospitality, a vocation of poverty, non-violence, silence, the efforts of prayer, obedience, generosity, exhibiting stigmata, entering solitude, or, I suppose among these and many others, squatting on top of a pillar.[35]

Stringfellow insists that whatever else may be affirmed about it, both spiritual maturity and spiritual fulfilment incorporate the whole person. This not only includes body, mind and soul, place, relationships and history, in Stringfellow's view it also incorporates the whole of creation.[36] He also notes that biblical spirituality not only includes a self-conscious relationship with oneself in the most radically personal sense, it simultaneously implicates us concretely in reconciliation with the rest of creation. As such, spirituality represents the most profoundly political reality available to human experience.[37]

As you reflect on these and similar questions it is important to remember that today all kinds of people have begun to use the word *spirituality*. These include people who practise a religion, secular people, liberal people, conservative people, socialists, Marxists, agnostics and atheists. Clearly, the word spirituality does not name the same level of experience or even the same kind of experience for everyone. It is also true that the word often struggles under the weight of popular, traditional, socio-cultural, religious and ideological baggage. As a result, a great many people today tend to view the word with a degree of scepticism. Some, because of the word's perceived subtext of other-worldliness, claim that it cannot easily be seen as reasonable and reflective. Others see it as naming something esoteric, or private, or eccentric that has more to do with the search for certainty than with life in the real world. Add to this the stereotypic materialist view that spirituality names a purely subjective phenomenon, a kind of sophisticated 'navel gazing', and it becomes clear why some have concluded that spirituality is at best irrelevant to 'real life' (do you notice the tacit definitions?) and at worst a menace to society.

It is in this context that important new research work needs to be undertaken. Both contemporary and future work in spirituality, for example, will have to face the challenge of rescuing received aspects of spirituality from their own negative history, particularly in terms of such key issues as socio-cultural engagement and the complete acknowledgment of the vigorous incarnational dynamism that is found in authentic Christianity. In fact, it is not religion, but human nature itself that is responsible for the negative impression that spirituality is escapist at best and delusional at worst. That is why a broadly based, positive understanding of spirituality is necessary. Peter Van Ness's definition is worth pondering. He defines spirituality as *the quest for attaining an optimal relationship between what one truly is and everything that is.*[38] It touches a lot of important bases. What other elements would you add?

### THE CHRISTIAN VISION
In the Christian vision, the human spirit, dancing with embodiment on the earth, names the creative centre of our whole manner of being in the world, and all the deep personal, social, ecological, and ethical consequences that flow from that creatively liberating mode of being. Spirituality, this embodied dance of spirit, is an inescapable part of being human, something we come to know as we come to know ourselves fully as persons who are loved by God. The Greek tradition speaks of Christian spirituality as a process of *theopoiesis*, literally *god-making*, a process of utter transformation usually referred to in English as deification. Western Christianity has been more reserved about *theopoiesis*, or *theosis* as it was later called, afraid, not without reason, that such an idea would be too easily misunderstood, too easily literalised.

The preference in the West has been to speak of a process of deep and utter transformation of life in God's grace. St John's Gospel supports the

Greek tradition (John 10:34). From its first beginnings Christian spirituality has sought its summit and its source, its vision of human wholeness, wholesomeness, integrity and compassionate being in Jesus of Nazareth, the Christ, and his simple but utterly deep call to a spirituality of passionate, creation-embracing love. To follow the Christian spiritual path is to choose to live to the full in Christ Jesus (Ephesians 3:21) not just as a compassionate symbol of human perfection, but as a historical person who actually lived what he taught. It is because Jesus is a real person that Christian spirituality is self-implicating of its very nature. It is self-implicating because his life reveals him as the perfect living image of the invisible God (Colossians 1:15).

Authentic Christian spirituality harmoniously embraces the totality of human living and personality: body, soul and spirit, our human nature and our human destiny, our personal, historical and social lives, our human desire and our human longing to transcend the limitations of existence. Humans long to discover liberating value and liberating meaning. Christians find this liberation in a personal experience of the divine, a personal experience of the living Christ, in the discovery shared with many sisters and brothers that God acts far more lavishly than we could ever imagine through the power of the Spirit at work in us (Ephesians 3:20). This experience brings us into a world of utter fullness, of utter awareness of a world vibrant with life, vibrant with Spirit, vibrant with promise, vibrant with the call to engage creatively in all that is: and the gifted capacity to respond deeply and do it. For those following the Christian way, spirituality emerges and develops as they engage more and more fully with the Holy Spirit, as they let the Spirit fill their minds and so shape their lives (Romans 8:6). At its best, Christian spirituality is not only self-implicating, it is always a life-changing force.

The very heart of Christian spirituality is a lived and living experience of God. The challenge is to live increasingly in its unmediated, unfiltered reality. Then we can become real human beings, the kind we are meant to be, fully open to human existence in the world, part of the historic struggle for a better world, a world in tune with God's loving designs. This means that purely individualistic understandings of life and spirituality cannot stand, because Christian spirituality cannot be thought of apart from others on the way. It cannot be thought of apart from the needs of the world and everyone in it. Its essential core is unmistakably prophetic, a call to walk in fields of justice and integrity, compassionately open to the other and the different, lovingly open to the goodness and beauty of God encountered in otherness and difference. This prophetically demanding stance reveals itself in the personal and communal search for the meaning of Jesus and the profound social and cosmic implications of his life and teaching.

People walking in the path traced out by Jesus show what it means to believe that God is on our side as human beings as we struggle for clarity of life; and in that struggle seek a commitment to heal injustice of every kind. In this way, Christian spirituality brings together contemplation and action, prayer, worship and creative engagement in the world. Christian spirituality recognises human freedom; it also recognises God's equally free appeal to human freedom. In this sense, spirituality touches our innermost and outermost experiences in very practical, yet deeply demanding, deeply transformative ways: Christian spirituality is called to save the world. Today that implies a spirituality that is biblically grounded, ecumenical, open to life in all its expressions, concerned for personal and social growth and development, ecologically responsible, and exquisitely respectful of difference.[39]

Christian spirituality, then, is a way of living that gives expression to ultimate meaning and value, a hopeful expression that finds its transformative power in a gifting God. It is an integrative process that incorporates our diverse experiences of faith and life into a relational and meaningful whole. Christian spirituality may be defined as *willing entry into the rhythms of Christ*; as *seeking the ultimate meaning and value of Christ expressed in the biblical narratives and the living reflection and practice of the Christian community over two millennia*. For Christians this ultimate meaning and value are found in and through love. This particular definition helps us to see that Christian spirituality operates on two levels, the personal and the communal. In early Christianity, spirituality meant *life lived according to the Spirit*. This is very apparent in the teaching of St Paul who emphasised the deeply personal, intensely experiential and transformative nature of spirituality as it was lived at that time and as it can still be lived today (1 Corinthians 2:14–15). Christian spirituality is *life attuned to the rhythms and orientations of the mind of Christ, lived in the power of the Spirit, lived interactively in the presence, the awesome presence of God*. Christian spirituality sings of a transformed consciousness in a transformed life.

Christian spirituality makes radically personal demands on those who take their Christian faith seriously and try to live it lovingly in the world. This is an interactive, situated process. In it things are seen differently; reality seen with a transformed mind. Christian spirituality unfolds as belief and life weave a new tapestry of existence in the world. What this implies is that Christian spirituality emerges out of a creative process that brings faith, personal and communal life, culture, history and the world dynamically together.[40] Christian spirituality faces the challenge of living a truly human life, a truly loving life, a life which is really human, really Spirit-filled, really prayer-filled. It means embracing a life destiny like Jesus, the pioneer and perfecter of every Christian's faith (Hebrews 12:2). It means living a new existence made possible in the Spirit of Christ.

Today Christian spirituality has to face not a crisis of identity, but a crisis of function in the world. Christian spirituality is challenged to rediscover the core Christian task in the world: to carry a treasure beyond price, a message of infinite love. In order to do this, Christians have to recognise an ancient problem, one Paul brought to the attention of the Corinthians two thousand years ago: the *vessel trap*. What is important is not the vessel, but the treasure that shows that the transcendent power is not ours but God's (2 Corinthians 4:7). Because of the variety of Church-related scandals that have afflicted believers over the past number of years it is perfectly understandable that many would fall into the vessel trap. We need a more contemplative vision than that – one that glimpses beyond the dreadful criminality and sin and betrayal caused by abuses of trust and privilege and power. We need to be able to glimpse beyond the shame and the disappointment, notice the soft glow, the still small voice, of renewed promise.

The only spirituality that will be taken seriously today is one that reveals the reality of *performative testimony*. This is not about *what we espouse*, but about *what we actually do* as believers and disciples of Christ. It is about the kinds of lives we live, as pastors and people, as parents and teachers of the next generation. It is not about being conservative or liberal: no, what we need to regain is a clear sense of the very congruence of our daily lives. What we need to rediscover today is how to be friends of God and prophets (Wisdom 7:27) in the reality of Western culture in the twenty-first century. We need to rediscover the mind of Christ. We need to rediscover how to be alive with Christ and walk confidently in the gifts we have been given (Eph 2:1-10). We need to be real. We need to be mystics in our own days. We need to let spirit song soar. We need to let Jesus live. Nothing else will do.

## THEMES AND QUESTIONS FOR FURTHER REFLECTION

1. When you use the word *spirituality*, what does it mean for you? How would you define it now?
2. Identify the challenges and opportunities found in the explosion of forms and contours in spirituality.
3. What is the essence of Christian spirituality? Do you see it as a life project?
4. Explain how spiritual meaning is uncovered in everyday life. What colours or underpins your present sense of spiritual meaning?

## FURTHER READING

Tony Hendra, *Father Joe* (London and New York: Penguin Books, 2004).

NOTES: 1. Val Plumwood, 'Belonging, Naming and Decolonisation' in Jean Hillier and Emma Rooksby, eds, *A Sense of Place*, Second Edition (Aldershot: Ashgate, 2005) 371–394 at 377–378.

2. See Victor L. Schermer, *Spirit and Psyche: A New Paradigm for Psychology, Psychoanalysis, and Psychotherapy*. Foreword by Kenneth Porter (London and New York: Jessica Kingsley Publishers, 2003) 21–40.

3. For a very good example of the challenges and difficulties involved in defining key elements of human experience see John P. Lizza, *Persons, Humanity, and the Definition of Death* (Baltimore: The Johns Hopkins University Press, 2006).

4. John Feehan, 'The Dipper's Acclaim' in *Resurgence*, November/December (2003) 7.

5. Quoted in Tomaš Spidlik, *Prayer: The Spirituality of the Christian East*, Volume 2. Translated by Anthony Gythiel (Kalamazoo: Cistercian Publications, 2005) 165.

6. See Robert H. Scharf, 'The Rhetoric of Experience and the Study of Religion' in Jensine Andresen and Robert K. C. Forman, eds, *Cognitive Models and Spiritual Maps: Interdisciplinary Explorations of Religious Experience* (Bowling Green, OH and Thoverton: Imprint Academic) Journal of Consciousness Studies 7 (2000) 11–12, 267–287.

7. See for example David Jaques, *Learning in Groups: A Handbook for Improving Groupwork*, Third Edition (London and New York: RoutledgeFalmer, 2000); Randy Y. Hirokawa and Marshall Scott Poole, *Communication and Group Decision Making*, Second Edition (Thousand Oaks, London, New Delhi: Sage Publications, 1996); David O. Moberg, ed., *Aging and Spirituality: Spiritual Dimensions of Aging Theory, Research, Practice, and Policy* (New York, London, Oxford: The Haworth Pastoral Press, 2001); Chris Segrin and Jeanne Flora, *Family Communication* (Mahwah, NJ: Lawrence Erlbaum Associates, 2005).

8. See Brian L. Lancaster, 'On the Relationship Between Cognitive Models and Spiritual Maps: Evidence from Hebrew Language Mysticism' in Jensine Andresen and Robert K. C. Forman, eds, *Cognitive Models and Spiritual Maps: Interdisciplinary Explorations of Religious Experience* op. cit. 231–250.

9. Laurel Kearns, 'Saving the Creation: Christian Environmentalism in the United States' in *Sociology of Religion* 57 (1996) 55–70.

10. See David O. Moberg, PhD, ed., *Aging and Spirituality: Spiritual Dimensions of Aging Theory, Research, Practice and Policy* (Binghampton, NY: The Haworth Pastoral Press, 2001).

11. Alister E. McGrath, *Christian Spirituality* (Oxford: Blackwell, 1999) 2.

12. See Rosemary Radford Ruether, *Gender, Ethnicity & Religion: Views from the Other Side* (Minneapolis: Fortress Press, 2002).

13. Sandra M. Schneiders, 'Theology and Spirituality: Strangers, Rivals, or

Partners?' in *Horizons* 13 (Fall, 1986) 253–274 at 253. For a bibliography of Sandra Schneiders' major writing see Bruce H. Lescher and Elizabeth Liebert, *Exploring Christian Spirituality: Essays in Honor of Sandra M. Schneiders, IHM* (New York/Mahwah NJ: Paulist Press, 2006) 215–223.

14. For an account of how these tools are used in the study of Christian spirituality see Elizabeth A. Dreyer & Mark Burrows, 'Spirituality as an Academic Discipline' in Elizabeth A. Dreyer & Mark Burrows, *Minding the Spirit: The Study of Christian Spirituality* (Baltimore and London: The Johns Hopkins University Press, 2005) 1–4 at 2; Sandra M. Schneiders, IHM, 'The Study of Christian Spirituality: Contours and Dynamics of a Discipline' in Elizabeth A. Dreyer & Mark Burrows, *Minding the Spirit: The Study of Christian Spirituality* op. cit. 5–24 at 21–22; Sandra M. Schneiders, IHM, 'A Hermeneutical Approach to the Study of Christian Spirituality' in Elizabeth A. Dreyer & Mark Burrows, *Minding the Spirit: The Study of Christian Spirituality* op. cit. 49–64 at 50; Mary Frohlich, RCSJ, 'Spiritual Discipline, Discipline of Spirituality' in Elizabeth A. Dreyer & Mark Burrows, *Minding the Spirit: The Study of Christian Spirituality* op. cit. 65–78 at 65.

15. See Mary Frohlich, RSCJ, 'Critical Interiority' in *Spiritus: A Journal of Christian Spirituality* 7 (2007) 1, 77–81 at 77; Mary Frohlich, RCSJ, 'Spiritual Discipline, Discipline of Spirituality' in Elizabeth A. Dreyer & Mark Burrows, *Minding the Spirit: The Study of Christian Spirituality* op. cit. 65–78.

16. For a discussion of Schneiders' approach to these issues see Judith A. Berling, 'Christian Spirituality: Intrinsically Interdisciplinary' in Bruce H. Lescher and Elizabeth Liebert, *Exploring Christian Spirituality* op. cit. 35–52. See Sandra M. Schneiders, 'Religion vs. Spirituality: A Contemporary Conundrum' in *Spiritus: A Journal of Christian Spirituality* 3 (2003) 2, 163–185; Sandra M. Schneiders, IHM, 'The Study of Christian Spirituality: Contours and Dynamics of a Discipline' in Elizabeth A. Dreyer & Mark Burrows, *Minding the Spirit: The Study of Christian Spirituality* op. cit. 5–24; Sandra M. Schneiders, IHM, 'A Hermeneutical Approach to the Study of Christian Spirituality' in Elizabeth A. Dreyer & Mark Burrows, *Minding the Spirit: The Study of Christian Spirituality* op. cit. 49–64; Sandra M. Schneiders, IHM, 'Christian Spirituality: Definitions, Methods, Types' in Philip Sheldrake, ed., *The New SCM Dictionary of Christian Spirituality* (London: SCM Press, 2005) 1–6.

17. Ronald Rolheiser, *Seeking Spirituality: Guidelines for a Christian Spirituality for the Twenty-first Century* (London, Sydney Auckland: Hodder & Stoughton, 1998) 7 & 11; Ronald Rolheiser, *The Shattered Lantern: Rediscovering a Felt Presence of God* (New York: Crossroads, 1995).

18. Philip Sheldrake, 'Christian Spirituality as a Way of Living Publicly: A Dialectic of the Mystical and the Prophetic' in *Spiritus: A Journal of Christian Spirituality* 3 (2003) 1, 19–37; Philip Sheldrake, 'Spirituality and its Critical Methodology' in Bruce H. Lescher and Elizabeth Liebert, *Exploring Christian Spirituality* op. cit. 15–34; Philip Sheldrake, 'What is Spirituality?' in Kenneth J. Collins, ed., *Exploring Christian Spirituality: An Ecumenical Reader* (Grand Rapids, MI: Baker Books, 2000) 21–42.

19. Ronald Rolheiser, *Seeking Spirituality*, op. cit. 6.

20. Ibid.

21. Neville Symington, *Emotion and Spirit: Questioning the Claims of Psychoanalysis and Religion* Foreword by John Stokes (London: Karnac Books, 1998) 46–48.

22. John Fulton, Michael P. Hornsby-Smith, Margaret Norris, *The Politics of Spirituality: A Study of a Renewal Process in an English Diocese* (Oxford: The Clarendon Press, 1995) 27–50.

23. Harold G. Koenig, David B. Larson, Michael E. McCullough, *Handbook of Religion and Health* (New York and Oxford: Oxford University Press, 2001) 17–23. See also Martin E. Marty, *When Faiths Collide* (Malden, MA and Oxford: Blackwell, 2005) 97–123.

24. Holly B. Nelson-Becker, 'Spiritual, Religious, Nonspiritual, and Nonreligious Narratives in Marginalized Older Adults: A Typology of Coping Styles' in Mark Brennan, Deborah Heiser, eds, *Spiritual Assessment and Intervention with Older Adults* (Binghamton, NY: The Haworth Pastoral Press, 2004) 21–38 at 22–23.

25. See Rogene A. Buchholz and Sandra B. Rosenthal, 'Spirituality, Consumption and Business: A Pragmatic Perspective' in Robert A. Giacalone and Carole L. Jurkiewicz, eds, *Handbook of Workplace Spirituality and Organizational Performance* (Armonk, NY and London: M. E. Sharpe, 2003) 152–163 at 153.

26. Riane Eisler and Alfonso Montuori, 'The Human Side of Spirituality' in Robert A. Giacalone and Carole L. Jankiewicz, eds, *Handbook of Workplace Spirituality and Organizational Performance* op. cit. 46–56.

27. David O. Moberg, 'The Reality and Centrality of Spirituality' in David O. Moberg, ed., *Aging and Spirituality: Spiritual Dimensions of Aging Theory, Research, Practice, and Policy* (Binghamton, NY: The Haworth Pastoral Press, 2001) 3–20.

28. Pam McCarroll, Thomas St. James O'Connor, Elizabeth Meakes, 'Assessing Plurality in Spirituality Definitions' in Augustine Meier, Thomas St James O'Connor, Peter VanKatwyck, eds, *Spirituality and Health: Multidisciplinary Explorations* (Waterloo: Wilfrid Laurier University Press, 2005) 43–60.

29. See Allan K. Fitzsimmons, *Defending Illusions: Federal Protection of Ecosystems*

(Lanham, Boulder, New York, London: Rowman & Littlefield Publishers, 1999) 115–138. See also Alexander Gillespie, *International Environmental Law, Policy and Ethics* (New York, Oxford: Oxford University Press, 1997, reprinted 2002) 62–81; Roger S. Gottlieb, ed., *This Sacred Earth: Religion, Nature, Environment* (London, New York: Routledge, 1996); F. Marina Shauffler, *Turning to Earth: Stories of Ecological Conversion* (Charlottesville and London: University of Virginia Press, 2003).

30. See Adam Possamai, *In Search of New Age Spiritualities* (Aldershot: Ashgate, 2005) 23–24.

31. Mark A. McIntosh, *Mystical Theology: The Integrity of Spirituality and Theology* (Oxford: Blackwell, 2005) 130–145.

32. Ibid. 134.

33. See Kees Waaijman, *Spirituality: Forms, Foundations, Methods* (Louvain: Peeters, 2002) 11–303.

34. See Unruh et al. 'Spirituality Unplugged' op. cit. 7–13; Zinnbauer et al. 'Religion and Spirituality' op. cit. pp. 550–552; Waaijman, *Spirituality*, op. cit. 307–309; S. Rose, 'Is the Term "Spirituality" a Word Everyone Uses, But Nobody Knows What Anyone Means By It?' in *Journal of Contemporary Religion* 16 (2002) 2, 193–207.

35. William Stringfellow, *The Politics of Spirituality* (Philadelphia: Westminster Press, 1984) 19.

36. Ibid. 22.

37. Ibid. 20–21.

38. Peter Van Ness, "Introduction: Spirituality and the Secular Quest,' in *Spirituality and the Secular Quest. World Spirituality: An Encyclopedic History of the Religious Quest*, vol. 22, edited by Peter Van Ness. (New York: Crossroad, 1996) 5.

39. See Richard J. Woods, *Christian Spirituality: God's Presence through the Ages. New Expanded Edition* (Maryknoll: Orbis Books, 2006) 274–276

40. See Alister E. McGrath, *Christian Spirituality: An Introduction* (Oxford: Blackwell, 1999) 9.

## CHAPTER 10

*Practices, Literacies and Discourses:
The Shape of Contemporary Spirituality*

*As a life project spirituality surfaces today in the interlocking
fields of practice that reveal the journey towards
coherence in lives touched by the sacred.*

## SPIRITUALITY AS A FIELD OF PRACTICE

Spirituality today, as a life project that finds expression through
practices, literacies and discourses, is a field of changing and contrasting
voices, allegiances and emphases. In this changing world, the study of
spirituality faces the difficult task of discerning the extent to which we
are still gripped by the high certainties of modernity's positivist myth of
unabated progress or have crossed the shifting threshold into the borderlands and in-between spaces of late modern and postmodern uncertainty
and pathos. This is a space where modern practices of demythologisation
and their rationalist ideologies begin to turn against themselves and seek
the re-enchantment of the world. This is the social turn that provides the
background for understanding what is happening in contemporary spirituality. It emerges in interlocking fields of practice that reveal the journey
towards coherence in lives touched by transcendence and the sacred.

The changes we are experiencing are global and interactive in nature.
They show many of the symptoms of technologically driven acceleration,
nowhere more clearly than in the information revolution and the practices
that frame it. This implies that the tempo of change tends to outpace the
capacity of people to incorporate it not only into their deep-seated socio-
political and socio-religious practices and discourses, but into their
spiritual and moral attitudes as well. It seems that the act of interpreting
the world is intimately linked with the practices that change it.[1] The
implications for the practice and study of spirituality are staggering. At
the very least, existential and experiential gaps and uncertainties arise
that impact deeply on the understanding and practice of spirituality
whether it is understood as a search for knowledge or a search for change.

This phenomenon seems to hold true regardless of whether mechanistic
or organic, traditional or modern, individualistic or communal, grass-

roots or organisational approaches to spirituality are adopted.[2] As earlier arrangements are eroded, an unoccupied space opens up in the spiritual-cultural landscape. This gap allows once repressed and marginalised spiritual practices to return. Implicitly and explicitly these also include a continuum of understandings of the nature of human being that range from the most fundamentalist to the most liberal. More importantly, issues of authenticity, sincerity, and honesty, as well as issues of authority and truth also arise. Here, authenticity, with its turn to the person and self-directed understandings and practices of authority, represents the more demanding, more painful ethical experience, not least because it raises 'how' rather than 'what' questions about spirituality and its tasks in the world.[3]

### ℭ The pathos of authenticity

The challenges we encounter in the particularities of context and the practices that shape them are already carriers of meaning, vital resources for spiritual reflection and practice.[4] More importantly, for spirituality the changing and declining ethos of the times paradoxically confronts us with the pathos of authenticity: the living experience of a hope being frustrated by the contingent and unpredictable realities of contemporary existence.[5] The pathos of authenticity arises in spirituality as a paradoxical recognition of our shared longing for a secure ground and a desire for life to the full (John 10:10). But this desire is confronted by an ever-shifting, ever out-of-reach experience in a world that exploitatively pits the sacred and the secular against each other in a consumer fantasy land where the siren calls of shallow ethics and empty promises abound.[6] Such is the uncertain, the sometimes cynical, and the frequently material-istic or greed-driven ground that so often gives rise to the anticlimax of authenticity, to its pathos, and to its challenges to self-implicating spiritual transformation in an uncertain milieu.

There are other challenges. Students and practitioners of spirituality alike are confronted today with epochal horizons shaped by dynamic historical and cultural forces that expose the positive and negative effects of attachment histories.[7] This is where the pathos of authenticity generates a field of practices. What happens when we are confronted by the world itself as image or sound byte, especially when that image or sound byte is the product of a burgeoning technology serving other agendas?[8] Why are people who seek to take spirituality seriously surprised when cultural conflicts arise in contexts where competing and absolutist constituencies seek to impose their own contested ethical visions on the body politic?

Then there is the challenge of media representations typified by a whole spectrum of conservative, liberal, religious, secular, materialist, and consumer dogmatisms. It is as if two resolute faiths, two resolute visions, are at cross-purposes in the world today: sacred visions of the future grounded in often disputed metaphysics, and contesting secular visions of the future grounded in an increasingly threadbare secular faith in the modernist myth of human, scientific and technological progress. This is the space where Christian spirituality is challenged to come to grips with its own understanding of self-emptying kenosis (Philippians 2:7), especially when it is associated with often unconsciously gendered positions of rank and power. All of these factors are embodied in fields of spiritual and cultural practices.

Gianni Vattimo's concept of cultural destabilisation represents a third challenge, especially for Christian spirituality as it attempts to understand contemporary reality and respond to the invitation to flourish in grace.[9] Christian spirituality is invited today to attend to what John Webster has described as the snares of modernity where Christian spirituality is challenged to find its way not only between nature and history or between self and non-self, but also between givenness and choice, and above all between human well-being and the freedom of God.[10] This journey is negotiated through fields of practices that allow us to investigate spirituality in its actual social context as phenomena such as agency, knowledge, beliefs, doctrines, language, ethics, power and technique surface and demand attention. But even as we do this, we need to be alert to the need for different, often conflicting intuitions about spiritual practices, about the purposes of spirituality, and of the need for different research methods in spiritually destabilised cultural contexts. Inherent in this need is the cry for a humbler, softer, more humane understanding of the human predicament.

Authentic spirituality will be better served by turning to forms of discourse and practice that do not aspire to totalise the multitude of contrasting and contesting human voices into a single universalising system. This must be particularly so in encounters with the voices that inhabit the borderlands, the culturally unapproved and in-between spaces of consensual and mainstream reality. The spiritual challenge is to undertake an adventure of difference as we attempt to find our way through the labyrinth that is the contested world in which we live.[11] What is at stake is spirituality's capacity to express itself actively in a new world even as it transcends the old. The call is for a mode of praxis that generates spirituality itself.[12] That is why we need to re-envision spirituality as a field of practices. It will allow us to imagine a third space in a world that is no longer spiritually homogeneous, a space between the passing world of modernity and its snares and the not-yet worlds of the truly postmodern and their as-yet mysterious possibilities.

## THE ADVANTAGE OF WEAK ONTOLOGY

All of this bespeaks a turn to ontology, the branch of philosophy that studies existence and the nature of being. Because spirituality engages with human existence I would like to view the actual state of contemporary spirituality through the lens of what Gianni Vattimo termed *weak ontology*.[13] I am alert to the problems Vattimo's approach brings in its train, but I believe that there are two very good intersecting reasons to bring weak ontology into conversation with spirituality when it is understood as a field of practices. The first is that in the postmodern context all basic paradigms of self, other and world are contestable. The second recognises that these very paradigms are unavoidable in the search for a reflective ethical and social life: it is within such parameters that spirituality surfaces. Practice theory is well placed to handle such challenges. These ideas suggest the value of a humbler position if valid dialogical practices are to emerge and orient spiritual conversations. Weak ontology not only represents a philosophy of actuality – and spirituality is the study of actuality – it also contests modernity's universalistic, atemporal, aggressive self-centrism and its intolerance of contradiction. More importantly for spirituality, weak ontology not only engages in a humbler process of reflection open to rethinking, healing, attention and respect, it is sufficiently strong to point towards definitive truth.[14]

A humbler ontology accepts that context, contingency, contestability, and history impact on the whole gamut of ethical, religious, spiritual and socio-political practices and ideas. Founded on an engaged self, an engaged contemplative self, weak ontology allows for an energetic understanding of existence and being. It is empathic, generative, contextual and responsive, concerned with experiential interaction. Weak ontology understands personal narratives. It is not aggressive; it does not domineer, it lets down walls; it overcomes itself by attending to the unspoken and the unspeakable; it is capable of delight; it is hospitable to the stranger and the strange, the residues, the sealed-off places of silence and the body; the repressed, marginalised places; and it is ready to meet other worlds. A softer, humbler ontology is ideally suited for the tasks of contemporary spirituality because it is at home in the places where the resurgence of spirituality is taking place in our times, the places of performative practice, the places of change and difference: the reality of indeterminate spaces that are simultaneously real and imagined, heterotopias, places of possibility, change, crisis and improvisation, spiritual counter-sites that stop us in our tracks.[15] By confronting our habitual assumptions heterotopias become apt places for disconcerting encounters with the radically Other.[16]

By allowing for processes of disagreement and correction, by being aware of pre-suppositions, hidden assumptions, frames of reference, horizons, expectations and distortions, weak ontology and a sense of heterotopia not only allows other voices to emerge, it also permits silenced voices to be heard again. It allows for finitude and the infinitely surprising. It allows for humanisation and the linked themes of complexity, experience, language, embodiment and its spatial and temporal situations. It also attends to such emotive issues as provocation, disillusionment, nostalgia, despair, and melancholia, significant issues in contemporary spirituality. In so doing, weak ontology also undermines narcissism and arrogance, the twin dangers of modernity's self-assured rationalism. Weak ontology is concerned with opening up spaces for change, spaces for new modes of thought, attention and action, spaces for arrays of practices. What is at stake is nothing less than a more open, more nuanced, more contingently alert, more contextually aware, more situated and more ethical form of spiritual practice. These are paradoxical times and they refuse a single unitary history or explanation. There are other truths yet to be developed.[17]

Claims based on strong ontologies have ceased to be universally compelling or convincing. The challenge today is to engage with grounding political and religious interpretations of the world in ways that reduce the pretexts for violence, cynicism and scorn, interpretations that allow the changing social context to open ways to mutual respect, care, engagement and thoughtful response. Reality is not simple. It is a rich and saturated phenomenon typified by a multiplicity of factors: entanglements, languages, historicity, cultures, and clusters of commitments to a growing range of concepts and ideologies. We live in complex, fragmented societies that use many interpretative models. This very complexity undermines the possibility of a unitary or privileged point of view; it challenges the search for objectivity. If these forces go unacknowledged in the study of spirituality, how are we to handle the ambiguities of cultural translation?[18] In this way, writers and commentators are confronted with the interplay of individual autonomy, society, self-interest, religion, and ethical knowledge, a potent brew that requires a steady hand! In such contexts, love alone and the justice it cries out for shine like guiding lights in the storm and the dark.

## POETICS AND PRACTICES

The interweaving of weak ontology, poetics, and practice theory with spirituality is guided by the assumption that the study of spirituality is best served by the methods and approaches of practical theology in dialogue with the human sciences. Contemporary forms of spirituality, as dynamic expressions of human life, constitute a relatively autonomous area of social, cultural, religious and philosophical practice that is currently in a resurgent state. From the human point of view, understandings of spirituality can only be helped by an honest and open conversation with the human and social sciences. If spirituality represents fields of practices, then it needs to engage with a recuperative hermeneutics of practice itself: though it must be said that poetics is not just another word for hermeneutics. Poetics is not about explaining texts. It is about what happens to us when we read spiritual texts or listen to spiritual narratives. It is about what begins to unfold in our minds and imaginations, in our lives and our relationships. Audacity of spirit is manifested in audacious practices. It is lived, not just merely said.

There lies the difference in a nutshell. Poetics and practices are about us, about the quality of the lives we choose to live, and the worlds we choose to construct by our living choices. Poetics and practices are about agency and action in the world. Both are needed if spiritual practitioners are to construct a broad, goal-oriented praxis capable of doing justice to a resurgent spirituality. Both are needed as the repressed dimensions of embodiment and soul return in response to the forces of postmodern emancipation whose winds of change carry with them real risks of fragmentation and superficiality. For Christian spirituality a goal-oriented praxis is challenged to respond with integrity to the human person situated in open or contested relation to Church in its local situations. Such open or contested relations emerge against the broader global contexts of human pathos that reveals implicit and explicit forms of political, gender-based, cultural and economic oppressions and exclusions. Spiritual audacity is needed to let Jesus live in such contexts.

Practice is an important theoretical construct today, one that is particularly relevant to the study and practice of spirituality.[19] Practice theory was designed for working with either living people or well-documented historical events, focal points shared with spirituality. Contemporary spirituality is about the practices of living people and the events through which they live. It is about repeated daily activities that individuals and groups enact as they undertake the spiritual journey and give it embodied expression. Sets of practices that gradually become habitual are set in train and become the compositional basis of an emerging style of life responsive to the realities of particular cultural-historical-religious milieux. Not unlike poetics, practice theory examines the routines and anomalies of daily life for evidence relating to the subject at hand – in this case, spiritually oriented identity-making transformative behaviours. Like poetics practice theory provides a suitable tool for modelling spiritual-cultural experience and behaviour, first because it offers a portal to how meaning is produced and maintained through repetitive patterns of activity, and second because such patterns are easily observed in practice.

A poetics understands spirituality as a mode of composition typified by a wealth of wide-ranging practices and their related rational, affective and active expressions. Narrative structures have effects. A poetics helps us to see spirituality as an interactive space where a wealth of everyday practices and metaphors make their presence felt. *Spirituality is a journey* is a typical example. Journey represents both a metaphor and a field of practice, a question of creative agency and imaginative action. Poetics also helps us to understand that spiritual-cultural practices operate according to their own functional logics and modes of metaphoric, enigmatic or paradoxical expression. Poetics and practices bring about effects. They can also disclose problems. As fields of practices, contemporary spiritualities are distinguished by complex, dynamic and multidimensional modes of inward and outward thought, feeling and action. Such fields are considered to be personally and socially relational in character. They are centres of relational interactions that take place simultaneously on interweaving levels of thinking, intuiting, sensing, feeling, affectivity and behaviour. In short, spirituality is innately experiential. It demands personal acquaintance with the practices that give it living expression.

Like other forms of discourse, spirituality is concerned with the meanings events and experiences have for people actively involved in contemporary contexts. Like discourse, spirituality is a space where human meaning-making occurs and finds discursive expression in fields of practices. Practices shape the transformative relationship with the true, the good and the beautiful, however they may be experienced in context. This raises an intriguing question. Is spirituality one or many fields of practices? The answer will depend on whether we can clearly differentiate, for example, between Eastern and Western spiritual practices, or between secular and religious spiritual practices, or between adult, adolescent and children's spiritual practices, between love-based and fear-based spiritual practices, or between the spiritual practices of women and men.

Even when differentiations are well grounded we are confronted by what they have in common: a shared interest in some kind of meaning-making, or some desire for liberation and healing, or some desire for comforting hope, as new situations are encountered and new practices demanded. What poetics and practice theory help us to do is to engage with the way fields of practices reveal a negotiated order that emerges in the human dance between social settings and contextual resources. Spirituality would add at least a third dimension to this dynamic interplay of social settings and contextual resources: the dance with transcendence and the transpersonal; and Christian spirituality would want to recognise the transforming dance with gifting Spirit and the God seeds that feed spirit. After all, spirituality is a domain of situated activity that mediates not only contexts and resources but beliefs, emotions, desires, personality preferences and a range of other psychospiritual and religious elements as well.

As a meaning-making, discursive activity, spirituality is organised by values and beliefs, by representations of needs, by aesthetics, by language, by religious receptivity or contestation, as well as the interplay of tragedy and serenity, sorrow and joy. These are part of the music of the often-discordant dance between the individual and the collective. Spirituality is often a site of personal and social struggle, a space where life is encountered in the raw, a space where the dark is as likely as the bright, and resistance as likely as receptivity. Spirituality emerges not only in the messy everyday conflicts and contingencies of life, but also in the ambiguities and ambivalences of the practices of every day. Spirituality emerges in our search for self-definition and self-understanding, and it is there as we attempt to make sense of our internal states and desires, our worldviews, our innermost selves.

Spirituality is not only present in the great themes of politics, religion, and the survival of the planet. It is also present – at least implicitly – in the seemingly trivial and casual conversations we engage in about daily experience, about people and relationships, about activities and events, about work and play, about needs and desires and the run-of-the-mill dimensions of commonplace lives. And it is there in the interweaving invitations and challenges of the social, cultural, religious and psychological aspects of our lives. What actually constitutes spiritual practice is not always readily apparent or well defined. The spiritual dimension of life does not exist in a vacuum. It dances in and out of the whole array of forces that impinge on individual and collective lives – the political, economic, social, historical, aesthetic, moral, religious, ecclesiastical and organisational aspects of human existence.

## THE PRACTICE TURN

The concept of practice is not as unambiguous as it may appear. Nor is clarity helped by divisions that mirror the – false? deceitful? – dichotomy often placed between theory and practice. There is no agreed theoretical definition of practice beyond a very basic understanding that practices are arrays of patterned human activity that tend to have socially recognised goals.[20] It is often difficult to define the activities that make up a particular field of practices. This is often the case in resurgent spiritualities, especially in their patchwork and eclectic expressions. At the same time, it is possible to identify a basic convergence of interest on the typical skills, techniques, assumptions, and tacit logics that underpin sets of activities. These four interconnected thematics already provide us with useful interpretative lenses for exploring the nature and expression of lived spirituality in contemporary – and historical – environments. There is also a convergence of interest among theorists on the embodied nature of practice. This is evident in the use within the worlds of religion and spirituality of pious objects and artefacts.

Practice accounts have the capacity to identify and underscore a wide range of observable phenomena. These include not only forms of knowledge, teaching, and levels of meaning, but also the types of action, engagement and modes of embodied and linguistic expression that arise within schools and traditions of spirituality. They also highlight the paradigms, stages of transformation and growth, and the development of sophisticated techniques within strands of spirituality. Practice accounts also draw attention to a range of identifiable components of fields of practices: power and empowerment, the impacts of and responses or reactions to the particularities of social systems and cultural traditions, the role of new and old personal and collective mythologies and histories. Thus, spirituality may be properly defined as a complex field of practice, or a complex of fields of practices, in which an indeterminate array of activities and their related components mark their presence and make their mark in personal, social, and religious lives.

Spirituality may be further defined as a field of embodied practices mediated by arrays of personal and/or group activities organised around some form of practical understanding or, more to the point, organised around a critically reflective spiritual praxis. The word *embodied* here is important. It highlights such aspects of spiritual practice as movements and postures, as well as spatial and sensual activities of many different kinds. It also draws attention to the view that practice is at root a body construct responding or reacting to socio-cultural or socio-religious spatial contexts. Practice is constitutive of body experience, and body experience is foundational to practice; the implications for disembodied visions of spiritual experience are not far to seek. Suffice it to remind ourselves that every level of human experience has a bio-neurological counterpart.

Practices arise in contexts of shared understanding. In spirituality, this is immediately evident in practices such as prayer, meditation or ritual, and in contemplative and mystical practices, especially those that belong to specific schools or traditions. Other contexts are equally illuminative regarding the effective omnipresence of practice and its linkages to shared understandings. Obvious examples include ecological and creational spiritualities, justice and social development spiritualities, gender-based and liberational spiritualities, workplace and business spiritualities, and the spiritualities emerging in the educational, health, psychotherapeutic, and caring professions. In all of these and more, practices shape the nature of spiritual interventions and interactions and impact on emerging understandings and interpretations.

Practices take place in spatial settings and subtly interact with them. Going apart to pray, seeking a quiet space to meditate, shaping liturgical and ritual spaces aesthetically and architecturally, writing icons, creating works of art and music to support spiritual awareness and attention, going into deserts or other spaces of retreat, setting out on pilgrimage, visiting sacred sites, climbing holy hills and mountains, seeking and discovering thin places: all are expressive of the wide world of embodied practices. The meaning of space itself within spirituality is in many ways a concomitant aspect of contextual practice and serves to construct spatial relatedness. Using light and darkness, colour, texture, shape and form and the many expressions of the artist's and architect's art is an essential component in the interweaving of space and practice in embodied form. It reminds us that practice becomes an essential component of critical praxis, especially when related inner states give rise to contextual results. The concept of praxis engages with practices precisely because embodied, spatial practice informs the critical reflection that defines praxis at its best. A praxis approach does not oppose theory to practice. By linking truth and action praxis allows them to interact dynamically in service of a goal. Praxis is dialogical.

Practice is a complex, multidimensional reality, but one that does not privilege one aspect or component over another in interpreting the social or religious or spiritual worlds in which practitioners of spirituality live. For example, language and discourse are practice phenomena, while institutions and structures are practice effects. However, they all interweave and interact with each other. Activity and meaning and the spaces in which they arise constitute a single interactive complex that impacts simultaneously on behaviour, feeling and thought. This interactive complex also impacts on the conscious and the unconscious flows and rhythms that frequently resist separate analysis. In fields of practices, persons, meaning systems, modes of expression, literacy and discourse, activities, personal and institutional roles all play their parts in the interweaving dance of embodied desire and hope, of expectation and loss, of suffering and joy and all the other dynamic components that mark spiritual experience. They can only be fully understood as interactive elements in the fields of practices in which they unfold their parts.

In spirituality, fields of practices arise in a range of interacting contexts: religious, ethical, embodied, political, social, cultural, developmental, liberational, mystical, and many others. Viewing spirituality through the lens of fields of practices and what they represent, especially in the case of self-incriminating practices, also permits us to identify, analyse and evaluate the interdependent patterns of practice that come to light in spiritual and mystical texts, narratives and other dialogical encounters. Attention to practice makes it possible to identify what grounds and organises the interweaving ebb and flow of spiritual or mystical experience in a given narrative account. Augustine's well-known 'Not Yet, Lord!' is a typical example of the impact of interacting yet contesting practices with their specific desires and languages. How often does willingness encounter wilfulness? How often in real life does the desire to pray uncover encounters with mutually contesting desires? Practice reveals the nature of the response. The person either prays or does not pray or at least not yet. The analysis of fields of spiritual practices also helps us to distinguish between patterns that are spiritually creative and enhancing and those that diminish, oppress or wound: the practices themselves reveal what orders and organises them.

In self-incriminating spirituality, practice itself becomes not only an expresser of meaning but also a shaper of what is perceived as normal and desirable in a person or in the life of a spiritual group. Practices become decisive in identifying and discerning such spiritualities. Moreover, the account an individual or group gives of a personal or collective spirituality reveals the force of practice, even in the local languages used to give it expression and in which its truth and authority claims are couched. Fields of practices order what is considered normal within a consensual spiritual system, and fields of practices also reveal meaning horizons and languages. Their interplay makes it possible to identify what is acceptable and what is inevitably repressed or marginalised by practitioners who consent to a spiritual school, system, or tradition.

Practices arise in ongoing activity and cannot be simply reduced to a set of either mental representations or images. Practices anchor the rules that constitute and define a particular form of spirituality through their repeated public enactment; they visibly emerge in situations with a history of use. While images and representations suggest meanings that emerge between knowers and the world, personal and group intentionality is clearly revealed in the situated nature of practice. Practices identify the behaviours and beliefs that correspond to the norms and traditions that characterise a given spirituality as it responds or reacts to actual situations. For example, a religious charism – the divine gift around which a religious community is organised – remains an a-historical, unincarnated abstraction in the absence of practical ways of ordering, communicating and expressing the gift and its service to the world.

Practice is where words, meanings and intentions are made flesh. Practice is what makes spirituality real in time and space. Practices organise and order spirituality in ways that imply worlds of meaning, understanding, knowledge, and ethical response that are made possible through the processes of situated embodiment that practice makes possible. This becomes even more relevant once it is noted that practices have, for better or worse, an observable tendency to take on a life of their own, regardless of individual or group intentions. Through creative, consistent and congruent usage, practices tend to become more refined and more open to transformative learning encounters with new practices;

unfortunately the opposite is also true. The creative and developmental side of this tendency is clearly visible in ongoing meditative and reflective practices. Like good wine, they tend to improve with age and congruent care. It also gives pause for thought on such pivotal elements in life and spirituality as agency, intentionality, knowledge, ethics, power, and even technique itself. The practice of practices indeed makes perfect.

FIELDS OF PRACTICES IN SPIRITUALITY

In spirituality, fields of practices surface in two major ways: through activist or engaged practices, and through what have been traditionally named devotional practices. What the two have in common are voluntary commitments and preparatory exercises. Then, an interactive field of practices is set in train in which some of the following will make their presence felt:

- lectio divina, rhythms of reading, meditation and prayer, especially prayer understood as conversation with God, of silent and vocal prayer, or written and spontaneous prayer, prostrations, bowings, and other embodied postures;
- engaging in breath prayer, aspiratory prayer, the Jesus Prayer;
- paradoxically risking the Void and opening to the All, paradoxically losing the alienated life to gain the true or contemplative life;
- contemplating, singing, chanting, letting jubilee soar, silences, groaning and exclamations, arms outspread, hands raised, hands clapping, hands joined;
- dancing, walking, sitting or kneeling in stillness, hands joined, arms outstretched, fingers fingering beads;
- reflective reading, spiritual exercises, twelve steps programmes, seven-storey mountains, wrestling with God;
- building relational bridges made of faithful, Spirit-informed devotional and spiritual practices;
- making and using religious and spiritual artefacts and objects;
- engaging in honest self-examination and self-reflection;
- confessing unworthiness and sin, patterns of diminishment and disorder, patterns of oppression and injustice, patterns that are destructive of the earth and the species we share it with;
- fasting and abstaining, preparing for death and heaven;
- intertwining active and receptive social rhythms;
- interweaving positive and negative referents, and facing their challenges;
- engaging in participatory practices, celebrating communal worship, marking religious festivals and seasons, celebrating carnival and other special days;

- participating in retreats, novenas, triduums;
- seeking solitude, going apart, engaging in intimately private practices (Matt 6:6);
- seeking spiritual guidance and conversation, joining prayer meetings and meditation groups;
- joining movements for justice, becoming active and engaged in seeking a better world for all;
- refusing to flee the contingencies of either history or politics;
- studying spirituality, attending workshops and conferences;
- painting religious art, writing icons, composing religious and spiritual texts, poems, music, songs, hymnody;
- keeping spiritual journals, writing spiritual biographies, reading and listening to spiritual testimonies.

Even the older tradition of hagiographical writing served devotional and spiritual practices. Their depictions show interweaving fields of inner and outer expressions of piety that in Christian terms become portals and bearers of Spirit.

Fields of practices ground, anchor and express the spiritual life. Even the gaps between written accounts of practices and their lived reality reveal spaces where God's seeds are to be found. Christian spirituality is full of fields of practices that cross traditions and cross-fertilise each other. Many trace their origins back to the Biblical tradition itself. Think of the work of poets such as Richard Crashaw, Robert Southwell, John Donne, George Herbert, William Blake, Gerard Manley Hopkins, and Patrick Kavanagh. Think of John of the Cross, Teresa of Avila, Ignatius of Loyola, Francis de Sales, Jane de Chantal, and more recently people like Dietrich Bonhoeffer, Edith Stein, Dorothy Day, Thomas Merton, Mother Teresa, and Oscar Romero. They cannot be understood apart from the fields of spiritual practices that not only contain and express their very lives but shape their every action. Even at the height of the Reformation, a wide range of shared activist and devotional practices characterised both Protestant and Catholic traditions. The sensual imagery of the Song of Songs recognises no boundaries.

At the level of spiritual practice, there is a broad, implicit ecumenism. Think of the root metaphor of the pilgrimage or journey of the soul. As a way of mapping and engaging with the journey to God, it traces its origins back to Elizabethan England and beyond to Bunyan, Chaucer and Dante, and then to the desert journeys of the people of Israel. Pilgrimage acts as an organising and ordering centre of practice; it is ever ancient and ever new, simultaneously a situated geographic activity and a deep inner purgative, illuminative, unitive activity, a world of transformative exper-iences and practices, and at the same time an interpretative framework and a mode of discourse. The self-same practice is there in the stories of Old Testament figures like Abraham and Sarah, Isaac, Jacob, Joseph, Moses, Rahab, Nehemiah, and in the foundational journey of Jesus from Nazareth to Jerusalem.

Journey and pilgrimage reveal a profoundly spiritual and theological understanding of embodied and geographically situated practices and activities. Embodied action is there in the situated activities that give participative expression to shared doctrinal themes such as grace, conversion, and redemption: metaphors of transformative journey, of *theosis*, and the activities that exemplify that journey and its purposes. The same is true of the forces of diremption that tear people apart and lead to violent separations. There, too, embodied actions and disruptive practices are revealed. Redemption and diremption are practices that point to the construction of a world-view, a meaning horizon, an interpretative structure. They point to either a mode of transformative and reformative visioning and anchoring action or its opposite. In Christian terms, journey as metaphor and field of practice spans the spaces between the birth, life, death and resurrection of Jesus as it finds form in embodied and situated practices that trace its transformative impact on the forces that tear people and the world apart.

The study of practices confronts us primarily with studies of real people living real lives because life rather than ideas about life is what comes to light when spirituality is approached as fields of soul revealing and spirit expressing practices. It brings the engaged and devotional practices and activities of real people to the fore. Spirituality is about spiritual exercises, about the practices that structure and construct spiritual experience, give it tone and colour, give it shape and form as it follows daily, weekly, monthly and yearly patterns, evoking themes, building transformative processes, healing violent conflicts, entering into the redemptive drama, into the journey of spiritual life as it dances its rhythmic way through time and space towards its transcendent goal. Focus on practice also reveals major shifts of allegiance and emphasis in spirituality. In postmodern contexts trust has become nomadic. It turns away from once-loved institutions and traditions no longer deemed trustworthy. It turns inwards to personal experience and authority, giving them precedence over other more communal forms of trust. Practices of change reveal what is in the ascendancy. Practices of change clearly reveal that once-repressed now-contesting practices are making a vigorous return. The future spirituality is unfolding in changing fields of practices.

## SPIRITUALITY AS A DOMAIN OF LITERACY AND DISCOURSE
Discourse, literacy, and practice are mutually constitutive. They come together in the nexus of practice, in the dynamic worlds of human

interaction and communication. Spirituality is a marvellous example of all of these elements at work. As well as being a domain of practice, spirituality is also a domain of literacy and discourse. Discourse highlights the nature of language as meaningful social action. It is a form of practice that takes place through oral or written, formal or informal events, texts and other communicative interactions.[21] Communication in spirituality is already a literacy practice where local meanings play their complex part in personal, communal and group experiences of spiritual conversation discourse.[22] Spirituality is a domain where literacy plays a vital role. A level of spiritual literacy appropriate to age, education, experience and development actively supports spiritual growth and development. Literacy points to other sets of social practices that give expression to the complexities of the different domains of human life: it is a social practice that structures information in specific ways.[23] Literacy practices come in a variety of forms: linguistic, emotional, visual, relational, professional, religious, spiritual. Literacy standards are important characteristics of such domains.

Reflect on the problem of the person with a Masters degree in a professional discipline whose spiritual or religious literacy ceased developing in primary school. There are inevitable literacy gaps that need attention if persons are to bring their professional and spiritual literacies to the same levels of critical fluency. Not surprisingly, then, one of the first difficulties encountered in the study and practice of spirituality is the gap that frequently exists at the level of essential spiritual or religious literacy. Growing in spirituality is not only about growing more proficient in a field of practice. Spiritual growth is also about growing in spiritual or religious literacy precisely because speech, conversation and conceptual awareness are essential elements of spirituality as embodied and situated practices. Literacy not only plays an important role in spiritual growth and development, something demanding time and effort; it also plays a pivotal role in the coordination and communication of individual and group learning and practice.

Practitioners of spirituality need to recognise that many forms of literacy and discourse reveal power relations. For example, levels of spiritual discourse and literacy are used to integrate and classify persons and social groupings. Who is a beginner? Who is advanced? How are such things determined? Literacy and discourse also serve to identify developmental stages and growth challenges.[24] Moreover, organisations and groups use discourse to practise power and exercise authority, usually with the consent of members.[25] Something similar happens in the case of influential individuals, such as teachers; though here the issue of consent becomes more complex because of the decision-making power teachers tend to have. On the other hand, discourse has become a somewhat loose term lacking formally agreed definition across disciplines. This is especially problematic when content is structurally or functionally subordinated to organisational or group goals, as is the case with traditions and schools of spirituality. Spiritual organisations can use discourse in a variety of ways to institutionalise, to legitimise, to take advantage of, and to inculcate organisational doctrines and dogma. In all of these cases, language serves as both the container and the means of organising and structuring inter-personal communication.[26]

By implication, then, spirituality needs to be alert to its language uses and their social implications. This is particularly so in the case of narratives and texts. Every text involves a third function situated between those of narrator and narratee. Texts and narratives produce a world, something that may or may not be familiar to the narratee, which becomes the text's world of reference, its text world.[27] Text worlds are also referred to as mental representations, mental models, mental spaces, and narrative worlds. Spiritual texts always produce text worlds that coincide with the text's narrative function. Spiritual practices, literacies and discourses also coincide with narrative functions and reference worlds, worlds that expose all the key elements of a narrator's spiritual vision, including characters, a sense of time and place, modes of acting, objects, and voices. The text world refers to the arrays of knowledge activated by a text: knowledge about the entities, states, terrains, values, events, and processes that connect to social knowledge and everyday life.[28]

In spirituality as elsewhere, text worlds make use of prior knowledge and common processing practices in their own construction. Moreover, spiritual discourse, whether spoken or written, needs to be understood as a communicative event where linguistic, cognitive, affective, and social actions converge in ways that, for better or worse, have shaping impacts on people. Spiritual discourse, especially when it takes the form of a text world or narrative model, has the power to activate an array of social and inter-subjective forces and forms of knowledge. Text-world models communicate spiritual roles, states, events, processes, stages, structures, functions, and identities.[29] Such models work by offering world-building elements in combination with propositions that advance its function. New worlds can also emerge, facilitated by words like *should, believe, hope, wish, desire, could, might, want, get, keep, clearly, apparently*.[30] Psychological, social and spiritual change is part of the package. Spiritual discourses are not neutral, nor are they always benign. If they were, there would be no such things as dark nights or spiritual emergencies, no such things as spiritual abuse or soul murder.

Spiritual literacies and discourses are complex social phenomena that often represent points of convergence. Not only do technological, cognit-ive, cultural, reflective, and experiential issues meet in the arena of literacy and discourse, but issues of perspective and definition arise as well. Literacy is the most social of practices. It epitomises the role of culture in human communication and it reveals the socio-cultural interactions that are part of every spirituality. Literacy channels and guides the most crucial of our personal and joint conversations and activities. It allows us to be active participants in communities and collectives. That is why being illiterate in a literate culture is so isolating. To be illiterate is to be without important means to become involved and communicate with others.[31] Spiritual illiteracy has the potential to cut people off from worlds of meaning, symbolism, ritual and the sacred. Sacred and spiritual texts become closed books. Spiritual illiteracy also has immense marginalising power in spiritual groups and at spiritual events and gatherings, especially when a degree of emotional, spiritual, ritual and mythological literacy is presumed among participants.

Literacies generate new ways of being in the world, new ways of dialogical relationality. Spiritualities and literacies invite us to go aside, to create reflective spaces, to engage knowingly with forms of transformative learning that have clear social consequences. Spiritualities and their interactive literacies also involve tensions with mainstream consensus realities. Furthermore, literacies and discourses incorporate what is taken for granted, the tacit theories of what we believe are normal and the right ways to think, feel and behave as spiritual practitioners. Literacies and discourses are also portals to what is different, challenging, demanding of change. In this way, they become carriers of difference and potential separation from the mainstream majority view. Conversely, literacies that take on a counter-cultural character can also lead to mainstream marginalisation.

In our daily lives, we all engage in overlapping discourses and make use of an array of literacies that correspond to context and situation. Where discourses and literacies do not mesh, they reveal a variety of gaps, contradictions, inconsistencies, incompatibilities and conflicts that are acted out through different social identities. In spirituality, such gaps represent the spaces of struggle and resistance. They represent the places of complicity with the inner and outer forces that diminish and denigrate our capacities for compassionate and humane interactions. They are the places that undermine the desire to live more congruent soul-based lives and engage more deeply with transformative praxis. These are also the spaces, for example, where work-identity and spiritual-identity lose their interactive congruence and go in different directions, creating worlds where professional and spiritual identities diverge and contradict each other. And in that diverging, larger integrities and values are lost. The challenge raised by practice, literacy and discourse is nothing less than the integrity of every spiritual involvement, the authenticity of each self-implicating spiritual engagement.

This aspect of practice, literacy and discourse becomes more influential as society becomes more pluralist and more fragmented. How does my professional discourse crosscut my family discourse? How do they in turn crosscut my religious and spiritual discourses? What happens when I lack the literacies needed to engage in such discourses or conversations? What happens when the theory behind a discourse does not translate into everyday life so that unconscious issues of power, trust, respect, fairness, equality, status, rank and privilege continue to make damaging impacts? What implicit messages do our inhabiting of simultaneously contra-dictory discourses convey? What happens when literacies and practices have alienating, isolating impacts? What happens when practices, literacies and discourses contradict consensual reality? What happens when practices, literacies and discourses are revealed as essentially self-referential? More importantly, what happens when discourses are decontextualised as so easily happens when formal languages are used? The problem is that discourses, including mainstream consensual discourses and conversations, are sometimes very difficult to distinguish from ideologies, especially when they claim to wear the garb of common sense.

There is an interesting point here. It is revealed every time we use a phrase such as 'That's how it is' or 'That's how I/we understand these things' or 'It is accepted that' or 'That's how I feel about' or 'In my experience'. Discourses reveal beliefs and the regular claims we make about definitions and judgements on the basis of these beliefs. They reveal the interweaving of language and practice in life choices, and show us why Wittgenstein famously described them as 'forms of life' statements. 'Forms of life' statements have social effects precisely because the uses of language are interwoven with the activities and practices, the patterns and configurations with which we engage life, not all of which are subject to free choice and the principles of personal integrity. Hope and grief are typical examples.[32] Other examples include language use itself, being religious, and having a culture. It has been suggested that 'forms of life' statements reveal a range of influential biological, human, cultural, and socio-linguistic dimensions.[33]

Again, different forms of life with their shared practices and shared judgments reflect different ways of seeing the world, ways on which the world itself impacts, ways in which the world itself acts as teacher. The implications for spirituality as an interweaving triad of fields of practices, literacies, and discourses are always close to hand. The problem then is about our capacity for ethical literacy. Are we able to reflect critically on the impact of our own 'form of life' statements and the choices they reveal? Are we alert to the uses and influences of social forms? Are we able to discern the bad from the merely silly?[34] What is at stake is our capacity to understand that patterns of discourse, literacy and practice in spirituality reflect particular ways of defining reality and constructing world-views, which in turn become moulders of identity. It is here that the role of what a person really values in sets of discourses, the practices that give them living expression, and the associated ways of knowing and communicating that are applied to life and the world, come to the fore. This is precisely how spirituality is shaped as a human characteristic: it surfaces performatively and self-incriminatingly in the interweaving worlds of personal, communal and organisational practices, literacies and discourses.

Spirituality clearly has to do with 'forms of life' statements; but it also has to do with the interacting literacies that inform all our spiritual discourses, be they psychological, philosophical, socio-cultural or theological in initial inspiration. The meanings of words are connected to cultural models, which in turn are embedded in social languages or discourses. Once we begin to speak about our spiritualities, we enter this terrain and the challenge then is to come to terms with the cultural and social forces shaping the language we choose to employ in telling our stories and in making sense of them. It is very easy to forget that what makes sense in one community of belief may not make any sense in another. Think for a moment about a conversation between an astronomer and an astrologer. They may have stars in common but there the similarities tend to stop as one engages in a mathematical discourse and the other in a discourse about the forces of destiny. Both believe that they are making sense. Or think of the theist and the atheist. The same word 'God' sits between them, but their sense-making around that word goes in opposite directions. The issue for spirituality here is an accurate awareness of how language works in conjunction with the sets of behaviour and expectations that identify us as individuals and groups and that interact communicatively with our discourse and conversational practices.

Discourses and literacies, like practices, are situated; they arise in contexts. The same is true of spirituality. To the extent that they share the same quality of literacy, spirituality and other forms of discourse emerge within a matrix of other social and cultural activities. Spiritual discourse, reflection and conversation not only reveal a situated literacy with its own historical and spatial contexts: places of pilgrimage are typical examples; they also reveal their own social structuring in language and practice typical of specific forms of life and experience. This structuring capacity becomes clear when we examine spiritualities that engage with and give – frequently tacit – expression to such themes as globalisation, justice, power relations, cultural and gendered identities, planetary and human ecology, liberational praxis, popular religiosity, capitalism, socialism, engaged mysticism and the like. Literacy, in the sense it is used here, is located in the interacting rhythms of time, space, practices and discourse, regardless of whether that discourse is communicated in oral or written form. Spirituality surfaces where arrays of channels of communication – auditory, visual, proprioceptive, kin-aesthetic, relational and social – converge and interact.

As a form of literacy, spirituality often finds itself in the unpredictable borderland spaces between institutions and the power or authority relations that sustain them. The contemporary mantra about being spiritual but not religious is indicative of this transitional space where trust shifts from more institutional to more personal forms of focus and more autonomous, more personally empowered discourse; but it also reveals a potentially tacit and unrecognised neo-liberal political agenda. More specifically, literacy is a social practice that issues in context-specific discourses, narratives and conversations. Spirituality is one such context. In this sense, spirituality identifies things people do with a particular form of literacy and its related forms of intelligence, including intellectual, emotional and spiritual intelligence. Spirituality is thus a social practice in which literacy plays a crucial role. Spiritual literacy then finds expression in context-specific narratives, texts, discourses and conversations. More specifically, as a social practice literacy is also evocative of values, attitudes, understandings, feelings, meaning horizons, assumptions and their related expectations, imagery, transformative learning, socio-religious and cultural identifications, as well as socio-cultural, socio-economic, socio-political and transpersonal relations.

Spirituality and its linked literacies are shaped by social rules, which organise and regulate practices and their expression in narrative and discourse. Practices in this sense bridge the spaces between personal and group or community environments. They surface in, shape and mediate the relationship between the inner and outer dimensions of individual life, and between individual, social and environmental worlds. Each of these settings calls for its own appropriate integrity and authenticity, its own appropriate spiritual logic and literacy. Spirituality represents a specific and yet fluid way of utilising literacy to orient and shape experience in specific directions: towards meaning, towards transcendence, towards transformation, but more specifically towards giving expression to the elusive and mysterious depths of soul. Spiritual practices are activities where the role of literacy is revealed in an array of activities that includes events, journeys, rituals and a wide variety of texts: those of everyday life and those that bespeak deep transformations; those that surface differences, and those that mediate spiritual coherence and integrity.[35]

Literacy supports the ways in which spiritual activities uncover and communicate the meaning and value of our embodied situations and relationships. It helps spirituality not only to make connections and engage with symbol systems, but also to shape identities and modes of relating to people, places and events. Like language itself, literacy is a shaper and moulder of visions and perceptions of reality. It clarifies by confronting what is clouded and obscured. I see this process all the time in my work with adult students when they begin to study spirituality. As language and literacy skills develop, whole new understandings emerge, and hitherto invisible vistas open up and offer new horizons for spiritual awareness, conversation and participation. This is so because such awareness embraces the entire knowing person: body, mind, heart, soul and spirit. It is a literacy that arises from the inner depths of a person. It is a literacy of recognition, of remembrance, of deeper awakening, a literacy of the deeper self, a literacy capable of all that is, a literacy that has learnt how to let Jesus live in word and truth.

Language, literacy, discourse, awareness, practice: such is the raw material of human spirituality. Against this background it becomes possible to re-define spirituality as *a complex convergence of language-in-action, literacy-in-action, discourse-in-action, awareness-in-action, and practice-in-action.* They are all tied in their own ways to what is going on in an individual or group's here-and-now living context: what they are doing or what they ought to be doing. Like spirituality, language, literacy, discourse, awareness and practice surface within and reveal the shaping influences of and resistances to the place-time events and issues of real-life contexts. In the interplays of individual and group response and resistance, language, literacy, discourse, awareness and practice reveal the underlying processes impacting on historically and politically shaped lives. Spirituality emerges dynamically in their dynamic interactions. They all flourish in local forms. They all reveal social participations. They all demand inter-subjective involvement

*Spirituality as the convergence of practices, literacies and discourses*

Where fields of awareness, practice, language, literacy, and discourse converge, spirituality is revealed. Spirituality emerges in the spaces where activist and devotional involvements become the focus of practical engagement. Spirituality is also revealed in the underlying processes by means of which inter-subjective understanding and transformative learning are attained. This is particularly so in the case of spiritual discourse.[36] People and the contextual lives of people become the decisive forces in understanding spirituality as a convergence of discourses, literacies and fields of practices. In this process, texts-as-archives are given a less important place than texts-as-spaces where writer and reader interact in a world of subtle subtexts and shared undertalk that open up new spiritual possibilities and directions, and where inter-subjective literacies are worked out in the dialogic encounter that allows spiritual meaning to arise. That is what it means when spiritual literacies and discourses are understood in inter-subjective terms and when spiritual or mystical texts are seen to facilitate processes of interaction and engagement.[37]

It is precisely for these reasons that spirituality can be approached as a complex field of interactive and inter-subjective practices, literacies and discourses, a complex field of contextual references, resonances, receptivities and resistances. Once we accept that spirituality is a human characteristic, we must be ready to view it in such social, relational and communicative terms. Certainly, from an academic point of view, it is easy enough to see spirituality as a 'discourse community' with its own rules, conventions, and paradigms of inquiry, all with their own attendant vocabularies and forms of discourse. The problem is, of course, that such approaches favour texts. Tacit knowledges become textual propositions, and literate learning is mistaken for literacy learning.[38]

In universities this is understandable, but it does not do any favours to the reality of spirituality as it is lived in the embodied situations of real lives. There, the daily interactions of literacies and practices rather than textual analysis form the primary stuff of contextually engaged spiritualities. The trick for those academically interested in spirituality is to know the difference. The study of contemporary spirituality has more in common with ethnography and social anthropology than with literary criticism; it calls for interactive fieldwork. A softer, humbler, generative, interactive and inter-subjective approach, respectful of oral literacies and oral narratives, will best serve the nature of soul-based, spirit-seeking lives, especially in the fragmented, pluralist societies where Western spirituality is once again challengingly resurgent. In the end, spirituality is always about depth, about the fact that in truly insightful spiritual lives there is no gap between spiritual awareness and spiritual action.

Conscious practice knits them together as a seamless garment, a dance in the service of life.

## THEMES AND QUESTIONS FOR FURTHER REFLECTION

1. Identify key practices that give genuine inner and outer expression to individual and communal spirituality. How transformative are such practices?
2. Discuss the importance of spiritual literacy to spiritual development. Are you able to engage in genuine spiritual conversations with other adults, and give a coherent adult account of your spirituality?
3. Describe how spiritual practices and conversations support life. How can they help to make a better, more responsive, more responsible world?

## FURTHER READING

Michael Casey, *Fully Human, Fully Divine: An Interactive Christology* (Chawton: Redemptorist Publications, 2004).

NOTES:    1. See for example, Gianni Vattimo, 'Gadamer and the Problem of Ontology' in Jeff Malpas, Ulrich Arnswald and Jens Kertscher, eds, *Gadamer's Century: Essays in Honor of Hans Georg Gadamer* (Cambridge, Mass: MIT Press, 2002) 299–306; and 'After Onto-Theology: Philosophy Between Science and Religion' in Mark A. Wrathall, ed., *Religion After Metaphysics* (Cambridge: Cambridge University Press, 2003) 29–36.

2. See John Fulton, Michael P. Hornsby-Smith, Margaret Norris, *The Politics of Spirituality: A Study of a Renewal Process in an English Diocese* (Oxford: The Clarendon Press, 1995) 27–50.

3. For a discussion of these issues see Jacob Golomb, *In Search of Authenticity: From Kierkegaard to Camus* (London & New York: Routledge, 1995).

4. See Gregory B. Stone, *The Death of the Troubadour: The Late Medieval Resistance to the Renaissance* (Philadelphia: University of Pennsylvania Press, 1994) 208.

5. My understanding of the term pathos of authenticity has been influenced by Gianni Vattimo. *La fine della modernità* (Milan: Garzanti, 1985); the English translation was published three years later, *The End of Modernity* (Baltimore: Johns Hopkins University Press, 1988).

6. See Marta Frascati-Lockhead, *Kenosis and Feminist Theology: The Challenge of Gianni Vattimo* (Albany, NY: State University of New York Press, 1998) 72; Daphne Erdinast-Vulcan, *The Strange Short Fiction of Joseph Conrad: Writing, Culture, and Subjectivity* (Oxford: Oxford University Press, 1999) 92; Chris

Bongie, *Exotic Memories: Literature, Colonialism, and the Fin de Siecle* (Stanford, CA: Stanford University Press, 1991) 23–28.

7. See Paulo Freire, Henry A. Giroux, Michael Peters, eds, *Education and the Postmodern Condition.* (Westport, CT: Bergin & Garvey, 1995) 17.

8. See Ronaldo Munck, *Cultural Politics in Latin America* (Basingstoke: Macmillan, 2000) 66.

9. Mary McClintock Fulkerson, 'Feminist Theology' in Kevin J. Vanhoozer, ed., *The Cambridge Companion to Postmodern Theolog.* (Cambridge: Cambridge University Press, 2003) 109–125 at 121–122.

10. John Webster, 'The Human Person' in Kevin J. Vanhoozer, ed., *The Cambridge Companion to Postmodern Theology.* op. cit. 219–234 at 229.

11. Felix Geyer, *Alienation, Ethnicity and Postmodernism* (Westport, CT: Greenwood Press 1996) 174; see also Chris Bongie. *Exotic Memories: Literature, Colonialism, and the Fin de Siecle,* op. cit. 25.

12. See Clayton Crockett, *A Theology of the Sublime* (London: Routledge, 2001) 18–20.

13. See, for example, Stephen K. White, *Sustaining Affirmation: The Strength of Weak Ontology in Political Theory* (Princeton: Princeton University Press, 2000); Gianni Vattimo. *Belief.* Trans. Luca D'Isanto & David Webb (Stanford, CA: Stanford University Press, 1999); Gianni Vattimo *La fine della modernità* (Milan: Garzanti, 1985); Gianni Vattimo & Pier Aldo Rovatti, eds, *Il pensiero debole* (Milan: Feltrinelli, 1983); Rene Girard, *Things Hidden Since the Foundation of the World* Trans. Michael Metteer & Stephen Bann (Stanford, CA: Stanford University Press, 1987); Marta Frascati-Lochhead, *Kenosis and Feminist Theology: The Challenge of Gianni Vattimo.* op. cit.

14. See Alicia De Alba, Edgar González-Gaudiano, Colin Lankshear, Michael Peters, *Curriculum in the Postmodern Condition* (New York: Peter Lang, 2000) 54. See also Valeria Finucci, *Renaissance Transactions: Ariosto and Tasso* (Durham, NC: Duke University Press, 1999) 3.

15. See Gianni Vattimo. 'From Utopia to Heterotopia,' in *The Transparent Society,* translated by David Webb (Cambridge: Polity Press, 1992) 62–75. See also Tabin Siebers, ed., *Heterotopia: Postmodern Utopia and the Body Politic* (Ann Arbor: University of Michigan Press, 1994).

16. See Thomas R. Flynn, 'Partially Desacralized Spaces: The Religious Availability of Foucault's Thought' in James Bernauer and Jeremy Carrette, eds, *Michel Foucault and Theology: The Politics of Religious Experience* (Aldershot: Ashgate, 2004) 143–156.

17. See Fred D'Agostino, *Free Public Reason: Making it up as We Go* (Oxford & New York: Oxford University Press, 1996) 112.

18. See Chris Bongie. *Islands and Exiles: The Creole Identities of Post-Colonial Literature* (Stanford, CA: Stanford University Press, 1998) 382.

19. My understanding of practice theory is grounded in a conversation with

the following texts: Pierre Bourdieu, *Outline of a Theory of Practice* (Cambridge: Cambridge University Press, 1977, thirteenth printing, 2003); Margaret Wetherell, Stephanie Taylor, Simon J. Yates, *Discourse Theory and Practice: A Reader* (London: Sage, 2002); Peter Jarvis, *Adult and Continuing Education: Theory and Practice* (London: Routledge, 1995); Norman Graves, ed., *Learner Managed Learning: Practice, Theory and Policy* (London: Routledge, 1993); Adele E. Clarke, *Situational Analysis: Grounded Theory After the Postmodern Turn* (London: Sage, 2005); Kate Cregan, *The Sociology of the Body* (London: Sage, 2006); Derek Layder, *Understanding Social Theory* Second Edition (London: Sage, 2005); Anthony Elliott and Larry Ray, eds, *Key Contemporary Social Theorists* (Oxford: Blackwell Publishers, 2003); Griff Foley, ed., *Dimensions of Adult Learning: Adult Education and Training in a Global Era* (Crows Nest, NSW: Allen & Unwin, 2004); Hedwig Meyer-Wilmes, Lieve Troch, Riet Bons-Storm, eds, *Feminist Perspectives in Pastoral Theology: Yearbook of the European Society of Women in Theological Research* (Leuven: Peeters, 1998); Edward Farley, *Practicing Gospel: Unconventional Thoughts on the Church's Ministry* (Louisville, KY: Westminster John Knox Press, 2003).

20. See Simeon J. Yates, 'Researching Internet Interaction: Sociolinguistics and Corpus Analysis' in Margaret Wetherell, Stephanie Taylor and Simon J. Yates, eds, *Discourse as Data: A Guide for Analysis* (London, Thousand Oaks, New Delhi: Sage/Open University, 2001) 93–146 at 101.

21. See Renata Fox and John Fox, *Organizational Discourse: A Language-Ideology-Power Perspective* (Westport, CT: Praeger, 2004) xi and 15.

22. See Teun A. van Dijk, 'Multidisciplinary CDA: A Plea for Diversity' in Ruth Wodak and Michael Meyer, eds, *Methods of Critical Discourse Analysis* (London, Thousand Oaks, New Delhi: Sage Publications, 2001) 95–120 at 103–106. See also Teun A. van Dijk, 'Principles of Critical Discourse Analysis' in Margaret Wetherell, Stephanie Taylor and Simeon J Yates, eds, *Discourse Theory and Practice: a Reader* (London, Thousand Oaks, New Delhi: Sage/Open University, 2001) 300–317 at 312–314.

23. See David Barton and Mary Hamilton, 'Literacy Practices' in David Barton, Mary Hamilton and Roz Ivanič, eds, *Situated Literacies: Reading and Writing in Context* (London & New York: Routledge, 2000) 7–15.

24. See James Paul Gee, *Social Linguistics and Literacies: Ideology in Discourses*, Second Edition (London: Taylor & Francis Ltd., 1996) ix. See also James Paul Gee, *An Introduction to Discourse Analysis: Theory and Method* (London and New York: Routledge, 1999).

25. See Renata Fox and John Fox, *Organizational Discourse*, op. cit. 8.

26. ibid. 22.

27. See Paul N. Werth, *Text Worlds: Representing Conceptual Space in Discourse* (London: Longman, 1999). See also Joanna Gavins, '"Too much blague?" An Exploration of the Text Worlds of Donald Barthelme's *Snow White*' in

Joanna Gavins and Gerard Steen, eds, *Cognitive Poetics in Practice* (London: Routledge, 2003) 129–144.

28. See Ross Chambers, *The Writing of Melancholy: Modes of Opposition in Early French Modernism.* Translated by Mary Seidman Trouille (Chicago and London: Chicago University Press, 1993) 1–23. See also Catherine Emmott, *Narrative Comprehension: A Discourse Perspective* (Oxford: Clarendon Press, 1997) 56–59; Renata Fox and John Fox, *Organizational Discourse*: op. cit. 36-39; Angela Carrasquillo and Vivian Rodriguez, *Language Minority Students in the Mainstream Classroom: Bilingual Education and Bilingualism*, 2nd Edition (Clevedon: Multilingual Matters, 2001) 87–90.

29. See Renata Fox and John Fox, *Organizational Discourse*, op. cit. 36. See also Robert de Beaugrande, *New Foundations for a Science of Text and Discourse: Cognition, Communication, and the Freedom of Access to Knowledge and Society* (Norwood, NJ: Ablex Publishing Corporation, 1997).

30. See Joanna Gavins, '"Too much blague?" An Exploration of the Text Worlds of Donald Barthelme's *Snow White*' op. cit. 130–132.

31. See Deborah Brandt, *Literacy as Involvement: The Acts of Writers, Readers, and Texts* (Carbondale, IL: Southern Illinois University Press, 1990) 1–11.

32. See, for example, Oswald Hanfling, *Wittgenstein and the Human Form of Life* (London & New York: Routledge, 2002). See also, Naomi Scheman, 'Forms of Life: Mapping the Rough Ground' in Hans Sluga, David G. Stern, eds, *The Cambridge Companion to Wittgenstein* (Cambridge: Cambridge University Press, 1996) 383–410.

33. See Nicholas F. Gier, *Wittgenstein and Phenomenology: A Comparative Study of the Later Wittgenstein, Husserl, Heidegger, and Merleau-Ponty* (Albany, NY: State University of New York Press, 1981) 18–21.

34. See Peter Munz, *Beyond Wittgenstein's Poker: New Light on Popper and Wittgenstein* (Aldershot: Ashgate Publishing Ltd., 2004) 89–100.

35. See David Barton and Mary Hamilton, 'Literacy Practices' op. cit. 8–10.

36. See Deborah Brandt, *Literacy as Involvement* op. cit. 96.

37. ibid. 99–100.

38. ibid. 119–120.

## CHAPTER 11

*Apophatic Spirituality and*
*Passionate Solidarity*

> *We need a spirituality informed by stillness in a noisy world*
> *and a passionate solidarity in a world of individualisms.*
> *Our shared humanity requires them.*

INTRODUCTION

A principal aim of authentic Christian spirituality today is the development and support of persons choosing to walk a path of love open to God, open to the traces of the divine in all that is, persons capable of building a caring civilisation of life in a globalising world. The primary social task of an emergent post-postmodern spirituality, then, will be to take a prophetically critical approach to the socio-cultural ethos that orients globalising consumer cultures. The task of such a spirituality will be to offer an alternative ethos, an alternative orientation, to people living in a world of consumer-driven individualisms. This will be a robust spirituality shared by people committed to respectful justice and passionately caring solidarity with all who suffer and all who are diminished in an exploitive world. It will be a wise spirituality informed by a critical praxis made possible by real commitments to contemplative stillness in a noisy world.

The word *ethos*, with its roots in ancient Greek philosophy, is important here. For example, in a famous fragment Heraclitus views ethos as more than the spirit or sense of an age. He understands it as an abode, an understanding taken up by Martin Heidegger in his *Letter on Humanism*. Heidegger rereads ethos as the place of human sojourn, the open space where human beings construct their lives, an abode that contains and preserves the essence of what it is to be human. There is a clue here to the nature of spirituality understood as the search for true humanity. This is how the word ethos needs to be understood by an emergent post-postmodern spirituality. Ethos is not only the space where we discover our human essence, it is our home, the place where we confront our human destiny. Ethos is also the space where we discover that we are in the vicinity of the divine, capable of nearness to God. Ethos is the place of encounter with truth, the place where the greatest good is to be met and unfolded. It is the place where spirituality grows and makes its authentically liberating mark. Ethos implies portals to good places in which we are divinely invited to dwell and make meaningful lives together.[1]

Here, then, is the basis for a new definition of spirituality: the search for, the recognition of, and the embrace of our true dwelling, that space of deepest encounter with the essence of what it is to be human, to dance joyfully in the vicinity of the divine, to take up the challenge of the cosmos, and respond compassionately and realistically to the realities of human contingency and ultimacy. In the Christian sense, our ethos, our dwelling is God discovered in the events of the age in which we live and have our being. Only in God is it possible to recognise, conserve and protect the essence of humanity, because ultimately God alone is our true good. Again, in the Christian sense, alienation from God is alienation from our essential nature. It is the loss of abode, of a sense of at-homeness in the cosmos, of a sense of the good, of a sense of creative presence and responsibility in the world, of a sense of our need for the sacred and the transcendent. Alienation from God makes it possible for us to become predators, focal points of destruction, bearers of violence, creators of fear; and humankind's alienation from its true essence is the great challenge facing an emergent post-postmodern spirituality.

From a Christian perspective, the absence of a sense of vicinity to the divine remakes our vision of humanity on too small a scale. We accept a reductive vision and then resent its myriad human and ecological consequences. Having killed God, having removed the divine from our human abode, having desacralised the world, is it any wonder that Eurocentric modernity set out to kill humans in vast numbers, and is still doing so? This is the pivotal challenge confronting a historically – and philosophically – aware emergent spirituality. The journey to inward transformation only makes sense to the extent that it has a collective impact; that it has social, political and ecological consequences. Otherwise the place where we dwell, the ethos that orients our lives, loses its openly receptive nature. Then it can become cold, an empty place inimical to real life, and the dangerous edge of a vast abyss.

In terms of the sacred and the spiritual, to kill God is to kill ourselves, and is to destroy our dwelling place. We lose contact with any truly liberating sense of who we are and how we are meant to be at one with all that is. All unthinkingly, Europe and the West have become places of lost people who, having exiled their God, now confuse their exile with freedom. The task of an emergent spirituality and the religiosity to which it can give rise is to shatter this frigid illusion, not confirm it. The irony is that God once killed, dead metaphors return to life, the gods return, the idols of yesteryear arise, work of our own hands. We killed

God because we wanted instant salvation, instant enlightenment on our own self-referred terms; we want gods and goddesses cut to our own measure even in their unpredictability. We seek a magical gnosis or an occult secret, and in the seeking confuse homelessness with being at home.[2] A desacralised and individualised world quickly loses a sense of the common good. The task of the emerging spirituality is the restoration of the sacred, the recreation of a landscape fit for people who desire to dwell in harmony with each other and the world.

The emerging spirituality will be particularly challenged by the need to rediscover the sacredness of humanity and all that is. It will be a contemplative and a mystical spirituality, one that discovers in the contemplative mode the truth of humanity in the face of Christ (2 Corinthians 4:6) and in that compassionately mirroring light rediscover the truth of the human situation and its deep need. In Christ we embrace with all of creation a Spirit-led destiny whose beginning and end is God (Revelations 1:8 and 22:13). In discovering our deep humanity we discover what lies beyond ego: we discover the worlds of soul and spirit and in that discovery learn that we have been created for life, for unimaginably great things (Psalm 126:3; Luke 1:49; 1 Corinthians 2:9; Ephesians 2:1–10). According to Martin Laird, we are built for contemplation, for a way of silence, for an uncharted way that has no map unless surrender is its name, surrender to watchful awareness and surrender to alert stillness, to the discovery of the sacred within where it is hidden with God in Christ.[3]

The emergent spirituality will keep in mind that the sense of the sacred and the sense of the nearness of God is the gift of the Divine Spirit to the human spirit, a gifting that healingly frees the human spirit from its proclivity to self-illusion, self-inflation, self-doubt and self-destruction.[4] In a busy, noisy world the coming spirituality will be challenged to create an ethos of stillness, a meditative and contemplative milieu where depth can be pursued and deeper loving. A contemplative attitude permits life to be touched at its deepest levels. Then the illusions built on the mists of self-reference and self-deceit can be identified and allowed to fall away before the warmth of a compassionately contemplative gaze.

In contemplative stillness the emerging spirituality will rediscover in the Spirit that God's love is reason enough for a life open to engaged mysticism.[5] In that divine love it will find the empowerment to reach out in caring solidarity to the other and the stranger, to freely embrace inter-individuality and the common good; and in lifting healing hands will bring emancipation and salvation to the world and everything the world is. The emerging spirituality will remind us that only God is God and that true spirituality beckons to an abode far beyond the ego's unaided capacity to construct meaning.[6] The emerging spirituality will bring us into new harmony with soul-song and spirit-dance. It will reconnect us to the audacity of spirit. It will show us again how to let Jesus live. Then the world can be changed. But that means confronting an ancient block to spirit, an ancient block that has major personal, social and psychospiritual implications for the times in which we live. Then we shall be in a better position to explore the parameters of a post-postmodern generative spirituality and embrace the future with loving hope.

## The Ancient Block: Akedia, Anhedonia and Apatheia

Since the fourth century, Christian spirituality has recognised that the single greatest obstacle to authentic spiritual life and development is an illness of the human soul known in the Greek as *akedia* (from the Greek for *not caring*). The earliest detailed study of akedia is found in the works of Evagrius Ponticus, a scholar-monk of the Egyptian Desert who died in 399. Evagrius was an astute student of what we today would call psychospirituality or contemplative psychology.[7] Akedia (*acedia, acedy* or *accidie* in English) is a complex psychospiritual state that is very common today. Medical statistics that highlight the growing global prevalence of chronic sadness and depression in all age cohorts indicate that akedia will be a significant on-going challenge to the emerging spirituality. Akedia is a confused, dark, desperate, deadening, dejected, despairing, despondent, discontented, discouraged, disinterested, fainthearted, indifferent, listless, uncaringly negligent and spiritually corrupting syndrome. Other symptoms such as apathy, aversion, anxiety, dissatisfaction, drowsiness, ennui, heaviness, rancour, somnolence, torpor, and unease also occur.

When acute akedia touches a life everything becomes pointless and insipid. The mind becomes darkened and unfocused, and instability ensues. The capacity for regularity, including the regular practice of spiritual disciplines such as prayer and meditation, is undermined, taste for them gone. Self-concern grows, negative introspection increases, unreality and illusion begin to dominate. So does soul-emptiness because the cause of akedia is within oneself, within one's self-image rather than one's life situation.[8] In effect, akedia is a kind of spiritual death that begets all the other spiritual ills. Paradoxically, it seems to denote a bipolar state in which the desire for gratifying contact with others and the passions of hate and suicidal aggression unconsciously battle for control. The mention of suicidal thoughts should come as no surprise since there is no depression in which they do not play some part;[9] and akedia is a form of reactive depression. It is worth considering whether akedia, as an aggravated condition of soul-loss, is a contributing factor to the present upsurge in suicide, especially among young males. Akedia also links with the signs of clinical depression. These include persistent sadness, difficulty concentrating and making decisions, anxiety, hopelessness, pessimism, guilt, feelings of worthlessness, insomnia, fatigue and loss of energy, and a range of other persistent physical and psychological symptoms.[10]

Apparently a cognitive-behavioural disorder, at the very least akedia represents a joyless state of weary tedium, fatigue, and boredom with life that can lead to psychopathic and other forms of illness; and, like reactive depressions, may trigger unipolar or endogenous depression. A cross-cultural psychological comparison suggests that akedia shares a symptomology with *anhedonia*, a psychiatric disorder with both physical and social symptoms that are also predominantly characterised by the loss of interest or pleasure in life. Anhedonia is one of the two main symptoms of a major depressive episode, and is also linked to schizophrenia. In ways that are strikingly similar to akedia, the condition has a range of social, occupational, inter-personal and personal implications. It involves a loss of emotional fluency characterised by emotional blunting and withdrawal. The will flags, energy drops, feelings become painful, the world becomes unreal, noise becomes troublesome, crowded and busy spaces become unpleasantly intolerable. At work anhedonia leads to a decline in enthusiasm, creativity, and the capacity for innovation. A lowering of confidence, commitment and general productivity also occurs.[11]

In Christian spirituality akedia has long been identified as a parasitic shadow presence, a depressed state that enervates every human act and robs it of spiritual significance and energy. Akedia has the capacity to take over the human mind, give it a negative tone, and destroy trust, creativity and focus. It thoroughly undermines the capacity to pray and meditate precisely because it is the polar opposite to contemplation. It opposes joy. It undermines engaged relationality. Akedia deflates and flattens love, and leads to a joyless, darkened, increasingly isolated and shadowed existence. Given its negative self-referent cognitive and behavioural nature, it is not difficult to see that akedia, as a depressed state where feeling and caring have been flattened, also has immense personal and social implications.

It is not difficult to see that akedia-anhedonia describes the dominant spiritual health challenge of our times: a state easily aggravated by the self-referred, competitive, fragmented and individualistic lifestyles that typify contemporary Western cultures; lifestyles all too prone to discontents, depressions, disappointments, and addictions. Akedia-anhedonia will be the dominant spiritual block to be faced by a post-postmodern spirituality. Everyone interested in the spiritual journey needs to be informed about akedia. Everyone engaged in spiritual accompaniment needs to be trained in its diagnosis and treatment. Everyone on an authentic spiritual path will be challenged to confront its diminishing impacts, signalled by de-energised complacency, avoidance, indifference to the wider needs of humanity, and a mildly-depressive self-centred concern.

The danger today as ever is that akedia is accepted as an acceptable part of life. The result is that the desired transformation of religious communities, parishes and Churches does not take place because akedia is neither identified nor taken seriously as a spiritual malaise. It remains a largely unnamed and unacknowledged state or way of being.

⟨ *The spiritual response: apatheia*

The spiritual antidote or response to akedia is to choose and then work towards its opposite, a state of serene stillness and quiet. This is an ideal state known in the Greek as *apatheia* (from *a-pathos*, unperturbed by what has been endured, especially outside influences). In contemporary terms, pathos refers to the painful impact of drives, needs, dependencies, compulsions, obsessions and imposed suffering of many kinds. Apatheia, on the other hand, remains unharmed by outside influences. Stillness remains intact without recourse to suppressive, repressive or projective ego-defensiveness. Apatheia is a state of quiet, humble, accurate, and emancipatory self-knowing where ego-referred concerns play a diminishing role as soul and spirit, those deeper, more holistic, more creative, questing and questioning centres play an increasingly central part in daily life.

Apatheia is the sign that a soul-based life has emerged, the end point of a healing and illuminating process that then becomes a new point of transformative departure in life. Mind and heart come together in ways that reveal the dynamic and fruitful reality of engaged contemplation. Apatheia denotes a freedom of spirit, a state of integrated tranquillity where love is born and portals to higher states of consciousness are opened. Apatheia is the natural state of a person who has been cleansed and healed of akedia and its parasitic distortions, diminishments and losses. However, in Christian spirituality apatheia was never used to denote a sinless state. What apatheia points to is a condition of psychospiritual integration and serenity, a human attribute and ideal that grows through participation in the transformative action of grace. It represents a freedom of being that emerges as a consequence of union with God.

Apatheia makes true audacity of spirit possible. It is difficult to conceive of true audacity of spirit in the absence of apatheia and its implications for good-humoured, contemplative realism. Apatheia is a Spirit-gifted quality of spiritual aliveness that embodies an interweaving of many different states. The list includes calm confidence, courage, equanimity, evenness of manner, freedom, harmony, inner peace, integrity, and openness. Apatheia builds a good-humoured serenity that utterly transforms personal and social engagement. This is possible because apatheia is capable of profound love, capable of relating to the other, capable of relating to God, capable of a serenely participative and relational spirituality. Apatheia is akin to the New Testament ideal of purity of heart, a state where the pain of anger, violence and other forms of emotional and spiritual suffering fall away, their place taken by compassion and love.

Apatheia may also be described as a state of mature mindfulness, of grounded sensitivity capable of a keen, loving, accurate and uncluttered awareness of the lifeworld in all its inner and outer dynamics. It names a profoundly healed and renewed humanity, a compassionate humaneness that is profoundly Christ-like: it reveals a richness of soul in harmony with all that is. At its best, apatheia denotes a state of compassion that arises from a place of deep inner peace, soul-based inner peace that is both a gift and an act of faith. It is simultaneously an expression of love and hope, exemplified by the gift of patient compassion.[12] How can we begin to imagine an emergent spirituality that does not remember the necessity for the contemplative growth that reveals the healing gift of apatheia?

## TOWARDS A POST-POSTMODERN SPIRITUALITY

The deconstructive mood of the postmodern and its suspicion of language points in the direction of a renewed conversation with the classical apophatic or non-discursive spiritual traditions and their quiet meditative embrace of the now. This orientation has already been influential in reshaping philosophical and theological reflection. The growth of interest in meditation and East–West interspiritual dialogue are strong indicators of just such a move, with implications for an emerging spiritual ethos. The turn to a non-discursive contemplative or apophatic model of spirituality will be of particular importance in the unfolding of the emergent spirituality, especially in its Christian expressions.

The postmodern mood of individualism presently supports lifestyles that are too restricted, too narrow, too small, too lacking in expansive creativity to develop a vibrantly social spirituality. Consequently, the emergent spirituality will have to come to terms with an array of divisive self-focused/other-focused polarisations if it is not to lose sight of its political and historical responsibilities. Another clue to the nature of the emergent spirituality is the ecological turn that now accepts the reality of a world crisis that confronts humankind with serious ethical, religious and spiritual challenges. Without the presence of an ecological awareness and the ethical conversion it demands, it is difficult to see how an emergent spirituality will be able to address the challenge of an ethos capable of confronting an unjust and exploitive world. This is why compassionate solidarity, one that respects the uniqueness of authentic individuality, must be the horizon against which the authenticity of an emergent spirituality is discerned.

Non-discursive or apophatic spirituality, compassionate and passionate social solidarity, an engaged ecological consciousness, and a turn to ethical integrity will be the four anchor points of a desirable spirituality for a post-postmodern world. What is desired is a good-humoured, compassionate, just, loving, emancipatory, respectful, and audaciously engaged mysticism that works for and desires the good of all. What is imagined here is a social poetics and a critical praxis grounded in the interplay of apophatic spirituality and compassionate solidarity. The reason is simple enough: there is ultimately nothing private about unitive, contemplative, or mystical experience. Because it is transformative it is incapable of not engaging with and touching other people's lives. The challenge for the Christian mystic is to make that engagement conscious through action in the world that flows from a personally transforming encounter with the living Christ (John 17:21). This encounter lies at the heart of both contemplative stillness and engaged activism. We are challenged to facilitate the emergence of a spirituality that will transform the world.

The postmodern milieu pits subjective and individualistic forms of spirituality against those with a more religious, communal or social shape. This will be a serious challenge for the emergent spirituality. Postmodern philosophy is also suspicious of the misuse and abuse of power. This suggests that the emerging spirituality will be challenged to walk gently and humbly in the world. It will also be challenged to resist and actively reject any kind of return to the totalitarian experiments that have bedevilled humanity throughout its history. However, the post-modern in its other turn towards individualism and relativism raises serious problems for a spirituality that seeks to embrace communal and social reality in the service of justice and equal respect for all. Our shared humanity and the dangerous remembrance of the crucifying passion of Jesus require a spirituality that embraces all of these forces. What we need is a spirituality that interweaves personal, social and planetary transformation; a spirituality revealing the kind of knitting a Julian of Norwich would speak of today.

## A Reflection on Meditative Technique

Over most of the last two thousand years the Western contemplative tradition has made use of a triad of Greek cognitive tools, an experiential mind-map to identify and negotiate the contemplative labyrinth. They help in removing the many layers of personal and cultural baggage that obscure unitive experience and generate powerful self- and reality-illusions. These tools help the contemplative to discover and then live out of the difference between mainstream, consensual, or politically correct states of knowing, and wisdom rooted in the gift of transforming love flowing from the mind of Christ. The three words used to name this experiential map are *apophasis, aphairesis* and *aporia*, words with deep roots in Greek philosophy. They were used by Plato, Aristotle and many others before being taken up and used experientially by the Christian contemplative and mystical tradition. These three words represent significant technical components in the development of a non-discursive or *apophatic* spirituality that favours and encourages stillness in a busy world. It is this form of spirituality that will be particularly relevant in shaping the contours of the emerging spirituality for a post-postmodern world.

### ℂ *Apophasis, aphairesis, and aporia*

*Apophasis*[13] is a refusal to allow reality to be imprisoned in language or in picture-knowing imagery. It favours a path of simultaneous openness and transcendence. *Aphairesis*[14] is the strategic refusal to stay in the domain of words and images by peeling them away. While *apophasis* transcends the limits of ego-centred awareness and is aswim in a world of unknowing, *aphairesis* clears the inessential away and removes whatever blocks the pure view. The layered accretions of experience, of cultural and psychological baggage, the prejudices and conditionings that obscure and limit mind are systematically cut away. The non-discursive path, by combining the experiential techniques of *apophasis* and *aphairesis*, makes it possible in meditation to intentionally remove recognisable features (think of abstract art as an example). Layer by layer, everything that stands in the way of is-ness is stripped away and a sudden gifted blossoming of enlightening love begins to flow.

By using *apophasis* and *aphairesis*, for example by attending to the process of breathing or by the repetition of an aspiration, the busy discursive mind is disrupted and quiet, non-discursive awareness is supported. In a now of God-gifted seeing a gap is opened through the veils of illusion and reality glimpsed. The socio-political implications of this experience of contemplative and mystical awareness are obvious. A person who has glimpsed reality with clarity must take a socially prophetic stance in favour of a transformed socio-cultural ethos or diminish integrity. The third Greek word that completes the experiential triad is *aporia* from the Greek *a* (without) and *poros* (way or passage). *Aporia* names a normally disorienting experience of cognitive arrest, a startling moment of puzzlement, or perplexity, or awe, or wonder, or amazement that crosscuts busy discursive knowing and brings it to an abrupt stop. In the contemplative tradition, the movement of *aporia* names the thought-stopping impact of loving wisdom coming to birth in the depths of the soul. A not-knowing, pregnant with meaning, arises. A more genuine wisdom is enabled to emerge as rigid boundaries give way to love's transformative power.

A new self-understanding is allowed to evolve, a new consciousness to emerge. Freedom from compulsiveness grows. Deep peace emerges as parasitic fears fall away. The power of a self-referenced lifestyle wanes. Polarising forces decrease and dualisms fall before a unitive Trinitarian love that creates a new congruence and a new sense of oneness with all that is. A changed field of receptiveness comes to the fore. Life ceases to be determined solely by self-interest. Concerns with hedonism, competition and defensive emotional distancing are confronted by concerns for relationality, interdependence, and socio-ecological integrity, and give way to them.

What is of particular relevance to the emerging spirituality is that as egocentric references and locations lose force, other-centred orientations and locations gradually come into harmonising play. A new way of living reality comes to the fore. When compassionately other-centred perception takes centre stage it becomes increasingly difficult to treat the world and the other as objects of exploitation, objects of egocentric manipulation. Apathies decay and motives become more open, more loving, more attentive. Interconnectedness and interdependence grow. Qualities of interest, openness and respectful receptivity come alive. More considerate, more caring and more vigorous participatory awareness becomes normal. A turning towards the other, towards the not-self, becomes a distinguishing mark, a sure test of contemplative maturity, openness and receptivity. Creativity finds new life. Compassionate humaneness becomes normal.

Wilfulness is recognised and dealt with in a still space where no self-referenced motivation can survive on its own, only the will of the One and the call of the Other. That which is beyond knowing confronts knowing. That which is beyond striving confronts striving. Regardless of willingness, that which is beyond will confronts human will. A pause, a kind of death, a moment of simultaneous possibility and impossibility is set in train. It challenges the completeness of knowledge, especially of self-knowledge. It challenges the completeness of striving, especially of self-striving and the sovereign self-willed autonomies self-knowledge and self-striving enigmatically suggest. An invitation to total transformation is laid bare in the paradoxical invitation to move in landscapes of utter self-transcendence.

The blending of *apophasis, aphairesis* and *aporia* represents what the Celts called a *caol áit*, a thin place, a space in the landscape where the sacred is palpably close at hand, a space that reveals the importance of spiritual geography. Through such a thin veil a new understanding of human and planetary solidarity is brought to birth as we become more experientially, more spiritually open to the ethical demands of life and all God's good creation. In that openness we refuse to make an idol of either knowledge or the grandiose knowing self. We recognise that God is always more than a grounding concept, and reality more than we can ever grasp. In such a space illusions of rank, status and privilege fall way and a humbled self is supported (Psalm 51:19). Authentic contemplation sets in train the process of letting go of privilege, rank and status, of letting knowledge of them go, of letting self-images based on them go. At last, God is freed from our human grasp.

Apophatic spirituality refuses to objectify the self just as it refuses to make God an object: it goes beyond the busyness of the discursive mind whose task is to construct mental objects, a dangerous capacity in an uncritical, unreflective consumer universe. Contemplative prayer is a practice and a discipline of letting go: letting concepts go, concepts of self, concepts of the other and the stranger, concepts of God. Letting them go, not simply postponing or deferring them. This is precisely what Evagrius of Ponticus calls pure prayer. 'You will not be able to pray purely if you are all caught up in material affairs and agitated with unremitting concerns. For prayer is the rejection of concepts.'[15]

## ℂ Technique

Technique is ever and always an external element whose purpose is akin to that of a scaffold that helps the contemplative to rise above the discursive mind and its chittering strings of words, its pizzicato images, in a lifting made possible by a few sacred sounds silently subvocalised. The echoing sound of a sacred word or a phrase transverses the empirical mind's restlessness and, in transversing it, liberates it, opening portals to immediate experience. The paradox is that language games liberate mind from the grip of language, not least by dislodging the sound of a word from reflection on its meaning. Attending to the sounds of words and phrases helps us to sail beyond the horizon of language. We rise above language on the lilting sounds of language. This is indeed the land of paradox: living by dying, finding by losing, being carried by sound as sound is carried on breath in a movement of transforming grace, paradoxically dancing while sitting still, singing silently while engaging with silent music. What limits and what liberates meet in the same place and dance a non-dance in a dancing stillness.

That is why the art, the discipline of meditation is to sit before the wall of boredom, to transcend its diffuse anger, to trust that seemingly barren wilderness state to liberate us from the desire for instantly gratifying enlightenment. There is a hidden door to be found in the wall of boredom, a door to a new space where a new identity and a new mode of illumined knowing awaits those who are patient (Revelations 2: 12). Learn to love the wall of boredom. Learn to love the diffuse anger that gives us the energy to walk away, but above all learn to let it go. Learn to love patiently the desire for instant enlightenment, and then lovingly let it go. The meditative discipline is to stay there on the edge of the abyss, willingly waiting for what limits to meet what liberates and for them to begin their new dance into a new stillness. That is the sole job of technique, to aid and orient willingness. Then, in the unitive space, difference is left behind. So is mind-dulling apathy. The meditator is drawn into the flow of graced absorption.

At this intersection, the words fall away and the melody soars. And then the intersection itself falls away and saving emancipation occurs. To contemplate is to sit at the intersection and be touched by the inexpressible and then seek to communicate it in falteringly inadequate yet discriminating expression. Here is the paradoxical rub: without language none of this could be expressed at all. We could not bring the expressible and the inexpressible to the point of unity. In the end it is about using language liberatingly by seeing through language. There where communicative action and inverse reality begins, the engaged participant grasps the art of contemplative and generative listening, of going beyond unexamined judgments, conclusions and assumptions and their unrecognised and hidden premises.

The application in spirituality is also straightforward. In the contemplative state, non-discursive thought takes on a pervasive quality. The quiet mind can overshadow all other thinking processes, even though they continue to operate in the background, as powerful potentials for dangerous distraction and tempting delusion. In contemplative practice, language is transcended, usually by using language as part of thought-disrupting meditative techniques. Christian *aspirations* (short, lovingly repeated prayer phrases carried by the breath) and *jubilatio* (free or spontaneous monophonic chanting), Zen *koans*, and Hindu *mantras* are well-known examples. In Christian practice the intention is to make things more difficult for conventional and habitual forms of thought in order to open portals to more appropriate, less tangible modes of graced awareness and experience.

In this way the engaged contemplative not only seeks to transcend all self-reference but in so doing is drawn, in Spirit-gifted serenity, through Christ, into an ever deepening communion with an invisible, incomprehensible, transcendent God (Colossians 1:15; 1 Timothy 1:17). This is a profoundly transformative process. The watchful, contemplative attention at the heart of spiritual solidarity flows from this deep encounter with Trinitarian Love. It enables contemplatives to see through the veils of illusion and recognise the sacred value of all with eyes opened by the Spirit of love. It enables the contemplative to listen to the common core of humanity and all of creation in ways that generate newness and the dynamic compassion that learns how to support our interdependent freedom.[16]

What is important here in terms of spiritual and contemplative practice is to understand that apophatic prayer is not a simple deferring or postponing of affirmative or kataphatic prayer: apophasis does not slip back to kataphasis. In piling concept onto concept and image onto image, for example, Julian of Norwich teaches that kataphatic prayer also has the power to disrupt the discursive mind and set soul free on the path to unitive contemplation. By moving beyond the flow of discursive modes of awareness both forms have the capacity to move beyond affirmative discourse into deeds. Even then a task of humble vigilance remains. Language has the capacity to create a fiction world centred on a fiction self.

In letting go of language or in swamping language or in disrupting language, the fiction world is radically challenged and so too the fiction self that displaces the other, and unthinkingly exploits or controls the other for self-serving reasons. That is why the authentic ascent into union must spiral into compassionate deeds, fruit of un-selfed love, action from a still point aglow with divinely transformative energy, full of the creative audacity of spirit, goaded by dangerous memory, and a zeal to let Jesus live. If language there be, it is a God-filled word that sets creative forces transformatively in train. Word and deed become one in the Word. Word and deed reveal the Word-made-flesh. The vanishing point of talk becomes the focal point of action, the new ground of unlimited possibility.

## ℂ *Discursive mind, non-discursive mind, and attention*

There are no shortcuts to transformed consciousness. It requires an understanding of two dimensions of mind, the *dianoia* or discursive mind and the *nous* or non-discursive mind. This is completed by the practice of watchful attention, or *nepsis* in Greek, in which the contemplative develops a consciously held metaposition. The capacity to maintain a metaposition is crucial to the development of a contemplative attitude. A metaposition is an overarching attention to or awareness of the qualities, states, and behavioural expressions of human consciousness, communication and action. It pays conscious attention to the array of ethical, psycho-logical, relational and spiritual challenges that arise in the development of a lovingly contemplative practice, a commitment that needs to be consistently sustained through contemplative practice. What is at stake is the quality of the transformed consciousness a transformed world requires.

The Greek *dianoia* represents the discursive mind and its involvements with everything to do with daily life. It is full of curiosity and easily distracted. *Dianoia*-mind encapsulates what we call today *ego consciousness*. It plays an important role in a developing spirituality, supporting various forms of conceptual and imaginative prayer and meditation practices. It is involved in intellectual learning and reflective writing. *Dianoia*-mind makes possible the conceptual reflection behind spiritual conversation and discourse, as well as the processes of affective choice that ground spiritual bricolage. It also plays an essential role in developing critically reflective approaches to, for example, socio-cultural, socio-economic and socio-ecological politics. However, stillness arises from the non-discursive or *nous*-mind, because *dianoia*-mind proves incapable of sustained attention to the unimaginable Other. That capacity is the gift of *nous*-mind, a gift that allows the intuition of the unimaginable Other to become a consistently conscious part of a lovingly enacted spirituality and the orientation of its daily praxis.

Martin Laird defines *nous*-mind as an intuitive spiritual intelligence that runs deeper than discourse. The movement to *nous*-mind names a transformative shift from the object of thinking to a watchful surrender to the vast silence of the heart.[17] It is also worth noting that in the history of Christian usage *nous* was sometimes understood as synonymous with spirit. Clear-minded attention and awareness – *nepsis* is related to not being drunk – are particularly required when discursive forces and concepts become compulsive and obsessive, addictive symptoms of a desire for control yet to encounter the liberation of love, yet to find the deep heart's core, yet to discover how to let Jesus and his dangerous memory live, how to allow unitive attention to God become the trans-formed resting place of the mind. The capacity to sustain clarity of awareness allows us to gently maintain a commitment to open, non-evaluative, non-discursive, God-attentive wakefulness and clarity, while unitive love displaces the incessant and often afflictive or painfully angry and defensive search for a sure 'spiritual' knowledge intended to keep our rigid security needs and defences intact. *Nepsis*-attention supports the clear stillness and still clarity of *nous*-mind even as it acts to transcend the divisions and blinkered attentions of *dianoia*-mind.

*Dianoia*-mind is mathematic and busy; *nous*-mind is poetic and still. *Nous*-mind begins where *dianoia*-mind ends: it represents the threshold of unitive possibility. It makes the trajectory towards transcendence possible by gently peeling off anything that would block it in a constant return to transcendent attention. In *nous*-mind, knowledge ceases to be propositional and multiform. It becomes intuitive, insightful, integrated, unified, one. Non-discursive *nous*-mind transcends concepts and constructs, images and mind-pictures. It is intuitive, capable of eternal truth, of truth simply seen as true. It represents deep soul-mind at work. *Nous*-mind lies at the heart of stillness. It represents dimensions of mind that are generally active only in mystics and contemplatives, those who have responded to the call to enter the domain of enactive spirituality. The emergent spirituality needs this enactive quality if it is to be a vehicle for personal and socio-cultural transformation and the construction of an appropriate abode for humankind.

## A Befriending Solidarity

The postmodern opens up a highly significant area of reflection for an emergent spirituality: the link between non-discursive spirituality and deconstruction on the one hand, and their implications for human solidarity on the other. Apophasis is the space traditionally available to spirituality when it is confronted by or indeed makes use of deconstructive logics. More importantly, for an emerging post-postmodern spirituality it has the potential to open up an inclusive space for unconditional human solidarity. The still point achievable through apophatic practice makes such a spirituality more likely especially when it supports an engaged spirituality that is serenely reasonable, acknowledges connectedness to all that is, and offers practical loving kindness to all. However, apophasis also reminds us that ordinary ways of knowing are incomplete. They are potentially distorting because of the presence of unconscious forces, drives, and needs, and a potentially toxic and parasitic mix of subjective experiences and cultural conditionings that have the power to seriously undermine social mutuality and receptivity. This demands an open, actively engaged, relational spirituality.

Nicholas Lash has summarised the heart of Christianity in the phrase, *we have been made capable of friendship*, a thought he honestly finds disturbing.[18] The reasons for this disturbance are not difficult to understand. They are there in the oppressive and exploitive, inhuman and violent colonial foundations of contemporary Western socio-economic and political well-being. Echoes of this history are evident in laws and regulations governing economic migration and refugee status. The politics of a spirituality grounded in a befriending solidarity runs utterly counter to this history, a history in which it is only too easy to collude and connive for personal and collective economic gain. This raises significant questions.

How are we to negotiate the interplay of globalising and localising forces today? How is this to happen in a Judeo-Christian culture that has largely abandoned its religious roots in favour of a purely economic vision of life in a desacralised world? How is this to happen if we have forgotten that we are made capable of friendship? How is this to happen if we restrict the parameters, the political, social and economic parameters, of a critically reflective solidarity of friendship only to our own class or to our own ethnic or religious or political group? How is this to happen if religion, spirituality and engaged mysticism are exiled from the political forum? How are we to break free of such conditions, such assumptions, such expectations and their predictable modes of thinking, feeling and being? We need to recuperate another, very different consciousness.

### ℂ Bonhoeffer

If spirituality is to take up the task of building a life-enhancing, spirit-nurturing ethos for humankind it must be capable of responding to a range of integrative and enactive tasks. The contemporary roots of this emphasis can be traced back to Dietrich Bonhoeffer's 1930 doctoral dissertation, *Sanctorum Communio*, in which he asked whether Christianity, and by extension Christian spirituality, had a definable social essence.[19] Bonhoeffer's response is to insist that Christian life is grounded in the engaged social enactment of agape/love. Bonhoeffer creatively imagined a mature spirituality able to dance before God in the midst of a secularised milieu, a dance not with divine omnipotence but with the reality of human weakness and powerlessness (Mark 8:14–21). He shows the way for a spirituality unafraid to question the consumer ethos of the age and respond creatively in a daringly and distinctively Christian way to its alienating and socially fragmenting challenges.

In Bonhoeffer's view, the social structure of personhood is innately and originally spiritual. An ethos, an abode in the cosmos or the spirit of an age that does not respond creatively to this innately spiritual force is doomed to fail because it will not be able to answer humankind's most original need. The human spirit is profoundly social and dialogical, and so must authentic spirituality be if it is to emerge as an effective mode of critical resistance in a consumerised world. In consequence, the emergent spirituality will be audaciously social or essentially irrelevant to the times and easily dismissed. Social solidarity will be definitive of a post-postmodern spirituality because it is definitive of the human person. A socially embodied spirituality will permit transcendence to find social expression in freedom for others, for the neighbour in reach, a freedom for empowering care and service, a loving solidarity with the plight of the world.

The emergent spirituality urges us to move beyond the limits of ordinary knowing, to reach out in love, transformingly graced love, in dialogical love and reverence, towards the radically other. This passionate energy has its own intensity. It is deeply and reverently aware of all that is. Love, compassionate and dialogically receptive love, love that knows its own reasons and becomes its own knowledge, then becomes its own driving force. Theologically, this means that authentic love of God must flow out into social solidarity. If this overflow of love does not happen, its passion is revealed as just another case of delusion, or compulsion, or manipulative narcissism. We are not separate from our environments. Our relationships take place in real contexts. Our capacity for creative and interactive dwelling and communality bespeaks the nature of our humanity. It is precisely through interactive, interconnected relationality and dwelling that we encounter our essential task as people on this planet. Whatever moves us away from this understanding diminishes who we are.

Christian personalism, which emphasises the unity, liberty, relational, and transcendent character of the human person, also reminds us that parasitic evil attacks the very roots of this loving relatedness and interconnectedness, this capacity for freedom, this transcendent value, this communal dwelling. Soul-based solidarity reminds us that we do have some control, that compassionate intentionality and its active expression are a viable force in human affairs. Unconditional love is the challenge a thorough-going Christian understanding of life places before contemporary spirituality. Here is the basis for the critical self-reflection on assumptions that opens the way to socially-relevant metanoia, to socially transformative spiritual learning, to an authentically passionate solidarity. The inverse perspective of the great icons teaches us that the starting point is within the viewer rather than in the depths of an image. The journey is ours, but what guides us is another matter.

### PASSIONATE SOLIDARITY[20]

Many of us connive with the forces of diminishment and live silent lives of unreflective conformity with the exploitive ways of a globalised consumer world. That is a serious challenge for spirituality today, especially a spirituality attempting to engage with and give vital expression to passionate solidarity. Spiritual practices that bespeak intentional solidarity with the plight of the world and the predicament of the disadvantaged who are treated like prey in it[21] have none of the qualities of flight or evasion that social conformism and its collusions inevitably beget, but they sometimes forget Habermas's point that solidarity is the other side of justice. Justice has to do with equal rights and equal respect for all; solidarity is a stance of compassionate empathy and care for the well-being of the other and the stranger. Justice and compassion are two aspects of a single social reality;[22] and a spirituality of passionate solidarity gives them both social and ecological significance. The one needs the other; and a spirituality of passionate solidarity needs them both. The challenge is to transform domination into love and collusion and connivance with domination into spirit-grounded courage.

That is why a spirituality that embraces solidarity needs to be both audacious and passionate. Justice, solidarity, and us: three words that promise a more responsible, more mutually receptive attitude towards the other. This is the vision that beckons a passionate spirituality of social and ecological solidarity forward today. It clearly responds to the signs of the times. But that response in some measure will mean discovering spiritually ethical ways of confronting the power elites who organise global markets exploitively to suit their own financial and power ends. In Dorothee Soelle's terms, a spirituality of passionate solidarity, then, is a spirituality, a mysticism of resistance.[23] A spirituality of resistance involves a profound metanoia: intentional changes in attitudes, affectivity, perceptions and action. A spirituality that embraces social and ecological solidarity is a spirituality that embraces a consistent and operative ethic of justice.

A spirituality of solidarity is often a protest, a taking of counter-cultural decisions. Yet it is a sensible and sensitive spirituality, concerned with the nitty-gritty problems and purposes of real lives in real situations in real locations. It is a spirituality that dances consciously in the landscapes of mutuality and responsibility. The choice is to affirm and respect the difference-bearing character of all human life. The call is to embrace the praxis of solidarity, dwelling compassionately together in common space in a mutually empowering dialogue that dances passionately with difference. The undersong of humanity is always intersubjective: we come to identity and to awareness in dialogue. Solidarity calls for a spirituality audacious enough to demand a justified moral account from political and state authority, especially when 'solidarities' have been engineered to legitimise the less than visible hand of state coercion. In so doing, solidarity gives spirituality an embodied standpoint that challenges it to break free of limiting and defensive postures, to break through the boundaries and limitations imposed by fear. A growing sense of solidarity is normal to a developing spirituality, moulding its reality in history, society and politics. It recognises that solidarity is a goal not a given, something to be created rather than uncovered, something that needs participation in the grace of God.

Solidarity is a call to humane action, action that is reciprocal and relational. It turns away from defensive and enemy-making forces. Conscious choice and intentionality are always at its root. Communion with God is its deeply empowering driving force. That is what Oscar Romeros and Dietrich Bonhoeffers, Helder Camaras and Dorothy Days and Edith Steins and Etty Hillesums and Agnes Bojaxhius do. This is what a Mahatma Gandhi, a Martin Luther King, a Dag Hammarskjöld and a Nelson Mandela do. Such is the call of engaged spirituality. A spirituality of passionate solidarity means choosing a future and standing in the challenging spaces where it needs to be built. It means choosing a future and responding contemplatively and actively to the God seeds in it and letting the systemic husks fall away.

The engaged mystic recognises both the delusion of omnipotence and the delusion of historic innocence, and actively recognises their twin dangers. The engaged mystic recognises the need for a personally and a socially transformative praxis. But then, the mystic's understanding of reality comes from a place where Christ has begun to live and dance anew (Ephesians 2:20). The capacity to receive the pain of another who remains radically other orients such a spirituality by activating a mode of thoughtful engagement focused beyond the defensively limiting boundaries of self-interest. The results are never narcissistically pleasing as the deaths of many courageous women and men living in brutal and violent places vividly demonstrate. From the perspective of spirituality, solidarity emerges to the extent that persons are prepared to enter the world of the other and so begin to express the nature of community as personal and the nature of person as communal.

Call, embodiment and communion are essential dimensions of the human person. At the heart of the person is a call to transcend self in dialogue with others. Embodiment teaches spirituality that no one can leave the human condition behind. Communion names a true community of unique persons. Integrity and integration dance at the crossroads where all three meet. In all of this, solidarity represents challenging ground where inter-dependent and interindividual dynamics are continually encountered. Solidarity gives rise to participation in all its relational forms. It identifies what is most personal and most social about each one of us. If participation fails, the portals to alienation and all its attendant ills are opened. In Christian spirituality all of this is summed up in the image of the neighbour. If neighbour is not perceived, community does not emerge. The Christian vision demands a spirituality of freedom-in-justice-and-love, a spirituality overflowing with creative promise for communion, community and mutual solidarity.

A spirituality of passionate solidarity has to be dynamic and adaptable of its very nature. There can be nothing rigid or static about it. It has to respond fluidly to the contours of the locations and situations that shape it and call it forth. It deals with bitter storms and it deals with fine summer afternoons. It embraces stillness, but it also connects with people and events because it is practical at root. It prays and meditates, but it also sings and dances, protests, gets involved in advocacy, and does what is necessary. It thinks of heaven but it lives and walks and works in the muddy messiness of the earth, seeking to improve and enhance the quality of life for as many as possible. It is inspired by the healing and liberating ministry of Jesus, and it knows what his passion means. It looks at the ideal he shared in his stories of a better way of life and it is saddened by the historical response and the continuing oppression, not just of women and men and children, but of the planet and all the flora and fauna with which men and women and children share it.

A spirituality grounded in solidarity understands that Jesus wanted women and men to be, well, real women and real men with real chances to embrace fuller lives. It seeks to live his stories with good enough congruence to make a difference and nudge the world in a better, less conniving, less oppressive direction. It reflects and meditates on Jesus' choices, his options, his solidarity with others, the marginalised, the untouchables, the publicans and sinners, the lepers, the littlest and the least. It reflects and meditates on the kinds of abuse and injustice, especially the religious abuse and injustice that Jesus confronted. It reflects on and reflects how he affirmed the dignity and humanity of the littlest and the least, and how he stood against the controlling hypocrisy of power elites. A spirituality grounded in solidarity notices, approves of and joins his struggle for liberated lives, lives touched by the bright promise he brought everywhere with him. It cooperates with the creation of the nobler world he sought when he spoke on hills and out of boats. It sees in him a living example of solidarity and empowering conviction, a conviction full of radiantly liberating grace and truth (John 1:14; Hebrews 1:3).

A spirituality of passionate solidarity grows out of solidarity with the passion of Christ, a solidarity that is situated, an expressive solidarity that finds its inspiration and challenge in the local spaces where prayer and work, meditation and emancipatory action make most sense, and where there is no evasive or delusional search for pie in the sky. A spirituality of solidarity must enter real situations, real locations, real histories, especially histories of oppression because that is where the face of a suffering Christ is glimpsed and his sad dirges sung. It is no longer enough to claim in some cautiously comforting way, some evasively transcendental way, that God is always with me even when I do not walk with God. Jesus knew a time of absence, a time of self-emptying, a dark time and a painful time, a tortured and abused time precisely because he chose to be with God and walk to his destiny in Jerusalem on God's terms. That is why the coming spirituality will be a spirituality of resistance. If it remains locked into self-referred postmodern fragment-ation it will have failed its call to radical engagement.

The real question is whether I am open to God on God's terms, whether I allow myself to be touched by the Spirit, whether I am willing to stand against the structures of oppression because that is what Jesus did in loving compassion and that is why he was executed. That is why I want to be like the woman at the well. That is why I wonder about Nicodemus. That is especially why I want to remember with theologians like J B Metz that it is impossible to create the structures of the domain of God on earth, only its premise, its hope-filled premise, to embrace its ideal in some graced way, to accept it as in some sense normative for me, and that is why I want to reflect on and consider the tasks and challenges of a Christian spirituality of solidarity. A spirituality of solidarity refuses to allow the links between the spiritual, religious and political implications of the gospel to be severed in the name of some kind of solipsist or self-referred mysticism that has already fled the world of history and politics and sought refuge in an inner world of fantasy transformations and their smoke and mirror magic.

There is nothing fictional or virtual about a spirituality of solidarity. Instead it demands an ethic of change that supports movements of reform rather than movements to preserve conformity to some safe status quo. A hope-guided spirituality of solidarity constantly seeks liberation from the

forces of apathy and disinvolvement that have always supported oppressive structures even when they are encountered in ostensibly religious
contexts. There can be nothing private about engaged spirituality,
precisely because there is nothing private about the gospel. The challenge
for a spirituality of solidarity is to engage with the gospel, keep it in the
public eye, and refuse power to the forces that seek to remove soul from
the world and entrap and enslave the human spirit. We need a gospel-
based hermeneutic of emancipation, not a consolidation of slavery.
Spirituality conceived as a compensatory or spare-time activity, or as a
product solely intended to comfort and reassure, or packaged only to
support individual well-being has no part to play in the construction of
emancipatory hope. Nor has a spirituality that limits options or only pays
lip-service to change while evading real social and ecological commitments.
Reality makes serious demands. The great test of spiritual integrity is the
capacity to follow a difficult, often radical and seemingly unrewarding
path of life with sustained congruence.

That is why integrity shines out like the dawn, like a bright torch
piercing the darkest night. As Jesus saw it, integrity has to do with what
he called poverty of spirit, accurate self-knowledge, knowledge not just
of who I am but more specifically of how I am and how I am impacting on
others out of my innate poverty and incompletion. It means accepting and
taking responsibility for this incompletion and what it does in the many
circumstances of life, this propensity for anxiety, for anger and fear, for
jealousy and envy, for apathy and indifference, for the pride and lust for
power that change how I am where I am. It means embracing responsibility for what happens when I fall for the delusion of omnipotence or
grandiosity, and when I fall for the delusion of innocence. Integrity is
about developing the gift for doing what is good regardless of how I am,
where I am or what others may think, and seeking to do it in honesty
because I have glimpsed a beauty and a goodness and a truth and seek to
respond to them and let them flower, learning like Jesus to live from the
heart and find treasures there to fill my empty hands with healing hints of
divine presence (Matthew 6:21).

As guardians of the memory of One who died that all might live, we
seek a life-affirming path to global sanity. But first we have to remember:
remember suffering and remember freedom and become poets who witness
to them both in the search for a world where isolation need never occur,
where fragmentation can be healed, where freedom is alive and suffering
meets compassionate response. That is the song of spiritual integrity in
a world seeking interdependent completion. Divine compassion is its
beating heart, its open space, its nurturing receptacle, its divine home –
a divine home that has no fixed edges to its passionate solidarity. That we
cannot control Divine compassion does not mean we cannot join its song:

that is the gift of Spirit, and this is a creating song that lies at the heart of the cosmos. It is a song that empowers us to change things in the direction of justice and freedom, of peace and joyful hope because it not only draws us into the truth and goodness and beauty of God's work. It draws us into the heart of the Trinity where both our treasure and our home lie. We are to make room for an expanded vision of the wondrous potential that is in us all and set it free to dance liberatingly in the world, dance a new world into being (Revelations 21:1).

THEMES AND QUESTIONS FOR FURTHER REFLECTION

1. Have you discovered with Thomas Merton that your spirituality is your own truest self? Is there room for others there?
2. Identify the importance of integrity and congruence in a mature spirituality. How are these to be unfolded in practice?
3. Have you developed a practice that favours stillness in a noisy world? Are you allowing that still space to be the foundation for your life choices?
4. Evaluate the importance of a spirituality of service, of passionate and friendly solidarity with your sisters and brothers, and all that is. What actual forms of action show this aspect of your spirituality?

FURTHER READING
Martin Laird, *Into the Silent Land: The Practice of Contemplation* (London: Darton, Longman and Todd, 2006)

NOTES:  1. Ann Hartle, *Michel de Montaigne: Accidental Philosopher* (Cambridge: Cambridge University Press, 2003) 155.

2. See Martin Heidegger, *Pathmarks,* edited by William McNeill (Cambridge: Cambridge University Press, 1998) 239–276; Joanna Hodge, *Heidegger and Ethics* (London and New York: Routledge, 1995) 24–26; Rudi Visker, 'In Respectful Contempt: Heidegger, Appropriation, Facticity' in James E. Faulconer and Mark A. Wrathall, eds, *Appropriating Heidegger* (Cambridge: Cambridge University Press, 2000) 137–154 at 144. See also Basilio Petrà, 'L'ethos del futuro: Etica e vita spirituale di fronte alle sfide del terzo millennio' in Natalino Valentini, ed., *Una spiritualità per il tempo presente* (Bologna: Edizioni Dehoniane Bologna, 2002) 114–132.

3. Martin Laird, *Into the Silent Land: The Practice of Contemplation* (London: Darton, Longman and Todd, 2006) 1–8.

4. James E. Loder, *The Logic of the Spirit: Human Development in Theological Perspective* (San Francisco: Jossey-Bass, 1998) 10.

5. Dorothee Soelle, *The Silent Cry: Mysticism and Resistance* (Minneapolis, MN: Fortress Press, 2001) 36–37.

6. James E. Loder, *The Logic of the Spirit: Human Development in Theological Perspective* op. cit. 257.

7. The best contemporary study on akedia has been done in German by Gabriel Bunge. The Italian translation of the fourth German edition has been consulted here: Gabriel Bunge, *Akedia: il male oscuro* (Magnano: Edizioni Qiqajon, 1999). For a significant overview see also Jean-Claude Larchet *Mental Disorders and Spiritual Healing: Teachings from the Early Christian East*. Translated by Rama P. Coomaraswamy and G. John Champoux (Hillsdale, NY: Sophia Perennis, 2005) 89–125. It is important to note that in the spiritual tradition many disorders held to have a psychic origin today were placed within the spiritual domain.

8. See Thomas Dubay, S.M. *Fire Within: St Teresa of Avila, St John of the Cross, and the Gospel-On Prayer* (San Francisco: Ignatius Press, 1989) 163–164.

9. See for example, Verena Kast, *The Creative Leap: Psychological Transformation Through Crisis*. Translated by Douglas Whitcher (Wilmette, IL:Chiron Publications, 1990) 31–49.

10. See Gerald G. May, M.D. *The Dark Night of the Soul: A Psychiatrist Explores the Connection Between Darkness and Spiritual Growth* (New York: HarperSanFrancisco, 2004) 155–159.

11. See Stéphanie Dubal and Roland Jouvent, 'Loss of Emotional Fluency as a Developmental Phenotype' in Jacqueline Nadal and Darwin Muir, eds, *Emotional Development: Recent Research Advances* (Oxford: Oxford University Press, 2005) 409–427; Abraham Myerson, *Foundations of Personality* (Whitefish, MT: Kessinger, 2004); Mario Maj et al., eds, *Personality Disorders* (Chichester: John Wiley & Sons, 2005); Adrian Raine, Todd Lencz, Sarnoff A. Mednick, eds, *Schizotypal Personality* (Cambridge: Cambridge University Press, 1995); David Watson, Roman Kotov, Wakiza Gamez, 'Basic Dimensions of Temperament in Relation to Personality and Psychopathology' in Robert F. Kruger and Jennifer L. Tackett, eds, *Personality and Psychopathology* (New York, London: The Guilford Press, 2006) 7–70; R. Wayne Pace, *Organizational Dynamism: Unleashing Power in the Workforce* (Westport, CT., London: Quorum Books, 2002) 15–26; John T. Cacioppo et al., eds, *Foundations in Social Neuroscience* (Cambridge, MS: MIT Press, 2002); Giovanni Stanghellini, *Disembodied Spirits and Deanimated Bodies: The Psychopathology of Common Sense* (Oxford: Oxford University Press, 2004); Mitchell D. Feldman and John F. Christensen, eds, *Behavioural Medicine in Primary Care: A Practical Guide*. Second edition (New York: Lange Medical Books/McGraw-Hill, 2003).

12. See for example, Jürgen Moltman, *The Crucified God: The Cross of Christ as the Foundation and Criticism of Christian Theology* (London: SCM Press, 2001) 277; Laura Swan, *The Forgotten Desert Mothers: Sayings, Lives and Stories of Early*

*Christian Women* (New York/Mahwah, NJ: Paulist Press, 2001) 25; David Bentley Hart, *The Beauty of the Infinite: The Aesthetics of Christian Truth* (Grand Rapids and Cambridge: Eerdmans Publishing, 2003) 190 & 375.

13. From the Greek *apo* (away) and *phanai* (to say), literally an unsaying.

14. From the Greek *apo* (away) and *hairein* (to take), literally a process of removal.

15. Evagrius Ponticus, *The Praktikos. Chapters on Prayer.* Translated with an introduction and notes by John Eudes Bamberger OCSO (Spencer, MS: Cistercian Publications, 1970) 66.

16. The textual origins of this approach in Christian spirituality are usually traced to a text entitled *The Mystical Theology* attributed to a sixth century monk now known as Pseudo-Dionysus although the tradition predates that work.

17. Martin Laird, *Into the Silent Land*, op. cit. 26–28.

18. Nicholas Lash, 'The Church in the State We're In' in L. Gregory Jones and James J. Buckley, eds, *Spirituality and Social Embodiment* (Oxford: Blackwell Publishers, 1997) 121–137 at 124.

19. Dietrich Bonhoeffer, *Sanctorum Communio: A Theological Study of the Sociology of the Church*, Dietrich Bonhoeffer Works, Volume 1, new edition (Minneapolis: Fortress Press, 1998). See also Clifford J. Green, *Bonhoeffer: A Theology of Sociality*, revised edition (Grand Rapids, MN and Cambridge: Eerdmans Publishing, 1999).

20. What follows is indebted to Dorothee Soelle, *The Silent Cry: Mysticism and Resistance* (Minneapolis, MN: Fortress Press, 2001); Thomas E. Reynolds, *The Broken Whole: Philosophical Steps Toward a Theology of Global Solidarity* (Albany, NY: State University of New York Press, 2006); Hanke Brunkhorst, *Solidarity: From Civic Friendship to a Global Community.* Translated by Jeffrey Flynn (Cambridge, MA, and London: MIT Press, 2005); Kurt Bayertz, ed., *Solidarity* (Dordrecht/Boston/London: Kluwer Academic Publishers, 1999); Kevin P. Doran, *Solidarity: A Synthesis of Personalism and Communalism in the Thought of Karol Wojtyla/Pope John Paul II* (New York: Peter Lang, 1996); Richard Rorty, *Contingency, Irony and Solidarity* (Cambridge: Cambridge University Press, 1989).

21. Dorothee Soelle, *The Silent Cry: Mysticism and Resistance* op. cit. 292.

22. See for example, Giovanna Borradori, *Philosophy in a Time of Terror: Dialogues with Jürgen Habermas and Jacques Derrida* (Chicago and London: The University of Chicago Press, 2003); Jiwei Ci, *The Two Faces of Justice* (Cambridge and London: Harvard University Press, 2006).

23. Dorothee Soelle, *The Silent Cry: Mysticism and Resistance* op. cit. 195.

## CHAPTER 12

*Reflections on a Spiritual Theology*

> *It is only by living completely in*
> *this world that one learns to believe.*
>
> DIETRICH BONHOEFFER

## INTRODUCTION

We in the West, for all our seeming prosperity and freedom, still dwell in the long dark shadow of the horrors of the twentieth century. We also live in the shadow of their inheritors who seek to legitimise violence in the kingdom of violence, a kingdom where difference is eliminated in the name of power. These shadowed, vengeful spaces demand a truly enlight-ened contemporary spiritual theology, one born from the domain of true peaceableness, midwived in a love that supports a true inclination towards peace. What is desired is a theology capable of explicating peace, capable of embracing difference, but above all capable of recognising the seductions and abuses of power.[1] As Merton would have it, we cannot build a vision of unity and peace on a casual indifference to essential Christian values.[2]

If we believe in the values of freedom, peace and unity those who consider themselves spiritual must commit themselves to supporting the proponents of freedom, peace and unity everywhere, even if the non-violent means of the peacemaker show little apparent fruit. Neither spirituality nor a theology in touch with the spiritual search can avoid the reality of human brutality and the brutality of the struggle for power even if we do not give Hobbes and his masterwork, *Leviathan*, the definitive word on the human capacity for brutality.[3] To do so would be to render the struggle for freedom, justice and peace unreal. The drive to freedom makes us human; the root of freedom lies at the heart of human reason, part of our capacity to make reasonable choices and embrace their consequences in favour of a better world. It is to the trace of true freedom and other-regard, to the conjunction of the divine and the human in these shadowed bloodied spaces that we now turn.

## BONHOEFFER'S CHALLENGE

Before he was executed for his principled opposition to Nazi tyranny and religious collusion with it in Germany, Dietrich Bonhoeffer, the Lutheran theologian and martyr, came to a startling conclusion: 'It is only by living completely in this world that one learns to believe.'[4] Coming reflectively to this conclusion, Bonhoeffer set in train a radical inversion of thinking, something entirely characteristic of his work as a theologian that has profound implications for contemporary spirituality. The immediate implication for us today is that Christian life and spirituality as engagement with God are authentic to the extent that they share three fundamental qualities. First, Christian life and spirituality are authentic to the extent that they are self-implicating. Second, Christian life and spirituality are authentic to the extent that they are ethically performative. Third, Christian life and spirituality are authentic to the extent that they are socially engaged in embracing, respecting and caring for life and creation in all its forms and expressions.

Responses to Bonhoeffer's view have implications that transcend his own times. They have specific implications for the attempt to do theology and embrace spirituality in a postmodern, consumer environment. Two further outcomes are particularly relevant. The first has to do with texts and bodies; the second with ethical responsibility for the kind of world we are constructing. A postmodern theology is appreciative of both texts and bodies and the ways they sometimes seem to merge as word is made flesh, and as they open up the possibilities of new experiences in new life and system worlds. Texts leave traces in bodies, and bodies leave traces in texts: *logos* – the Greek for *word* – and life cannot be ultimately separated. The images we have of bodies and lives affect how bodies and lives are respected or exploited. Auschwitz and the Holocaust, sexual exploitation, commercially farming bodies for body parts, and all forms of power-motivated violence and torture make the point. Power brands and marks bodies and lives, and a consumer world commodifies them and renders them effortlessly and unthinkingly disposable.

The second outcome of Bonhoeffer's thought is that both spirituality and theology are authentic to the extent that they have accepted ethical responsibility for the kind of world we are tacitly and explicitly constructing, and for our personal and collective collusions with the globalising tyrannies of our times. We have the capacity to take on a calculated attitude toward the world and live from that attitude and its expectations. Such purposeful attitudes are the stuff of moral and spiritual choice; they shape our interactions with self, others, society, God and all that is. How do we hear the call of the world? What sort of purposes have we embraced for our lives? As we construct our comforting spiritualities, are we trying to invent pasts without shadows, conceive fantasy spiritualities just right for never-never-lands, or conjure tired theologies for times that exist only in soothing dreams? Without an ethical stance, neither theology nor spirituality has the integrity to stand prophetically before the world and call it to account. We construct worlds on the basis of agendas, however tacit or unconscious they may be.

There is a disturbing challenge here. In the absence of political and historical responsibility, spirituality can become a parasitic creature of connivance; theology can become an other-worldly artefact. In a Nazi jail, Bonhoeffer recognised and definitively embraced the this-worldly nature of Christian spirituality and theology and followed its self-implications to the end.[5] Others, male and female, young and old, have done no less, and so their bodies became texts and their lives stories we can keep at a distance when we favour neat and comforting theologies and their neat and comforting categories and certainties. Spiritualities and theologies that are disconnected from reality, regardless of their idealisms, remain unconvincing in late modern and postmodern contexts. They lack the grounding force of context, situation and location. They lack embodied integrity, and they respond poorly to the mystical-political demands of existence.[6] Such theologies will have little or no relevance to the search for a post-postmodern spirituality.

Standing on the fault-line opened up by Bonhoeffer's profound insight two forms of spirituality and theology are thrown into sharp relief. The first is grounded in a radical altruism that confronts oppressive and unjust situations. The second remains detached and indifferent to such conditions. It experiences no sense of social responsibility, sees no connection between spirituality and the social demand authentic spirituality always makes.[7] And there's the rub. Radical altruism of this kind is grounded in an imperative, an embodied call to give thought to the living and to the qualities, pieties, and values of the living.[8] This is the dark space where the challenge the contemporary world offers spirituality emerges in its full starkness, where the truth claims of spirit laid bare and set audaciously to work in the world comes under public scrutiny. What price self-implication at that point? The postmodern demands the reality of integrity, of being real, of a real being revealed in a real doing. Its concern is not with modern relevance, but – and this may sound ironical – with coherence. Life and gospel must be all of a piece if either is to be taken seriously.

For Bonhoeffer, gospel and life became inseparable. Gospel and human life converged and became identical. In prison, he came to a prophetic conclusion: 'There remains an experience of incomparable value, that we have learned to see the great events of world history for once from below, from the perspective of those who are excluded, suspected, maltreated, powerless, oppressed, and scorned, in short, the sufferers.'[9] Both theology and spirituality are challenged to view history from the perspective of the victims, the voiceless ones, whoever or wherever they may be. If this vector is absent from spirituality and theology, something essential to the Christian vision is lost, or worse still, deliberately excluded. A claimed enlightenment that marginalises the already marginalised or silences the already silenced is an illusion in need of shattering: this is not the path Jesus proposed for himself or those who follow in his way (John 15:13).

The wake-up call for spirituality and theology today is nothing other than the call to recognise the predicament of life in the full flowering of its enigmatic paradoxality. Real life confronts us everywhere with the enigma and the paradox of God: that which we do not know, that which confronts us with limit, with the full meaning of finitude. In the words of the great Hebrew poet Yehuda Amikhai, '[a]fter Auschwitz there is a new theology' if there is any theology at all because the Jews who died there confront us with the irrationality of the world.[10] Bonhoeffer would have understood what Amikhai meant by this enigmatic new theology when he wrote, 'God is the beyond in the midst of our life. The God who is with us is the God who forsakes us.'[11] A spirituality or a theology that aspires to be real, to be coherent, to be more than fanciful cannot fail to take account of the victims of evil and injustice.

If I understand Bonhoeffer correctly, contemporary spirituality and theology must engage openly with the complexity and brutality of life, with what happens at the margins of both society and belief; with otherness and difference, with presence and absence, with poverty and injustice, with pain and suffering, with all the forces of diminishment in the world. Spirituality and theology in Merton's terms must also engage with the poorer, less splendid means to human unity. These less splendid means are always available to us in meditative and contemplative silence, in prayer, fasting, and almsgiving. They may be less visible than other forms of Christian activism but they have this advantage: they explicitly look to God, a God whose traces have not fully disappeared from the world.[12] They too are a means to critical communal and personal self-reflection, to a mode of prayer that becomes the basis for action, to a practice of fasting that becomes the basis of solidarity, and to an understanding of alms-giving that opens the way to caring ethically for the other.

Spirituality and theology must also be in dialogue with the needs of the planet. They must also be in dialogue with the publicly repressed dimensions of devotion, with folk religion, with grassroots pieties and popular religiosities: with the messy spiritual bricolages and patchworks of everyday and their juxtaposing of visual images, patterns and texts. If nothing else, these factors raise questions of everyday recognition and interaction for spirituality and theology: the aesthetics of piety has its own significance.[13] As they work together, spirituality and theology can risk open dialogue with all of the uncomfortable, challenging, disconcerting, disturbing, disorienting and alarming aspects of contemporary life. They both fail the test of critical questioning, critical reality, if they do not. In fact, Bonhoeffer's theological inversion suggests the need for deep dialogical listening: listening constructively to God within a tradition, listening cooperatively to sibling traditions, listening reciprocally in an interfaith and intercultural mode to the different world traditions, listening openly to secular knowledges, listening above all to the undersong of Spirit in the voiceless and repressed.

A spiritual theology grounded in Trinity is challenged at the very least to wake up and deal with otherness and difference in a dialogically respectful fashion open to generating a better future, a more just world. If this state of wakefulness is absent, spirituality and theology will likely lend themselves to neutralising rather than valuing the disturbing challenge of otherness and difference. What happens when otherness and difference are the best words to struggle with God who is otherness and difference? What happens when the world itself is revealed as a carnival of otherness and difference, or as a grotesque parody of what God's Trinitarian love desires? The gospel images of Peter, with his capacity for sleep first at Tabor and then at Gethsemane, raise interesting questions for those who work and live in postmodern contexts. A spiritual theology today is above all challenged to listen: and that requires the capacity to be alert, aware and awake.

A spiritual theology that fails to grasp the challenge of carnival and parody, that fails to recognise the many voices and many faces people lay bare, quickly becomes irrelevant to the shaping of contemporary sociopolitical and economic reality and reactions to it. This potential irrelevancy becomes all the more poignant when never-ending consumption is presented as the yellow-brick road to human happiness, when new atrocities and slaveries are the invisible price others pay for that deceitful and ephemeral vision. The challenge is to make sure that otherness does not remain other, that difference does not remain different, and suffering meets empathic solidarity. As Wendy Farley so poignantly put it, "tragic suffering cannot be atoned for; it must be defied."[14] In listening to other and different forms of spirituality with their discourses of belief and desire, in listening to radical suffering, we are in fact listening to our brothers and sisters who share the human predicament with us, who are also audaciously seeking spirit-based ways of engaging creatively with creation's dilemmas and threats, its pains and sufferings.

Peace and human integrity, economic and political systems that are congruent with the best interests of the planet and all its life forms, are the goal and the prize. Neither spirituality nor theology is a manifesto for escapist illusion. Spirituality is about nothing less than life itself, life in the world of contingent realities, their challenges and predicaments. Spirituality and theology are about being fully alive on this planet, responsively and responsibly provoked by what is happening to it; being fully alive with our brothers and sisters and what is happening to them; being fully alive before God, fully open to the lively, joyous life of God and its implications for our creational being here and now: the ethical and creative implications for the human spirit seeking to live audaciously in the world and dance before God-as-Trinity.

## GOD-AS-TRINITY AND CHRISTIAN SPIRITUALITY

From earliest times there has been a linkage, sometimes stronger, sometimes weaker, between Christian spirituality and the question of God, especially the question of God-as-Trinity. The link tends to be anchored in an intuition that divine life in all its loving fullness has active implications for human life, certainly the life of the spiritually engaged believer whose expressed and operative or functional beliefs have achieved a quality of congruence. This intuition translates into a conviction that human life is graciously drawn into divine communion by the transform-ative and empowering action of the Divine Spirit and by the saving-healing love of Jesus Christ drawing people into the creative and eternally re-creative embrace of the Father-Mother God. Operative Christian spirituality is Trinitarian in a dynamic analogy of the divine *perichoresis*/dance. Spirituality is invited to engage in something like the Trinitarian dance of mutual intimacy, relationship, union, and fullness of love.[15]

The Trinitarian vision in spirituality opens the way to understanding the fullness of life that is offered to us as pure gift (John 10:10). It also opens up the immeasurable reality of graced wholeness and holiness.[16] Twenty years ago Walter Kasper identified Trinity as the foundational grammar of Christian experience.[17] Michael Downey has developed this image. He views Trinity as the foundational grammar of Christian spirit-uality, a grammar that is at once life orienting and a transforming gift.[18] As Catherine LaCugna put it, the doctrine of the Trinity in Christian spirituality is less about the abstract nature of God or a point of view that sees God in isolation from the daily realities of life; it is "a teaching about God's life with us and our life with each other."[19] Today, such a statement would include an equally firm reference to our life with nature and the cosmos as creation groans for completion under the growing burden of human corruption (Romans 8: 20-22).

A theology of the Trinity lies at the heart of Christian spirituality on two major grounds. On the one hand it orients Christian spirituality in profoundly loving and creatively relational directions because God is Love (1 John 4: 8); on the other it anchors spirituality in a dynamic experience of the healing-saving and creative character of divine love. The question for contemporary Christian spirituality is its groundedness in a life-orienting awareness of the dynamic relationship between God's inner reality and God's self-communication, a relationship that leaves traces as it flows through grace in human experience and teaches new music to the human spirit. Trinitarian spirituality challenges us to be lovingly, responsibly, creatively and imaginatively responsive to the pressing challenges and questions of the times precisely because Trinitarian spirituality reveals the undersong of Divine care for the whole of creation.

Through gifting spiritual experience people discover that they are image-of-God-as-Trinity, the *imago Trinitatis*, a discovery that has immense implications for how people come to terms with their personal and communal being-in-the-world and the responsibilities that give that mode of being historic expression. In fact, transformation that is grounded in experience and understanding of God-as-Trinity has governing implications for the Christian understanding of the spiritual life, for its inner and outer spiritual congruence. This is an understanding anchored in the integrity of love and the on-going communication and sharing of love in and for the world.[20] God-as-Trinity is evocatively explored by Michael Downey in a creative cluster that images God as *Giver, Given* and *Gift/ing of Love*, or as *originating Love, the self-expression of Love,* and *the inexhaustible self-giving of Love*.[21]

Trinitarian spirituality is a love-impelled journey in gifting love to ever deepening communion between us, the whole of creation, and God-as-Trinity in ways that respect equality and diversity, mutuality and reciprocity, interdependence and individuality and the transforming flow of charity-love. For that reason a Trinitarian spirituality has constantly unfolding ethical implications. Christian mystics dance in intimate relationship with the Trinity in a transformative unfolding of the mystery of Trinitarian love. Trinity is the Living Spring from which all creative life and love ultimately flow, a flow that finds insistently imaginative and lovingly committed relational expression in the world as it journeys towards fulfilment in a loving God. Trinity not only shapes and forms the mystical experience in Christianity; it constantly challenges and questions the authenticity of spirituality and its expressed orientation towards active engagement in the construction of a better world.

This is what the unfolding of the *imago Trinitatis* means in practice as it informs such pivotal spiritual practices as prayer, meditation, contemplation and practical forms of discipline engaged in by the Christian who has rediscovered them as channels of Trinitarian love. The same is true of Christian worship understood as an on-going action of profound gratitude for Trinitarian Love, the very Love that created us and to which we are invited to return. This is what *theosis*/deification implies in practice as it enters the deepening rhythms of the fullness of God, a fullness measured by the Cross and the dangerous memory of Jesus the Teacher. We live Trinity to the extent that we let Jesus teach us, transformingly live in us and through us in the world and, in the words of Julian of Norwich, make all things well. Julian developed a vision of the Trinity that is still fresh today. Her descriptive clusters open an imaginatively beautiful way of entering into and unfolding the mystery of God-as-Trinity: *Might, Wisdom, Love; Joy, Bliss, Delight; Maker, Keeper, Lover; Fatherhood, Motherhood, Lord*.[22] Julian's is a homely love. It responds to an invitation to be at home with God-as-Trinity, partakers in God's divine nature (2 Peter 1 : 4).

Gregory of Nyssa (died circa 395), one of the great figures in Christian spirituality and theology, also engaged highly imagistic and subtly eroticised language in his descriptions of the ascent of the soul to transforming intimacy with God-as-Trinity. He images God-as-Trinity in an image cluster full of the sensuality of perfumed oil poured out in an eternal flow of mutual Love in which God-as-Trinity is revealed as the *Anointer, the Anointed One, and the Anointing*.[23] Gregory's descriptive language has profound implications for understandings of what happens to human identity, especially rigidly gendered definitions of human identity, at different moments along the spiritual way. Gregory opens the door to a relationally anchored understanding of the human person in Christian spirituality, but one that reveals an identity that, as ascent to the Trinity unfolds, becomes increasingly open to disconcerting shifts and reversals as deeper metaphor opens doors to identity-altering implications.

In his *Commentary on the Song of Songs* Gregory presents the ascent into Trinitarian intimacy, which he places at the centre of Christian spirituality, as dynamic, transformative, and certainly relational. He also identifies a range of gender identity sea changes and reversals that have the capacity to generate profound semantic and psychospiritual shock for the unwary or the unattuned who believe contemporary individualistic visions of the gendered person to be the last word on the matter.[24] Spiritual transformation in Gregory's subtle vision changes every aspect of human identity, lifts it beyond the prison of fixed imagination. The transformed life is, in Sarah Coakley's terms, the matrix where the radically transformative encounter between God-as-Trinity and the human person is laid bare.[25] In that process and encounter both the relational and the salvational trajectories of Christian spirituality find their transforming anchorage. In this light, the encounter between God and the human person not only implies radical shifts in thinking about God, it also implies radical shifts in thinking about ourselves and our identity in relation to God-as-Trinity.

For Gregory of Nyssa, this is an experiential encounter in which the Holy Spirit acts as the point of entry into the Divine. The implication is that Christian spirituality is a grounding process of transformation made possible by *the Spirit*, prepared by *the Son*, and wrought by *the Father-Mother*. All of this process takes place as one motion, one communion. Spirituality is visioned as the touch of the *Bridegroom* drawing the mystic into a dark world of utterly transformative and radically disconcerting unknowing: the sharp tip of the *loving arrow* that wounds the soul is none other than the Divine Spirit. Gregory challenges us to break free of fixated images and their fixating limits. He reminds us that God-as-Trinity provides Christian spirituality with an unlimited horizon. Gregory also teaches us that a transformative appreciation of such a horizon requires a constantly renewed imagination open to the reality of awe and wonder and their creatively practical expression in the world. He shows us a horizon ablaze with creative power, with the forces of healing and saving, and replete with re-echoing blessings and empowerments whose purpose is to change the world.

Following Gregory, it is essential to insist that the whole point of the Trinitarian vision in Christian spirituality is an utterly transformative outcome that transcends and challenges both gendered accounts of human reality and, just as importantly, fixed gender projections onto God, especially those that hide adolescing and superego traits.[26] The process of transformation envisaged by Gregory is very different to what we generally encounter today. It has profoundly subtle implications for every aspect of human identity-in-the-world in ways that pose powerful questions for gendered accounts of human identity and gendered accounts of God. Gerald O'Collins has drawn attention to an image cluster that speaks loudly into this dimension of spiritual experience, one that unambiguously images God-as-Trinity as *Lover, Beloved*, and *Equal Friend*, or as *Eternal Lover, Divine Beloved*, and *Empowering Friend*.[27] Gregory of Nyssa has explored the transformative implications of such an embrace.

The Christian mystic swims under the uplifting wings of that wondrous Trinitarian horizon and its indeterminate array of transformative gifts and potentials. The Trinitarian horizon is a dancing place full of songs that overflow into life, songs of communion and healing, of saving and life to the full, and of possible new worlds. Christian spirituality is about communion in all its many forms and permutations: if communion is lost and the love of communion, spirituality loses its Christian stamp. Christian spirituality insists on the personal nature of the experience of the Trinitarian horizon and the journey in its light. Christian spirituality insists on the intimacy and the invitation to intimacy that beats at its deep heart's core. This is the lesson of Trinity, a dynamic lesson full of the rhythms of creation and love. In Gregory's terms, the hand of the *Bridegroom* is ever outstretched in intimate invitation, the *Spirit arrow* is always carried on the wind to human hearts, and the creative care of *Father-Mother God* is ever near, ever at hand.

Three expressions in particular seem to dance at the centre of Trinitarian spirituality: a dynamic movement of loving availability, the mutuality of reciprocal love, and compassionate self-giving. They are important because they reveal the nature of authentic intimacy. These three phrases take on more explicit importance when they are set in the context of contemporary postmodern consumer culture and its tendencies towards value drift, relational fragmentation, consumer-driven superficiality, apparent individualism, conformist mimicry, and counterfeit existences. These forces strongly impact prevailing views of the self, society and the cosmos. Set against such a backdrop a dynamic movement of loving availability, mutually reciprocal love and compassionate self-giving have the liberating potential to generate a different way forward for the human spirit.

Such a way forward is essential in an emerging culture struggling to experience patterns of respectful inclusivity and equality that transcend prevailing dominator-connivance models of human relationship, as well as socio-economic, political and other forms of human organisation. In a world viewed in organic rather than mechanical terms, where the self is understood relationally rather than in isolation, and where ecological crisis is now self-evident, spirituality is confronted by an array of new challenges. This is particularly so as women and men struggle to rediscover what it means to be *imago dei* and *imago Trinitatis* in postmodern contexts: masculine and feminine visions of divine beauty glimpsed now but always moving towards a final fulfilment that makes on-going practical, ethical and compassionate demands.

At the same time, a more inclusive understanding of society is struggling to emerge from the shadows of domination and the horrors of the twentieth century. The times now seem to favour more caring visions of process and becoming. In spirituality a more feminine attention to spiritual process and care has begun to healthily counteract prevailing masculine goal-oriented understandings of spirituality and spiritual development. A spirituality of mutuality demands increasing attention, a mutuality that is more responsive to visions of wise and loving living, to demands for radical equality, to the need for a more resourceful vision of communion-in-diversity.

There are traces of God-as-Trinity hidden in all of these patterns of change, especially those that confront radical individualism and challenge ideologically driven movements of social fragmentation, marginalisation and socio-economic inequality and injustice. The fact is that Christian spirituality is authentic to the extent that it is lived out in the loving embrace of the living God, in loving communion with the living God, in a loving movement towards the living God, in joyful worship of the living God that reverberates in human history and translates into compassionate, just and practical projects and processes.

Christian spirituality is also challenged to dance through terrains of depth and mystery to the music of a Triune Love made known in the seeking of our good and that of all creation, a seeking that makes us God's special treasure and fills us with a yearning to glimpse the glorious light of the Trinity in the face of Christ (2 Corinthians 4: 6). At the same time, the Christian spiritual tradition reminds us that a Trinitarian spirituality dances ultimately to an apophatic corrective. This corrective reminds us to respect the limits of image and imagination when they focus on an utterly transcendent God, a God who is utterly Other, invisible in a light that is a dazzling darkness.

How can naïve understandings fully express a God who is silent in a vibrant silence full of angel song and *alleluyahs* that transcend human imagining? The apophatic corrective fully recognises the dangers of simplistic interpretations of God. Yet the *imago Trinitatis* also reminds us that Trinity is our place of origin and our only satisfying place of return: spirituality is what we do in freedom as we giftingly journey along this spiral of life and love. Spirituality is ultimately *a path into the freedom of intimacy with Love and the utterly radical transformation such graced intimacy brings.* God-as-Trinity teaches us a lesson well known to mystics. Freedom grows as intimacy with God grows, as the chain of Trinitarian love grows; intimacy grounded in a paradoxical dependence and surrender, a consenting willingness that is paradoxically never complete yet blossoms in an unexpected and indescribably awesome liberation. Reflection on God-as-Trinity also teaches us that love must blossom as service in the world or lose its essential Christian imprint.

That imprint is the reason why Christian spirituality is an ongoing, ever deepening, ever ascending, ever transforming, ever loving, ever healing, ever creative process. It is also the reason why Christian spirituality continually engages in a communion of friendship that unfolds an ecology of compassion big enough to embrace the whole planet and everyone and everything in it. Such compassion has a non-judgmental character honed in willing service that is grounded in prayer, worship and meditation and the spiritual maturity they support. That is how Christian spirituality ultimately reflects the love of the Trinity: it resonates to *Eternal Lover, Divine Beloved,* and *Empowering Friend* in the Trinitarian Dance that makes and remakes the world. Ultimately, Trinitarian spirituality teaches us the secret of stable Christian self-respect, a self-respect readied for the rhythms of a new song and a new life in a dance of knowledge and love whose Horizon is eternal.[28]

MERTON AND THE CREATIVE IMAGINATION
What happens to theology when it is dynamically engaged through the lens of a living spirituality, a Christian spirituality that has perceived the

dynamically transformative significance of gracious change for the better, and trusted the potentials of gifted, joyous life? What happens when Christian spirituality is radically internalised and practised? What happens to theology when it encounters the audacity of the human spirit? Taking a clue from Thomas Merton, I suggest that a contemporary spiritual theology will find its natural location in the potentially liberating spaces where imagination and contemplative experience meet in the landscape of radical love.[29] It is through the capacity to re-imagine the world and God and their possible relationships in transforming love that a contemporary spiritual theology may find creative new ways to dialogue with and live generously, generatively and audaciously in a world in flux.

To paraphrase Merton, the renewal of the self, the new creation of the new human self in Christ, is one of the most significant themes in Christian thought today. It is a question of learning how to be alive in Christ, to let Jesus live in the contemporary world through the practice of an engaged Christian mysticism. What is at stake is the renewal of life, a process of rebirthing renewal that favours a better, more just, more equitable world. But this requires the capacity to break free of the tiredness of the old ways; it requires a renewed audacity: the courage to stand before an exploitive world and cry, 'Enough!' The answers and the audacity are to be found in the realms of silent meditation, meditation that connects us to the Source, brings us back to the Unity of the beginning. It is a question of accessing hidden Wisdom, of walking a path that performatively balances meditative stillness with action for justice.[30] This is the journey of contemplative imagination.

### ℭ Contemplative imagination

Imagination works in different ways in theology and spirituality. What is called dialectical imagination helps us to uncover experiences of distance and transcendence, experiences of the hiddenness and absence and majesty of God. What is called analogical imagination helps us to uncover experiences of the nearness and presence of God, of a God present in history; it helps us to uncover the traces of the Divine in creation and in people's lives.[31] Spirituality can teach theology a third form of imagination. Contemplative imagination bridges the difference between dialogical and analogical imagination. It knows how to remain true to both: to Divine reality in its transcendent majesty as well as to the traces of the Divine in the particularities of the human condition.

Contemplative imagination is spiritual vision audaciously confronting and piercing self-mirroring mists of inebriating illusion. The challenge of spiritual theology today is to see through the false transparency of the world in order to birth a more radical, more connected, more sacral vision. If spirituality and theology cannot work together to do this, there is something profoundly amiss with their self-understanding and their call to serve the truth of justice and freedom. When they bridge the gap and dance together, they become a profoundly imaginative poetic event, opening doors to possible new worlds: they help us to make holy ground.[32] The encounter with the sacred, with the wisely empowering Divine, takes place through imagination and is made human through it. Christologically grounded imagination is profoundly incarnational in such contexts: the symbolic becomes sacramental and is made flesh; the sacramental prayer becomes performance, doing what it says.

Contemplative imagination encourages a movement away from self-interest, however enlightened. In that move the emptiness of the post-modern sign is revealed. Imagination must be illuminated if it is not to fall victim to its own capacity for fictional distortion. The chances are excellent that if a Christological illumination is absent, its place will be taken by a contrary position, perhaps by a Manichean imagination that makes all human effort evil.[33] This does not mean that spirituality is an imaginary thing, something merely notional. Quite the opposite; it means precisely that spiritual experience is real and that the creativity of the spiritual or mystical or contemplative imagination expresses itself in real ways in real locations through real operations and real expressions of human creativity: the proof is in their emancipating power. Being is revealed in doing just as love is.

By drawing us into the creativity necessary to unfold meaning, to encounter it as invitation, fact and event, contemplative imagination not only allows us to see into our own predicament, but because meaning has its dangerous aspects, it also allows us to glimpse metaphorically and to encounter however briefly the awesomely beautiful ways of divine creation as they flirt with us in memories, stories, gestures, rituals, icons and the workings and blessings of nature. The close, imaginative, loving attention that the meditative mind turns to human experience is capable of catching glimpses of God everywhere: it is *capax dei*, open to God. In Merton's view, contemplative imagination has the power to cross beyond the boundaries of the material world. Imagination makes it possible to encounter possible worlds.[34] Contemplative imagination is able to see in the fogs of confusion.

Properly understood, creative imagination is a force for transformation precisely because it allows new possibilities to be glimpsed in the paradoxically dark light of contemplation. Importantly, for Merton the cognitive and creative functions of the imagination interact profoundly in the act of 'seeing'.[35] Seeing is also a theological reality: in seeing us, God gifts us with a superior reality in which we also discover God.[36] In this sense, seeing denotes epiphany: it allows God to be glimpsed in a sudden leap of illuminating intuition. Seeing allows the Centre to be entered through the contemplative gaze. It makes a new life visible.[37] Seeing, even as metaphor, allows us to understand the nature of contemplative imagination; and it reveals its theological necessity if holiness and the things of the spirit are to be more fully investigated.

A clear example is the way imagery, the way evocative poetry and music and dance, the way authentic iconography, the way spiritual biography enriches our experience of the world. These are facts of experience because the truth of the icon, the true image that simultaneously scrutinises and entrances the human heart, is located in the here-and-now world of visual phenomena. As we stay with these facts, however, they become events, lifeworlds that trigger transformative process. Creative imagination is also found at the heart of figurative language; and figurative language is cognitively realistic: it dances with reason and affectivity in the workings of the human mind and heart. It traces the pathways to soul, finds its way to a place deeper than memory.[38]

Contemplative imagination makes it possible for spirituality to be creative, transformative, generative, responsible. It makes it possible for spirituality to find and explore a wide range of linguistic and non-linguistic expressions that transcend the dangers of disjunction and compartmentalisation of life. In such a way, a spiritual theology acts as a conscious metaposition, an awareness of the guiding qualities of awareness: it knows the moon's reflection on the water for what it is, a hint, a flirt, a thin place opening portals to other-where, where the Divine *perichoresis*, the life-embracing dance of Trinitarian Love, may be imagined beyond the stillness and the silence of the Void.[39] The creativity of contemplative imagination makes Rublev-like icons of hopeful, fruitful, aesthetic, responsible wholeness possible.

Contemplative imagination discovers the way to the good, the true and the beautiful regardless of the contingent starting point. Hopelessness, on the other hand, tells us that creative imagination has been cowed and is dying, making way for defensive rigidities and self-protective flights into narcissistic unreality. Healing comes with entry into the imaginative inscapes of new life. Not surprisingly, the major challenge to authentically creative imagination is to cross the threshold of pain. This demands a departing from positions of ego-inflation in the face of the human condition in both its extroverted and introverted forms. The former leads to exploitive modes of defensive refusal to acknowledge suffering, to divert it projectively and leave it in the outer nothing-to-do-with-me world. The latter opens up a secret world of narcissistic self-interest and impractical ivory-tower idealism poisonously laced with angry disappointment. It also raises the challenge of an over-sensitive relationship to evil and suffering and victimhood that leads to the loss of meaning and the rise of irritated cynicism.

Mature spirituality finds a middle space between these two. It inhabits the fluctuating middle ground of reality and embraces a humbler position. Liberating good-news has been embraced, ego-inflation has been left behind, and a deeper, self-transcending meaning is discovered as soul seeks depth and spirit finds wings, wings lifted on Holy Breath, wings soaring into realms of personal and social transformation. In such self-transcendence imagination rises above trajectories of either cynical defence or hopeless defeat. Instead, it detects and follows the traces of meaning, beauty and possibility that each graced now, each kairos moment, presents in the concrete realities of time and place.

Imagination is the human faculty that joins the contemplative self with the universe and reveals the nature of the human and cosmic condition as it enters a process of seeking transcendence and completion. Without imagination, it becomes impossible to detect the shallowness of the contemporary infatuation with the consumer myth and its marginalisations of depth and interiority. That is why so many of us are left prey to inferior dreams and shallow, dissatisfying desires. I believe that Ross Labrie is right when he argues that in Merton's view Western culture, having severed its connection with the religious and wisdom traditions that had supported and encouraged the interior life, has been left with a vacuum filled by the products of inferior imaginations, the empty simulacra of postmodern signs.[40] The challenge to contemporary Western spirituality and its accompanying theological reflection is to confront this vacuum in every way possible.

Creative imagination is not just literal or allegorical; it has both spiritual and ethical dimensions that bring their own interpretative challenges and movements to bear.[41] It also allows us to imagine the imageless, to find words that evoke stillness and silence, and the awesome absence of words. In the end, Merton's imagination is not so much psychological as ontological, a place of being beyond images of being.[42] It is in this space that Merton's tendency to use imagination, contemplation, mysticism, and intuition interchangeably as ways of naming avenues to wisdom makes sense.[43] Contemplative imagination gives us the power to see into the heart of things. Without it, the world remains lost to us in its concrete Spirit-blest materiality.

### ℂ Critiques of power

As an activity, a spiritual theology is eschatological, leaning towards a definitive future; it is contingent, recognising the things that are unpredictable in life, beyond individual control. A spiritual theology also needs to understand the fragility of the human person facing principalities and powers. But so many horrors haunt the twentieth century, so much destruction and sorrow, that inherited views of the world and its relationship with the Divine are themselves in crisis. Thus, a critique of power, of its uses and abuses, has to be an inherent part of the critical reflection grounding a contemporary spiritual theology. Critiques of power always shake loose the collusions and complacencies we have left unexamined, unadmitted, and perhaps, even, resistingly unrecognised.

Confronted with power relations and their omnipresence, meaning becomes a very dangerous location. Our personal (and academic?) blind spots, deaf spots and dumb spots would be revealed. Our unrecognised 'colonial' biases, our parasitic uses of earlier theologies, our ethnophobias and gender biases, our Eurocentric and anthropocentric visions of God, persons, the world and their interactions would be exposed and called into question.[44] These are uncomfortable spaces, but they are also the squares where metanoia plays its pipes and invites us to join the dance of transformation. On the other hand, creative imagination has the astonishing power to envision how to restore a living unity of being: but there is an assumed price to pay. Are we open to the continuing ethical and spiritually self-implicating response demanded by such a vision?

## The Theological Challenge

A spiritual theology that does not struggle with questions about God and the world, with horror and hope and our individual and collective responsibility for the world, may be temporarily comforting but in no way liberating and so of little earthly use. A merely comforting or entertaining spirituality represents a kind of early twenty-first-century socio-political anodyne, a tranquilliser for mystical-spiritual shock; an avoidance of the crisis of personal and collective culture; a sterile leisure pursuit never intended to disturb an individual or group's prevailing compromises or narcissistically deluded comfort and security zones. A forthright spiritual theology rages with compassion, battles with monsters, resurrects persons, and practices thoughtfulness as it dances through friendship and strangeness to build hospitable communities.[45]

An authentic spiritual theology must confront the crisis of transformation that faces the prevailing Western spiritual collage, its Eastern–Western patchwork collage: the cut-and-paste spirituality that reduces the wild symphonic and unbridled power of spirit to a comforting gurgle and hum that robs spirituality of its transformative power. Translation is not transformation; surface change simply rearranges the furniture. Today more than ever, spiritual theology must face the challenge of radical transformation and emancipation. Transformation is not an easy thing to embrace: it has a shattering effect on the satisfied self and evicts it from its defensive entrenchments. The challenge is to find the power in faith to resist evil with the tough wisdom of Job.[46]

For authentic transformation to happen, unexamined psychospiritual, religious and societal structures must be questioned and confronted with change, a process that requires disturbance: a disorienting dilemma, a crisis, or an ethically insightful but disruptive moment of mutuality. Then more radical modes of being in the world, being before God, being in the presence of difference, being confronted by absence and suffering can break through our sterile, antiseptic performances and reveal something more foundational, something more courageous and determined, something embodied and lived. As Johann Baptist Metz would suggest, if the cross is not heard, resurrection hope becomes suspect. In a world that airbrushes crucified people out of collective awareness, hope comes cheap. True hope hopes with the victims and learns to sing their songs on riverbanks of suffering.[47]

At such moments, imagination uncovers creative potentials but it also brings to the surface tensions of meaning. The problem is that the word *theology* tends to be quite ambiguous today, raising any number of questions seeking explanation, including the problem of second-hand spiritual experience.[48] In raising the question of spiritual theology, two questions in particular need to be faced. What makes theology spiritual? What makes theology part of the great Christian tradition? Answers to these questions are particularly relevant today given the range of alternative visions of the world and of the spirit that are instantly available in the information omniverse. In the world of spirituality, what makes Christian thinking and doing different? What makes Christian understandings of ethical responsibility in the world distinct? What makes Christian spiritual practice easy to recognise?

The first answer to such questions lies in the model Jesus proposes of relating creatively to the world and to the human condition. Christian spiritual theology engages with the details of what it means to follow Jesus to Jerusalem and beyond. The second has to do with what happens to weakness, pain and suffering in this life, to the forces of transgression and diminishment. Are they left behind or do they become the dark medium of encounter with God? In both senses, a Christian spiritual theology is fundamentally oriented by the causal and sacramental nature of the Christ-event, especially the memory of his passion, death and resurrection, even when other reflective and linguistic visions and resources come into play. In either case, an authentic spiritual theology today protests against depersonalising forces: a spiritual theology is not just a repository of abstract information about God, or even strategic programmes focused on God.[49] The role of spirituality is to keep the focus on lived experience; the role of theology is to keep the living focus on God.[50] The role of both together is to dance to the eschatological, hope-filled rhythms of radical Christian experience as the Christ-event persistently uncovers challenges that address the orientations of social and communal solidarity and structures Christian responses. Do they lean towards the comfortable? Do they lean towards the exploited? Do they risk transgressing the prevailing political and social consensus? Do they trigger audacity of spirit?

The Christ-event, the symbols, rituals and other expressions that have carried it into history, that create its mythos and ethos, express a call to breach the experiential limits of our comfortable personal and social slumbers and resistances. A spiritual theology that discloses these concerns, that allows itself to be systematically confronted by them, is in touch with reality. It does not fear the political and social implications of a crucified Christ. In the shadow of the crucifixion, the Christ-event continually confronts us with the question of theodicy: with the reality of weakness, suffering and horror, and the possibility of hope and meaning. Spiritual theology emerges as an engagement with this question to the extent that its challenge is perceived and lived reflectively. Spiritual theology is itself a spiritual practice, a praxis leading to a living conversation with all of life, not just the nice bits.

As a Christian spiritual practice, spiritual theology is always challenged to unfold its Christological and Trinitarian implications. The challenge is to recognise how these implications are to be unfolded in ways that remain true to the Christian vision recorded in our normative and authoritative texts. It is difficult to see how this can be done today without critical conversations with the human sciences; and this means that spiritual theology needs to acknowledge its links to an ethically grounded practical theology. In the end, spiritual theology is challenged to do something new: identify and offer transformative possibilities to a Western world gorging on empty signs, signs emptied of fire and transformative potential and packaged for a consumer world seeking the fantasy of comfortable happiness.

How do we handle the interweaving beliefs, meanings, feelings, locations, moods, tones, presences and absences that shape the complex particularities of historical and contemporary contexts spiritual theology is called on to process? How are we to unfold the context-laden felt-meanings of the past in profoundly different cultural realities?[51] The answers open up in a world of critically lived experience that refuses evasion. The Christ-event and the Trinity remain at the heart of the Christian evaluation of truth and value; they are the primary lens through which history and politics are viewed. Spiritual theology is a process of engaged reflection in which contemplative imagination and belief, language and culture, history and politics, and audacious questioning dance to a music originating in the mystery of a Triune love echoed by a community of worshipping disciples. Otherwise spirituality will continue its isolating, fragmenting postmodern drift into unquestioned, uncontested individualism.

### SPIRITUALITY: PRESENCING AND PRESENCE LEARNING

Contemporary spirituality calls people to live with audaciously discerning wisdom in the exploitive world of globalising processes where people become easily discounted units of production, consumer citizens valued only for their consumption. But how is this to be done if we have forgotten how to be contemplatively present to the world and its contingent realities? Spiritual theology has to rediscover a mode of presence that leads to transformative learning, a learning serving an emergent spirituality in an emergent milieu that allows little space for the reassurance of bogus self-images much less spurious social constructions of the self.[52] Only a gracious awareness of presence of the divine and human other will make this emancipatory process possible.

This healingly liberating process has to do with learning through presencing, a learning that requires a contemplative mode of awareness, one that enters the flow and becomes present to the whole with integrative contemplative immediacy. Presencing opens us to emergent being. Presencing calls on us to stand in the now, open to kairos time, open to grace, as it makes new demands on the now.[53] Presencing confronts us with the eschatological proviso that is an essential part of Christian spirituality: no one human version of the future can make an unconditional claim on us. And yet we must presence ourselves for the future, discover ourselves as graced participators in the construction of what we are meant to be. This eschatological proviso has another implication. Because Christian spirituality stands in the shadow of the Cross and chooses before God to remember those who suffer, it subverts time-conditioned understandings of theological relevance and reasonableness in favour of being real in the now.

The eschatological proviso or condition that is inherent to Christian spirituality triggers its own mode of graced struggle and expression, because in Christianity ultimate liberation is God's gift alone. However, while its primary task is to prevent any particular understanding of the eschatological future from being rigidly applied, the proviso does not tell us how this is to be done in practice. Its task is to constantly challenge Christian spirituality to identify and engage critically with the forces of human and planetary emancipation, open to God's inviting call. At the same time, while the concept of an eschatological condition reminds us of the dangers inherent in any kind of human utopia, it does not mean that we are citizens of two histories, one religious the other secular. The challenge is to live reflectively and transformatively in both of them, to let their songs become a single song, their dance a gloriously incarnated dance. When religious and secular belonging are set in opposition to each other they give rise to conflicts, misunderstandings and obscurities that challenge religious and secular allegiance. Nevertheless, spiritual theology is always challenged to become real in and through concrete historical projects open to an emergent future and its beckoning potentials.[54]

Presencing as a method first engages with inward openness and reflection in order to make outer action more open to the emergent future and the changes it requires. Presencing attempts to learn from the emerging future even as it learnt from the past: in this, it is meditative and contemplative, and, irony of ironies, is already in use in the world of business precisely in the service of future change.[55] Presence in this sense has to do with nearness, with nearing and drawing near, creating a context for a new understanding. The act of presencing allows us to pierce through to the boundaries of our cultural understandings of being and God and the things of the spirit, and transcend their illusory limits. Instead of favouring a horizon grounded totally in the past, presencing allows us to discover the horizon of the future, to become alert to it, to recognise its non-local nature and use it in the search for new understandings. Eschatological hope informed by love is the light that guides a spiritual theology that is open to grasping the seeds of a beckoning future already, but not yet, here.

Presence learning makes it impossible to ignore our dark side. It throws into stark relief our shadowed, encrusted spirits, all our refusals, denials, untruths, repressions, our unanswered invitations to live life deeply and fully, and all our defensive forms of living. What is at stake is the maturing of the human spirit as it faces the future as John the Baptiser did in a wilderness (Luke 1:80). Too many of us want stability in a world of change when what is demanded of us is an open reciprocity, the willingness to go beyond difference in the name of justice and respect, especially in dangerous times.[56] By searching for stability in a world of changing realities we run the risk of becoming oblivious to highest presence.[57] The critical meditation required by presencing and presence learning, therefore, challenges us with how willing we are to construct a personal and social identity open to the future, an identity that permits the human and divine spheres to dance a new dance together, sing a new, more open identity into being.

We tend to identify ourselves through tangles of gender, status, rank and privilege, and through their related snarls of ethnicity and locality. Such factors position us and represent us. They say who we are in the consensual world, and they say who we are not. These tangles and snarls decide our social position and our social worth. They position our utterances and conversations even when some of them are borrowed, and others spontaneous and deeply personal. Presencing and presence learning remind us that we emerge in transitional landscapes that define us only until we begin new journeys, new cultural, new spiritual journeys that challenge us with questions that are ever ancient, ever new, ever unfolding from the future in the present. Presencing and presence learning require an openness and readiness to change. Presencing makes us alert to God-seeds and Divine traces in the transitoriness of time itself. Presence learning challenges us to respond in practical action: action that is always creative, always emancipatory, always inspired by love, always facing the future.

Who is God for me? What sort of mind-set do I bring to such a question? What is a person for me? What do I bring to such a question? What is the world for me? What city, what labyrinth, what desert does it symbolically or imaginatively evoke for me? Do persons and the world represent responsibilities to be cared for or resources to be ruthlessly exploited? What agendas move me? What aims and goals do I bring to bear on my relationships and responsibilities? Do my views of God and persons and the world ever meet anywhere? Do they influence and inform each other in any way? Do they have any practical implications for how I choose to live? How do I confront injustice? How do I confront evil and suffering? How do I deal with the past? How do I embrace or evade the rhythms of time and the challenges of place? How do I take flight from or engage in history and politics, and nature and freedom and their various necessities? Am I open to the emerging future? Do I seek a better world? Is there any activism in my spiritual reverie?

These were never simple questions. They are more unsettling at a time when Western culture is struggling through a series of critical paradigm shifts. Contesting voices challenge the authority of the narratives on which traditional religious and spiritual beliefs and truth claims are based. Not even the traditional structure of the family is exempt from the processes of re-invention: and none of this should come as a surprise. Not only do we live in the shadow of the twentieth century; we are bearers of a postmodern culture, responding to radically new perspectives that touch every aspect of life. We have experienced the capacity of consumerism to overwhelm all the practices of everyday life where even truth becomes a packaged commodity with a short shelf-life and its regulated sell-by date. In the consumer world, even truth is a simulacrum, a window mannequin selling counterfeit wares.

We know the interplays of pleasure and displeasure, of surprise, delight and disappointment as we wend our nomadic ways through the new labyrinths: the shopping malls of evanescent meaning, not even noticing their subversive subtexts. We have been touched by the fragmentation of the times and have not noticed how the cracks make space for repressed experiences to spill into the light of cultural day. We have been subject to the marketeers' spins, their smoke-and-mirrors magic as they persuade us to link conspicuous consumption with spiritual meaning, and we don't even notice the banality of it all, its one-dimensional profit-driven banality and corruption. We haven't even noticed that our whole economy is based on a yesteryear vice: greed is the new virtue that makes our economic prosperity possible. Without it, consumption would not grow and we all know what that would mean to our comfortably domesticated existences. The emergent spiritual theology in the West has a basic task: to make us all uncomfortable. What is needed is the luminosity of awareness tending towards transformative metanoia in the encounter with an emerging future that flows from God in love.

## Lonergan, Metanoia and Conversion

Luminous awareness implies a mind that is fully alive to the possibility of insight, a mind fully alive to discovery, a mind aware while engaged in sensing, thinking, or willing. According to Bernard Lonergan, as we attend in our spiritual reflection to our own awareness the quality of our consciousness itself becomes a subject for self-inquiry that leads in turn to self-understanding and self-knowledge. Our awareness reveals itself now as self-presence, now as flow, direction, interest, or concern. In meditation, we discover through personal experience the patterned nature and directional flow of consciousness itself. We observe how it flows through a variety of levels: empirical, intelligent, rational, or existential. We notice how it moves from experiencing to inquiring-into-experience. We discover the unity of the stream of consciousness. We discover how it expands selfhood. We are thrown into a process of desiring to know; we are reoriented to knowledge and obligation; and we discover intentionality as we become aware that objects are to be understood as answers to a question.[58]

We discover that the self emerges in the tension between the questioner and the questioned, and we discover something liberating. We discover what we are truly seeking: the true self. We discover that all authentic inquiry is at root a search for authentic existence. Once we understand that true inquiry is a search for the true self, we can imagine why consciousness must open up to everything: to the unconscious and the buried realms of personal and collective unawareness; to elementary symbolisms and archetypal forces; to affectivity in all its pain, glory and complexity; to aesthetics and the wonder of beauty; to ethics and the challenges of value and valuing; to others in their very otherness; to presencing Being as a call to life. Through it all consciousness is challenged to open up to a revealing God who remains mysteriously hidden.

In the process we discover the call to embrace integration at many different levels: from the molecular to the neurological, from the physical to the cosmic, from nature to soul and spirit and love and beyond in an upwardly directed dynamism carried on the gifting wings of Spirit Breath. We discover in this dynamic a below and an above, an inner and an outer, the boundaries around which all the vital dimensions of spiritual experience unfold: psychic vitality, symbolic mindfulness, dark nights, transformative dilemmas, purifications, spiritual enlightenments, movements of prayer, psychospiritual healings, personal and social liberations, engagements in history and politics, the withdrawals of blame, the disidentifying from projections, and unitive experiences.

Such experiences allow us to encounter the horizon of experience itself and there we are challenged to understand, judge, decide and be responsible. We also discover that consciousness is not to be confused with the contents of consciousness. Consciousness is not the perception of mental operations; it is more than that, more mysterious, something of indeterminate extent. There is a sense, too, in which subjectivity and the self it expresses always remain mysterious, beyond exhaustive unfolding. But we can always ask questions; we can always explore; we can move towards heightened awareness. In the end, it is always a question of our quality of openness, openness to change, openness to conversion, to the transformative metanoia through which soul-making and soul-based living are made real. For that to happen, something else needs to be destabilised and transcended.

### ℭ Metanoia unfolding

Metanoia must come into play. Quite simply, metanoia, a turning about, a change of direction, a change of mind, a change of heart, is at once an insight, a moment of awareness, and a process of spiritual and ethical maturation. It challenges us to sense, think, choose and take personal responsibility for soul-based living and the creation of a soul-based identity that unfolds in a synergy of transforming love and grace. Linguistically *metanoia* is linked to the Greek *nous*, which means mind; and so metanoia signifies a fundamental change of mind, a change in how we actually think about things, more specifically how we handle our habitually operative beliefs and perceptions, our experiences of spontaneous felt meaning. In effect, metanoia names a total change of life that confronts us with the abyss that lies just beyond the borders of conscious identity. Metanoia is personal and social, a divine gift and a human task, a grace and a divinely cooperative adventure, a stepping into the as-yet unknown. It happens in a relational field where others play their different roles and is defined, at least in part, by a transformed relationality that exposes psychic, aesthetic, personal and communal, intellectual, ethical and religious obligations and graced potentials for personal and social change: personal mystery unfolds in social history.[59]

Genuine metanoia simultaneously reveals and energises the movement away from the forces of personal, social and creational diminishment, from oppressions and connivance with oppressions, from exploitations and collusions with exploitations, with the complicating tangles and kinks of greed and power and self-serving ambition, and the conspicuous consumption it is embraced to serve. Metanoia also denotes the sadness that comes from having spent time in and devoted imagination and energy to such spaces, even as that sadness is healed and transcended. Metanoia is a movement of transcendence, a journey into expanding circles of reconciliation with self, others, creation and God, a journey towards an eschatological or future completion always tantalisingly just beyond reach. It constantly calls for the turning around of life in all its ways and forms. It calls for the turning around of all relationships and every horizon of meaning and experience. Ultimately metanoia names a rescued mind, a renewed heart, and a transformed understanding.

Metanoia is a turning point in life, a new beginning, a point where thoughts, values, feelings, attitudes and actions change direction. It is an inner change with all-embracing inward and outward implications and responsibilities. Metanoia is about coming to our senses, coming to a right-mindedness, a right understanding of the true nature of things and our relationships with them. Metanoia is a movement towards intellectual, psychic, ethical and religious liberation. In the process of metanoia, we move from a state of foolishness to a state of wisdom. We learn to listen to another song, to soul-song and its attunement to God, to all that is in God's good creation. In metanoia time, we are reconnected to Divine Wisdom and walk again in the luminous splendour of God's liberating light. Metanoia graciously reveals the mind as capable of graced participation with God. It reveals soul and spirit as divine image and likeness. Metanoia authentically humanises us, teaches us to be compassionate and humane in all our ways.

In a mysterious encounter with grace, metanoia makes mind and heart and soul and spirit capable of harmoniously discerning the Good, the True, and the Beautiful. It teaches us how to respond to their undersong in everything, especially in things that are good and acceptable and perfect (Romans 12:2). Metanoia is the graced embrace of the life of God and all the liberating and transforming differentiations that implies. It allows us entry into the transforming flow of Divine Love; and it sets our feet on the straight path to spiritual fulfilment. This is what conversion, from the Latin *conversio*, to turn around, to start over, really means, and it is a good word, despite its historical baggage, for what spirituality is ultimately about: a dynamic process of freely embraced self transformation characterised by interplays of flow and differentiation that involve deep and complex interactions leading to intellectual, philosophical, narrative, psychological, ethical, spiritual, theological and socio-political change. Emotion and practice, loyalties, psychologies and anthropologies are also involved, as is a turning away from whatever corrupts being and the cognitive errors that permit it. What is at stake is the transformative effect of new knowledge.

❲ *Personal transformation*

From a theological point of view, Lonergan's understanding of the human person and human transformation is framed in not dissimilar terms. It is characterised by a clear focus on the developing human subject, a focus that is an essential theme in any contemporary spiritual theology worth attention. Given this developmental turn, it is not surprising that Lonergan's understanding of human consciousness is framed in terms of flow and differentiation. While these two positions point to the developing, rational and willing nature of the human subject, they also open the way for a third movement: the movement from self to others and God. It is here that Lonergan's understanding of conversion makes its presence felt. This third position brings affectivity clearly into the picture and delineates his understanding of self-transcending conversion. Self-transcendence is understood as the capacity to develop a relationship with others and God grounded in openness to intellectual, psychic, moral and religious conversion.[60] The interactive nature of these four levels clearly demonstrates that conversion denotes and requires a socially and relationally open stance towards others and God.

Intellectual conversion and psychic conversion come first in the process of transformation. They open the way for the others. Intellectual conversion begins when we are ready to do more than merely look at life, to do more than gape at it without understanding. It begins when we move beyond looking and, more specifically, become open to appraising truth claims on the basis of adequate evidence and reasoning. Intellectual conversion is present when we are authentically able to experience, understand, judge, and decide about our own experiencing, understanding, judging, and deciding. It means taking responsibility for our self-appropriations as knowers. It bespeaks a movement of the true self as intellectual conversion begins to dance with its aesthetic-dramatic counterpart, psychic conversion. And so begins a ballet that brings the intellectual or cognitive, psychic, moral, and religious dimensions of the self interweavingly to the fore. Psychic conversion keeps spiritual theology in touch with the deep inner mystery of the human subject such theology is invited to explore.

According to Robert Doran, psychic conversion, which can occur before or after intellectual conversion, names the awakening of the capacity for active personal engagement with the inner world of symbolic consciousness.[61] The level of symbolic consciousness is encountered where the conscious and unconscious dimensions of mind meet. It represents an elemental or mythic level of mind full of images, forces and powers. This is the transitional space where psychic integration is challenged to emerge in ways that mediate appropriate sensitivity. Symbolic consciousness leads in turn to the development of a transformed ego ready to serve the deeper mysteries of soul. It turns to what is interior, temporal, generic, and religious; it turns away from what is exterior, spatial, specific, and profane. Symbolic consciousness works on the imaginal-aesthetic-dramatic rather than the cognitional level of consciousness and results in a process of affective integration that brings together the mysteriously indeterminate array of opposites that constitutes the Self. It challenges us to learn about and work with the impacting dynamics of elemental and archetypal symbols, affect-laden images and sensations, or archaic emotional forces, as they weave their liminal, mediating way through our minds, bodies and lives.

We live and respond in symbolic and mediated worlds. That is why symbolic sensitivity is essential to a coherent spiritual theology. If nothing else, it helps spirituality to appreciate the force and power of image and imagination. Like its three siblings, psychic conversion, then, is the beginning of a transformative process rather than an isolated goal or event. Dreamwork and related forms of imaginative and transformative meditation, reflection, journaling and reflective reading are typical of the creative and imaginative ways working at this level requires: the range of symbolic possibility is indeterminate in extent, especially when it encounters and enters the domains of otherness and difference. Such work is innately pragmatic in its openness to change, opening the door to a renewed self-affirmation lit by transforming intention. Working reflectively at this level helps to create the basis for an interiorly differentiated consciousness to emerge and dance with a religiously differentiated consciousness: these two are foundational to a spiritual theology worthy of the name.

Moral conversion and religious conversion also reveal an aesthetic base that responds to and is structured by the drama of affective and symbolic interactions, and allows the intentions of the human heart to be read in a moral and a religious key. Moral conversion signifies a shift at the level of our values as a result of being intellectually or religiously open. It implies that our values are more important than our egocentric satisfactions, wants and needs. Moral conversion lifts us beyond the wilderness of bias and its censoring potentials. Religious conversion quite simply means falling in love with God, being flooded with love (Romans 5:5): it opens the eyes of love to the power and empowerment of love. Religious conversion reorients heart and mind towards God.

This, in Christian terms, is a lovingly-graced-embraced-transformed openness, a mode of transformed relational being that serves as the ground of genuine self-appropriation: the fruitful acceptance of self-presence, which sets the true, the contemplative self free to dance with God. Coherent self-presence transformingly touches every level of personal and relational living. It unfolds in an interlocking series of changes and developments that radically transform understandings, values, and relationships with self, others, the cosmos and God. Understood in this four-fold way, conversion becomes the pivot of a spiritual theology that is open not just to conclusions about life but also to the principles that make congruent conclusions possible.

An understanding of the processes and dynamics of conversion is the concrete foundation of a wise spiritual theology. In this process, religious conversion usually comes first, preparing the way for moral conversion. These in turn generate the basis for deeper intellectual and psychic conversion; and so the spiral of transformation flows and differentiates. This presupposes the capacity to ask questions at increasingly higher levels of contemplative awareness and objectivity, a questioning that intensifies when the question of intentionality is brought to bear. Like all theology, spiritual theology is confronted by the intention of being, an intention with an unlimited reach that lies at the heart of meaning. This is what makes the move between description and evaluation so important for a spiritual theology seeking deeper understanding, even if the basis of that understanding is essentially heuristic and contemplative. This must be the case in spirituality precisely because we stand in contemplative solidarity with our brothers and sisters in an awesomely beckoning landscape that borders the spaces of both knowing and unknowing; and that makes the difference to the unfolding of a consistent spiritual theology.

Of course, conversion can be blocked, skewed, refused, dead-ended. It can run into ego defence mechanisms tuned with varying degrees of subtlety to detect threats to the ego-world. Various alienating forces can warp it, especially the personal and group biases and agendas, be they dramatic or banal, which lie at the heart of the deteriorating social situations we see all around us. Conversion runs in the opposite direction. It ultimately means that we transformingly embrace our intellectual, aesthetic, psychic, moral, and religious orientation toward the good. Conversion denotes a posture of the whole person, body and mind, soul and spirit. It transforms the ways of knowing, discerning, acting and loving that make us authentic human beings, especially where others, creation and God are concerned. Complacency, the refusal or avoidance of experiencing, understanding, judging and deciding, is the opposite of conversion and leads us onto paths surfaced with politically correct relativisms evasive of historical obligation and political responsibility. Discerning judgment then places us in an appropriate position to share with others. Without the experience of a personal encounter with Spirit, how are we to offer insightful data to help the spiritual encounter of another?

Conversion reminds spiritual theology that it must find its foundations within the concrete structures at work in human beings. It reminds spiritual theology that it stands within a cultural matrix working with its own categories in ways intended to uncover life-enhancing values. Conversion reminds spiritual theology that it must keep returning to the transcendental precepts that call us to be attentive, be intelligent, be reasonable, be responsible, and then to be loving in ways obedient to grace, and disclosive of its dynamic synergies and potentials for participation. Conversion reminds spiritual theology of its transformative vocation, and the call to live that vocation in transformative, prayerful praxis open to an agapic purification of social and political commitments. The challenge is to move from description to explanation in the context of the times. The challenge is to do this in a way that permits spirituality to engage with the transcendental aspirations of the human spirit in the spaces where they are confronted by the transformative demands of an absolutely free divine revelation and grace and the call to a spiritually differentiated consciousness unashamed of its Christian heritage and identity.

### ℭ A hint of Lonergan's spirituality

In Lonergan's thought spirituality is linked to his understanding of the foundational dynamics of religious conversion and the experience of divine love that lies at its heart. For Lonergan Romans 5: 5 is the classic statement of the centrality of love to the Christian vision.[62] The text not only focuses attention on the dynamic ascendancy of love in Christian spirituality, it also discloses a profoundly Trinitarian image of the unrestricted love of God flooding the inmost human heart through the inpouring of the Holy Spirit. The experience of an inpouring of unrestricted love anchors religious conversion as Lonergan describes it. In Lonergan's vision religious experience is essential to the realisation of the spiritual self; and in Christian terms, the inpouring of divine love is the portal to this experience and its transformative potential. The inpouring of divine love has the power to beget a trajectory of return towards God. Love describes a dynamic process whose ultimate goal, *vertical finality* in Lonergan's terms, is found only in God: and grace is what makes the difference.[63]

Spirituality, then, names the reorientation of every aspect of life in response to love as it unfolds within the domains of authentic, self-transcending choice and commitment. It names a state of being consciously in love with God in the concrete realities of human existence. Authentic Christian spirituality is grounded in a lovingly transformed motivation that is anchored, effected and sustained by the gracious inpouring of divine love. It brings to light the life-transforming outflow of the inflow of grace revealing the transformative action of the Holy Spirit. Spirituality is the art of being attentive to the experience of unrestricted love, intelligent in probing its depths, reasonable in evaluating its insights, responsible in anchoring the actions that flow from love in valid insights, and above all by loving in the manner of Jesus Christ.

There is a complex understanding of love at work here. It includes a range of experiential possibilities weaving through a dance of love: God's love for us; our experience of God's love grounded in a faith judgment; our experience of loving God; our experience of being immersed in the infinite ocean of God's love; our experience of unconditional, unmerited love. The dance allows us to see love as a divine gift that actively stirs up love itself as its own graciously evoked response. In this light spirituality unfolds as the unfolding of love in the world, the inner world of the heart and the outer world of action. Lonergan's is a love-based spirituality that is brought to maturity by grace, by the inpouring of the Holy Spirit. It is a love-based spirituality demanding loving authenticity within the contingent realities of life and their blocking power.

Love is the first experiential step on the way to a more profound, more critical view of reality achieved through a process of critically reflective discovery that leads in turn to a positive understanding of the Christian faith. This positive understanding, according to Lonergan, favours an explanatory over an expository role. Against this background, love itself is shown to have significant characteristics: it is receptive and responsive, it is developmental, it is active and dynamic, it is motivationally reflective, and it is free as it unfolds in an ascending spiral towards God. Love is lived out on the three levels of nature, reason, and grace, levels that unfold the divine presence and reveal the divine trajectory of love.[64] Love is the key and grace makes all the difference. Our task is to undertake the self-transcending journey.

### RAHNER'S SPIRITUAL VISION

Karl Rahner is one of the outstanding theologians of the Spirit, and so of spirituality, in the twentieth century.[65] In his vision the gap between theology and spirituality disappears. Rahner developed a theological vision spiritually grounded in the lived experience of God in everyday life. He taught that every man and woman has the capacity to experience God in the rhythms and flows of their own daily lives, an experience resonating with shaping immediacy. It is this moulding and orienting sense of immediacy, of the empowering presence of Spirit, which informs Rahner's spirituality and gives it its unique flavour.

The same conviction lies at the heart of Rahner's immense theological enterprise. Since the experience of God as it is conceived by Rahner is immediate, it requires no further proof: it is self-evident from lived human experience, a claim that has staggering implications in a consumer culture informed by an increasingly unconscious operative or functional atheism. How does such unconscious, such functionally uncritical atheism influence and colour the experienced absence of the divine in the lives of many Western people today? In Rahner's vision, instead, God can be known immediately by grace even if God is beyond the world, utterly trans-cendent, utterly mysterious, yet reaching out in gracious freedom to humankind and all of the cosmos.

This knowing takes place in the freedom of faith, a transcendent knowing in faith that brings people to an encounter with God as the very ground of human freedom. Spirituality is what unfolds when human freedom begins to dance in loving faith and hope with a transcendent God in the unfolding of a thoroughly humanising grace. This is a mystical dance, a dance with the glowingly dazzling darkness of God experienced in a vibrantly mindful stillness that lies beyond all imagining. And this transforming, liberating dance is for all. It is an innately non-elitist dance of surrender to unsayable Mystery. It is a surrender in the bright dark place where language and image fails while paradoxically opening the way to a dazzlingly unsayable world of transcendent life beyond the empirical world of everyday that even more paradoxically demands a real life in this contingent reality we call home. In the everyday world we respond to the rhythms and the beat of ultimate Mystery, of an indwelling God who graces and empowers the flow of human deification.

Deification is what happens through the universal, dynamic and trans-forming presence in human lives of the Holy Spirit (1 Timothy 2: 4). In Rahner's vision, the transforming presence of the Holy Spirit generates an existential structure (a *supernatural existential*) that makes spiritual experience, mysticism, and the process of deification possible. This *supernatural exis-tential*, as Rahner termed it, makes union with God possible because it structures, empowers and activates the very human longing for God that God desires to satisfy. In Christ, in the loving heart of Christ, we humans are openness to God, being transformed by God's self-gift in Christ and the Spirit, being transformed by God's nearness to us in our everyday lives. To live spiritually in this frame, is to live in God's gracious closeness, sharing through Christ and the Spirit in God's life alive in the Christian community and its sacraments, experiencing the nearness of God every-where and in everything.

There are, of course, privileged moments when this closeness is exper-ienced more vividly and dynamically, when the experience of grace is more finely tuned and full of life. Examples include moments of specially empowered courage in the face of malevolent hostility or of suffering and death; of love that reaches beyond all self-interest; forgiveness that is utterly forgetful of self; of profound trust in God's enlivening presence; and a lively response to God's invitation and call in difficult circum-stances. All such experiences reveal the immediacy and vibrancy of God's loving presence in everyday. Their impact is made plain in changes to the general orientation of life itself. There is nothing of flight from the world in any of this, nothing of evasion of the realities of everyday. What there is, instead, is the challenge to find God at the centre and to keep God at the centre of everyday life by identifying with Christ, by putting on the mind of Christ and the compassionate manner of Christ.

To live in the Holy Spirit, to release the creativity of the human spirit is to taste the utter freedom of God. This in turn generates and grounds a true inner freedom in the face of the world and its contingencies, a willingness to become freely engaged in the transformation of the world. A mature spirituality finds its centre of gravity, its equilibrium, in the dynamic space between inner freedom and the demands of the world. It finds a discerning path and sings a discerning song as it dances in discernment to Spirit music. It finds the measure of a God-centred life in a faith that recognises and responds to the offer of Spirit-shaped freedom. Such is the great horizon of Rahner's spiritual vision, a vision unapologetically grounded in experiential knowledge of God where it becomes increasingly impossible to separate life and work.

This is a spirituality and a theology that knows how to speak to God from the depths of the human heart in the realities of everyday. In the end, Rahner envisions a spirituality that overcomes all the artificial splits the human imagination can create in order to rationalise its resistances to the freedom that God alone can offer, a God who comes to us one by one, a God who comes to each one of us in the unique realities of everyday personal and communal existence and invites us in the very experience of our own limitations to go beyond ourselves. Rahner teaches us to take experience seriously. He teaches us that transcendence names our capacity for the dynamisms of transcendence and love that structure and orientate healthy spiritual processes and transitions. He teaches us that the human spirit is revealed in self presence, in the courage to ask real questions that unfold as love, and in the renewing creativity that finds the traces of God even in the shattered fragments of human dreams.

How can this be? It can be because we are fundamentally religious, fundamentally oriented towards the infinite. Rahner teaches us that Christian life reveals an invitation to mysticism grounded in the immediacy of God's self-presence, grounded in the experience of God as the depth dimension in human experience, grounded in the hustle and bustle of everyday life, grounded in a personally unique experience of grace-based, faith-based, love-based, hope-based union with the Holy Spirit within a community of brothers and sisters in Christ engaged in the world. It is in the end a spiralling journey of prayer that, arising from the depths of the human heart, reaches into the Heart of God in a flow of eternal and ever-deepening return. What, then, defines spirituality for Karl Rahner? Spirituality is encounter, lovingly transformative personal encounter with the Mystery of God in everyday even when that encounter also subsumes an ecclesial dimension and even when that dimension remains in need of development. As Thomas Merton noted in a letter to Dr John C. Wu written in 1961, "it seems to me that mysticism flourishes most purely right in the middle of the ordinary."[66] Merton neatly sums up Rahner's vision, a vision of immense importance to the healthy unfolding of contemporary spirituality, Christian or otherwise.

## A LIFE IN GRACE

Following in Rahner's footsteps, Christian spirituality may be defined as *everyday life in the grace of God*. Just as the word nature points in the direction of human capacities and energies so the word grace refers to divine life. Linguistically, grace comes from the Greek *charis*, a word with a range of meanings including fascination, beauty, generosity, benefaction, goodwill towards, delight in, unity, and favoured recognition.[67] It translates the Hebrew *hen* with its marvellous imagery of a benevolent gaze from on high. Grace is the freely and spontaneously given gift to humanity of the very life of God. It is given generously and is intended to lead to gracious action in human lives and relationships. The Greek tradition always adds the word *pneuma*/spirit to *charis*/grace: *pneuma*/spirit accentuates the divine origin of *charis*/grace as a free gift. The Latin *gratia*/grace, which translates the Greek, also rings with tones of divine benevolence and goodness.

Grace is the presence of the Trinity in the human heart. Grace is the gifting that empowers us to live according to the Spirit (Romans 8:9). Grace draws us to Trinity in love and, as Jesus promises, Trinity makes a loving home in us (John 14:23). These are clear references to divine action. However, medieval theology introduced an interesting distinction. The term 'uncreated grace' was used to refer directly to God, and in particular to the Holy Spirit given to us. The term 'created grace' was used to refer to those gifts of the Spirit active in the human soul that are considered supernatural, that do not belong to purely human concepts of perfection. Faith in God is a typical example. It is the term 'created grace' that permits us to speak of human cooperation and participation with grace and to see unique differences in the way people live spiritual lives in response to grace.

Grace helps us understand our natural capacity for transcendence. It helps us to understand how grace and freedom can grow together in the cooperative relationship between a person and God. Grace, freedom and human goodness are not opposed to each other. They sing and dance together towards newness of life in the history of people and in the history of the world. Grace is the foundation of all processes of spiritual growth and is the basis of the process of deification, *theosis*. Grace is a mode of being. It is universal and relational, its dynamism touches every aspect of life be it interior or exterior: in the Hebrew tradition God is present everywhere. Grace is God's hold on our very being. Grace is God's power renewing our nature, finding dynamic expression in the virtues that accompany grace and reveal cooperation with it. Grace allows us to operate harmoniously in the spheres of life that are human and divine because grace invites cooperation, cooperation that encounters the resistances grounded in hidden fears and similar psychospiritual forces.

Grace offers the vision and possibility of a human person fully alive, brimming with the audacity of spirit, able to let Jesus live in every aspect of life, always alert to the challenges of dangerous memory and the forces of diminishment, exploitation and evil rampant in our world. When we speak of grace today we speak of turning away from such forces. We speak of the active desire for a better, more just world. When we speak of grace today we are speaking of something real, something essential to the human experience of spirit before God, something uncovered in the wonderful and terrible realities of life as we live it today. We encounter the gift of grace in the world as it is, in the lifeworlds and in the systemworlds of our daily lives. We encounter grace in myriad different songs and dances, in art, in narrative, in poetry, in the faces and voices of men and women learning to love tenderly, act justly and walk humbly before their God; and we encounter grace in the endless creativity of children joyfully at play. They all point to a generous, loving God who gave us Jesus, and who continues to be active in the world through the blessed action of the Holy Spirit. Grace is the life of the Trinity touching our world, drawing it to a beautiful, a lavishly generous future. Our freedom and our glory is our capacity to embrace the vision to the full and make it real here and now. Our cooperation gives glory to God.[68] Let a new song rise!

THEMES AND QUESTIONS FOR FURTHER REFLECTION

1. How does Bonhoeffer's challenge relate to your personal spirituality?
2. Give reasons for the necessity of a non-elitist understanding of spirituality today. Outline several ways mature spirituality responds to the encounters and resistances of everyday.
3. Is your spirituality open to an emerging future? Describe the impact that thought of the future has on how you handle the complexities and demands of life in the present.
4. Why is metanoia/conversion a grounding element in a transformative spirituality? Describe life and growth supporting ways of responding to the inner and outer challenges of grace and presence.

FURTHER READING

Susan Rakoczy, *Great Mystics and Social Justice: Walking on the Two Feet of Love* (New York/Mahwah, NJ: Paulist Press, 2006)

NOTES:
1. See Gerard Loughlin, 'René Girard (b. 1923): Introduction' in Graham Ward, ed., *The Postmodern God: A Theological Reader* (Oxford: Blackwell Publishing, 1997, reprinted 2004) 96–104.

2. Thomas Merton, *Essential Writings*. Selected with an Introduction by Christine M. Bochen (Maryknoll, NY: Orbis Books, 2005) 180.

3. Thomas Hobbes, *Leviathan: Revised Student Edition*. Edited by Richard Tuck (Cambridge: Cambridge University Press, 1996).

4. Dietrich Bonhoeffer, *Prisoner for God: Letters and Papers from Prison* Eberhard Bethge, ed., translated by Reginald H. Fuller (New York: Macmillan, 1960) 169. With five other members of his resistance group Dietrich Bonhoeffer was hanged in Flossenbürg concentration camp on the morning of 9 April 1945 on charges of treason following the assassination attempt on Adolph Hitler. According to the camp doctor at Flossenbürg Dietrich prayed before his execution and had been peaceful and composed. The Third Reich ended a month later. See also Renate Wind, *Dietrich Bonhoeffer: A Spoke in the Wheel* translated by John Bowden (Grand Rapids, MN: Eerdmans, 1992) 172–180.

5. See G. B. Kelly & F. B. Nelson, *The Cost of Moral Leadership: The Spirituality of Dietrich Bonhoeffer* (Grand Rapids, MI: Eerdmans, 2003) 93–96.

6. See James Matthew Ashley, *Interruptions: Mysticism, Politics and Theology in the Work of Johann Baptist Metz* (Notre Dame: University of Notre Dame Press, 2002) 191.

7. See Edith Wyschogrod, *Saints and Postmodernism: Revisioning Moral Philosophy* (Chicago: University of Chicago Press, 1990) 127–128.

8. See Edith Wyschogrod, 'Pythagorean Bodies and the Body of Altruism,' in Stephen G. Post, Lynn G. Underwood, Jeffrey P. Schloss & William B. Hurlbut, *Altruism & Altruistic Love: Science, Philosophy, & Religion in Dialogue* (Oxford: Oxford University Press, 2002) 29–38.

9. Quoted in Renate Wind, *Dietrich Bonhoeffer: A Spoke in the Wheel* op. cit. 166.

10. Quoted in Reuven Tsur, *On the Shore of Nothingness: A Study in Cognitive Poetics* (Exeter: Imprint Academic, 2003) 82.

11. Quoted in Renate Wind, *Dietrich Bonhoeffer: A Spoke in the Wheel* op. cit. 167.

12. Thomas Merton, *Essential Writings* op. cit. 178–185.

13. See David Morgan, *Visual Piety: A History and Theory of Popular Religious Images* (Berkeley and London: University of California Press, 1999) 21–26.

14. Wendy Farley, *Tragic Vision and Divine Compassion: A Contemporary Theodicy* (Louisville, KY: Westminster/John Knox Press, 1990) 29.

15. See Stephen T. Davis, 'Perichoretic Monotheism: A Defence of a Social Theory of Trinity' in Melville Y. Stewart, ed., *The Holy Trinity* (Dordrecht/Boston/London: Kluwer Academic Publishers, 2003) 35–52. See also Michael Downey, *Understanding Christian Spirituality* (New York/Mahwah, NJ: Paulist Press, 1997) 44–45.

16. See Anne Hunt, *Trinity: Nexus of the Mysteries of the Christian Faith* (Maryknoll, NY: Orbis Books, 2006) 184.

17. Walter Kasper, *The God of Jesus Christ*. Translated by Matthew J. O'Connell (New York: Crossroads, 1988) 311.

18. Michael Downey, *Altogether Gift: A Trinitarian Spirituality* (Maryknoll, NY: Orbis Books, 2000) 47.

19. Catherine LaCugna, *God for Us: The Trinity and Christian Life* (San Francisco: HarperCollins, 1993) 1.

20. See Philip Sheldrake, *Spirituality and Theology: Christian Living and the Doctrine of God* (London: Darton, Longman & Todd, 1998) 47–53.

21. Michael Downey, *Altogether Gift*, op.cit. 58–59, 67.

22. Philip Sheldrake, *Spirituality and Theology*, op.cit. 75–83, 107–118.

23. See Boris Bobrinskoy, *The Mystery of the Trinity: Trinitarian Experience and Vision in the Biblical and Patristic Tradition* (Crestwood, NY: St Vladimir Seminary Press, 1999) 249.

24. See Sarah Coakley, '"Persons" in the "Social" Doctrine of the Trinity: A Critique of Current Analytic Discussion' in Stephen T. Davis, Daniel Kendall, and Gerald O'Collin, eds, *The Trinity: An Interdisciplinary Symposium on the Trinity* (Oxford: Oxford University Press, 2001) 123–144.

25. Ibid. 125.

26. See John J. Shea, *Finding God Again: Spirituality for Adults* (Lanham and Oxford: Rowman & Littlefield Publishers, 2005).

27. Gerald O'Collins, *The Tripersonal God: Understanding and Interpreting the Trinity* (London: Geoffrey Chapman, 1999) 192–203.

28. See James Earl Massey, 'Faith and Christian Life in the Afro-American Spirituals' in Timothy George, ed., *God the Holy Trinity: Reflections on Christian Faith and Practice* (Grand Rapids, MN: Baker Academic, 2006) 57–68.

29. See Ross Labrie, *Thomas Merton and the Inclusive Imagination* (Columbia, MO: University of Missouri Press, 2001) 10.

30. Thomas Merton, *Essential Writings* op. cit. 62-67.

31. See Jill Y. Crainshaw, *Wise and Discerning Hearts: An Introduction to Wisdom Liturgical Theology* (Collegeville, MN: The Liturgical Press, 2000) 58–59.

32. See for example, Nicholas Zurbrugg, 'Baudrillard and the Ambiguities of Radical Illusion' in *Performance Research: A Journal of Performing Arts* 1 (1996) 3, 1–5.

33. See George A. Kilcourse Jr., *Flannery O'Connor's Religious Imagination: A World with Everything off Balance* (New York, Mahwah, NJ: Paulist Press, 2001) 90–123.

34. See Ross Labrie, *Thomas Merton and the Inclusive Imagination*, op. cit. 177.

35. Ibid. 163.

36. See John Laughlin, *Reading Thomas Merton: A Guide to His Life and Work* (Philadelphia: Xlibris, 2000) 43.

37. See Susan M. Tiberghien, *Circling to the Centre: One Woman's Encounter with Silent Prayer* (New York/Mahwah, NJ: Paulist Press, 2000) 65–66.

38. Ross Labrie, *Thomas Merton and the Inclusive Imagination* op. cit. 102.

39. The word *perichoresis* was used by St John Damascene (c.675–c.750) to depict the unity of Divine life. It paints a dynamic picture of intimacy and of pure reciprocity that does not result in confusion or loss of identity in the Trinity. It suggests a circle of shared life.

40. See Ross Labrie, *Thomas Merton and the Inclusive Imagination*, op. cit. 181.

41. For a detailed exploration of these ideas see the following: Donald L. Gelpi, *Experiencing God: A Theology of Human Emergence* (New York: Paulist Press, 1978). This classic book has been recently reprinted by University Press of America; Andrew Greeley, *The Catholic Myth: The Behavior and Beliefs of American Catholics* (New York: Scribner, 1990) chap. 3: 'Do Catholics Imagine Differently?' 34–62; Noel Dermot O'Donoghue 'Mystical Imagination' in J. P. Mackey *Religious Imagination* (Edinburgh: Edinburgh University Press, 1986) 186–205; J. R. Barth S. J. *Romanticism and Transcendence: Wordsworth, Coleridge, and the Religious Imagination* (Columbia, MO: University of Missouri Press, 2003).

42. See Ross Labrie, *Thomas Merton and the Inclusive Imagination* op. cit. 151.

43. Ibid. 6 & 22–23.

44. See P. Ochs, 'Revised: Comparative Religious Traditions' in *Journal of the American Academy of Religion* 74 (2006) 2, 483–494.

45. See John Swinton, *Raging with Compassion: Pastoral Responses to the Problem of Evil* (Grand Rapids/Cambridge: Eerdmans Publishing, 2007).

46. Ibid. 69–89.

47. James Matthew Ashley, *Interruptions*: op. cit. 193.

48. See Mark and Louise Zwick, *The Catholic Worker Movement: Intellectual and Spiritual Origins* (New York/Mahwah, NJ: Paulist Press, 2005) 201.

49. See Eugene H. Peterson, *Christ Plays in Ten Thousand Places: A Conversation in Spiritual Theology* (Grand Rapids and Cambridge: Eerdmans Publishing, 2005) 1–9.

50. Ibid. 47.

51. D. Brown, 'What is a Christian Theology?' in H. J. Cargas and B. Lee *Religious Experience and Process Theology: The Pastoral Implications of a Major Modern Movement* (New York: Paulist Press, 1976) 41–52 at 45.

52. Mark A. McIntosh, *Mystical Theology: The Integrity of Spirituality and Theology* (Oxford: Blackwell, 2005) 5–6.

53. For a discussion of presencing see Martin Heidegger, *Basic Concepts*. Translated by Gary E. Aylesworth. (Bloomington & Indianapolis:

Indiana University Press, 1998); see also Carol J. White, *Time and Death: Heidegger's Understanding of Finitude.* Edited by Mark Ralkowski with a Forward by Hubert L. Dreyfus. (Aldershot: Ashgate, 2005).

54. For a discussion of eschatology and its proviso see Mark A. McIntosh, *Mystical Theology,* op. cit. 185–187; see also Declan Marmion, *A Spirituality of Everyday Faith: A Theological Investigation of the Notion of Spirituality in Karl Rahner* (Louvain: Peeters Press, 1998) 298–299; David G. Kamitsuka, *Theology and Contemporary Culture: Liberation, Postliberal and Revisionary Perspectives* (Cambridge: Cambridge University Press, 1999) 137–138; Hans Schwartz, *Theology in a Global Context: The Last Two Hundred Years* (Grand Rapids, Cambridge: Eerdmans Publishing, 2005) 442, 545; Ivan Petrella, *The Future of Liberation Theology: An Argument and a Manifesto* (Aldershot: Ashgate, 2004) 126–128, 139 n23.

55. See for example Peter M. Senge and Claus Otto Scharmer, 'Community Action Research: Learning as a Community of Practitioners, Consultants and Researchers' in Peter Reason and Hilary Bradbury, eds, *Handbook of Action Research: The Concise Paperback Edition* (London: Sage, 2006) 195–206.

56. See Elisabeth Louise Thomas, ed., *Emmanuel Levinas: Ethics, Justice and the Human Beyond Being.* (New York & London: Routledge, 2004).

57. See Gary Banham, 'Derrida, the Messianic, and Eschatology' in Philip Goodchild, ed., *Rethinking Philosophy of Religion: Approaches from Continental Philosophy* (New York: Fordham University Press, 2002) 123–136.

58. See Robert M. Doran, *What is Systematic Theology?* (Toronto Buffalo London: University of Toronto Press, 2005); Robert M. Doran, *Theology and the Dialectics of History* (Toronto: University of Toronto Press, 1990); Robert M. Doran, *Theological Foundations: Intentionality and Psyche* vol. 1, (Milwaukee: Marquette University Press, 1995); Thomas J. McPartland, *Lonergan and the Philosophy of Historical Existence* (Columbia, MO: University of Missouri Press, 2001); Michele Saracino, *On Being Human: A Conversation with Lonergan and Levinas* (Milwaukee: Marquette University Press, 2003); Matthew C. Ogilvie, *Faith Seeking Understanding: The Functional Specialty, 'Systematics', in Bernard Lonergan's Method in Theology* (Milwaukee: Marquette University Press, 2001).

59. See, for example, Bernard Tyrell, 'Passages and Conversions' in Matthew L. Lamb, ed., *Creativity and Method: Essays in Honor of Bernard Lonergan, S.J.* (Milwaukee: Marquette University Press, 1981) 11–33; William P. Loewe. *The College Student's Introduction to Christology* (Collegeville, MN: The Liturgical Press, 1996) 69–85; Murray A. Rae. *Kierkegaard's Vision of the Incarnation: By Faith Transformed* (Oxford: The Clarendon Press, 1997) 140–171; Horst Balz and Gerhard Schneider, eds, *Exegetical Dictionary of the New Testament.* Volume Two. (Grand Rapids, MN: Eerdmans, 2000) 415–419; Donald L. Gelpi, *The Firstborn of Many: A Christology for Converting Christians* vol. 1, (Milwaukee: Marquette University Press, 2001);

Adrian T. Peperzak, *The Quest for Meaning: Friends of Wisdom from Plato to Levinas* (New York: Fordham University Press, 2003) 48–72; Dwight Longenecker, *Adventures in Orthodoxy: The Marvels of the Christian Creed and the Audacity of Belief* (Leominster: Gracewing, 2003) 139–146; Massimo Leone, *Religious Conversion and Identity: The Semiotic Analysis of Texts* (New York: Routledge, 2003); Andrew Collier, *On Christian Belief: A Defence of a Cognitive Conception of Religious Belief in a Christian Context* (New York: Routledge, 2003); Zeba A. Crook. *Reconceptualising Conversion: Patronage, Loyalty and Conversion in the Religions of the Ancient Mediterranean* (Berlin & New York: Walter de Gruyter, 2004).

60. Lonergan scholar Robert Doran added psychic conversion to Lonergan's original triad.

61. Psychic conversion surfaces the foundational role of what Doran refers to as a transformed archetypal psychology. For an in-depth discussion of psychic conversion see his *Theological Foundations: Intentionality and Psyche* vol. 1 op. cit. 25–104.

62. See for example Robert C. Croken and Robert Doran, eds, *Collected Works of Bernard Lonergan: Philosophical and Theological Papers 1965–1980* (Toronto, Buffalo, London: University of Toronto Press, 2004) 38–41.

63. See Tatha Wiley, *Original Sin: Origins, Developments, Contemporary Meanings* (New York/Mahwah, NJ: Paulist Press, 2002) 181–182.

64. See Jim Kanaris, *Bernard Lonergan's Philosophy of Religion: From Philosophy of God to Philosophy of Religious Studies* (Albany, NY: State University of New York Press. 2002) 61–99.

65. There is a vast literature on this theme. This resume has developed in conversation with the work of Declan Marmion, 'The Notion of Spirituality in Karl Rahner' in *Louvain Studies* 21 (1996) 61–86 and in personal conversation with the author; John J O'Donnell, *Karl Rahner: Life in the Spirit* (Rome: Gregorian, 2004); Philip Endean, *Karl Rahner and Ignatian Spirituality* (Oxford: Oxford University Press, 2001); Harvey D. Egan, 'Theology and Spirituality' in Declan Marmion and Mary E. Hines, eds, *The Cambridge Companion to Karl Rahner* (Cambridge: Cambridge University Press, 2005) 13–28; David B. Perrin, 'Mysticism' in Arthur Holder, ed., *The Blackwell Companion to Christian Spirituality* (Malden and Oxford: Blackwell Publishing, 2005) 442–458.

66. William H. Shannon, ed., *The Hidden Ground of Love: The Letters of Thomas Merton on Religious Experience and Social Concerns* (London: Collins flame, 1990) 621.

67. See James D. G. Dunn, *The Theology of Paul the Apostle* (Grand Rapids, Cambridge: Eerdmans Publishing, 2006) 321.

68. See Elizabeth Dreyer, *Manifestations of Grace* (Collegeville, MN: The Liturgical Press, 1990).

# The Challenging Future of Christian Spirituality

The fullness of life is a promise, not a utopia.
It is our promised spiritual abode, our living ethos;
but it is also our challenge to prophetic
 communion with all that is.

The nature of the human spirit is revealed
in the creative drive, the struggle
to construct coherence in all the domains of life:
to remain open to ultimacy,
to dance in irrepressible self-transcendence,
to explore potentiality,
to engage in transformative action,
to refuse the lure of confusion,
to seek the hidden order in chaos.

The human spirit is creatively relational,
but needs to be awakened,
unbound from its perversity,
its fears, its desperation.

The human spirit needs to be rediscovered,
met, owned, appropriated,
received inwardly and set free,
whether through crisis, or tragedy,
or moments of grateful joy.

The task of spirit is to refocus life,
open it to transforming dance,
respond to the deep music of soul,
move to deeper rhythms
that hint of divine promise:

*spirit needs to be drawn*
*out of isolation by the inviting Spirit,*
*Nourisher of spirit,*
*drawing to divine intimacy.*

*Such is the underlying dynamic*
*and structure of spirituality:*
*it offers a path through*
*the cosmic loneliness*
*of a disenchanted world,*
*a world cut off from*
*any sense of the sacred.*

*In walking the spiritual path*
*the human spirit rediscovers*
*its own deep nature: made*
*to find a home, a bright home*
*in the cosmos.*
*If we do not find our way*
*How dire will the consequences be?*[1]

Where does the future of Christian spirituality lie? The future of Christian spirituality lies in the rediscovery of human existence as real, as that real existence really unfolds before God in the audacity that is the gift of the Spirit of Jesus Christ. In the light of St John's gospel, Christian spirituality affirms that spirituality is about life to the full (John 10:10). It affirms that the fullness of life is a right and a promise, not a dreamlike utopia. The fullness of life is our promised spiritual abode, our living ethos, the profoundly relational dance we dance with the Divine Spirit. Christian spirituality is the process of coming alive in grace to the fullness of grateful living, and the proof of it lies in its mindful, whole-hearted, dynamic living. It challenges us to discover and openly live from the taproot of our very being; to dance from the heart in the embrace of an extraordinary power; and in that place of fullness and wholeness a deeper silence begins to reign, a silence that reaches God. In that moment of illumination we understand the fullness of being alive.[2]

Only paradox is big enough to hold such fullness: we become expectantly unexpectant and yet give birth to something new: a new release of energy, the construction of a new pattern of meaning, the blossoming of a new quality of relationality, a new ground of coherence and integrity. After all, all human activity is embodied and existent, and Christian spirituality is meant to be incarnational, spirit made flesh in real lives and real actions. Christian spirituality is about reality, about making, a purposeful making characterised by the qualities of imagination and understanding, by the qualities of heartfelt prayer and grateful contemplation that make existential insight and judgment possible. Christian spirituality is a poetic action in the world, a straining against two poles, the one human the other divine; and in that creative tension Spirit song arises and dances its empowering transformations. Contemplative vision makes the difference. By paradoxically allowing us to see beyond the prevailing illusions of our times contemplative vision shows us how to cooperate with what the Spirit is really doing in the world. Contemplative vision teaches us that the freedom of the Spirit is the freedom to create, to innovate, to dance creatively with the eternally new.[3]

Christian spirituality is not about some vague spirit: it is about the Spirit of Jesus Christ. It is not some kind of abstract discourse on the human soul, or even about some kind of generic personal depth or self-transparency achieved through meditative disciplines. Christian spirituality is the choice to walk in the path of Jesus Christ, according to his Spirit, and this is a graced path. As a graced path, the Christian spiritual life is quite specific, defined by its own lifestyle, its own literacies and discourses, and its own stances, ethics and practices. It is specific about the kind of human life that is proposed, it is specific about the centrality of Jesus to this proposal, and it is specific about the life-giving role of the Spirit in unfolding what is proposed. What is proposed is that we become, in the grace of the Spirit, *a new creation in Christ* (2 Corinthians 5:17), someone who does not live by bread alone, someone who is fed by every word that comes from the mouth of God (Matthew 4:4). What is proposed is that we discover a new identity visioned through a contemplative imagination that is interiorly free, nourished on grace, and capable of deep authenticity and integrity. This is the identity that unfolds as we learn to say to Jesus Christ: "You are my truth, my liberating, my loving truth; you are my measure of what it means to be fully human, fully transparent in my embodied humanity. Teach me to let you live!"

Christian spirituality freely embraces the dangerous memory of Jesus, and lives the rhythms of that remembrance concretely in the world of today, facing the real challenges of these times. Christian spirituality lets Jesus live: and there is nothing abstract or merely notional in any of it. Christian spirituality is a process that unfolds in real lives in real situations, in real places facing real challenges. It is a narrow path, a challenging journey, a dangerous way that responds poorly to resistance and baulking (Exodus 4: 24). Christian spirituality demands encounter with the deeper, unregenerated realities of life. It opens the way to an awesome encounter with the depths of Immensity. Christian spirituality bespeaks a Holy One who is simultaneously everywhere and nowhere, paradoxically present in absence and absent in presence: a Holy One to be joyfully trusted not placated, exultantly honoured not managed (Isaiah 12:6; Zephaniah 3:14). Christian spirituality is a way of encounter with the sacred in life, with what the ancient Irish called a *caol áit*, a thin place where opposites dance and make new possibilities soar and sing, such that absence and presence lead beyond themselves to a place where height becomes depth and depth height and all the normal boundaries blur and make unitive transformation possible.

In these thin, almost boundariless contemplative places new levels of spiritual awareness are plumbed and scaled. Theological insight plays its informing part in this process, so does critical reflection on what it means to become fully human journeying along the loving way of Jesus Christ. So does critical reflection on the nature of human structures and their far from neutral impacts, as well as reflection on questions of human solidarity, on the nature of human relationships, and on the challenge to individualism of an ethic of solidarity and service. So does critical reflection on questions of history and the orientations of social choice with their implications for future generations. Christian spirituality demands that we break free of the limiting forces of self-interest as Jesus did and become responsively and ethically conscious on a much wider scale. All of these themes become personal in Christian spirituality, all of them become issues of a personal as well as a collective responsibility that finds its model in Jesus as he wends his way through the land making a difference as a prophet and a healer, as a teacher of liberating truth and an activist for justice, as he reveals in his life and his words the true nature of a compassionate God, the One-who-suffers-with-us.

Christian spirituality grows in 'the grace of the Lord Jesus' (Acts 15:11). It grows through a process of cooperative participation that begins in understanding, leads to the possibility of choice, and becomes a committed decision. These stages interweave and interact with each other, constantly revisited, constantly renewed. They recognise the significance of mediations: of the wise accompaniment of others, of community, of engagement in ritual and worship, of sacramental encounters with grace, of shared spiritual intimacy, of love. This is not a path one undertakes alone, even though it remains a very personal choice, a very personal commitment, a process of personalisation within a community that offers support and encouragement to all on the way. Others are not left behind; embodiment and its social and relational implications are not left behind, spirit and its relational implications are not bypassed, time is not abandoned: individualistic fragmentation and isolation are recognised as the spiritual dead-ends they are, their illusions clearly noted.

Authentic Christian spirituality does not abandon the human situation: it journeys to the heart of it with Jesus and many sisters and brothers. It lovingly seeks a better, a more compassionate, more equitable, more just world, and in the seeking is guided by a reasonableness and goodness of heart, is motivated by a profoundly religious conviction. Christian spirituality lovingly holds inward and outward concerns in a dynamic equilibrium, favouring engaged prayer, engaged meditation, engaged contemplation, engaged mysticism: forms of prayer, meditation, contemplation, and mysticism that lead by their very nature to transformative action and involvement in the world. It is a spirituality that walks in the pathways of the world: the inner world and the outer world knowing that they are in the end inseparable, all of a piece. And along the way no-one or no-thing is excluded from compassionate recognition, from loving action in the manner of Jesus Christ.

This is an ethical spirituality that recognises its historical, its political, its social, its cultural, its ecological, and its economic responsibilities. It does not seek to avoid them. It learns from Jesus that fig trees (Luke 13:6-9) and vines (John 15:1-2; Isaiah 5:1-2) need care if the planet is to survive the depredations of modernity and we are not to end up eating sour grapes, or have our lives rolled up like leaves from a grapevine or green figs from a fig tree (Isaiah 34:4). Christian spirituality breathes in the world; it is meant to give life to the world, to let light shine deeply and liberatingly in the world. Christian spirituality is the dance of body, soul and Holy Spirit along the ways of the world. The Russian saint Theophane the Recluse put this vision very succinctly: the Christian participates in the Holy Spirit, a participation that is indispensable because the one who does not have the Spirit of Christ is not in Christ. The Spirit is the birth water of Christian spirituality, the rain that gives it life and sustains it in being. The Spirit is the breathing in the breath of Christian spirituality. The Spirit gives the colour to its flowering, and all the colours come together in Christ, the Singer of the songs of life, the Dancer dancing saving-healing in our midst.

Christians dance at the edges of a new Spirit-shaped identity, responding to its changing rhythms and its lilting tones. Spirituality sings of life; it sings of the ways we allow faith to shape us in the world. Understood in Hebrew terms, faith is a journey. It has to do with the way the person of faith actually walks in the light of belief in God, walks as someone seeking to be always creatively and caringly present. Faith has to do with seeking with others to walk humbly in the world, to do good, be kindly, practise justice, fight oppression, defend the weak and support the voiceless (Micah 6:8; Isaiah 1:11-17). Authentic Christian spirituality in this light lets justice flow like water and integrity like an ever-flowing stream (Amos 5:24). Effective Christian life, in fact, is possible only to the extent that we have developed, in cooperation with the Spirit, a vital spiritual centre that lets go of narcissistic, self-absorbed practices and approaches, that refuses to succumb to the seductions of corrupting power and violence and the actions that diminish life and the planet.

Christian spirituality is in fact a response to the gift of a love given unconditionally that allows us to live life according to a different spirit, the spirit of Jesus. In postmodern contexts Christian spirituality rediscovers itself as living before the face of Jesus Christ, the other who embodies the world's suffering and hope. It supports a spirituality of life in this world, open to the questioning of the other. Christian spirituality points us to the Spirit's presence in the contingencies of human life and history. It favours the full flourishing of Spirit-shaped human life in all its wonderful diversity. This is an engaged, wisdom-based spirituality rooted in lived stories emerging in diverse landscapes that find genuine ways of bearing prophetic witness to a world in need of the healing and peace that love alone can bring. This is a spirituality alive to the need for dangerous memory, one that recognises the reality of evil and oppression in the world, one alive to the task of transforming the world. This is a spirituality that lets Jesus live.

Basic to all forms of Christian spirituality, then, are an understanding of the human person, an understanding of the meaning and message of Jesus and his incarnation, an understanding of the role of the Church community, an understanding of sin and evil and moral living, an understanding of the need for grace and salvation, an understanding of God's presence in creation, and an understanding of death and human destiny. Christian spirituality is profoundly relational in essence and involves the challenge to live the loving life in all circumstances in ways that thoroughly respect personhood and its irreplaceable uniqueness. As history, even recent history, shows, these dominant themes of compassion and respect are not easy to live by nor are they comfortable in the ordinary sense of that word. Down the years, failures in these areas have had disastrous consequences for victims of abuse and exploitation

In Christianity, people are initiated into a way of living in the Spirit that is not just individual, but has both socio-political and culture-centric forms and engagements. This second level of spirituality tends to be shared mostly through narrative and conversation in groups and workshops, since spirituality is arguably still an oral culture maintained and transmitted through intimate conversation and the telling of stories, through reflective dialogue and honest debate. Today, many such conversations take place on the internet, especially through spiritual blogging sites. This represents a fascinating new venue for spiritual sharing and renewal, a venue that in and of itself represents a new and interesting form of interconnectedness. We need to emphasise the culture-centric nature of spirituality and respect all the contexts in which it occurs. These include groups and communities, whatever form they take; family, support, or activist/ministry groups, as well as various kinds of church-related, educational, therapeutic, aid and development groups; and the array of spiritual groups dedicated more explicitly to prayer, meditation, and spiritual growth.

At these culture-centric levels, Christian spirituality tends to become more nuanced, giving expression to different spiritual traditions and/or communities, so giving rise to different schools and expressions of spirituality in the Church, in society, and in the world at large. In Christianity, such schools attempt in characteristic ways to live gospel values in everyday life in ways that have authentic cultural significance. They are challenged to do this today particularly in regard to techno-economic exploitation, the socio-political impacts of secular ideology, reductive materialism, consumerism, poverty, and social injustice. They must also take into account ecological politics as well as contemporary postmodern science with its interest in the sacred potential of matter in general and human experience in particular. In other words, compassionate and emancipatory activism is a core aspect of authentic Christian spirituality and, as we are learning today, mysticism has a prophetic, socially engaged, political side seeking authentic expression in the world's painful spaces.

Christian spirituality brings together all the dimensions of the human person and all the dimensions of the human personality in the transforming energy of the Spirit: mind, affectivity, behaviour, heart, soul, spirit, will and body. Clothed in Christ (Galatians 3:27), the person, desiring relatedness and no longer making distinctions between one individual and the next, is creatively empowered to bring the beauty of transformed spirit into living environments, into society, into the whole world. The fulcrum of Christian spirituality is the following of Christ, the *sequela Christi*. There is nothing abstract here; it is all real, and it empowers us for deepening responsibility and involvement as we dance in the diverging spaces between mind and heart, in the contrary spaces of paradox, and in the conflicts and dissensions that are so often the stuff of life, especially when stances grounded in integrity bring rejection (Jeremiah 15:10). In the end, Christian spirituality is *an option for Jesus Christ in prophetic communion with brothers and sisters responding to the signs of the times*, signs that challenge us to care for all that is. Those who take up the spiritual adventure cease to live as isolated individuals. They embrace the challenge to build a more humane world. Are we ready for that challenge today? Have we the audacity of spirit?

NOTES:    1. See James E. Loder, *The Logic of the Spirit: Human Development in Theological Perspective* (San Francisco: Jossey-Bass, 1998); James E. Loder, W. Jim Neidhardt, *The Knight's Move: The Relational Logic of the Spirit in Theology and Science* (Colorado Springs, CO: Helmers & Howard, 1992).

2. See David Steindl-Rast, *Gratefulness, the Heart of Prayer: An Approach to Life in Fullness* (New York/Mahwah, NJ: Paulist Press, 1984).

3. See Francesca Aran Murphy, *Art and Intellect in Etienne Gilson* (Columbia, MO: University of Missouri Press, 2004) 107, 286, 302.

# Index